T0231939

INTELLIGENT IMAGE PROCESSING

Adaptive and Learning Systems for Signal Processing, Communications, and Control

Editor: Simon Haykin

INTELLIGENT IMAGE PROCESSING

Steve Mann

University of Toronto

The Institute of Electrical and Electronics Engineers, Inc., New York

A JOHN WILEY & SONS, INC., PUBLICATION

Library of Congress Cataloging-in-Publication Data

Mann, Steve, 1962-
    Intelligent image processing / by Steve Mann.
        p. cm. - - (Wiley series on adaptive and learning systems for signal processing,
    communications, and control)
    "A Wiley-Interscience publication."
    ISBN 0-471-40637-6 (cloth : alk. paper)
        1. Image processing, 2. Computational intelligence. I. Title. II. Adaptive and learning
    systems for signal processing, communications, and control.

TA1637 .M33 2002
621.36′7–dc21   2001024228

10 9 8 7 6 5 4 3 2 1

CONTENTS

6 VideoOrbits: The Projective Geometry Renaissance   233

Appendixes

PREFACE

This book has evolved from the author's course on personal imaging taught at the University of Toronto, since fall 1998. It also presents original material from the author's own experience in inventing, designing, building, and using wearable computers and personal imaging systems since the early 1970s.

The idea behind this book is to provide the student with the fundamental knowledge needed in the rapidly growing field of personal imaging. This field is often referred to colloquially as wearable computing, mediated (or augmented) 'reality,' personal technologies, mobile multimedia, and so on. Rather than trying to address all aspects of personal imaging, the book places a particular emphasis on the fundamentals.

New concepts of image content are essential to multimedia communications. Human beings obtain their main sensory information from their visual system. Accordingly, visual communication is essential for creating an intimate connection between the human and the machine. Visual information processing also provides the greatest technical challenges because of the bandwidth and complexity that is involved.

A computationally mediated visual reality is a natural extension of the next-generation computing machines. Already we have witnessed a pivotal shift from mainframe computers to personal/personalizable computers owned and operated by individual end users. We have also witnessed a fundamental change in the nature of computing from large mathematical "batch job" *calculations* to the use of computers as a *communications* medium. The explosive growth of the Internet (which is primarily a communications medium as opposed to a calculations medium), and more recently the World Wide Web, is a harbinger of what will evolve into a completely computer-mediated world. Likely in the immediate future we will see all aspects of life handled online and connected.

This will not be done by implanting devices into the brain — at least not in this course — but rather by noninvasively "tapping" the highest bandwidth "pipe" into the brain, namely the eye. This "eye tap" forms the basis for devices that are being currently built into eyeglasses (prototypes are also being built into contact lenses) to tap into the mind's eye.

The way EyeTap technology will be used is to cause inanimate objects to suddenly come to life as nodes on a virtual computer network. For example, as one walks past an old building, the building will come to life with hyperlinks on its surface, even though the building itself is not wired for network connections. The hyperlinks are created as a shared imagined reality that wearers of the EyeTap technology simultaneously experience. When one enters a grocery store with eyes tapped, a milk carton may convey a unique message from a spouse, reminding the wearer of the EyeTap technology to pick up some milk on the way home from work.

EyeTap technology is not merely about a computer screen inside eyeglasses. Rather, it is about enabling a shared visual experience that connects multiple perceptions of individuals into a collective consciousness.

EyeTap technology could have many commercial applications. It could emerge as an industrially critical form of communications technology. The WearTel™ phone, for example, uses EyeTap technology to allow individuals to see each other's point of view. Traditional videoconferencing that merely provides a picture of the other person has consistently been a marketplace failure everywhere it has been introduced. There is little cogent and compelling need for seeing a picture of the person one is talking to, especially since most of the time the caller already knows what the other person looks like, not to mention the fact that many people do not want to have to get dressed when they get up in the morning to answer the phone, and so on.

However, the WearTel phone provides a view of what the other person is looking at, rather than merely a view of the other person. This one level of indirection turns out to have a very existential property, namely that of facilitating a virtual being with the other person rather than just seeing the other person.

It may turn out to be far more useful for us to exchange points of view with others in this manner. Exchange of viewpoints is made possible with EyeTap technology by way of the miniature laser light source inside the WearTel eyeglass-based phone. The light scans across the retinas of both parties and swaps the image information so that each person sees what the other person is looking at. The WearTel phone, in effect, let's someone "be you" rather than just "see you." By letting others put themselves in your shoes and see the world from your point of view, a very powerful communications medium could result.

This book shows how the eye is tapped by a handheld device like WearTel or by EyeTap eyeglasses or contact lenses, allowing us to create personal documentaries of our lives, shot from a first-person perspective. Turning the eye itself into a camera will radically change the way pictures are taken, memories are kept, and events are documented. (The reader anxious to get a glimpse of this should check the Electronic News Gathering wear project at http://engwear.org, and some of the related sites such as http://eyetap.org or run a search engine on "eyetap.") Apparatuses like this invention will further help the visually challenged see better and perhaps help those with a visual memory disorder remember things better. It is conceivable that with the large aging population of the near future, attention to this invention will be on the rise.

The book is organized as follows:

1. *Humanistic intelligence:* The first chapter introduces the general ideas behind wearable computing, personal technologies, and the like. It gives a historical overview ranging from the original photographic motivations of personal cybernetics in the 1970s, to the fabric-based computers of the 1980s, and to the modern EyeTap systems. This chapter traces personal cybernetics from its obscure beginnings as a cumbersome wearable lighting and photographic control system to its more refined embodiments. The motivating factor in humanistic intelligence is that we realize the close synergy between the intelligence that arises from the human being in the feedback loop of a truly personal computational process.

2. *Personal imaging:* This chapter ponders the fundamental question as to where on the body the imaging system should be situated. In terms of image acquisition and display various systems have been tried. Among these is the author's wearable radar vision system for the visually challenged which is introduced, described, and compared with other systems.

3. *The EyeTap principle:* This chapter provides the fundamental basis for noninvasively tapping into the mind's eye. The EyeTap principle pertains to replacing, in whole or in part, each ray of light that would otherwise pass through the lens of at least one eye of the wearer, with a synthetic ray of light responsive to the output of a processor. Some of the fundamental concepts covered in this chapter are the EyeTap principle; analysis glass, synthesis glass, and the collinearity criterion; effective location of the camera in at least one eye of the wearer; practical embodiments of the EyeTap principle; the laser EyeTap camera; tapping the mind's eye with a computer-controlled laser (replacing each ray of light that would otherwise enter the eye with laser light); the author's fully functional laser EyeTap eyeglasses; infinite depth of focus EyeTap products and devices; and practical solutions for the visually challenged.

4. *Photoquantigraphic imaging:* This chapter addresses the basic question of how much light is desirable. In particular, when replacing each ray of light with synthetic light, one must know how much synthetic light to use. The analysis portion of the apparatus is described. Since it is based on a camera or camera-like device, a procedure for determining the quantity of light entering the camera is formulated.

5. *Antihomomorphic vector spaces and image processing in lightspace:* This chapter introduces a multidimensional variant of photoquantigraphic imaging in which the response of the image to light is determined. The discussion of lightspace includes the application of personal imaging to the creation of pictures done in a genre of "painting with lightvectors." This application takes us back to the very first application of wearable computers and mediated reality, namely that of collaborative production of visual art in a mediated reality space.

6. *VideoOrbits:*   The final chapter covers camera-based head-tracking in the context of algebraic projective geometry. This chapter sets forth the theoretical framework for personal imaging.

STEVE MANN

University of Toronto

1

HUMANISTIC INTELLIGENCE AS A BASIS FOR INTELLIGENT IMAGE PROCESSING

Personal imaging is an integrated personal technologies, personal communicators, and mobile multimedia methodology. In particular, personal imaging devices are characterized by an "always ready" usage model, and comprise a device or devices that are typically carried or worn so that they are always with us [1].

An important theoretical development in the field of personal imaging is that of humanistic intelligence (HI). HI is a new information-processing framework in which the processing apparatus is inextricably intertwined with the natural capabilities of our human body and intelligence. Rather than trying to emulate human intelligence, HI recognizes that the human brain is perhaps the best neural network of its kind, and that there are many new signal processing applications, within the domain of personal imaging, that can make use of this excellent but often overlooked processor that we already have attached to our bodies. Devices that embody HI are worn (or carried) continuously during all facets of ordinary day-to-day living. Through long-term adaptation they begin to function as a true extension of the mind and body.

1.1 HUMANISTIC INTELLIGENCE

HI is a new form of "intelligence." Its goal is to not only work in extremely close synergy with the human user, rather than as a separate entity, but, more important, to arise, in part, because of the very **existence** of the human user [2]. This close synergy is achieved through an intelligent user-interface to signal-processing hardware that is both in *close physical proximity* to the user and is *constant*.

1

There are two kinds of constancy: one is called *operational constancy*, and the other is called *interactional constancy* [2]. Operational constancy also refers to an always ready-to-run condition, in the sense that although the apparatus may have power-saving ("sleep") modes, it is never completely "dead" or shut down or in a temporary inoperable state that would require noticeable time from which to be "awakened."

The other kind of constancy, called interactional constancy, refers to a constancy of user-interface. It is the constancy of user-interface that separates systems embodying a *personal imaging* architecture from other *personal* devices, such as pocket calculators, personal digital assistants (PDAs), and other *imaging* devices, such as handheld video cameras.

For example, a handheld calculator left turned on but carried in a shirt pocket lacks interactional constancy, since it is not always ready to be interacted with (e.g., there is a noticeable delay in taking it out of the pocket and getting ready to interact with it). Similarly a handheld camera that is either left turned on or is designed such that it responds instantly, still lacks interactional constancy because it takes time to bring the viewfinder up to the eye in order to look through it. In order for it to have interactional constancy, it would need to always be held up to the eye, even when not in use. Only if one were to walk around holding the camera viewfinder up to the eye during every waking moment, could we say it is has true interactional constancy at all times.

By interactionally constant, what is meant is that the inputs and outputs of the device are always potentially active. Interactionally constant implies operationally constant, but operationally constant does not necessarily imply interactionally constant. The examples above of a pocket calculator worn in a shirt pocket, and left on all the time, or of a handheld camera even if turned on all the time, are said to lack interactional constancy because they cannot be used in this state (e.g., one still has to pull the calculator out of the pocket or hold the camera viewfinder up to the eye to see the display, enter numbers, or compose a picture). A wristwatch is a borderline case. Although it operates constantly in order to continue to keep proper time, and it is wearable; one must make some degree of conscious effort to orient it within one's field of vision in order to interact with it.

1.1.1 Why Humanistic Intelligence

It is not, at first, obvious why one might want devices such as cameras to be operationally constant. However, we will later see why it is desirable to have certain personal electronics devices, such as cameras and signal-processing hardware, be on constantly, for example, to facilitate new forms of intelligence that assist the user in new ways.

Devices embodying HI are not merely intelligent signal processors that a user might wear or carry in close proximity to the body but are devices that turn the user into part of an intelligent control system where the user becomes an integral part of the feedback loop.

1.1.2 Humanistic Intelligence Does Not Necessarily Mean "User-Friendly"

Devices embodying HI often require that the user learn a new skill set. Such devices are therefore not necessarily easy to adapt to. Just as it takes a young child many years to become proficient at using his or her hands, some of the devices that implement HI have taken years of use before they began to truly behave as if they were natural extensions of the mind and body. Thus in terms of human-computer interaction [3], the goal is not just to construct a device that can model (and learn from) the user but, more important, to construct a device in which the user also must learn from the device. Therefore, in order to facilitate the latter, devices embodying HI should provide a constant user-interface—one that is not so sophisticated and intelligent that it confuses the user.

Although the HI device may implement very sophisticated signal-processing algorithms, the cause-and-effect relationship of this processing to its input (typically from the environment or the user's actions) should be clearly and continuously visible to the user, even when the user is not directly and intentionally interacting with the apparatus. Accordingly the most successful examples of HI afford the user a very tight feedback loop of system observability (ability to perceive how the signal processing hardware is responding to the environment and the user), even when the controllability of the device is not engaged (e.g., at times when the user is not issuing direct commands to the apparatus). A simple example is the viewfinder of a wearable camera system, which provides framing, a photographic point of view, and facilitates the provision to the user of a general awareness of the visual effects of the camera's own image processing algorithms, even when pictures are not being taken. Thus a camera embodying HI puts the human operator in the feedback loop of the imaging process, even when the operator only wishes to take pictures occasionally. A more sophisticated example of HI is a biofeedback-controlled wearable camera system, in which the biofeedback process happens continuously, whether or not a picture is actually being taken. In this sense the user becomes one with the machine, over a long period of time, even if the machine is only directly used (e.g., to actually take a picture) occasionally.

Humanistic intelligence attempts to both build upon, as well as re-contextualize, concepts in *intelligent signal processing* [4,5], and related concepts such as neural networks [4,6,7], fuzzy logic [8,9], and artificial intelligence [10]. Humanistic intelligence also suggests a new goal for signal processing hardware, that is, in a truly personal way, to directly assist rather than replace or emulate human intelligence. What is needed to facilitate this vision is a simple and truly personal computational image-processing framework that empowers the human intellect. It should be noted that this framework, which arose in the 1970s and early 1980s, is in many ways similar to Doug Engelbart's vision that arose in the 1940s while he was a radar engineer, but that there are also some important differences. Engelbart, while seeing images on a radar screen, envisioned that the cathode ray screen could also display letters of the alphabet, as well as computer-generated pictures and graphical content, and thus envisioned computing as an interactive experience for manipulating words and pictures. Engelbart envisioned the mainframe computer as a tool for augmented intelligence and augmented communication, in which a number of people in a large amphitheatre could interact with one another using a large mainframe computer [11,12]. While Engelbart himself did not seem to understand the significance of the personal computer, his ideas are certainly embodied in modern personal computing.

What is now described is a means of realizing a similar vision, but with the computational resources re-situated in a different context, namely the truly personal space of the user. The idea here is to move the tools of augmented intelligence, augmented communication, computationally mediated visual communication, and imaging technologies directly onto the body. This will give rise to not only a new genre of truly personal image computing but to some new capabilities and affordances arising from direct physical contact between the computational imaging apparatus and the human mind and body. Most notably, a new family of applications arises categorized as "personal imaging," in which the body-worn apparatus facilitates an augmenting and computational mediating of the human sensory capabilities, namely vision. Thus the augmenting of human memory translates directly to a visual associative memory in which the apparatus might, for example, play previously recorded video back into the wearer's eyeglass mounted display, in the manner of a *visual thesaurus* [13] or *visual memory prosthetic* [14].

1.2 "WEARCOMP" AS MEANS OF REALIZING HUMANISTIC INTELLIGENCE

WearComp [1] is now proposed as an apparatus upon which a practical realization of HI can be built as well as a research tool for new studies in intelligent image processing.

1.2.1 Basic Principles of WearComp

WearComp will now be defined in terms of its three basic modes of operation.

Operational Modes of WearComp
The three operational modes in this new interaction between human and computer, as illustrated in Figure 1.1 are:

- *Constancy:* The computer runs continuously, and is "always ready" to interact with the user. Unlike a handheld device, laptop computer, or PDA, it does not need to be opened up and turned on prior to use. The signal flow from human to computer, and computer to human, depicted in Figure 1.1a runs continuously to provide a constant user-interface.

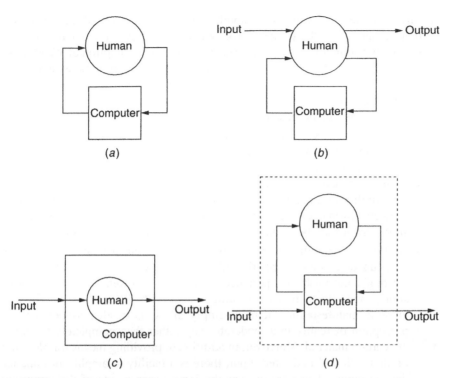

Figure 1.1 The three basic operational modes of WearComp. (a) Signal flow paths for a computer system that runs continuously, constantly attentive to the user's input, and constantly providing information to the user. Over time, constancy leads to a symbiosis in which the user and computer become part of each other's feedback loops. (b) Signal flow path for augmented intelligence and augmented reality. Interaction with the computer is secondary to another primary activity, such as walking, attending a meeting, or perhaps doing something that requires full hand-to-eye coordination, like running down stairs or playing volleyball. Because the other primary activity is often one that requires the human to be attentive to the environment as well as unencumbered, the computer must be able to operate in the background to augment the primary experience, for example, by providing a map of a building interior, and other information, through the use of computer graphics overlays superimposed on top of the real world. (c) WearComp can be used like clothing to encapsulate the user and function as a protective shell, whether to protect us from cold, protect us from physical attack (as traditionally facilitated by armor), or to provide privacy (by concealing personal information and personal attributes from others). In terms of signal flow, this encapsulation facilitates the possible mediation of incoming information to permit solitude, and the possible mediation of outgoing information to permit privacy. It is not so much the absolute blocking of these information channels that is important; it is the fact that the wearer can control to what extent, and when, these channels are blocked, modified, attenuated, or amplified, in various degrees, that makes WearComp much more empowering to the user than other similar forms of portable computing. (d) An equivalent depiction of encapsulation (mediation) redrawn to give it a similar form to that of (a) and (b), where the encapsulation is understood to comprise a separate protective shell.

- *Augmentation:* Traditional computing paradigms are based on the notion that computing is the primary task. WearComp, however, is based on the notion that computing is *not* the primary task. The assumption of WearComp is that the user will be doing something else at the same time as doing the computing. Thus the computer should serve to augment the intellect, or augment the senses. The signal flow between human and computer, in the augmentational mode of operation, is depicted in Figure 1.1*b*.

- *Mediation:* Unlike handheld devices, laptop computers, and PDAs, WearComp can encapsulate the user (Figure 1.1*c*). It does not necessarily need to completely enclose us, but the basic concept of mediation allows for whatever degree of encapsulation might be desired, since it affords us the possibility of a greater degree of encapsulation than traditional portable computers. Moreover there are two aspects to this encapsulation, one or both of which may be implemented in varying degrees, as desired:

  - *Solitude:* The ability of WearComp to mediate our perception will allow it to function as an information filter, and allow us to block out material we might not wish to experience, whether it be offensive advertising or simply a desire to replace existing media with different media. In less extreme manifestations, it may simply allow us to alter aspects of our perception of reality in a moderate way rather than completely blocking out certain material. Moreover, in addition to providing means for blocking or attenuation of undesired input, there is a facility to amplify or enhance desired inputs. This control over the input space is one of the important contributors to the most fundamental issue in this new framework, namely that of user empowerment.

  - *Privacy:* Mediation allows us to block or modify information leaving our encapsulated space. In the same way that ordinary clothing prevents others from seeing our naked bodies, WearComp may, for example, serve as an intermediary for interacting with untrusted systems, such as third party implementations of digital anonymous cash or other electronic transactions with untrusted parties. In the same way that martial artists, especially stick fighters, wear a long black robe that comes right down to the ground in order to hide the placement of their feet from their opponent, WearComp can also be used to clothe our otherwise transparent movements in cyberspace. Although other technologies, like desktop computers, can, to a limited degree, help us protect our privacy with programs like Pretty Good Privacy (PGP), the primary weakness of these systems is the space between them and their user. It is generally far easier for an attacker to compromise the link between the human and the computer (perhaps through a so-called Trojan horse or other planted virus) when they are separate entities. Thus a personal information system owned, operated, and controlled by the wearer can be used to create a new level of personal privacy because it can be made much more personal, for example, so that it is always worn, except perhaps during showering, and therefore less likely to fall prey to attacks upon the hardware itself. Moreover the close synergy between the human and computers makes it harder to attack directly, for example, as one might look over a person's shoulder while they are typing or hide a video camera in the ceiling above their keyboard.[1]

Because of its ability to encapsulate us, such as in embodiments of WearComp that are actually articles of clothing in direct contact with our flesh, it may also be able to make measurements of various physiological quantities. Thus the signal flow depicted in Figure 1.1a is also enhanced by the encapsulation as depicted in Figure 1.1c. To make this signal flow more explicit, Figure 1.1c has been redrawn, in Figure 1.1d, where the computer and human are depicted as two separate entities within an optional protective shell that may be opened or partially opened if a mixture of augmented and mediated interaction is desired.

Note that these three basic modes of operation are not mutually exclusive in the sense that the first is embodied in both of the other two. These other two are also not necessarily meant to be implemented in isolation. Actual embodiments of WearComp typically incorporate aspects of both augmented and mediated modes of operation. Thus WearComp is a framework for enabling and combining various aspects of each of these three basic modes of operation. Collectively, the space of possible signal flows giving rise to this entire space of possibilities, is depicted in Figure 1.2. The signal paths typically comprise vector quantities. Thus multiple parallel signal paths are depicted in this figure to remind the reader of this vector nature of the signals.

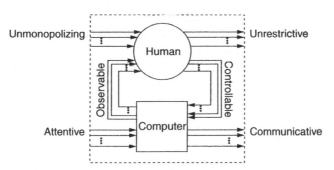

Figure 1.2 Six signal flow paths for the new mode of human–computer interaction provided by WearComp. These six signal flow paths each define one of the six attributes of WearComp.

---

[1] For the purposes of this discussion, privacy is not so much the absolute blocking or concealment of personal information, rather, it is the ability to control or modulate this outbound information channel. For example, one may want certain members of one's immediate family to have greater access to personal information than the general public. Such a family-area network may be implemented with an appropriate access control list and a cryptographic communications protocol.

1.2.2 The Six Basic Signal Flow Paths of WearComp

There are six informational flow paths associated with this new human–machine symbiosis. These signal flow paths each define one of the basic underlying principles of WearComp, and are each described, in what follows, from the human's point of view. Implicit in these six properties is that the computer system is also operationally constant and personal (inextricably intertwined with the user). The six signal flow paths are:

1. *Unmonopolizing of the user's attention:* It does not necessarily cut one off from the outside world like a virtual reality game does. One can attend to other matters while using the apparatus. It is built with the assumption that computing will be a secondary activity rather than a primary focus of attention. Ideally it will provide enhanced sensory capabilities. It may, however, facilitate mediation (augmenting, altering, or deliberately diminishing) these sensory capabilities.

2. *Unrestrictive to the user:* Ambulatory, mobile, roving — one can do other things while using it. For example, one can type while jogging or running down stairs.

3. *Observable by the user:* It can get the user's attention continuously if the user wants it to. The output medium is constantly perceptible by the wearer. It is sufficient that it be almost-always-observable within reasonable limitations such as the fact that a camera viewfinder or computer screen is not visible during the blinking of the eyes.

4. *Controllable by the user:* Responsive. The user can take control of it at any time the user wishes. Even in automated processes the user should be able to manually override the automation to break open the control loop and become part of the loop at any time the user wants to. Examples of this controllability might include a "Halt" button the user can invoke as an application mindlessly opens all 50 documents that were highlighted when the user accidentally pressed "Enter."

5. *Attentive to the environment:* Environmentally aware, multimodal, multi-sensory. (As a result this ultimately gives the user increased situational awareness.)

6. *Communicative to others:* WearComp can be used as a communications medium when the user wishes. Expressive: WearComp allows the wearer to be expressive through the medium, whether as a direct communications medium to others or as means of assisting the user in the production of expressive or communicative media.

1.2.3 Affordances and Capabilities of a WearComp-Based Personal Imaging system

There are numerous capabilities and affordances of WearComp. These include:

- *Photographic/videographic memory:* Perfect recall of previously collected information, especially visual information (*visual memory* [15]).

- *Shared memory:* In a collective sense, two or more individuals may share in their collective consciousness, so that one may have a recall of information that one need not have experienced personally.
- *Connected collective humanistic intelligence:* In a collective sense, two or more individuals may collaborate while one or more of them is doing another primary task.
- *Personal safety:* In contrast to a centralized surveillance network built into the architecture of the city, a personal safety system is built into the architecture (clothing) of the individual. This framework has the potential to lead to a distributed "intelligence" system of sorts, as opposed to the centralized "intelligence" gathering efforts of traditional video surveillance networks.
- *Tetherless operation:* WearComp affords and requires mobility, and the freedom from the need to be connected by wire to an electrical outlet, or communications line.
- *Synergy:* Rather than attempting to emulate human intelligence in the computer, as is a common goal of research in artificial intelligence (AI), the goal of WearComp is to produce a synergistic combination of human and machine, in which the human performs tasks that it is better at, while the computer performs tasks that it is better at. Over an extended period of time, WearComp begins to function as a true extension of the mind and body, and the user no longer feels as if it is a separate entity. In fact the user will often adapt to the apparatus to such a degree that when taking it off, its absence will feel uncomfortable. This is not much different than the way that we adapt to shoes and certain clothing so that being without these things would make most of us feel extremely uncomfortable (whether in a public setting, or in an environment in which we have come to be accustomed to the protection that shoes and clothing provide). This intimate and constant bonding is such that the combined capability resulting in a synergistic whole far exceeds the sum of its components.
- *Quality of life:* WearComp is capable of enhancing day-to-day experiences, not just in the workplace, but in all facets of daily life. It has the capability to enhance the overall quality of life for many people.

1.3 PRACTICAL EMBODIMENTS OF HUMANISTIC INTELLIGENCE

The WearComp apparatus consists of a battery-powered wearable Internet-connected [16] computer system with miniature eyeglass-mounted screen and appropriate optics to form the virtual image equivalent to an ordinary desktop multimedia computer. However, because the apparatus is tetherless, it travels with the user, presenting a computer screen that either appears superimposed on top of the real world, or represents the real world as a video image [17].

Advances in low-power microelectronics [18] have propelled us into a pivotal era in which we will become inextricably intertwined with computational technology. Computer systems will become part of our everyday lives in a much more immediate and intimate way than in the past.

Physical proximity and constancy were simultaneously realized by the WearComp project[2] of the 1970s and early 1980s (Figure 1.3). This was a first attempt at building an intelligent "photographer's assistant" around the body, and it comprised a computer system attached to the body. A display means was constantly visible to one or both eyes, and the means of signal input included a series of pushbutton switches and a pointing device (Figure 1.4) that the wearer could hold in one hand to function as a keyboard and mouse do, but still be able to operate the device while walking around. In this way the apparatus re-situated the functionality of a desktop multimedia computer with mouse, keyboard, and video screen, as a physical extension of the user's body. While the size and weight reductions of WearComp over the last 20 years have been quite dramatic, the basic qualitative elements and functionality have remained essentially the same, apart from the obvious increase in computational power.

However, what makes WearComp particularly useful in new and interesting ways, and what makes it particularly suitable as a basis for HI, is the collection of other input devices. Not all of these devices are found on a desktop multimedia computer.

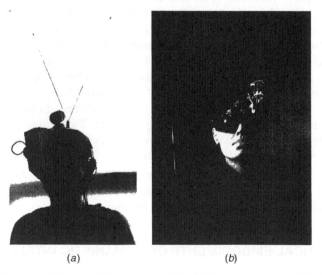

(a)   (b)

Figure 1.3 Early embodiments of the author's original "photographer's assistant" application of personal Imaging. (a) Author wearing WearComp2, an early 1980s backpack-based signal-processing and personal imaging system with right eye display. Two antennas operating at different frequencies facilitated wireless communications over a full-duplex radio link. (b) WearComp4, a late 1980s clothing-based signal processing and personal imaging system with left eye display and beamsplitter. Separate antennas facilitated simultaneous voice, video, and data communication.

---

[2] For a detailed historical account of the WearComp project, and other related projects, see [19,20].

   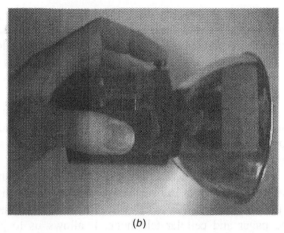

(a)   (b)

Figure 1.4 Author using some early input devices ("keyboards" and "mice") for WearComp. (a) 1970s: Input device comprising pushbutton switches mounted to a wooden hand-grip. (b) 1980s: Input device comprising microswitches mounted to the handle of an electronic flash. These devices also incorporated a detachable joystick (controlling two potentiometers), designed as a pointing device for use in conjunction with the WearComp project.

In typical embodiments of WearComp these measurement (input) devices include the following:

- Wearable portable miniature sensors such as cameras, often oriented to have the same field of view as the wearer, thus providing the computer with the wearer's "first-person" perspective.
- One or more additional cameras that afford alternate points of view (e.g., a rear-looking camera with a view of what is directly behind the wearer).
- Sets of microphones, typically comprising one set to capture the sounds of someone talking to the wearer (typically a linear array across the top of the wearer's eyeglasses), and a second set to capture the wearer's own speech so the WearComp system can easily distinguish between these two.
- Biosensors, comprising not just heart rate but full ECG waveform, as well as respiration, skin conductivity, sweat level, and other quantities [21], each available as a continuous (sufficiently sampled) time-varying voltage. Typically these are connected to the wearable central processing unit through an eight-channel analog to digital converter.
- Footstep sensors typically comprising an array of transducers inside each shoe.
- Wearable radar systems in the form of antenna arrays sewn into clothing. These typically operate in the 24.36 GHz range.

The last three, in particular, are not found on standard desktop computers, and even the first three, which often are found on standard desktop computers, appear in a different context in WearComp than they do on a desktop computer. For example, in WearComp the camera does not show an image of the user, as it does typically on a desktop computer, but rather it provides information about the user's environment. Furthermore the general philosophy, as will be described in Chapter 4, is to regard all of the input devices as measurement devices. Even something as simple as a camera is regarded as a measuring instrument within the proposed signal-processing framework.

Certain applications use only a subset of these devices but include all of them in the design facilitates rapid prototyping and experimentation with new applications. Most embodiments of WearComp are modular so that devices can be removed when they are not being used.

A side effect of this WearComp apparatus is that it replaces much of the personal electronics that we carry in our day-to-day living. It enables us to interact with others through its wireless data communications link, and therefore replaces the pager and cellular telephone. It allows us to perform basic computations, and thus replaces the pocket calculator, laptop computer, and personal data assistant (PDA). It can record data from its many inputs, and therefore it replaces and subsumes the portable dictating machine, camcorder, and the photographic camera. And it can reproduce ("play back") audiovisual data, so it subsumes the portable audio cassette player. It keeps time, as any computer does, and this may be displayed when desired, rendering a wristwatch obsolete. (A calendar program that produces audible, vibrotactile, or other output also renders the alarm clock obsolete.)

However, WearComp goes beyond replacing all of these items, because not only is it currently far smaller and far less obtrusive than the sum of what it replaces, but these functions are interwoven seamlessly, so that they work together in a mutually assistive fashion. Furthermore entirely new functionalities, and new forms of interaction, arise such as enhanced sensory capabilities.

1.3.1 Building Signal-Processing Devices Directly Into Fabric

The wearable signal-processing apparatus of the 1970s and early 1980s was cumbersome at best. An effort was directed toward not only reducing its size and weight but, more important, reducing its undesirable and somewhat obtrusive appearance. An effort was also directed at making an apparatus of a given size and weight more comfortable to wear and bearable to the user [1] by bringing components in closer proximity to the body, thereby reducing torques and moments of inertia. Starting in 1982, Eleveld and Mann [20] began to build circuitry directly into clothing. The term "smart clothing" refers to variations of WearComp that are built directly into clothing and are characterized by (or at least an attempt at) making components distributed rather than lumped, whenever possible or practical.

It was found [20] that the same apparatus could be made much more comfortable by bringing the components closer to the body. This had the effect of reducing the torque felt bearing the load as well as the moment of inertia felt in moving around.

More recent related work by others [22], also involves building circuits into clothing. A garment is constructed as a monitoring device to determine the location of a bullet entry. The WearComp differs from this monitoring apparatus in the sense that the WearComp is totally reconfigurable in the field, and also in the sense that it embodies HI (the apparatus reported in [22] performs a monitoring function but does not facilitate wearer interaction, and therefore is not an embodiment of HI).

Figure 1.5 Author's personal imaging system equipped with sensors for measuring biological signals. The sunglasses in the upper right are equipped with built in video cameras and display system. These look like ordinary sunglasses when worn (wires are concealed inside the eyeglass holder). At the left side of the picture is an 8 channel analog to digital converter together with a collection of biological sensors, both manufactured by Thought Technologies Limited, of Canada. At the lower right is an input device called the "twiddler," manufactured by HandyKey, and to the left of that is a Sony Lithium Ion camcorder battery with custom-made battery holder. In the lower central area of the image is the computer, equipped with special-purpose video-processing/video capture hardware (visible as the top stack on this stack of PC104 boards). This computer, although somewhat bulky, may be concealed in the small of the back, underneath an ordinary sweater. To the left of the computer, is a serial to fiber-optic converter that provides communications to the 8 channel analog to digital converter over a fiber-optic link. Its purpose is primarily one of safety, to isolate high voltages used in the computer and peripherals (e.g., the 500 volts or so present in the sunglasses) from the biological sensors, which are in close proximity, and typically with very good connection, to the body of the wearer.

1.3.2 Multidimensional Signal Input for Humanistic Intelligence

The close physical proximity of WearComp to the body, as described earlier, facilitates a new form of signal processing.[3] Because the apparatus is in direct contact with the body, it may be equipped with various sensory devices. For example, a tension transducer (pictured leftmost, running the height of the picture from top to bottom, in Figure 1.5) is typically threaded through and around the undershirt-based WearComp, at stomach height, so that it measures respiration. Electrodes are also installed in such a manner that they are in contact with the wearer's heart. Various other sensors, such as an array of transducers in each shoe [24] and a wearable radar system are also included as sensory inputs to the processor. The ProComp™ eight channel analog to digital converter, along with some of the input devices that are sold with it, is pictured in Figure 1.5 together with the CPU from WearComp6.

More Than Just a Health Status Monitor
It is important to realize that the WearComp apparatus is not merely a biological signal logging device, as is often used in the medical community. It rather enables new forms of real-time signal processing for HI. A simple example might include a biofeedback-driven video camera.

---

[3] The first wearable computers equipped with multichannel biosensors were built by the author during the 1980s inspired by a collaboration with Dr. Ghista of McMaster University. Later, in 1995, the author put together an improved apparatus based on a Compaq Contura Aero 486/33 with a ProComp™ eight channel analog to digital converter, worn in a Mountainsmith waist bag, and sensors from Thought Technologies Limited. The author subsequently assisted Healey in duplicating this system for use in trying to understand human emotions [23].

2

WHERE ON THE BODY IS THE BEST PLACE FOR A PERSONAL IMAGING SYSTEM?

This chapter considers the question of where to place the sensory and display apparatus on the body. Although the final conclusion is that both should be placed, effectively, right within the eye itself, various other possibilities are considered and explained first. In terms of the various desirable properties the apparatus should be:

- *Covert:* It must not have an unusual appearance that may cause objections or ostracization owing to the unusual physical appearance. It is known, for instance, that blind or visually challenged persons are very concerned about their physical appearance notwithstanding their own inability to see their own appearance.
- *Incidentalist:* Others cannot determine whether or not the apparatus is in use, even when it is not entirely covert. For example, its operation should not convey an outward intentionality.
- *Natural:* The apparatus must provide a natural user interface, such as may be given by a first-person perspective.
- *Cybernetic:* It must not require conscious thought or effort to operate.

These attributes are desired in range, if not in adjustment to that point of the range of operational modes. Thus, for example, it may be desired that the apparatus be highly visible at times as when using it for a personal safety device to deter crime. Then one may wish it to be very obvious that video is being recorded and transmitted. So ideally in these situations the desired attributes are affordances rather than constraints. For example, the apparatus may be ideally covert but with an additional means of making it obvious *when desired.* Such an additional means may include a display viewable by others, or a blinking red light indicating transmission of video data. Thus the system would ideally be operable over a wide range of obviousness levels, over a wide range of incidentalism levels, and the like.

Introduction: Evolution toward Personal Imaging

Computing first evolved from large mainframe business machines, to smaller so-called personal computers that fit on our desks. We are now at a pivotal era in which computers are becoming not only pervasive but also even more personal, in the form of miniature devices we carry or wear.

An equally radical change has taken place in the way we acquire, store, and process visual photographic information. Cameras have evolved from heavy equipment in mule-drawn carriages, to devices one can conceal in a shirt button, or build into a contact lens. Storage media have evolved from large glass plates to Internet Web servers in which pictures are wirelessly transmitted to the Web.

In addition to downsizing, there is a growing trend to a more personal element of imaging, which parallels the growth of the personal computer. The trend can be seen below:

- *Wet plate process:* Large glass plates that must be prepared in a darkroom tent. Apparatus requires mule-drawn carriages or the like for transport.
- *Dry plates:* Premade, individual sheets typically 8 by 10 or 4 by 5 inches are available so it was possible for one person to haul apparatus in a backpack.
- *Film:* a flexible image recording medium that is also available in rolls so that it can be moved through the camera with a motor. Apparatus may be carried easily by one person.
- *Electronic imaging:* For example, Vidicon tube recording on analog videotape.
- *Advanced electronic imaging:* For example, solid state sensor arrays, image capture on computer hard drives.
- *Laser EyeTap:* The eye itself is made to function as the camera, to effortlessly capture whatever one looks at. The size and weight of the apparatus is negligible. It may be controlled by brainwave activity, using biofeedback, so that pictures are taken automatically during exciting moments in life.

Originally, only pictures of very important people or events were ever recorded. However, imaging became more personal as cameras became affordable and more pervasive, leading to the concept of family albums. It is known that when there is a fire or flood, the first thing that people will try to save is the family photo album. It is considered priceless and irreplaceable to the family, yet family albums often turn up in flea markets and church sales for pennies. Clearly, the value of one's collection of pictures is a very personal matter; that is, family albums are often of little value outside the personal context. Accordingly an important aspect of personal imaging is the individuality, and the individual personal value of the picture as a prosthesis of memory.

Past generations had only a handful of pictures, perhaps just one or two glass plates that depicted important points in their life, such as a wedding. As cameras became cheaper, people captured images in much greater numbers, but still a small enough number to easily sort through and paste into a small number of picture albums.

However, today's generation of personal imaging devices include handheld digital cameras that double as still and movie cameras, and often capture thousands of pictures before any need for any to be deleted. The family of the future will be faced with a huge database of images, and thus there are obvious problems with storage, compression, retrieval, and sorting, for example.

Tomorrow's generation of personal imaging devices will include mass-produced versions of the special laser EyeTap eyeglasses that allow the eye itself to function as a camera, as well as contact lens computers that might capture a person's entire life on digital video. These pictures will be transmitted wirelessly to friends and relatives, and the notion of a family album will be far more complete, compelling, and collaborative, in the sense that it will be a shared real-time videographic experience space.

Personal imaging is not just about family albums, though. It will also radically change the way large-scale productions such as feature-length movies are made. Traditionally movie cameras were large and cumbersome, and were fixed to heavy tripods. With the advent of the portable camera, it was possible to capture real-world events. Presently, as cameras, even the professional cameras get smaller and lighter, a new "point-of-eye" genre has emerged. Sports and other events can now be covered from the eye perspective of the participant so that the viewer feels as if he or she is actually experiencing the event. This adds a personal element to imaging. Thus personal imaging also suggests new photographic and movie genres In the future it will be possible to include an EyeTap camera of sufficiently high resolution into a contact lens so that a high-quality cinematographic experience can be recorded.

This chapter addresses the fundamental question as to where on the body a personal imaging system is best located. The chapter follows an organization given by the following evolution from portable imaging systems to EyeTap mediated reality imaging systems:

1. Portable imaging systems.
2. Personal handheld imaging systems.
3. Personal handheld systems with concomitant cover activity (e.g., the VideoClips system).
4. Wearable camera systems and concomitant cover activity (e.g., the wrist-watch videoconferencing computer).
5. Wearable "always ready" systems such as the telepointer reality augmenter.
6. Wearable imaging systems with eyeworn display (e.g., the wearable radar vision system).
7. Headworn camera systems and reality mediators.
8. EyeTap (eye itself as camera) systems.

2.1   PORTABLE IMAGING SYSTEMS

Imaging systems have evolved from once cumbersome cameras with large glass plates to portable film-based systems.

2.2   PERSONAL HANDHELD SYSTEMS

Next these portable cameras evolved into small handheld devices that could be operated by one person. The quality and functionality of modern cameras allows a *personal imaging* system to replace an entire film crew. This gave rise to new genres of cinematography and news reporting.

2.3   CONCOMITANT COVER ACTIVITIES AND THE VIDEOCLIPS CAMERA SYSTEM

Concomitant cover activity pertains generally to a new photographic or video system typically consisting of a portable personal imaging computer system. It includes new apparatus for personal documentary photography and videography, as well as personal machine vision and visual intelligence. In this section a personal computer vision system with viewfinder and personal video annotation capability is introduced. The system integrates the process of making a personal handwritten diary, or the like, with the capture of video, from an optimal point of vantage and camera angle. This enables us to keep a new form of personal diary, as well as to create documentary video. Video of a subject such as an official behind a counter may be captured by a customer or patron of an establishment, in such a manner that the official cannot readily determine whether or not video is being captured together with the handwritten notes or annotations.

2.3.1   Rationale for Incidentalist Imaging Systems with Concomitant Cover Activity

In photography (and in movie and video production), as well as in a day-to-day visual intelligence computational framework, it is often desirable to capture events or visual information in a natural manner with minimal intervention or disturbance. A possible scenario to be considered is that of face-to-face conversation between two individuals, where one of the individuals wishes to make an annotated video diary of the conversation without disrupting the natural flow of the conversation. In this context, it is desirable to create a personal video diary or personal documentary, or to have some kind of personal photographic or video-graphic memory aid that forms the visual equivalent of what the electronic organizers and personal digital assistants do to help us remember textual or syntactic information.

Current state-of-the-art photographic or video apparatus creates a visual disturbance to others and attracts considerable attention on account of the gesture of bringing the camera up to the eye. Even if the size of the camera could be reduced to the point of being negligible (e.g., suppose that the whole apparatus is made no bigger than the eyecup of a typical camera viewfinder), the very gesture of bringing a device up to the eye would still be unnatural and would attract considerable attention, especially in large public establishments like department stores, or establishments owned by criminal or questionable organizations (some gambling casinos come to mind) where photography is often prohibited.

However, it is in these very establishments in which a visitor or customer may wish to have a video record of the clerk's statement of the refund policy or the terms of a sale. Just as department stores often keep a video recording of all transactions (and often even a video recording of all activity within the establishment, sometimes including a video recording of customers in the fitting rooms), the goal of the present invention is to assist a customer who may wish to keep a video record of a transaction, interaction with a clerk, manager, refund explanation, or the like.

Already there exist a variety of covert cameras such a camera concealed beneath the jewel of a necktie clip, cameras concealed in baseball caps, and cameras concealed in eyeglasses. However, such cameras tend to produce inferior images, not just because of the technical limitations imposed by their small size but, more important, because they lack a viewfinder system (a means of viewing the image to adjust camera angle, orientation, exposure, etc., for the best composition). Because of the lack of viewfinder system, the subject matter of traditional covert cameras is not necessarily centered well in the viewfinder, or even captured by the camera at all, and thus these covert cameras are not well suited to personal documentary or for use in a personal photographic/videographic memory assistant or a personal machine vision system.

2.3.2   Incidentalist Imaging Systems with Concomitant Cover Activity

Rather than necessarily being covert, what is proposed is a camera and viewfinder system with "concomitant cover activity" for unobtrusively capturing video of exceptionally high compositional quality and possibly even artistic merit.

In particular, the personal imaging device does not need to be necessarily covert. It may be designed so that the subject of the picture or video cannot readily determine whether or not the apparatus is recording. Just as some department stores have dark domes on their ceilings so that customers do not know whether or not there are cameras in the domes (or which domes have cameras and even which way the cameras are pointed where there are cameras in the domes), the "concomitant cover activity" creates a situation in which a department store clerk and others will not know whether or not a customer's personal memory assistant is recording video. This uncertainty is created by having the camera positioned so that it will typically be pointed at a person at all times, whether or not it is actually being used.

What is described in this section is an incidentalist video capture system based on a Personal Digital Assistants (PDA), clipboard, or other handheld devices that contain a forward-pointing camera, so that a person using it will naturally aim the camera without conscious or apparent intent.

The clipboard version of this invention is a kind of visual equivalent to Stifelman's audio notebook (Lisa J. Stifelman, *Augmenting Real-World Objects: A Paper-Based Audio Notebook*, CHI'96 Conference Companion, pp. 199–200, April 1996), and the general ideas of pen-based computing.

A typical embodiment of the invention consists of a handheld pen-based computer (see Fig. 2.1) or a combination clipboard and pen-based computer input device (see Fig. 2.2).

A camera is built into the clipboard, with the optical axis of the lens facing the direction from bottom to top of the clipboard. During normal face-to-face conversation the person holding the clipboard will tend to point the camera at the other person while taking written notes of the conversation. In this manner the intentionality (whether or not the person taking written notes is intending to point the camera at the other person) is masked by the fact that the camera will always be pointed at the other person by virtue of its placement in the clipboard. Thus the camera lens opening need not necessarily be covert, and could be deliberately accentuated (e.g., made more visible) if desired. To understand why it might be desirable to make it more visible, one can look to the cameras in department stores, which are often placed in large dark smoked plexiglass domes. In this

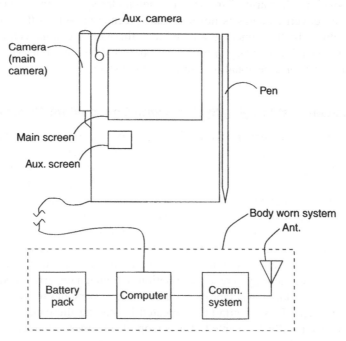

Figure 2.1 Diagram of a simple embodiment of the invention having a camera borne by a personal digital assistant (PDA). The PDA has a separate display attached to it to function as a viewfinder for the camera.

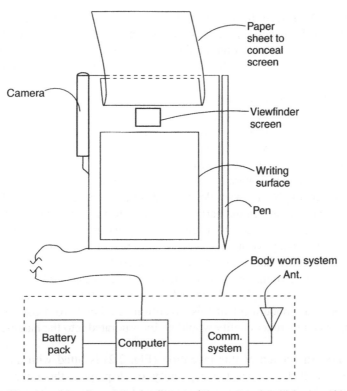

Figure 2.2 Diagram of an alternate embodiment of the system in which a graphics tablet is concealed under a pad of paper and an electronic pen is concealed inside an ordinary ink pen so that all of the writing on the paper is captured and recorded electronically together with video from the subject in front of the user of the clipboard while the notes are being taken.

way they are neither hidden nor visible, but rather they serve as an uncertain deterrent to criminal conduct. While they could easily be hidden inside smoke detectors, ventilation slots, or small openings, the idea of the dome is to make the camera conceptually visible yet completely hidden. In a similar manner a large lens opening on the clipboard may, at times, be desirable, so that the subject will be reminded that there could be a recording but will be uncertain as to whether or not such a recording is actually taking place. Alternatively, a large dark shiny plexiglass strip, made from darkly smoked plexiglass (typically 1 cm high and 22 cm across), is installed across the top of the clipboard as a subtle yet visible deterrent to criminal behavior. One or more miniature cameras are then installed behind the dark plexiglass, looking forward through it. In other embodiments, a camera is installed in a PDA, and then the top of the PDA is covered with dark smoky plexiglass.

The video camera (see Fig. 2.1) captures a view of a person standing in front of the user of the PDA and displays the image on an auxiliary screen, which may be easily concealed by the user's hand while the user is writing or pretending to write on the PDA screen. In commercial manufacture of this device the auxiliary screen may not be necessary; it may be implemented as a window displaying the camera's view on a portion of the main screen, or overlaid on the main screen. Annotations made on the main screen are captured and stored together with videoclips from the camera so that there is a unified database in which the notes and annotations are linked with the video. An optional second camera may be present if the user wishes to make a video recording of himself/herself while recording another person with the main camera. In this way, both sides of the conversation may be simultaneously recorded by the two cameras. The resulting recordings could be edited later, and there could be a cut back and forth between the two cameras to follow the natural flow of the conversation. Such a recording might, for example, be used for an investigative journalism story on corrupt organizations. In the early research prototypes, an additional wire was run up the sleeve of the user into a separate body-worn pack powered by its own battery pack. The body-worn pack typically contained a computer system which houses video capture hardware and is connected to a communications system with packet radio terminal node controller (high-level data link controller with modem) and radio; this typically establishes a wireless Internet connection. In the final commercial embodiment of this invention, the body-worn pack will likely disappear, since this functionality would be incorporated into the handheld device itself.

The clipboard version of this invention (Fig. 2.2) is fitted with an electronic display system that includes the capability of displaying the image from the camera. The display serves then as a viewfinder for aiming the camera at the subject. Moreover the display is constructed so that it is visible only to the user of the clipboard or, at least, so that the subject of the picture cannot readily see the display. Concealment of the display may be accomplished through the use of a honeycomb filter placed over the display. Such honeycomb filters are common in photography, where they are placed over lights to make the light sources behave more directionally. They are also sometimes placed over traffic lights where there is a wye intersection, for the lights to be seen from one direction in order that the traffic lights not confuse drivers on another branch of a wye intersection that faces almost the same way. Alternatively, the display may be designed to provide an inherently narrow field of view, or other barriers may be constructed to prevent the subject from seeing the screen.

The video camera (see Fig. 2.2) displays on a miniature screen mounted to the clipboard. A folded-back piece of paper conceals the screen. The rest of the sheets of paper are placed slightly below the top sheet so that the user can write on them in a natural fashion. From the perspective of someone facing the user (the subject), the clipboard will have the appearance of a normal clipboard in which the top sheet appears to be part of the stack. The pen is a combined electronic pen and real pen so that the user can simultaneously write on the paper with real ink, as well as make an electronic annotation by virtue of a graphics tablet below the stack of paper, provided that the stack is not excessively thick. In this way there is a computer database linking the real physical paper with its pen strokes and the video recorded of the subject. From a legal point of view, real physical pen strokes may have some forensic value that the electronic material may not (e.g., if the department store owner asks the customer to sign something, or even just to sign for a credit card transaction, the customer may place it over the pad and use the special pen to capture the signature in the customer's own computer and index it to the video record). In this research prototype there is a wire going from the clipboard, up the sleeve of the user. This wire would be eliminated in the commercially produced version of the apparatus, by construction of a self-contained video clipboard with miniature built-in computer, or by use of a wireless communications link to a very small body-worn intelligent image-processing computer.

The function of the camera is integrated with the clipboard. This way textual information, as well as drawings, may be stored in a computer system, together with pictures or videoclips. (Hereafter still pictures and segments of video will both be referred to as videoclips, with the understanding that a still picture is just a video sequence that is one frame in length.)

Since videoclips are stored in the computer together with other information, these videoclips may be recalled by an associative memory working together with that other information. Thus tools like the UNIX "grep" command may be applied to videoclips by virtue of the associated textual information which typically resides as a videographic header. For example, one can grep for the word "meijer," and may find various videoclips taken during conversations with clerks in the Meijer department store. Thus such a videographic memory system may give rise to a memory recall of previous videoclips taken during previous visits to this department store, provided that one has been diligent enough to write down (e.g., enter textually) the name of the department store upon each visit.

Videoclips are typically time-stamped (e.g., there exist file creation dates) and GPS-stamped (e.g., there exists global positioning system headers from last valid readout) so that one can search on setting (time + place).

Thus the video clipboard may be programmed so that the act of simply taking notes causes previous related videoclips to play back automatically in a separate window (in addition to the viewfinder window, which should always remain active for continued proper aiming of the camera). Such a video clipboard may, for example, assist in a refund explanation by providing the customer with an index into previous visual information to accompany previous notes taken during a purchase. This system is especially beneficial when encountering department store representatives who do not wear name tags and who refuse to identify themselves by name (as is often the case when they know they have done something wrong, or illegal).

This apparatus allows the user to take notes with pen and paper (or pen and screen) and continuously record video together with the written notes. Even if there is insufficient memory to capture a continuous video recording, the invention can be designed so that the user will always end up with the ability to produce a picture from something that was seen a couple of minutes ago. This may be useful to everyone in the sense that we may not want to miss a great photo opportunity, and often great photo opportunities only become known to us after we have had time to think about something we previously saw. At the very least, if, for example, a department store owner or manager becomes angry and insulting to the customer, the customer may retroactively record the event by opening a circular buffer.

2.3.3 Applications of Concomitant Cover Activity and Incidentalist Imaging

An imaging apparatus might also be of use in personal safety. Although there are a growing number of video surveillance cameras installed in the environment allegedly for public safety, there have been recent questions as to the true benefit of such centralized surveillance infrastructures. Notably there have been several instances where such centralized infrastructure has been abused by its owners (as in roundups and detainment of peaceful demonstrators). Moreover public safety systems may fail to protect individuals against crimes committed by members of the organizations that installed the systems. Therefore embodiments of the invention often implement the storage and retrieval of images by transmitting and recording images at one or more remote locations. In one embodiment of the invention, images were transmitted and recorded in different countries so that they would be difficult to destroy in the event that the perpetrator of a crime or other misconduct might wish to do so.

Moreover, as an artistic tool of personal expression, the apparatus allows the user to record, from a new perspective, experiences that have been difficult to so record in the past. For example, a customer might be able to record an argument with a fraudulent business owner from a very close camera angle. This is possible because a clipboard may be extended outward toward the person without violating personal space in the same way as might be necessary to do the same with a camera hidden in a tie clip, baseball cap, or sunglasses. Since a clipboard may extend outward from the body, it may be placed closer to the subject than the normal eye viewpoint in normal face-to-face conversation. As a result the camera can capture a close-up view of the subject.

Furthermore the invention is useful as a new communications medium, in the context of collaborative photography, collaborative videography, and telepresence. One way in which the invention can be useful for telepresence is in the creation of video orbits (collections of pictures that exist in approximately the same orbit of the projective group of coordinate transformations as will be described in Chapter 6). A video orbit can be constructed using the clipboard embodiment in which a small rubber bump is made on the bottom of the clipboard right under the camera's center of projection. In this way, when the clipboard is rested upon a surface such as a countertop, it can be panned around this fixed point so that video recorded from the camera can be used to assemble a panorama or orbit of greater spatial extent than a single picture. Similarly with the wristwatch embodiment, a small rubber bump on the bottom of the wristband allows the wearer to place the wrist upon a countertop and rotate the entire arm and wrist about a fixed point. Either embodiment is well suited to shooting a high-quality panoramic picture or orbit of an official behind a high counter, as is typically found at a department store, bank, or other organization.

Moreover the invention may perform other useful tasks such as functioning as a personal safety device and crime deterrent by virtue of its ability to maintain a video diary transmitted and recorded at multiple remote locations. As a tool for photojournalists and reporters, the invention has clear advantages over other competing technologies.

2.4 THE WRISTWATCH VIDEOPHONE: A FULLY FUNCTIONAL "ALWAYS READY" PROTOTYPE

An example of a convenient wearable "always ready" personal imaging system is the wristwatch videoconferencing system (Fig. 2.3). In this picture Eric Moncrieff is wearing the wristwatch that was designed by the author, and Stephen Ross (a former student) is pictured on the XF86 screen as a 24 bit true color visual.

Concealed inside the watch there is also a broadcast quality full color video camera. The current embodiment requires the support of a separate device that is ordinarily concealed underneath clothing (that device processes the images and transmits live video to the Internet at about seven frames per second in full 24 bit color). Presently we are working on building an embodiment of this invention in which all of the processing and the communications device fit inside the wristwatch so that a separate device doesn't need to be worn elsewhere on the body for the wristwatch videoconferencing system to work.

 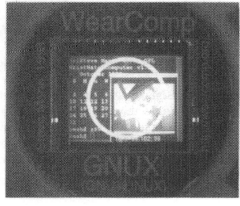

(a)   (b)

Figure 2.3 The wristwatch videoconferencing computer running the videoconferencing application underneath a transparent clock, running XF86 under the GNUX (GNU + Linux) operating system: (a) Worn while in use; (b) Close-up of screen with GNUX "cal" program running together with video window and transparent clock.

The computer programs, such as the VideoOrbits electronic newsgathering programs, developed as part of this research are distributed freely under GNU GPL.

This system, designed and built by the author in 1998, was the world's first Linux wristwatch, and the GNU Linux operating system was used in various demonstrations in 1999. It became the highlight of ISSCC 2000, when it was run by the author to remotely deliver a presentation:

ISSCC: 'Dick Tracy' watch watchers disagree

By Peter Clarke EE Times (02/08/00, 9:12 p.m. EST)

SAN FRANCISCO — Panelists at a Monday evening (Feb. 7) panel session at the International Solid State Circuits Conference (ISSCC) here failed to agree on when the public will be able to buy a "Dick Tracy" style watch for Christmas, with estimates ranging from almost immediately to not within the next decade.

Steve Mann, a professor at the University of Toronto, was hailed as the father of the wearable computer and the ISSCC's first virtual panelist, by moderator Woodward Yang of Harvard University (Cambridge Mass.).

. . .

Not surprisingly, Mann was generally upbeat at least about the technical possibilities of distributed body-worn computing, showing that he had already developed a combination wristwatch and imaging device that can send and receive video over short distances.

Meanwhile, in the debate from the floor that followed the panel discussion, ideas were thrown up, such as shoes as a mobile phone — powered by the mechanical energy of walking, and using the Dick Tracy watch as the user interface — and a more distributed model where spectacles are used to provide the visual interface; an ear piece to provide audio; and even clothing to provide a key-pad or display.

and finally appeared on the cover of *Linux Journal*, July 2000, issue 75, together with a feature article.

Although it was a useful invention, the idea of a wristwatch videoconferencing computer is fundamentally flawed, not so much because of the difficulty in inventing, designing, and building it but rather because it is difficult to operate without conscious thought and effort. In many ways the wristwatch computer was a failure not because of technology limitations but because it was not a very good idea to start with, when the goal is constant online connectivity that drops below the conscious level of awareness. The failure arose because of the need to lift the hand and shift focus of attention to the wrist.

2.5 TELEPOINTER: WEARABLE HANDS-FREE COMPLETELY SELF-CONTAINED VISUAL AUGMENTED REALITY

The obvious alternative to the flawed notion of a wristwatch computer is an eyeglass-based system because it would provide a constancy of interaction and allow the apparatus to provide operational modes that drop below the conscious level of awareness. However, before we consider eyeglass-based systems, let us consider some other possibilities, especially in situations where reality only needs to be augmented (e.g., where nothing needs to be mediated, filtered, or blocked from view).

The telepointer is one such other possibility. The telepointer is a wearable hands-free, headwear-free device that allows the wearer to experience a visual collaborative telepresence, with text, graphics, and a shared cursor, displayed directly on real-world objects. A mobile person wears the device clipped onto his tie, which sends motion pictures to a video projector at a base (home) where another person can see everything the wearer sees. When the person at the base points a laser pointer at the projected image of the wearer's site, the wearer's aremac's[1] servo's points a laser at the same thing the wearer is looking at. It is completely portable and can be used almost anywhere, since it does not rely on infrastructure. It is operated through a reality user interface (RUI) that allows the person at the base to have direct interaction with the real world of the wearer, establishing a kind of computing that is completely free of metaphors, in the sense that a laser at the base controls the wearable laser aremac.

2.5.1 No Need for Headwear or Eyewear If Only Augmenting

Using a reality mediator (to be described in the next section) to do only augmented reality (which is a special case of mediated reality) is overkill. Therefore, if all that is desired is augmented reality (e.g., if no diminished reality or altered/mediated reality is needed), the telepointer is proposed as a direct user interface.

The wearable portion of the apparatus, denoted WEAR STATION in Figure 2.4, contains a camera, denoted WEAR CAM, that can send pictures thousands of miles away to the other portion of the apparatus, denoted BASE STATION, where the motion picture is stabilized by VideoOrbits (running on a base station computer denoted BASE COMP) and then shown by a projector, denoted PROJ., at the base station. Rays of light denoted PROJ. LIGHT reach a beamsplitter, denoted B.B.S., in the apparatus of the base station, and are partially reflected; some projected rays are considered wasted light and denoted PROJ. WASTE. Some of the light from the projector will also pass through beamsplitter B.B.S., and emerge as light rays denoted BASE LIGHT. The projected image thus appears upon a wall or other projection surface denoted as SCREEN. A person at the base station can point to projected images of any of the SUBJECT MATTER by simply pointing a laser pointer at the SCREEN where images of the SUBJECT MATTER appear. A camera at the base station, denoted as BASE CAM provides an image of the screen to the base station computer (denoted BASE COMP), by way of beamsplitter B.B.S. The BASE CAM is usually equipped with a filter, denoted FILT., which is a narrowband bandpass filter having a passband to pass light from the laser pointer being used. Thus the BASE CAM will capture an image primarily of the laser dot on the screen, and especially since a laser

---

[1] An aremac is to a projector as a camera is to a scanner. The aremac directs light at 3-D objects.

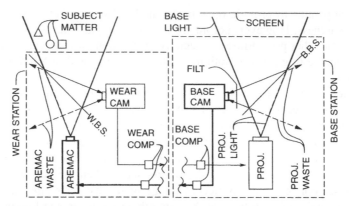

Figure 2.4 Telepointer system for collaborative visual telepresence without the need for eyewear or headwear or infrastructural support: The wearable apparatus is depicted on the left; the remote site is depicted on the right. The author wears the WEAR STATION, while his wife remotely watches on a video projector, at BASE STATION. She does not need to use a mouse, keyboard, or other computerlike device to interact with the author. She simply points a laser pointer at objects displayed on the SCREEN. For example, while the author is shopping, she can remotely see what's in front of him projected on the livingroom wall. When he's shopping, she sees pictures of the grocery store shelves transmitted from the grocery store to the livingroom wall. She points her laser pointer at these images of objects, and this pointing action teleoperates a servo-mounted laser pointer in the apparatus worn by the author. When she points her laser pointer at the picture of the 1% milk, the author sees a red dot appear on the actual carton of 1% milk in the store. The user interface metaphor is very simple, because there is none. This is an example of a reality user interface: when she points her laser at an image of the milk carton, the author's laser points at the milk carton itself. Both parties see their respective red dots in the same place. If she scribbles a circle around the milk carton, the author will see the same circle scribbled around the milk carton.

pointer is typically quite bright compared to a projector, the image captured by BASE CAM can be very easily made, by an appropriate exposure setting of the BASE CAM, to be black everywhere except for a small point of light from which it can be determined where the laser pointer is pointing.

The BASE CAM transmits a signal back to the WEAR COMP, which controls a device called an AREMAC, after destabilizing the coordinates (to match the more jerky coordinate system of the WEAR CAM). SUBJECT MATTER within the field of illumination of the AREMAC scatters light from the AREMAC so that the output of AREMAC is visible to the person wearing the WEAR STATION. A beamsplitter, denoted W.B.S., of the WEAR STATION, diverts some light from SUBJECT MATTER to the wearable camera, WEAR CAM, while allowing SUBJECT MATTER to also be illuminated by the AREMAC.

This shared telepresence facilitates collaboration, which is especially effective when combined with the voice communications capability afforded by the use of a wearable hands-free voice communications link together with the telepointer apparatus. (Typically the WEAR STATION provides a common data communications link having voice, video, and data communications routed through the WEAR COMP.)

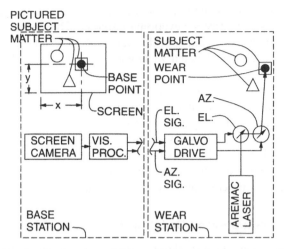

Figure 2.5 Details of the telepointer (TM) aremac and its operation. For simplicity the livingroom or manager's office is depicted on the left, where the manager can point at the screen with a laser pointer. The photo studio, or grocery store, as the case may be, is depicted on the right, where a body-worn laser aremac is used to direct the beam at objects in the scene.

Figure 2.5 illustrates how the telepointer works to use a laser pointer (e.g., in the livingroom) to control an aremac (wearable computer controlled laser in the grocery store). For simplicity, Figure 2.5 corresponds to only the portion of the signal flow path shown in bold lines of Figure 2.4.

SUBJECT MATTER in front of the wearer of the WEAR STATION is transmitted and displayed as PICTURED SUBJECT MATTER on the projection screen. The screen is updated, typically, as a live video image in a graphical browser such as glynx, while the WEAR STATION transmits live video of the SUBJECT MATTER.

One or more persons at the base station are sitting at a desk, or on a sofa, watching the large projection screen, and pointing at this large projection screen using a laser pointer. The laser pointer makes, upon the screen, a bright red dot, designated in the figure as BASE POINT.

The BASE CAM, denoted in this figure as SCREEN CAMERA, is connected to a vision processor (denoted VIS. PROC.) of the BASE COMP, which simply determines the coordinates of the brightest point in the image seen by the SCREEN CAMERA. The SCREEN CAMERA does not need to be a high-quality camera, since it will only be used to see where the laser pointer is pointing. A cheap black- and white-camera will suffice for this purpose.

Selection of the brightest pixel will tell us the coordinates, but a better estimate can be made by using the vision processor to determine the coordinates of a bright red blob, BASE POINT, to subpixel accuracy. This helps reduce the resolution needed, so that smaller images can be used, and therefore cheaper processing hardware and a lower-resolution camera can be used for the SCREEN CAMERA.

These coordinates are sent as signals denoted EL. SIG. and AZ. SIG. and are received at the WEAR STATION. They are fed to a galvo drive mechanism (servo) that controls two galvos. Coordinate signal AZ. SIG. drives azimuthal galvo AZ. Coordinate signal EL. SIG. drives elevational galvo EL. These galvos are calibrated by the unit denoted as GALVO DRIVE in the figure. As a result the AREMAC LASER is directed to form a red dot, denoted WEAR POINT, on the object that the person at the base station is pointing at from her livingroom or office.

The AREMAC LASER together with the GALVO DRIVE and galvos EL and AZ together comprise the device called an aremac, which is generally concealed in a brooch pinned to a shirt, or in a tie clip attached to a necktie, or is built into a necklace. The author generally wears this device on a necktie. The aremac and WEAR CAM must be registered, mounted together (e.g., on the same tie clip), and properly calibrated. The aremac and WEAR CAM are typically housed in a hemispherical dome where the two are combined by way of beamsplitter W.B.S.

2.5.2   Computer-Supported Collaborative Living (CSCL)

While much has been written about computer-supported collaborative work (CSCW), there is more to life than work, and more to living than pleasing one's employer. The apparatus of the invention can be incorporated into ordinary day-to-day living, and used for such "tasks" as buying a house, a used car, a new sofa, or groceries while a remote spouse collaborates on the purchase decision.

Figure 2.6 shows the author wearing the WEAR STATION in a grocery store where photography and videography are strictly prohibited. Figure 2.7 shows a close-up view of the necktie clip portion of the apparatus.

Figure 2.6 Wearable portion of apparatus, as worn by author. The necktie-mounted visual augmented reality system requires no headwear or eyewear. The apparatus is concealed in a smoked plexiglass dome of wine-dark opacity. The dark dome reduces the laser output to safe levels, while at the same time making the apparatus blatantly covert. The dome matches the decor of nearly any department store or gambling casino. When the author has asked department store security staff what's inside their dark ceilings domes, he's been called "paranoid," or told that they are light fixtures or temperature sensors. Now the same security guards are wondering what's inside this dome.

Figure 2.7 Necktie clip portion. The necktie-mounted visual augmented reality system. A smoked plexiglass dome of wine-dark opacity is used to conceal the inner components. Wiring from these components to a body-concealed computer runs through the crack in the front of the shirt. The necktie helps conceal the wiring.

2.6 PORTABLE PERSONAL PULSE DOPPLER RADAR VISION SYSTEM BASED ON TIME–FREQUENCY ANALYSIS AND q-CHIRPLET TRANSFORM

"Today we saw Mary Baker Eddy with one eye!" — a deliberately cryptic sentence inserted into a commercial shortwave broadcast to secretly inform colleagues across the Atlantic of the successful radar imaging of a building (spire of Christian Science building; Mary Baker Eddy, founder) with just one antenna for both receiving and transmitting. Prior to this time, radar systems required two separate antennas, one to transmit, and the other to receive.

Telepointer, the necktie worn dome ("tiedome") of the previous section bears a great similarity to radar, and how radar in general works. In many ways the telepointer tiedome is quite similar to the radomes used for radar antennas. The telepointer was a front-facing two-way imaging apparatus. We now consider a backward-facing imaging apparatus built into a dome that is worn on the back.

Time–frequency and q-chirplet-based signal processing is applied to data from a small portable battery-operated pulse Doppler radar vision system designed and built by the author. The radar system and computer are housed in a miniature radome backpack together with video cameras operating in various spectral bands, to be backward-looking, like an eye in the back of the head. Therefore all the ground clutter is moving away from the radar when the user walks forward, and is easy to ignore because the radar has separate in-phase and quadrature channels that allow it to distinguish between negative and positive Doppler. A small portable battery powered computer built into the miniature radome allows the entire system to be operated while attached to the user's body. The fundamental hypothesis upon which the system operates is that actions such as an attack or pickpocket by someone sneaking up behind the user, or an automobile on a collision course from behind the user, are governed by accelerational intentionality. Intentionality can change abruptly and gives rise to application of roughly constant force against constant mass. Thus the physical dynamics of most situations lead to piecewise uniform acceleration, for which the Doppler returns are piecewise quadratic chirps. These q-chirps are observable as peaks in the q-chirplet transform [28].

2.6.1 Radar Vision: Background, Previous Work

Haykin coined the term "radar vision" in the context of applying methodology of machine vision to radar systems [5]. Traditionally radar systems were not coherent, but recent advances have made the designing and building of coherent radar systems possible [25]. Coherent radar systems, especially when having separate in-phase and quadrature components (e.g., providing a complex-valued output), are particularly well suited to Doppler radar signal processing [26] (e.g., see Fig. 2.8). Time–frequency analysis makes an implicit assumption of short-time stationarity, which, in the context of Doppler radar, is isomorphic to an assumption of short-time constant velocity. Thus the underlying assumption is that the velocity is piecewise constant. This assumption is preferable to simply taking a Fourier transform over the entire data record, but we can do better by modeling the underlying physical phenomena.

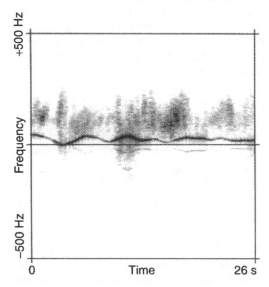

Figure 2.8 Sliding window Fourier transform of small but dangerous floating iceberg fragment as seen by an experimental pulse Doppler X-band marine radar system having separate in-phase and quadrature components. The radar output is a complex-valued signal for which we can distinguish between positive and negative frequencies. The chosen window comprises a family of discrete prolate spheroidal sequences [27]. The unique sinusoidally varying frequency signature of iceberg fragments gave rise to the formulation of the w-chirplet transform [28]. Safer navigation of oceangoing vessels was thus made possible.

Instead of simply using sines and cosines, as in traditional Fourier analysis, sets of parameterized functions are now often used for signal analysis and representation. The wavelet transform [29,30] is one such example having parameters of time and scale. The chirplet transform [28,31,32,33] has recently emerged as a new kind of signal representation. Chirplets include sets of parameterized signals having polynomial phase (piecewise cubic, piecewise quadratic, etc.) [28], sinusoidally varying phase, and projectively varying periodicity. Each kind of chirplet is optimized for a particular problem. For example, warbling chirplets (w-chirplets), also known as warblets [28], were designed for processing Doppler returns from floating iceberg fragments that bob around in a sinusoidal manner as seen in Figure 2.8. The sinusoidally varying phase of the w-chirplet matches the sinusoidally varying motion of iceberg fragments driven by ocean waves.

Of all the different kinds of chirplets, it will be argued that the q-chirplets (quadratic phase chirplets) are the best suited to processing of Doppler returns from land-based radar where accelerational intentionality is assumed. Q-chirplets are based on q-chirps (also called "linear FM"), $\exp(2\pi i(a + bt + ct^2))$ with phase a, frequency b, and chirpiness c. The Gaussian q-chirplet,

$$\psi_{t_0,b,c,\sigma} = \frac{1}{\sqrt{2\pi}\sigma} \exp\left(2\pi i(a + bt_c + ct_c^2) - \frac{1}{2}\left(\frac{t_c}{\sigma}\right)^2\right) \Big/ \sqrt{2\pi}\sigma$$

is a common form of q-chirplet [28], where $t_c = t - t_0$ is a movable time axis. There are four meaningful parameters, phase a being of lesser interest when looking at the magnitude of

$$\langle \psi_{t_0,b,c,\sigma} | z(t) \rangle \tag{2.1}$$

which is the q-chirplet transform of signal $z(t)$ taken with a Gaussian window. Q-chirplets are also related to the fractional Fourier transform [34].

2.6.2 Apparatus, Method, and Experiments

Variations of the apparatus to be described were originally designed and built by the author for assisting the blind. However, the apparatus has many uses beyond use by the blind or visually challenged. For example, we are all blind to objects and hazards that are behind us, since we only have eyes in the forward-looking portion of our heads.

A key assumption is that objects in front of us deserve our undivided attention, whereas objects behind us only require attention at certain times when there is a threat. Thus an important aspect of the apparatus is an intelligent rearview system that alerts us when there is danger lurking behind us, but otherwise does not distract us from what is in front of us. Unlike a rearview mirror on a helmet (or a miniature rearview camera with eyeglass-based display), the radar vision system is an intelligent system that provides us with timely information only when needed, so that we do not suffer from information overload.

Rearview Clutter is Negative Doppler

A key inventive step is the use of a rearview radar system whereby ground clutter is moving away from the radar while the user is going forward. This rearview configuration comprises a backpack in which the radome is behind the user and facing backward.

This experimental apparatus was designed and built by the author in the mid-1980s, from low-power components for portable battery-powered operation. A variation of the apparatus, having several sensing instruments, including radar, and camera systems operating in various spectral bands, including infrared, is shown in Figure 2.9. The radome is also optically transmissive in the visible and infrared. A general description of radomes may be found in http://www.radome.net/, although the emphasis has traditionally been on

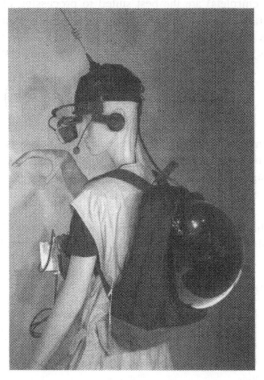

Figure 2.9 Early personal safety device (PSD) with radar vision system designed and built by the author, as pictured on exhibit at List Visual Arts Center, Cambridge, MA (October 1997). The system contains several sensing instruments, including radar, and camera systems operating in various spectral bands, including infrared. The headworn viewfinder display shows what is behind the user when targets of interest or concern appear from behind. The experience of using the apparatus is perhaps somewhat like having eyes in the back of the head, but with extra signal processing as the machine functions like an extension of the brain to provide visual intelligence. As a result the user experiences a sixth or seventh sense as a radar vision system. The antenna on the hat was for an early wireless Internet connection allowing multiple users to communicate with each other and with remote base stations.

radomes the size of a large building rather than in sizes meant for a battery-operated portable system.

Note that the museum artifact pictured in Figure 2.9 is a very crude early embodiment of the system. The author has since designed and built many newer systems that are now so small that they are almost completely invisible.

On the Physical Rationale for the q-Chirplet

The apparatus is meant to detect persons such as stalkers, attackers, assailants, or pickpockets sneaking up behind the user, or to detect hazardous situations, such as arising from drunk drivers or other vehicular traffic notations.

It is assumed that attackers, assailants, pickpockets, as well as ordinary pedestrian, bicycle, and vehicular traffic, are governed by a principle of accelerational intentionality. The principle of accelerational intentionality means that an individual attacker (or a vehicle driven by an individual person) is governed by a fixed degree of acceleration that is changed instantaneously and held roughly constant over a certain time interval. For example, an assailant is capable of a certain degree of exertion defined by the person's degree of fitness

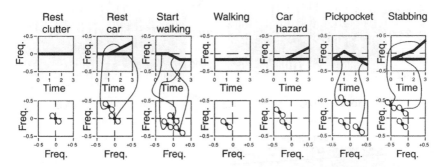

Figure 2.10 Seven examples illustrating the principle of accelerational intentionality, with time-frequency distribution shown at top, and corresponding chirplet transform frequency–frequency distribution below. REST CLUTTER: Radar return when the author (wearing the radar) is standing still. REST CAR: A car parked behind the author is set in motion when its driver steps on the accelerator; a roughly constant force of the engine is exerted against the constant mass of the car while the author (wearing the radar) is standing still. START WALKING: The author stands still for one second, and then decides to start walking. The decision to start walking is instantaneous, but the human body applies a roughly constant degree of force to its constant mass, causing it to accelerate until it reaches the desired walking speed. This takes approximately 1 second. Finally the author walks at this speed for another one second. All of the clutter behind the author (ground, buildings, lamp posts, etc.) is moving away from the author, so it moves into negative frequencies. WALKING: At a constant pace all of the clutter has a constant (negative) frequency. CAR HAZARD: While the author is walking forward, a parked car is switched into gear at time 1 second. It accelerates toward the author. The system detects this situation as a possible hazard, and brings an image up on the screen. PICKPOCKET: Rare but unique radar signature of a person lunging up behind the author and then suddenly switching to a decelerating mode (at time 1 second), causing reduction in velocity to match that of the author (at time 2 seconds) followed by a retreat away from the author. STABBING: Acceleration of attacker's body toward author, followed by a swing of the arm (initiated at time 2 seconds) toward the author.

which is unlikely to change over the short time period of an attack. The instant the attacker spots a wallet in a victim's back pocket, the attacker may accelerate by applying a roughly constant force (defined by his fixed degree of physical fitness) against the constant mass of the attacker's own body. This gives rise to uniform acceleration which shows up as a straight line in the time–frequency distribution.

Some examples following the principle of accelerational intentionality are illustrated in Figure 2.10.

Examples of Chirplet Transforms of Radar Data

A typical example of a radar data test set, comprising half a second (4,000 points) of radar data (starting from $t = 1.5$ seconds and running to $t = 2$ seconds in the "car3E" dataset) is shown in Figure 2.11. Here we see a two-dimensional slice known as frequency–frequency analysis [28] taken through the chirplet

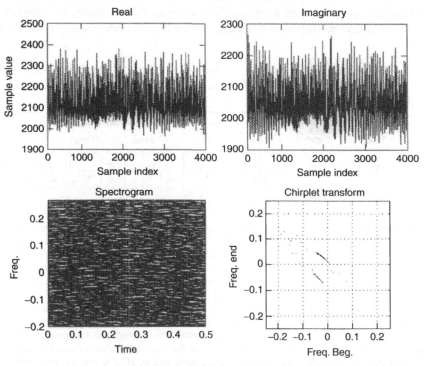

Figure 2.11 Most radar systems do not provide separate real and imaginary components and therefore cannot distinguish between positive and negative frequencies (e.g., whether an object is moving toward the radar or going away from it). The author's radar system provides in-phase and quadrature components: REAL and IMAG (imaginary) plots for 4,000 points (half a second) of radar data are shown. The author was walking at a brisk pace, while a car was accelerating toward the author. From the time–frequency distribution of these data we see the ground clutter moving away and the car accelerating toward the author. The chirplet transform shows two distinct peaks, one corresponding to all of the ground clutter (which is all moving away at the same speed) and the other corresponding to the accelerating car.

transform, in which the window size σ is kept constant, and the time origin t_0 is also kept constant. The two degrees of freedom of frequency b and chirpiness c are parameterized in terms of instantaneous frequency at the beginning and end of the data record, to satisfy the Nyquist chirplet criterion [28]. Here we see a peak for each of the two targets: the ground clutter (e.g., the whole world) moving away; and the car accelerating toward the radar. Other examples of chirplet transforms from the miniature radar set are shown in Figure 2.12.

Calibration of the Radar

The radar is a crude home-built system, operating at approximately 24 gigahertz, and having an interface to an Industry Standards Association (ISA) bus. Due to the high frequency involved, such a system is difficult to calibrate perfectly, or even closely. Thus there is a good deal of distortion, such as mirroring in the FREQ = 0 axis, as shown in Figure 2.13. Once the radar was calibrated, data could be analyzed with surprising accuracy, despite the crude and simple construction of the apparatus.

Experimental Results

Radar targets were classified based on their q-chirplet transforms, with approximately 90% accuracy, using the mathematical framework and methods described in [28] and [35]. Some examples of the radar data are shown as time–frequency distributions in Figure 2.14.

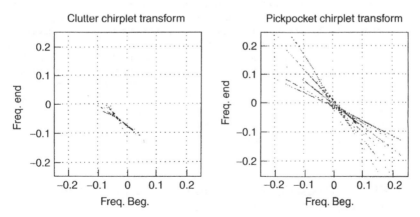

Figure 2.12 Chirplet transforms for ground clutter only, and pickpocket only. Ground clutter falls in the lower left quadrant because it is moving away from the radar at both the beginning and end of any time record (window). Note that the pickpocket is the only kind of activity that appears in the lower right-hand quadrant of the chirplet transform. Whenever there is any substantial energy content in this quadrant, we can be very certain there is a pickpocket present.

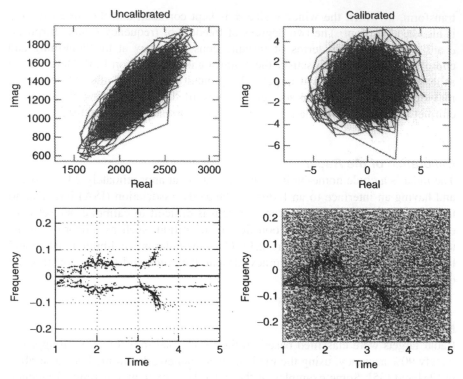

Figure 2.13 The author's home-built radar generates a great deal of distortion. Notice, for example, that a plot of real versus imaginary data shows a strong correlation between real and imaginary axes, and also an unequal gain in the real and imaginary axes, respectively (note that the unequal signal strength of REAL and IMAG returns in the previous figure as well). Note further that the dc offset gives rise to a strong signal at $f = 0$, even though there was nothing moving at exactly the same speed as the author (e.g., nothing that could have given rise to a strong signal at $f = 0$). Rather than trying to calibrate the radar exactly, and to remove dc offset in the circuits (all circuits were dc coupled), and risk losing low-frequency components, the author mitigated these problems by applying a calibration program to the data. This procedure subtracted the dc offset inherent in the system, and computed the inverse of the complex Choleski factorization of the covariance matrix (e.g., covz defined as covariance of real and imaginary parts), which was then applied to the data. Notice how the CALIBRATED data forms an approximately isotropic circular blob centered at the origin when plotted as REAL versus IMAGINARY. Notice also the removal of the mirroring in the FREQ = 0 axis in the CALIBRATED data, which was quite strong in the UNCALIBRATED data.

2.7   WHEN BOTH CAMERA AND DISPLAY ARE HEADWORN: PERSONAL IMAGING AND MEDIATED REALITY

When both the image acquisition and image display embody a headworn first-person perspective (e.g., computer takes input from a headworn camera and provides output to a headworn display), a new and useful kind of experience results, beyond merely augmenting the real world with a virtual world.

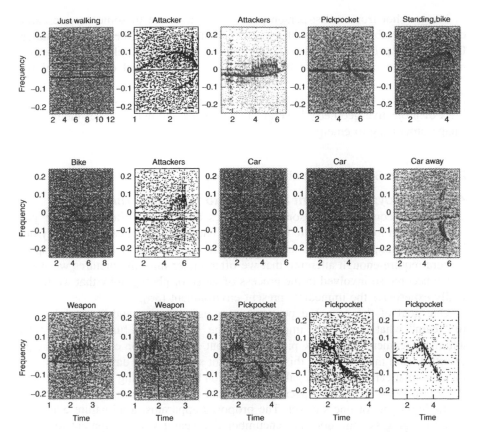

Figure 2.14 Various test scenarios were designed in which volunteers carried metal objects to simulate weapons, or lunged toward the author with pieces of metal to simulate an attack. Pickpockets were simulated by having volunteers sneak up behind the author and then retreat. The "pickpocket signature" is a unique radar signature in which the beginning and ending frequency fall on either side of the frequency defined by author's walking Doppler frequency. It was found that of all the radar signatures, the pickpocket signature was the most unique, and easiest to classify. The car plot in the middle of the array of plots was misclassified as a stabbing. It appears the driver stepped on the accelerator lightly at about time 1 second. Then just before time 3 seconds it appears that the driver had a sudden change of intentionality (perhaps suddenly realized lateness, or perhaps suddenly saw that the coast was clear) and stepped further on the accelerator, giving rise to an acceleration signature having two distinct portions.

Images shot from a first-person perspective give rise to some new research directions, notably new forms of image processing based on the fact that smaller, lighter cameras can track and orient themselves much faster, relative to the effort needed to move one's entire body. The mass (and general dynamics) of the camera is becoming small as compared to that of the body, so the ultimate limiting factor becomes the physical constraint of moving one's body. Accordingly the laws of projective geometry have greater influence, allowing newer methods of image processing to emerge.

2.7.1   Some Simple Illustrative Examples

Always Ready: From "Point and Click" to "Look and Think"

Current-day commercial personal electronics devices we often carry are just useful enough for us to tolerate but not good enough to significantly simplify our lives. For example, when we are on vacation, our camcorder and photographic camera require enough attention that we often either miss the pictures we want, or we become so involved in the process of video or photography that we fail to really experience the immediate present environment [36].

One goal of the proposed personal imaging apparatus and methodology is to "learn" what is visually important to the wearer, and function as a fully automatic camera that takes pictures without the need for conscious thought or effort from the wearer. In this way it might summarize a day's activities, and then automatically generate a gallery exhibition by transmitting desired images to the World Wide Web, or to specific friends and relatives who might be interested in the highlights of one's travel. The proposed apparatus, a miniature eyeglass-based imaging system, does not encumber the wearer with equipment to carry, or with the need to remember to use it. Yet, because it is recording all the time into a circular buffer [20] and merely overwriting that which is unimportant, it is *always ready*. Although the current embodiment of the invention is still in prototype stage, and is somewhat cumbersome enough that one might not wear it constantly, it is easy to imagine how, with commercial manufacture and miniaturization, smaller and lighter computational hardware could be built directly into ordinary glasses. Making the apparatus small enough to comfortably wear at all times will lead to a truly constant user-interface.

In the context of the *always ready* framework, when the signal-processing hardware detects something that might be of interest, recording can begin in a retroactive sense (e.g., a command may be issued to start recording from 30 seconds ago), and the decision can later be confirmed with human input. Of course this apparatus raises some important privacy questions discussed previously, and also addressed elsewhere in the literature [37,38].

The system might use the inputs from the biosensors on the body, as a multidimensional feature vector with which to classify content as important or unimportant. For example, it might automatically record a baby's first steps, as the parent's eyeglasses and clothing-based intelligent signal processor make an inference based on the thrill of the experience. It is often moments like these that we fail to capture on film: by the time we find the camera and load it with film, the moment has passed us by.

Personal Safety Device for Reducing Crime

A simple example of where it would be desirable that the device operate by itself, without conscious thought or effort, is in an extreme situation such as might happen if the wearer is attacked by a robber wielding a gun and demanding cash. In this kind of situation it is desirable that the apparatus function autonomously, without conscious effort from the wearer, even though the wearer might be aware of the signal-processing activities of the measuring (sensory) apparatus he or she is wearing.

As a simplified example of how the processing might be done, we know that the wearer's heart rate, averaged over a sufficient time window, would likely increase dramatically[2] with no corresponding increase in footstep rate (in fact footsteps would probably slow at the request of the gunman). The computer would then make an inference from the data, and predict a high visual saliency. (If we simply take heart rate divided by footstep rate, we can get a first-order approximation of the visual saliency index.) A high visual saliency would trigger recording from the wearer's camera at maximal frame rate, and also send these images together with appropriate messages to friends and relatives who would look at the images to determine whether it was a false alarm or real danger.[3]

Such a system is, in effect, using the wearer's brain as part of its processing pipeline. It is the wearer who sees the gun, and not the WearComp apparatus (e.g., a much harder problem would be to build an intelligent machine vision system to process the video from the camera and determine that a crime is being committed). Thus HI (intelligent signal processing arising, in part, because of the very existence of the human user) has solved a problem that would not be possible using machine-only intelligence.

Furthermore, this example introduces the concept of 'collective connected HI', because the signal processing systems also rely on those friends and relatives to look at the imagery that is wirelessly send from the eyeglass-mounted video camera and make a decision as to whether it is a false alarm or real attack.

---

[2] The heart may stop, or skip a beat at first, but over time, on average, experience tells us that our heart beats faster when frightened, unless the victim is killed in which case the apparatus should detect the absence of a heart beat.

[3] It has been suggested that the robber might become aware that his or her victim is wearing a personal safety device and try to eliminate the device or perhaps even target it for theft. In anticipation of these possible problems, personal safety devices operate by continuous transmission of images, so that the assailant cannot erase or destroy the images depicting the crime. Moreover the device itself, owing to its customized nature, would be unattractive and of little value to others, much as are undergarments, a mouthguard, or prescription eyeglasses. Furthermore devices could be protected by a password embedded into a CPLD that functions as a finite state machine, making them inoperable by anyone but the owner. To protect against passwords being extracted through torture, a personal distress password may be provided to the assailant by the wearer. The personal distress password unlocks the system but puts it into a special tracking and distress notification mode.

Thus the concept of HI has become blurred across geographical boundaries, and between more than one human and more than one computer.

The Retro-autofocus Example: Human in the Signal-Processing Loop

The preceding two examples dealt with systems that use the human brain, with its unique processing capability, as one of their components. In this way the whole system operates without conscious thought or effort. The effect is to provide a feedback loop of which subconscious or involuntary processes become an integral part.

An important aspect of HI is that the will power of the user may be inserted into or removed from the feedback loop of the entire process at any time. A very simple example, taken from everyday experience, rather than another new invention, is now presented.

One of the simplest examples of HI is that which happens with some of the early autofocus single-lens reflex (SLR) cameras in which autofocus was a retrofit feature. The autofocus motor would typically turn the lens barrel, but the operator could also grab onto the lens barrel while the autofocus mechanism was making it turn. Typically the operator could "fight" with the motor, and easily overpower it, since the motor was of sufficiently low torque. This kind of interaction is useful, for example, when shooting through a glass window at a distant object, where there are two or three local minima of the autofocus error function (e.g., focus on particles of dust on the glass itself, focus on a reflection in the glass, and focus on the distant object). Thus when the operator wishes to focus on the distant object and the camera system is caught in one of the other local minima (e.g., focused on the glass), the user merely grasps the lens barrel, swings it around to the approximate desired location (as though focusing crudely by hand, on the desired object of interest), and lets go. The camera will then take over and bring the desired object into sharp focus.

This very simple example illustrates a sort of humanistic intelligent signal processing in which the intelligent autofocus electronics of the camera work in close synergy with the intellectual capabilities of the camera operator. It is this aspect of HI that allows the human to step into and out of the loop at any time that makes it a powerful paradigm for intelligent signal processing.

2.7.2 Mediated Reality

A good way to bring the human into the loop is through the concept of mediated reality. Virtual reality allows us to experience a new visual world, but deprives us of the ability to see the actual world in which we live. Indeed, many VR game spaces are enclosed with railings, and the like, so that players do not fall down as they replace their reality with a new space and are therefore blind to the real world.

Augmented reality attempts to bring together the real and virtual. The general spirit and intent of augmented reality (AR) is to *add* virtual objects to the real world. A typical AR apparatus might consist of a video display with partially transparent visor, upon which computer-generated information is *overlaid* over the view of the real world.

In this section, we will see how MR forms a basis for personal imaging and a possible new genre of documentary video, electronic news gathering, and the like.

MR differs from typical AR in two respects:

1. The general spirit of MR, like typical AR, includes *adding* virtual objects but also the desire to *take away*, *alter*, or more generally to visually "mediate" real objects. Thus MR affords the apparatus the ability to augment, diminish, or otherwise alter our perception of reality.

2. Typically an AR apparatus is tethered to a computer workstation that is connected to an ac outlet, or constrains the user to some other specific site (a workcell, helicopter cockpit, etc.). What is proposed (and reduced to practice) in this chapter is a system that facilitates the augmenting, diminishing, or altering of the visual perception of reality in the context of ordinary day-to-day living.

MR uses a body-worn apparatus where both the *real* and *virtual* objects are placed on an equal footing, in the sense that both are presented together via a synthetic medium (e.g., a video display).

Successful implementations have been realized by *viewing* the real world using a head-mounted display (HMD) fitted with video cameras, body-worn processing, and/or bidirectional wireless communications to one or more remote computers, or supercomputing facilities. This portability enabled various forms of the apparatus to be tested extensively in everyday circumstances, such as while riding the bus, shopping, banking, and various other day-to-day interactions.

The proposed approach shows promise in applications where it is desired to have the ability to reconfigure reality. For example, color may be deliberately diminished or completely removed from the real world at certain times when it is desired to highlight parts of a virtual world with graphic objects having unique colors. The fact that vision may be *completely* reconfigured also suggests utility to the visually handicapped.

2.7.3   Historical Background Leading to the Invention of the Reality Mediator

Ivan Sutherland, a pioneer in the field of computer graphics, described a head-mounted display with half-silvered mirrors so that the wearer could see a virtual world superimposed on reality [39,40], giving rise to AR.

Others have adopted Sutherland's concept of a head-mounted display (HMD) but generally without the see-through capability. An artificial environment in which the user cannot see through the display is generally referred as a virtual reality (VR) environment. One of the reasons that Sutherland's approach was not more ubiquitously adopted is that he did not merge the virtual object (a simple cube) with the real world in a meaningful way. Steve Feiner's group was responsible for demonstrating the viability of AR as a field of research, using sonar (Logitech 3D trackers) to track the real world so that the real and virtual worlds could be registered [41,42]. Other research groups [43] have contributed to this development. Some research in AR arises from work in telepresence [44].

AR, although lesser known than VR, is currently used in some specific applications. Helicopter pilots often use a see-through visor that superimposes virtual objects over one eye, and the F18 fighter jet, for example, has a beamsplitter just inside the windshield that serves as a heads-up display (HUD), projecting a virtual image that provides the pilot with important information.

The general spirit of AR is to *add* computer graphics or the like to the real world. A typical AR apparatus does this with beamsplitter(s) so that the user sees directly through the apparatus while simultaneously viewing a computer screen.

The goal of this chapter is to consider a wireless (untethered) personal imaging apparatus worn over the eyes that in real time, computationally *reconfigures* reality. The apparatus allows the wearer to augment, diminish, or otherwise alter the perception of reality in addition to simply adding to reality. This "mediation" of reality may be thought of as a *filtering* operation applied to reality and then a combining operation to insert *overlays* (Fig. 2.15*a*). Equivalently the addition of computer-generated material may be regarded as arising from the filtering operation itself (Fig. 2.15*b*).

2.7.4   Practical Use of Mediated Reality

The author has found color-reduced reality mediation to be quite useful. For example, while comfortably seated in an airplane or commuter train, one can read text on the RM-based computer screen (e.g., read email), and at the same time "tone down" the surroundings so they take on a lesser role. One does not

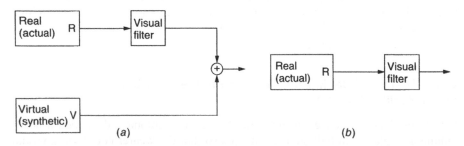

Figure 2.15 Two equivalent interpretations of mediated reality (MR). (a) Besides the ability to add computer-generated (synthetic) material to the wearer's visual world, there is potential to alter reality through a "visual filter." The coordinate transformation embodied in the visual filter may either be inserted into the virtual channel, or the graphics may be rendered in the coordinate system of the filtered reality channel so that the real and virtual channels are in register. (b) The visual filter need not be a *linear system*. The visual filter may itself embody the ability to create computer-generated objects and therefore subsume the "virtual" channel.

wish to completely block one's surroundings as in reading a newspaper, which can easily cover up most of a person's visual field.

Color-reduced reality mediation allows one to focus primarily on the virtual world. It might, for example, be comprised of email, a computer source file, and other miscellaneous work, running in emacs19, with colorful text, where the text colors are chosen so that no black, white, or gray text (text colors that would get "lost" in the medicated reality) is used. The experience is like reading a newspaper printed in brightly colored text on a transparent material, behind which the world moves about in black and white. One is completely aware of the world behind the "newspaper," but it does not distract one's ability to read the "paper."

Alternatively, the real world could be left in color, but the color mediated slightly so that unique and distinct colors could be reserved for virtual objects and graphics overlays. In addition to this "chromatic mediation," other forms of mediated reality have been found to be useful.

2.7.5   Personal Imaging as a Tool for Photojournalists and Reporters

In the early and mid-1990s the author experimented with personal imaging as a means of creating personal documentary, and in sharing this personal documentary video on the World Wide Web, in the form of *wearable wireless webcam* [45].

Several new and interesting forms of collaboration emerged. Occasionally the author serendipitously encountered newsworthy events while wearing the apparatus. Some were natural disasters which traditional journalists were unavailable to cover on the short notice involved, despite the importance for coverage of these events.

An example of how the author functioned as a 'roving reporter' is illustrated in Figure 2.16. This shows how computer-supported collaborative photojournalism (CSCP) emerged from *wearable wireless webcam*. Multiple images can be combined to produce a picture good enough for a full-page newspaper-size feature photograph despite the fact that each image had relatively low resolution. The manner in which pictures can be combined will be discussed in Chapters 4, 5, and 6.

In another instance of CSCP the author encountered a flood in the basement of a building and notified the police of the flood. However, without any conscious effort, the fact that the author walked past the event and noticed it resulted in its being recorded and transmitted wirelessly to remote sites. Thus the author was subsequently able to notify a newspaper of this transmission (wirelessly notifying the newspaper's editorial offices through email). The very high resolution images of tremendously high dynamic range and tonal fidelity were retrieved by the newspaper's editorial office and published in the newspaper. The quality of the images was higher than is typical for the newspaper, suggesting that wearable wireless webcam can rival the photographic technical quality and resolution of professional photographers armed with the best cameras available on the market.

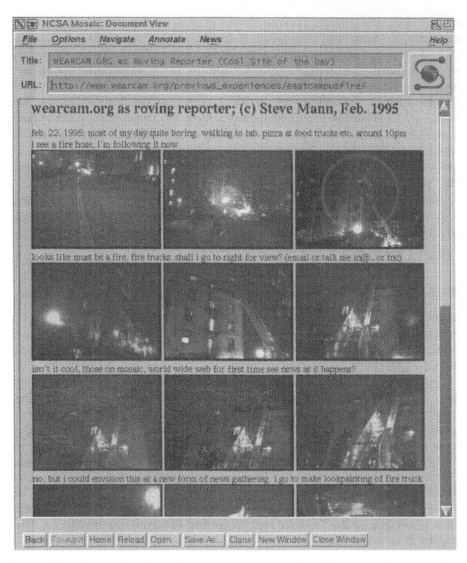

Figure 2.16 Serendipitously arising computer-supported collaborative photojournalism (CSCP). Author encountered an event serendipitously through ordinary everyday activity. As it turned out later, the newspapers had wanted to get this event covered but could not reach any of their photojournalists in time. The author, however, was able to offer hundreds of pictures of the event, wirelessly transmitted, while the event was still happening. Furthermore a collaboration with a large number of remote viewers enabled a new form of CSCP.

It is this "always ready" nature of mediated reality, of living life through the camera viewfinder, that makes it more successful than the other embodiments such as VideoClips or the wristwatch system described previously. In particular, the reality mediator embodies the concepts of incidentalist imaging, while at the same time providing a constancy of interaction with the real world. Thus, for example, the same retroactive recording capabilities of the VideoClips system are present in a more available way.

Registration between Real and Virtual Worlds

Alignment of the real and virtual worlds is very important, as indicated in the following statement by Ronald Azuma [46]:

> Unfortunately, registration is a difficult problem, for a number of reasons. First, the human visual system is very good at detecting even small misregistrations, because of the resolution of the fovea and the sensitivity of the human visual system to differences. Errors of just a few pixels are noticeable. Second, errors that can be tolerated in Virtual Environments are not acceptable in Augmented Reality. Incorrect viewing parameters, misalignments in the Head-Mounted Display, errors in the head-tracking system, and other problems that often occur in HMD-based systems may not cause detectable problems in Virtual Environments, but they are big problems in Augmented Reality. Finally, there's system delay: the time interval between measuring the head location to superimposing the corresponding graphic images on the real world. The total system delay makes the virtual objects appear to "lag behind" their real counterparts as the user moves around. The result is that in most Augmented Reality systems, the virtual objects appear to "swim around" the real objects ....
>
> *Until the registration problem is solved, Augmented Reality may never be accepted in serious applications.* (emphasis added)

The problem with different implementations of AR is that once registration is attained, if the eyeglasses shift ever so slightly or slip down the wearer's nose, the real and virtual worlds will not remain in perfect alignment.

Using the mediated reality (i.e., illusory transparency) approach, the illusion of transparency is perfectly coupled with the virtual world once the signals corresponding to the real and virtual worlds are put into register and combined into one signal. Not all applications lend themselves to easy registration at the signal level, but those that do call for the illusory transparency approach of mediated reality as opposed to an augmented reality overlay. In mediated reality, when eyeglasses slide down one's nose or shift slightly (or significantly for that matter), both the real and virtual worlds move together and remain in perfect register. Since they are both of the same medium (e.g., video), once registration is attained between the real and virtual video signals, the registration remains regardless of how eyeglasses might slide around on the wearer or how the wearer's eyes are focused or positioned with respect to the eyeglasses.

Another important point is that despite perfect registration, in a see-through visor (with beamsplitter, etc.) real objects will lie in different depth planes. In comparison, virtual objects are generally flat (i.e., in each eye) to the extent that their distance is at a particular focus (apart from the variations in binocular disparity of the virtual world). This is not so much a problem if all objects are far away as is often the case in aircraft (e.g., in the fighter jets using HUDs), but in many ground applications (e.g., in a typical building interior) the differing depth planes destroy the illusion of unity between real and virtual worlds.

With the illusory transparency approach of mediated reality, the real and virtual worlds exist in the same medium. They therefore are not only registered in location but also in depth. Any depth limitations of the display device affect both the virtual and real environments in exactly the same way.

Transformation of the Perceptual World

Even without computer graphics overlays mediated realities can be useful. For example, the color-blinding eyeglasses might allow an artist to study relationships between light and shade. While this experience may not be what the average person will want, especially given the cumbersome nature of past embodiments of RM, there are at least some users who would wear an expensive and cumbersome apparatus in order to see the world in a different light. Already, for example, artists have been known to travel halfway around the world to see the morning light in Italy. As the cost and size of the RM diminish, there could be a growing demand for glasses that also alter tonal range, allowing artists to manipulate contrast, color, and the like.

MR glasses could, in principle, be used to synthesize the effect of ordinary eyeglasses, but with a computer-controlled prescription that would modify itself, while conducting automatically scheduled eye tests on the user.

The RM might also reverse the direction of all outgoing light rays to allow the wearer to live in "upside-down" experiments in psychology. Although the majority of RM users of the future may have no desire to live in an upside-down, left-right-reversed, or sideways rotated world, these visual worlds serve as illustrative examples of possible extreme reality mediation that the author has experimented with extensively.

In his 1896 paper [47], George Stratton reported on experiments in which he wore eyeglasses that inverted his visual field of view. Stratton argued that since the image upon the retina was inverted, it seemed reasonable to examine the effect of presenting the retina with an "upright image."

His "upside-down" eye glasses consisted of two lenses of equal focal length, spaced two focal lengths, so that rays of light entering from the top would emerge from the bottom, and vice versa. Stratton, upon first wearing the glasses, reported seeing the world upside-down, but, after an adaptation period of several days, was able to function completely normally with the glasses on.

Dolezal [48] describes other types of optical transformations besides the *inversion* explored by Stratton, such as *displacement, reversal, tilt, magnification*, and *scrambling*. Kohler [49] discusses transformations of the perceptual world.

In general, 'optical transformations' could be realized by selecting a particular *linear time-invariant system* as the visual filter in Figure 2.15. (A good description of *linear time-invariant systems* may be found in a communications or electrical engineering textbook such as [50].)

The optical transformation to grayscale, described earlier, could also be realized by a visual filter (Fig. 2.15a) that is a linear time-invariant system, in particular, a *linear integral operator* [51]. For each ray of light, a linear time-invariant system collapses all wavelengths into a single quantity giving rise to a ray of light with a flat spectrum emerging from the other side.

Of course, the visual filter of Figure 2.15*b* cannot actually be realized through a *linear system* but through an equivalent *nonlinear* filter arising from incorporating the generation of virtual objects into the filtering operation.

2.7.6   Practical Implementations of the RM

Illusory Transparency

Ideally a holographic video camera and holographic video display can be used to create a perfect illusion of transparency. However, since the visor or eyeglasses of the reality mediator may be relatively well fixed with respect to the wearer, there is not really a great need for full parallax holographic video. The fixed nature of the visor conveniently prevents the wearer from moving the head with respect to the apparatus to *look around* within the visor itself. Instead, the act of looking around is accomplished when the user and the visor move together to explore the space. Thus two views, one for each eye, suffice to create a reasonable illusion of transparency.

Others [43,44,52] have explored video-based illusory transparency, augmenting it with virtual overlays. Nagao, in the context of his handheld TV set with single handheld camera [52], calls it "video see-through."

It is worth noting that whenever illusory transparency is used, as in the work of [43,44,52] reality will be mediated whether or not that mediation was intended. At the very least this mediation takes on the form of limited dynamic range and color, along with some kind of distortion that can be modeled as a 2D coordinate transformation. Since this mediation is inevitable, it is worthwhile to attempt to exploit it, or at least plan for it, in the design of the apparatus. A visual filter may even be used to attempt to mitigate the distortion.

A practical color stereo reality mediator (RM) may be made from video cameras and display. One example, made from a display having 480 lines of resolution, is shown in Figure 2.17. The maximum possible visual bandwidth is desired, even if the RM is to be used to create *diminished reality*, in which the apparatus of Figure 2.17 is used to reduce colorvision or resolution. This is done by applying the appropriate visual filter for the desired degree of degradation in a controlled manner automated by a computer. For example, color could be gradually reduced over the course of a day, under program control of the body-worn computer, to the extent that one would gradually move toward living in a grayscale world but not even realize it.

In the experiment the cameras were mounted the correct interocular distance apart and had the same field of view as the display devices used. With the cameras connected directly to the displays, the illusion of transparency was realized to some degree, at least to the extent that each ray of light entering the apparatus (e.g., absorbed and quantified by the cameras) appeared to emerge (by way of the display) at roughly the same angle.

Figure 2.17   An embodiment of author's reality mediator as of late 1994. The color stereo head-mounted display (VR4) has two cameras mounted to it. The intercamera distance and field of view match approximately author's interocular distance and field of view with the apparatus removed. The components around author's waist comprise radio communications equipment (video transmitter and receiver). The antennas are located at the back of the head-mount to balance the weight of the cameras, so that the unit is not front-heavy. ©Steve Mann, 1994.

Although there was no depth-from-focus capability, there was enough depth perception remaining on account of the stereo disparity for the author to function somewhat normally with the apparatus. Depth from focus is what is sacrificed in working with a nonholographic RM.

A first step in using a reality mediator is to wear it for a while to become accustomed to its characteristics. Unlike in typical beamsplitter implementations of augmented reality, transparency, if desired, is synthesized, and therefore only as good as the components used to make the RM. The author wore the apparatus in identity map configuration (cameras connected directly to the displays) for several days. He found it easy to walk around the building, up and down stairs, through doorways, to and from the lab, and so forth. There were, however, difficulties in instances of high dynamic range, such as in reading fine print (e.g., a restaurant menu or a department store receipt printed in faint ink).

The unusual appearance of the apparatus was itself a hindrance in daily activities (when the author wore the apparatus to formal dinner banquets, weddings, etc.), but after a while people became accustomed to the apparatus.

It was considered important to incorporate the computational apparatus into ordinary day-to-day activities, rather than limit its use to specific limited-duration experiments as Stratton and others had done with their optical apparatuses.

The attempt to create an illusion of transparency was itself a useful experiment because it established some working knowledge of what can be performed when vision is *diminished* to RS170 resolution and field of view is somewhat limited by the apparatus.

Knowing what can be performed when reality is mediated (e.g., diminished) through the limitations of a particular HMD (e.g., the VR4) would be useful to researchers who are designing VR environments for that HMD, because it establishes a sort of *upper bound* on "how good" a VR environment could ever hope to be when presented through that particular HMD. A reality mediator may also be useful to those who are really only interested in designing a traditional beamsplitter-based AR system because the RM could be used as a development tool, and could also be used to explore new conceptual frameworks.

2.7.7 Mediated Presence

McGreevy [53] also explored the use of a head-mounted display directly connected to two cameras, although his apparatus had no computational or processing capability. His head-mounted camera/display system was a very simple form of reality mediator, where the mediation was fixed (e.g., since there was no processing or computer control).

He was interested in showing that despite his two subjects having essentially immediate response (no delay) and also the luxury of perfect (e.g., unmediated) touch, hearing, smell, and so on, they had much difficulty adapting to the mediated visual reality in which they were placed. This showed that no matter how good a VR or telepresence simulation could be, there would still be significant limitations imposed by the interface between that simulation and the user — the HMD.

However, in his experiments he also noted that the system deprived the user of both color and stereo vision. Even though it had two cameras: "The lack of stereo vision provided in the head-mounted display prompted both of his experimental subjects to use alternative cues to make spatial judgements [53]"[4] (Both subjects would move their heads back and forth to perceive depth from the induced motion parallax.)

Something McGreevy appeared less interested in, which is far more important in the context of this course, is the notion of a deliberately diminished reality, and this underscores the important difference between mediated reality and augmented reality. Notably, living in a deliberately diminished reality allows us to come closer to what others will experience when they share this experience of reality (at a later time, a different place, or both).

Not all of the systems built by the author used stereo cameras and displays. In fact the author has found that the depth-deprived (2D) world of a single camera

---

[4] I have been unsuccessful in contacting McGreevy to determine how he routed the signals from two cameras into a nonstereo display.

input, sometimes also deliberately diminished in other ways, could give rise to a new genre of cinematography and other related experiences.

To be able to experiment with diminished reality in a controlled manner, it is desirable to first attain a system that can come close to passing reality through with more bandwidth than desired. In this way the exact desired bandwidth can be found experimentally. The system of Figure 2.17 overcame some of the problems associated with McGreevy's system, in having 34 times more visual bandwidth. It was just at the point where it was possible to conduct much of daily life through this illusion of transparency. The degree of reality could be reduced down to the level of McGreevy's system, and less, in a computer-controlled environment to find out how much visual bandwidth is needed for the user to conduct daily affairs. (The visual bandwidth may be crudely calculated as the number of pixels times two for stereo, times another three for color, although there is redundancy because left and right, as well as color channels are quite similar to one another.) For various tasks it was found that there was a certain point at which it was possible to function in the RM. In particular, anything below about $\frac{1}{8}$ of the system's full bandwidth made most tasks very difficult, or impossible. Once it becomes possible to live within the shortcomings of the RM's ability to be transparent, new and interesting experiments may be performed.

2.7.8 Video Mediation

After the apparatus is worn long enough for one to become comfortable with the illusory transparency, mediation of the reality can begin. In the early days of this research (up until the early to mid-1990s) the author attained a virtual WearComp system by wearing the I/O portion of the computer (display and input devices including camera) while situating the actual computer remotely.

The remote situation of the computer was attained by establishing a full-duplex video communications channel between the display/camera portion of the reality mediator and the host computer(s). In particular, a high-quality communications link (called the "inbound-channel") was used to send the video from the author's cameras to the remote computer(s). A lower-quality communications link (the "outbound channel") was used to carry the processed signal from the computer back to the HMD. This apparatus is depicted in a simple diagram (Fig. 2.18). Ideally both the inbound and outbound channels would be of high quality, but the inbound channel affects both the base station's view of the images and the wearable display, while the outbound channel affects only the wearable display. Therefore the better channel (typically the microwave communications link) is used for the inbound channel.

Originally communication was based on antennas that the author had installed on the roof of the tallest building in the city. Later one of the antennas was moved to another rooftop to improve inbound/outbound channel separation. The apparatus provided good coverage on the university campus, moderate coverage over a good part of the city, and some coverage from a nearby city. With this remote computational approach, the author was able to simulate the operation

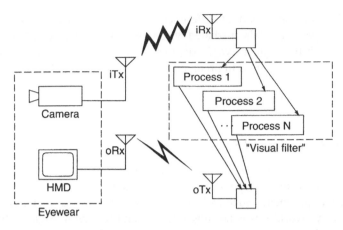

Figure 2.18 Simple implementation of a reality mediator (RM). The stereo camera (implemented as two separate cameras) sends video to one or more computer systems over a high-quality microwave communications link, called the "inbound channel." The computer system(s) send back the processed image over a UHF communications link called the "outbound channel." Note the designations "i" for inbound (e.g., iTx denotes inbound transmitter) and "o" for outbound. The designation "visual filter" refers to the process(es) that mediate(s) the visual reality and possibly insert "virtual" objects into the reality stream.

of future more recent generations of WearComp, even though they were, at the time, not technologically feasible in a self-contained body-worn package.

To a very limited extent, looking through a camcorder provides a mediated reality experience, because we see the real world (usually in black and white, or in color but with a very limited color fidelity) together with virtual text objects, such as shutter speed and other information about the camera. If, for example, the camcorder has a black and white viewfinder, the visual filter (the color-blindness one experiences while looking through the viewfinder with the other eye closed) is likely unintentional in the sense that the manufacturer likely would have rather provided a full-color viewfinder. This is a very trivial example of a mediated reality environment where the filtering operation is *unintentional* but nevertheless present.

Although the color-blinding effect of looking through a camcorder may be undesirable most of the time, there are times when it is desirable. The diminished reality it affords may be a desired artifact of the reality mediator (e.g., where the user chooses to remove color from the scene either to tone-down reality or to accentuate the perceptual differences between light and shade). The fact is that a mediated reality system need not function as just a reality enhancer, but rather, it may enhance, alter, or deliberately *degrade* reality.

Stuart Anstis [54], using a camcorder that had a "negation" switch on the viewfinder, experimented with living in a "negated" world. He walked around holding the camcorder up to one eye, looking through it, and observed that he was unable to learn to recognize faces in a negated world. His negation experiment bore a similarity to Stratton's inversion experiment mentioned in

Section 2.7.5, but the important difference within the context of this chapter is that Anstis experienced his mediated visual world through a video signal. In some sense both the regular eyeglasses that people wear, as well as the special glasses researchers have used in prism adaptation experiments [49,48], are reality mediators. However, it appears that Anstis was among the first to explore, in detail, an electronically mediated world.

2.7.9 The Reconfigured Eyes

Using the reality mediator, the author repeated the classic experiments like those of Stratton and Anstis (e.g., living in an upside-down or negated world), as well as some new experiments, such as learning to live in a world rotated 90 degrees. In this sideways world it was not possible to adapt to having each of the images rotated by 90 degrees separately. The cameras had to be rotated together in order for the mapping to be learned by adaptation (Fig. 2.19).

Figure 2.19 Living in a "Rot 90" world. It was found necessary to rotate both cameras rather than just one. Thus it does not seem possible to fully adapt to, say, a prism that rotates the image of each eye, but the use of cameras allows the up-down placement of the "eyes." The parallax, now in the up-down direction, affords a similar sense depth as we normally experience with eyes spaced from left to right together with left-right parallax.

The video-based RM (Fig. 2.17) permits one to experience any coordinate transformation that can be expressed as a mapping from a 2-D domain to a 2-D range, in real time (30 frames/s = 60 fields/s) in full color, because a full-size remote computer (e.g., a remotely located base station such as an SGI reality engine) is used to perform the coordinate transformations. This apparatus allows one to experiment with various computationally generated coordinate transformations both indoors and outdoors, in a variety of different practical situations. Examples of some useful coordinate transformations appear in Figure 2.20.

Researchers at Johns Hopkins University have been experimenting with the use of cameras and head-mounted displays for helping the visually handicapped. Their approach has been to use the optics of the cameras for magnification, together with the contrast adjustments of the video display to increase apparent scene contrast [55]. They also talk about using *image remapping* in the future:

One of the most exciting developments in the field of low vision is the Low Vision Enhancement System (LVES). This is an electronic vision enhancement system that provides contrast enhancement .... *Future enhancements* to the device include text manipulation, autofocus and *image remapping*. (quote from their WWW page [55], emphasis added)

 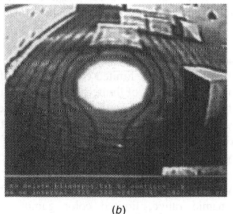

(a)   (b)

Figure 2.20 Living in coordinate-transformed worlds. Color video images are transmitted, coordinate-transformed, and then received back at 30 frames/s — the full frame-rate of the VR4 display device. (a) This visual filter would allow a person with very poor vision to read (due to the central portion of the visual field being hyperfoveated for a very high degree of magnification in this area), yet still have good peripheral vision (due to a wide visual field of view arising from demagnified periphery). (b) This visual filter would allow a person with a *scotoma* (a blind or dark spot in the visual field) to see more clearly, once having learned the mapping. The visual filter also provides edge enhancement in addition the coordinate transformation. Note the distortion in the cobblestones on the ground and the outdoor stone sculptures.

Their research effort suggests the utility of the real-time visual mappings (Fig. 2.20) previously already implemented using the apparatus of Figure 2.17.

The idea of living in a coordinate transformed world has been explored extensively by other authors [49,48], using optical methods (prisms, etc.). Much could be written about the author's experiences in various electronically coordinate transformed worlds, but a detailed account of all the various experiences is beyond the scope of this chapter. Of note, however, the author has observed that visual filters differing slightly from the identity (e.g., rotation by a few degrees) had a more lasting impression when removing the apparatus (e.g., being left incapacitated for a greater time period upon removal of the apparatus) than visual filters far from the identity (e.g., rotation by 180 degrees upside-down). Furthermore the visual filters close to the identity tended to leave an opposite aftereffect (e.g., causing the author to consistently reach too high after taking off the RM where the images had been translated down slightly, or reach too far clockwise after removing the RM that had been rotating images a few degrees counterclockwise). Visual filters far from the identity (e.g., reversal or upside-down mappings) did not leave an opposite aftereffect: the author would *not* see the world as being upside-down upon removing upside-down glasses.

This phenomenon might be thought of as being analogous to learning a second language (either a natural language or computer language). When the second language is similar to the one we already know, we make more mistakes switching back and forth than when the two are distinct. When two (or more) adaptation spaces were distinct, for example, in the case of the identity map and the rotation operation ("rot 90"), it was possible to mentally sustain a dual adaptation space and switch back and forth between the identity operator and the "rot 90" operator without one causing lasting aftereffects in the other.

Regardless of how much care is taken in creating the illusion of transparency, there will be a variety of flaws. Not the least of these are limited resolution, lack of dynamic range, limited color (mapping from the full spectrum of visible light to three responses of limited color gamut), and improper alignment and placement of the cameras. In Figure 2.17, for example, the cameras are mounted *above* the eyes. Even if they are mounted in front of the eyes, they will extend, causing the wearer to assume the visual capabilities of some hypothetical organism that has eyes that stick out of its head some three or four inches.

After wearing the apparatus for an extended period of time, the author eventually adapted, despite its flaws, whether these be unintended (limited dynamic range, limited color gamut, etc.), or intended (e.g., deliberately presenting an upside-down image). It appears that in some sense the visual reconfiguration is subsumed and induced into the brain. This way, the apparatus may act as an extension of the body and the mind. Conscious effort is no longer needed in order to use the machine.

Extended Baseline

Having the cameras above the display (as in Fig. 2.17) induced some parallax error for nearby objects, so the author tried mounting the cameras at the

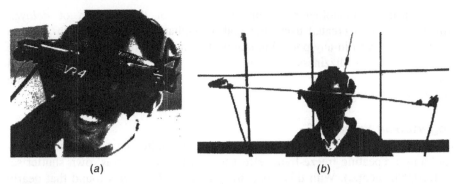

(a)   (b)

Figure 2.21 Giant's eyes: Extended baseline. (a) With a 212 mm baseline, author could function in most everyday tasks but would see crosseyed at close conversational distances. (b) With a 1 m baseline, author could not function in most situations but had a greatly enhanced sense of depth for distant objects (e.g., while looking out across the river). Wires from the cameras go down into author's waist bag containing the rest of the apparatus. Inbound transmit antenna is just visible behind author's head.

sides (Fig. 2.21a). This gave an interocular distance of approximately 212 mm, resulting in an enhanced sense of depth. Objects appeared smaller and closer than they really were so that the world looked like a reduced-scale model of reality. While walking home that day (wearing the apparatus), the author felt a need to duck down to avoid hitting what appeared to be a low tree branch. However, recollection from previous walks home had been that there were no low branches on the tree, and, removing the RM, it was observed that the tree branch that appeared to be within arm's reach was several feet in the air. After this enhanced depth perception was adapted to, the cameras were mounted on a 1 m baseline for further experimentation. Crossing the street provided an illusion of small toy cars moving back and forth very close, giving the feeling that one might just push them out of the way, but better judgment served to wait until there was a clearing in the traffic before crossing the road to get to the river. Looking out across the river provided an illusion that the skyscrapers on the other side were within arm's reach in both distance and height.

Delayed Illusory Transparency

Suppose that we had a hypothetical glass of very high refractive index. (Science fiction writer Bob Shaw refers to such glass as *slowglass* [56]. In Shaw's story, a murder is committed and a piece of slowglass is found at the scene of the crime, the glass being turned around as curious onlookers wait for the light present during the crime to emerge from the other side.) Every ray of light that enters one side of the glass comes out the other side unchanged, but simply delayed. A visor made from *slowglass* would present the viewer with a full-parallax delayed view of a particular scene, playing back with the realism of the idealized *holographic video* display discussed previously.

A practical (nonholographic) implementation of this illusion of *delayed transparency* was created using the reality mediator (Fig. 2.17) with a video delay. As is found in any poor simulation of virtual reality, wearing slowglasses induces a similar dizziness and nausea to reality. After experimenting with various delays, one will develop an appreciation of the importance of moving the information through the RM in a timely fashion to avoid this unpleasant delay.

Edgertonian Sampling

Instead of a fixed delay of the video signal, the author next experimented by applying a repeating freeze-frame effect to it (with the cameras' own shutter set to 1/10,000 second). With this video *sample and hold*, it was found that nearly periodic patterns would appear to freeze at certain speeds. For example, while looking out the window of a car, periodic railings that were a complete blur without the RM would snap into sharp focus with the RM. Slight differences in each strut of the railing would create interesting patterns that would dance about revealing slight irregularities in the structure. (Regarding the nearly periodic structure as a true periodic signal plus noise, the noise is what gave rise to the interesting patterns.) Looking out at another car, traveling at approximately the same speed, it was easy to read the writing on the tires, and count the number of bolts on the wheel rims. Looking at airplanes in flight, the number of blades on the spinning propellers could be counted, depending on the sampling rate in the RM the blades would appear to rotate slowly backward or forward the same way objects do under the stroboscopic light experiments of Harold Edgerton [57]. By manually adjusting the processing parameters of the RM, many things that escape normal vision could be seen.

Intelligent Adaptive RM Sampler

By adding machine vision (some rudimentary intelligence) to the incoming video, the RM may be used to decide what sampling rate to apply. For example, it may recognize a nearly periodic or cyclostationary signal and adjust the sampling rate to lock onto the signal, much like a phase-locked loop. A sufficiently advanced RM with eye tracking and other sensors might make inferences about what the wearer would like to see, and for example, when looking at a group of airplanes in flight would freeze the propeller on the one that the wearer is concentrating on.

Wyckoff's World

One of the problems with the RM is the limited dynamic range of CCDs. One possible solution is to operate at a higher frame rate than needed, while underexposing, say, odd frames and overexposing even frames. The shadow detail may then be derived from the overexposed stream, the highlight detail from the underexposed stream, and the midtones from a combination of the two streams. The resulting extended-response video may be displayed on a conventional HMD by using Stockham's *homomorphic filter* [58] as the visual filter. The principle of extending dynamic range by simultaneously using sensors of different sensitivity is known as the Wyckoff principle [59] (to be described in Chapter 4), in honor of Charles Wyckoff. Using a Wyckoff composite, one can be outside on bright sunny days and see shadow detail when looking into open doorways to dark interiors, as well as see detail in bright objects like the sun.

The Wyckoff principle is also useful in the context of night vision because of the high contrasts encountered at night. In the Wyckoff world one can read wattage rating numbers printed on a lightbulb and also see into the darkness off in the distance behind the lamp, neither brightness extreme of which is visible to the naked eye.

2.8 PARTIALLY MEDIATED REALITY

Artificial reality is a term defined by Myron Krueger to describe video-based, computer-mediated interactive media [39]. His apparatus consisted of a video display (screen) with a camera above it that projected a 2-D outline of the user together with spritelike objects. Krueger's environment is a partially mediated reality in the sense that within the screen the reality is mediated, but the user is also free to look around the room and see unmediated real objects. For example, the part of the user's visual field that shows his or her "reflection" (a left-right reversed video image of the camera is superimposed with computer graphic objects) is a mediated-reality zone, while the periphery (e.g., the user's own feet seen by looking straight down) is outside this mediation zone.

The artificial life interactive video environment (ALIVE) [60] is similar to Krueger's environment. In ALIVE users see themselves in a "magic mirror" created by displaying a left-right reversed video image from a camera above the screen. Virtual objects, appear, for example, a virtual dog will come over and greet the user. ALIVE is also a partially mediated reality.

2.8.1 Monocular Mediation

A camera and a display device completely covering only one eye (Fig. 2.22*a*) can be used to create a partially mediated reality. In the apparatus of Figure 2.22*a*, the right eye sees a green image (processed NTSC on a VGA display) that becomes fused with the unobstructed (full-color) view through the left eye.

Often the mediated and unmediated zones are in poor register, and one cannot fuse them. The poor register may even be deliberate, such as when the author has the right eye in a rotated ("rot 90") world even though this means that he cannot see in stereo in a meaningful way. However, one is more able to switch concentration back and forth between the mediated and nonmediated worlds. One can selectively decide to concentrate on one or the other of these two worlds.

An RM made from a camera and a virtual vision television set permits a mediation of even lesser scope to take place. Not only does it play into just one eye, but the field of view of the display only covers part of that eye (Fig. 2.22*b*). The visor is transparent so that both eyes can see the real world (although the left eye is partially blocked). With these glasses one might see an object with both

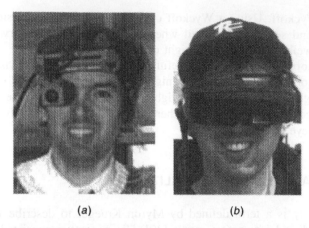

(a)   (b)

Figure 2.22 Partially mediated reality. (a) Half MR: Author's right eye is *completely* immersed in a mediated reality environment arising from a camera on the right, while the left eye is free to see unmediated real-world objects. (b) Substantially less than half MR: Author's left eye is *partially* immersed in a mediated reality environment arising from a camera also on the left. © Betty and Steve Mann, July 1995.

eyes, through the transparent visor, and then look over to the mediation zone where the left eye sees "through" the illusion of transparency in the display. Again, one can switch attention back and forth between the mediated reality and ordinary vision. Depending on the application or intent, there may be desire to register or to deliberately misregister the possibly overlapping direct and mediated zones.

2.9 SEEING "EYE-TO-EYE"

With two personal imaging systems, configured as reality mediators of the kind depicted in Figure 2.22b, the author set the output radio communications of one to the input of the other, and vice versa, so that an exchange of viewpoints resulted (each person would see out through the other person's eyes). The virtual vision glasses allowed the wearer to concentrate mainly on what was in one's own visual field of view (because of the transparent visor) but at the same time have a general awareness of the other person's visual field. This "seeing eye-to-eye" allowed for an interesting form of collaboration. Seeing eye-to-eye through the apparatus of Figure 2.17 requires a *picture in picture* process (unless one wishes to endure the nauseating experience of looking *only* through the other person's eyes), usually having the wearer's own view occupy most of the space, while using the apparatus of Figure 2.22b does not require any processing at all.

Usually, when we communicate (e.g., by voice or video), we expect the message to be received and concentrated on, while when "seeing eye-to-eye," there is not the expectation that the message will *always* be seen by the other person. Serendipity is the idea. Each participant sometimes pays attention and sometimes not.

2.10 EXERCISES, PROBLEM SETS, AND HOMEWORK

2.10.1 Viewfinders

Virtual reality (VR) systems block out the real world. For example, if you could make a VR headset portable, tetherless, and wireless, you could still not safely walk around while wearing it; you would bump into objects in the real world. A VR headset functions much like a blindfold as far as the real world is concerned.

Mediated reality (MR), as described in the next chapter, allows one to see a modified version of the real world. A reality mediator is a system that allows the wearer to augment, deliberately diminish, or otherwise alter his/her perception of visual reality, or to allow others (other people or computer programs) to alter his/her perception of reality. Allowing others to alter one's perception of reality can serve as a useful communications medium. For example, the wearable face-recognizer operates when the wearer allows the WearComp (wearable computational system) to alter his/her perception of reality by inserting a virtual name tag on top of the face of someone the system recognizes. See `http://wearcam.org/aaai_disabled.ps.gz`.

The newest reality mediators allow one to experience "life through the screen" (e.g., life as experienced through a viewfinder). The concept of living visual life through the viewfinder, as opposed to using a camera as a device that is carried and looked through occasionally, is what gives rise to this new form of interaction. Accordingly it is necessary that viewfinders be understood.

To prepare for the material in the next chapter (Chapter 3), and especially that of Chapter 4, it will be helpful to acquire an understanding of how camera viewfinders work. If you are taking this course for credit, your group will be given a small low-cost instamatic film camera to break apart in order to learn how viewfinders work. Before disassembling the camera try to answer the following questions, with particular reference to cheap "rangefinder" type cameras, as they are the most enlightening and interesting to study in the context of mediated reality: Why do the edges of viewfinders appear somewhat sharp? That is, why is it that a viewfinder can provide a sharply defined boundary? Some viewfinders have a reticle or graticule, or some form of crosshairs. Why is it that these appear sharply focused to the eye, though there is no part of the camera sufficiently far enough away to focus on?

Reality mediators have been built into ordinary sunglasses. How do you think it is possible that the screen appears in sharp focus? If you simply place an object (e.g., a piece of newspaper) inside your sunglasses, you will not likely be able to see the text in sharp focus because it is too close to your eyes to focus on. A magnifying lens between your eye and the newsprint could make it appear sharp, but the rest of the world will be blurry. How does a camera viewfinder make the graticule, reticle, or crosshairs sharp while keeping the scene appearing sharp as well.

After thinking about this, take apart the camera and see the answer. Try to answer the same questions now that you have seen how the camera viewfinder is made. Now you should understand how things may be overlaid onto the real world.

2.10.2 Viewfinders Inside Sunglasses

Sunglasses and camera parts (e.g., pocket 110 rangefinder cameras) will be handed out to each group of people taking the course for credit, or they can be readily obtained. Devise a means of projecting a reticle, graticule, crosshairs, or the like into the glasses, preferably with everything concealed inside the glasses. It should be possible to see objects through the glasses together with some form of viewfinder markings, and the like.

Use the engineering principles taught in the class, and improvise upon them if you wish. [Hint: Consider using some of the lenses in the camera, including possibly the objective lens of the camera that is normally not part of the viewfinder.]

Be careful not to wear the glasses while walking around, as there is the possibility of eye damage should you fall or bump into something. Care should be taken not to have objects too close to the eye.

Glasses should be handed in, and the resulting viewfinder implementations will be evaluated as a solution to this problem.

2.10.3 Mediated Reality

Explain the underlying principle of the WearCam invention. How does it allow one to alter one's perception of visual reality? How does it allow one to allow others to alter one's perception of visual reality?

How does it allow one to do this over a portion of the visual field of view, as opposed to doing it over the entire field of view?

2.10.4 Visual Vicarious Documentary

Say you want to make a documentary video of your daily life, and you have a small, lightweight camcorder that you can bolt to the brim of a hardhat.

What are some of the likely problems you might encounter? Apart from the cumbersome nature of the apparatus, what are the fundamental issues of living in a mediated reality environment?

Would you be able to play a competitive game of volleyball, and the like, while viewing the world only through camera(s)? If not, why not?

Why might you want to mount the viewfinder upside-down or sideways, with respect to the camera (i.e., so that you would see the world upside-down or sideways when looking through the apparatus)?

2.10.5   Aremac Field of View

What is the approximate field of view of the aremac (in this case, a simple head-mounted display) of the WearComp your group has been assigned? If you did not sign out a WearComp, you may want to look at one before or after class.

What are the horizontal FOV and the vertical FOV? What solid angle of cone would circumscribe the FOV? For example, what's the bounding cone angle needed?

Devise a simple way to measure the field of view.

2.10.6   Matching Camera and Aremac

What kind of camera matches the field of view of the aremac you measured in the previous question? Would a wide-angle camera match the aremac? What about a telephoto camera?

2.10.7   Finding the Right Camera

Say you find a company that manufactures a camera that has a field of view approximating that of the aremac. How could you test whether or not the field of view was exactly right? The Connectix QuickCam has approximately the correct field of view. Obtain the vf.c program, and compile and run it on the wearcomp with the QuickCam as input.

2.10.8   Testing the Camera

The QuickCam does not have *exactly* the right field of view but it's pretty close. Is it too wide or too tele?

3

THE EYETAP PRINCIPLE: EFFECTIVELY LOCATING THE CAMERA INSIDE THE EYE AS AN ALTERNATIVE TO WEARABLE CAMERA SYSTEMS

This chapter discloses the operational principles of the EyeTap reality mediator, both in its idealized form and as practical embodiments of the invention. The inner workings of the reality mediator, in particular, its optical arrangement, are described.

3.1 A PERSONAL IMAGING SYSTEM FOR LIFELONG VIDEO CAPTURE

A device that measures and resynthesizes light that would otherwise pass through the lens of an eye of a user is described. The device diverts at least a portion of eyeward-bound light into a measurement system that measures how much light would have entered the eye in the absence of the device. In one embodiment, the device uses a focus control to reconstruct light in a depth plane that moves to follow subject matter of interest. In another embodiment, the device reconstructs light in a wide range of depth planes, in some cases having infinite or near-infinite depth of field. The device has at least one mode of operation in which it reconstructs these rays of light, under the control of a portable computational system. Additionally the device has other modes of operation in which it can, by program control, cause the user to experience an altered visual perception of reality. The device is useful as a visual communications system, for electronic newsgathering, or to assist the visually challenged.

3.2 THE EYETAP PRINCIPLE

The EyeTap reality mediator is characterized by three components: a lightspace analysis system; a lightspace modification system; and a lightspace synthesis system.

To understand how the reality mediator works, consider the first of these three components, namely the device called a "lightspace analyzer" (Fig. 3.1). The lightspace analyzer absorbs and quantifies incoming light. Typically (but not necessarily) it is completely opaque. It provides a numerical description (e.g., it turns light into numbers). It is not necessarily flat (e.g., it is drawn as curved to emphasize this point).

The second component, the lightspace modifier, is typically a processor (WearComp, etc.) and will be described later, in relation to the first and third components.

The third component is the "lightspace synthesizer" (Fig. 3.2). The lightspace synthesizer turns an input (stream of numbers) into the corresponding rays of light.

Now suppose that we connect the output of the lightspace analyzer to the input of the lightspace synthesizer (Fig. 3.3). What we now have is an illusory transparency.

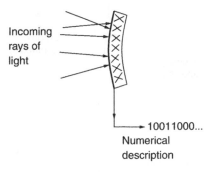

Figure 3.1 Lightspace analyzer absorbs and quantifies every ray of incoming light. It converts every incoming ray of light into a numerical description. Here the lightspace analyzer is depicted as a piece of glass. Typically (although not necessarily) it is completely opaque.

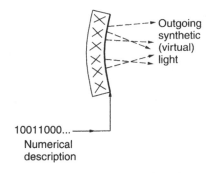

Figure 3.2 The lightspace synthesizer produces rays of light in response to a numerical input. An incoming numerical description provides information pertaining to each ray of outgoing light that the device produces. Here the lightspace synthesizer is also depicted as a special piece of glass.

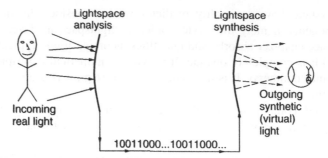

Figure 3.3 Illusory transparency formed by connecting the output of the lightspace analysis glass to the input of the lightspace synthesis glass.

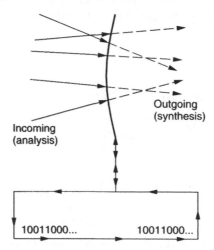

Figure 3.4 Collinear illusory transparency formed by bringing together the analysis glass and the synthesis glass to which it is connected.

Moreover suppose that we could bring the lightspace analyzer glass into direct contact with the lightspace synthesizer glass. Placing the two back-to-back would create a collinear illusory transparency in which any emergent ray of virtual light would be collinear with the incoming ray of real light that gave rise to it (Fig. 3.4).

Now a natural question to ask is: Why make all this effort in a simple illusion of transparency, when we can just as easily purchase a small piece of clear glass?

The answer is the second component, the lightspace modifier, which gives us the ability to modify our perception of visual reality. This ability is typically achieved by inserting a WearComp between the lightspace analyzer and the lightspace synthesizer (Fig. 3.5). The result is a computational means of altering the visual perception of reality.

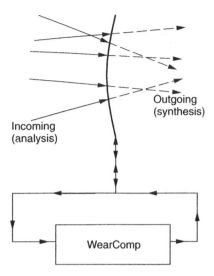

Figure 3.5   Reality mediator satisfying the collinearity (EyeTap) condition.

In summary:

1. A lightspace analyzer converts incoming light into numbers.
2. A lightspace modifier (i.e., a processor that is typically body-worn) alters the lightspace by processing these numbers.
3. A lightspace synthesizer converts these numbers back into light.

3.2.1 "Lightspace Glasses"

A visor made from the lightspace analysis glass and lightspace synthesis glass could clearly be used as a virtual reality (VR) display because of the *synthesis* capability. It could absorb and quantify all the incoming rays of light and then simply ignore this information, while the *synthesis* portion of the glass could create a virtual environment for the user. (See Fig. 3.6, top panel.)

Now, in addition to creating the illusion of allowing light to pass right through, the visor also can create new rays of light, having nothing to do with the rays of light coming into it. The combined illusion of transparency and the new light provides the wearer with an AR experience (Fig. 3.6, middle panel). Finally, the glasses could be used to alter the perception of visual reality, as described previously in this chapter and the previous chapter (Fig. 3.6, bottom panel). Thus VR is a special case of AR which is a special case of MR.

3.3   PRACTICAL EMBODIMENTS OF EYETAP

In practice, there are other embodiments of this invention than the one described above. One of these practical embodiments will now be described.

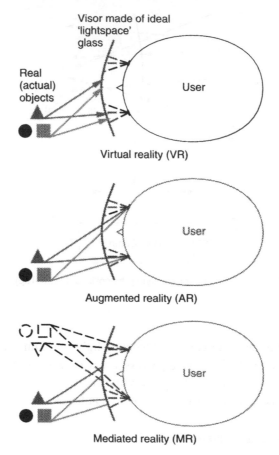

Figure 3.6 Eyeglasses made from lightspace analysis and lightspace synthesis systems can be used for virtual reality, augmented reality, or mediated reality. Such a glass, made into a visor, could produce a virtual reality (VR) experience by ignoring all rays of light from the real world, and generating rays of light that simulate a virtual world. Rays of light from real (actual) objects indicated by solid shaded lines; rays of light from the display device itself indicated by dashed lines. The device could also produce a typical augmented reality (AR) experience by creating the "illusion of transparency" and also generating rays of light to make computer-generated "overlays." Furthermore it could "mediate" the visual experience, allowing the perception of reality itself to be altered. In this figure a less useful (except in the domain of psychophysical experiments) but illustrative example is shown: objects are *left-right reversed* before being presented to the viewer.

A display system is said to be *orthoscopic* when the recording and viewing arrangement is such that rays of light enter the eye at the same angle as they would have if the person viewing the display were at the camera's location. The concept of being *orthoscopic* is generalized to the lightspace passing through the reality-mediator; the ideal reality-mediator is capable of being (and thus facilitates):

1. orthospatial (collinear)
   a. orthoscopic
   b. orthofocal
2. orthotonal
   a. orthoquantigraphic (quantigraphic overlays)
   b. orthospectral (nonmetameric overlays)
3. orthotemporal (nonlagging overlays)

An ideal reality mediator is such that it is capable of producing an illusion of transparency over some or all of the visual field of view, and thus meets all of the criteria above.

Although, in practice, there are often slight, (and sometimes even deliberate large) deviations from these criteria (e.g., violations of the orthotemporal characteristic are useful for embodiments implementing a photographic/videographic memory recall, or "WearCam flashbacks" [61]), it is preferable that the criteria be achievable in at least some modes of operation. Thus these criteria must be met in the system design, so that they can be deliberately violated at certain specific instants. This is better than not being able to meet them at all, which takes away an important capability.

Extended time periods of use without being able to meet these criteria have a more detrimental effect on performing other tasks through the camera. Of course, there are more detrimental flashbacks upon removal of the camera after it has been worn for many hours while doing tasks that require good hand-to-eye coordination.

3.3.1 Practical Embodiments of the Invention

The criteria listed above are typically only implemented in a discrete sense (e.g., discrete sampling of a discrete frame rate, which itself imposes limitations on sense of transparency, just as in virtual reality [62]). Typically the apparatus turns the lightspace into a numerical description of finite word length, and finite sampling for processing, after which the processed numerical description is converted back to the lightspace, within the limitations of this numerical representation.

3.3.2 Importance of the Collinearity Criterion

The most important criterion is the orthospatial criterion for mitigation of any resulting mismatch between viewfinder image and the real world that would otherwise create an unnatural mapping. Indeed, anyone who has walked around holding a small camcorder up to his or her eye for several hours a day will obtain an understanding of the ill psychophysical effects that result. Eventually such adverse effects as nausea, and flashbacks, may persist even after the camera is removed. There is also the question as to whether or not such a so-called mediated reality might, over a long period of time, cause brain damage, such as damage to the visual cortex, in the sense that learning (including the learning of new spatial mappings) permanently alters the brain.

This consideration is particularly important if one wishes to photograph, film, or make video recordings of the experience of eating or playing volleyball, and the like, by doing the task while concentrating primarily on the eye that is looking through the camera viewfinder. Indeed, since known cameras were never intended to be used this way (to record events from a first-person perspective while looking through the viewfinder), it is not surprising that performance of any of the apparatus known in the prior art is poor in this usage.

The embodiments of the wearable camera system sometimes give rise to a small displacement between the actual location of the camera, and the location of the virtual image of the viewfinder. Therefore either the parallax must be corrected by a vision system, followed by 3D coordinate transformation, followed by rerendering, or if the video is fed through directly, the wearer must learn to make this compensation mentally. When this mental task is imposed upon the wearer, when performing tasks at close range, such as looking into a microscope while wearing the glasses, there is a discrepancy that is difficult to learn, and it may give rise to unpleasant psychophysical effects such as nausea or "flashbacks."

If an eyetap is not properly designed, initially one wearing the eyetap will tend to put the microscope eyepiece up to an eye rather than to the camera, if the camera is not the eye. As a result the apparatus will fail to record exactly the wearer's experience, unless the camera is the wearer's own eye. Effectively locating the cameras elsewhere (other than in at least one eye of the wearer) does not give rise to a proper eyetap, as there will always be some error. It is preferred that the apparatus record exactly the wearer's experience. Thus, if the wearer looks into a microscope, the eyetap should record that experience for others to observe vicariously through at least one eye of the wearer. Although the wearer can learn the difference between the camera position and the eye position, it is preferable that this not be required, for otherwise, as previously described, long-term usage may lead to undesirable flashback effects.

3.3.3 Exact Identity Mapping: The Orthoscopic Reality Mediator

It is easy to imagine a camera connected to a television screen, and carefully arranged in such a way that the television screen displays exactly what is blocked by the screen so that an illusory transparency results. Moreover it is easy to imagine a portable miniature device that accomplishes this situation, especially given the proliferation of consumer camcorder systems (e.g., portable cameras with built in displays), see Figure 3.7.

We may try to achieve the condition shown in Figure 3.7 with a handheld camcorder, perhaps miniaturized to fit into a helmet-mounted apparatus, but it is impossible to line up the images exactly with what would appear in the absence of the apparatus. We can better understand this problem by referring to Figure 3.8. In Figure 3.8 we imagine that the objective lens of the camera is much larger than

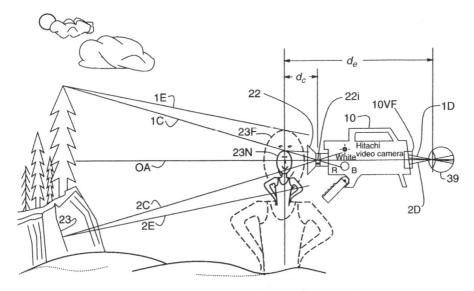

Figure 3.7 A modern camcorder (denoted by the reference numeral 10 in the figure) could, in principle, have its zoom setting set for unity magnification. Distant objects 23 appear to the eye to be identical in size and position while one looks through the camcorder as they would in the absence of the camcorder. However, nearby subject matter 23 N will be distance d_e, which is closer to the effective center of projection of the camcorder than distance d_e to the effective center of projection of the eye. The eye is denoted by reference numeral 39, while the camera iris denoted 22i defines the center of projection of the camera lens 22. For distant subject matter the difference in location between iris 22i and eye 39 is negligible, but for nearby subject matter it is not. Therefore nearby subject matter will be magnified as denoted by the dotted line figure having reference numeral 23 F. Alternatively, setting the camcorder zoom for unity magnification for nearby subject matter will result in significantly less than unity magnification for distant subject matter. Thus there is no zoom setting that will make both near and far subject matter simultaneously appear as it would in the absence of the camcorder.

it really is. It captures all eyeward bound rays of light, for which we can imagine that it processes these rays in a collinear fashion. However, this reasoning is pure fiction, and breaks down as soon as we consider the scene that has some depth of field, such as is shown in Figure 3.9.

Thus we may regard the apparatus consisting of a camera and display as being modeled by a fictionally large camera opening, but only over subject matter confined to a plane.

Even if the lens of the camera has sufficient depth of focus to form an image of subject matter at various depths, this collinearity criterion will only hold at one such depth, as shown in Figure 3.10. This same argument may be made for the camera being off-axis. Thus, when the subject matter is confined to a single plane, the illusory transparency can be sustained even when the camera is off-axis, as shown in Figure 3.11.

Some real-world examples are shown in Figure 3.12. An important limitation is that the system obviously only works for a particular viewpoint and for

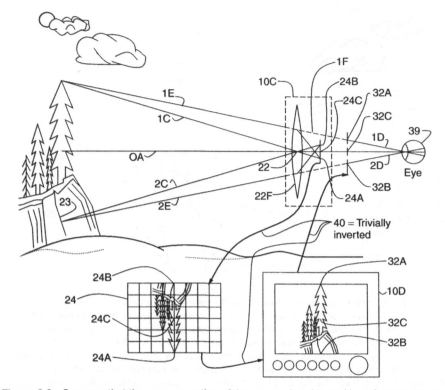

Figure 3.8 Suppose that the camera portion of the camcorder, denoted by reference numeral 10C, were fitted with a very large objective lens 22F. This lens would collect eyeward bound rays of light 1E and 2E. It would also collect rays of light coming toward the center of projection of lens 22. Rays of light coming toward this camera center of projection are denoted 1C and 2C. Lens 22 converges rays 1E and 1C to point 24A on the camera sensor element. Likewise rays of light 2C and 2E are focused to point 24B. Ordinarily the image (denoted by reference numeral 24) is upside down in a camera, but cameras and displays are designed so that when the signal from a camera is fed to a display (e.g., a TV set) it shows rightside up. Thus the image appears with point 32A of the display creating rays of light such as denoted 1D. Ray 1D is collinear with eyeward bound ray 1E. Ray 1D is response to, and collinear with ray 1E that would have entered the eye in the absence of the apparatus. Likewise, by similar reasoning, ray 2D is responsive to, and collinear with, eyeward bound ray 2E. It should be noted, however, that the large lens 22F is just an element of fiction. Thus lens 22F is a fictional lens because a true lens should be represented by its center of projection; that is, its behavior should not change other than by depth of focus, diffraction, and amount of light passed when its iris is opened or closed. Therefore we could replace lens 22F with a pinhole lens and simply imagine lens 22 to have captured rays 1E and 2E, when it actually only captures rays 1C and 2C.

subject matter in a particular depth plane. This same setup could obviously be miniaturized and concealed in ordinary looking sunglasses, in which case the limitation to a particular viewpoint is not a problem (since the sunglasses could be anchored to a fixed viewpoint with respect to at least one eye of a user). However, the other important limitation, that the system only works for subject matter in the same depth plane, remains.

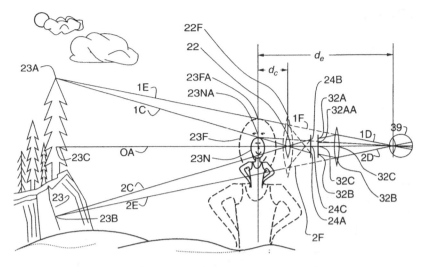

Figure 3.9 The small lens 22 shown in solid lines collects rays of light 1C and 2C. Consider, for example, eyeward bound ray of light 1E, which may be imagined to be collected by a large fictional lens 22F (when in fact ray 1C is captured by the actual lens 22), and focused to point 24A. The sensor element collecting light at point 24A is displayed as point 32A on the camcorder viewfinder, which is then viewed by magnifying lens and emerges as ray 1D into eye 39. It should be noted that the top of nearby subject matter 23N also images to point 24A and is displayed at point 32A, emerging as ray 1D as well. Thus nearby subject matter 23N will appear as shown in the dotted line denoted 23F, with the top point appearing as 23FA even though the actual point should appear as 23NA (e.g., would appear as point 23NA in the absence of the apparatus).

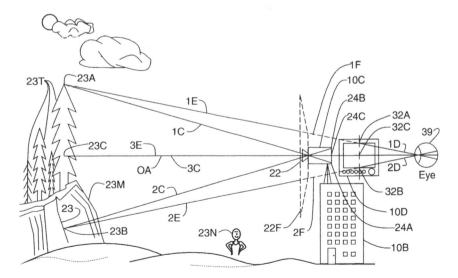

Figure 3.10 Camera 10C may therefore be regarded as having a large fictional lens 22F, despite the actual much smaller lens 22, so long as we limit our consideration to a single depth plane and exclude from consideration subject matter 23N not in that same depth plane.

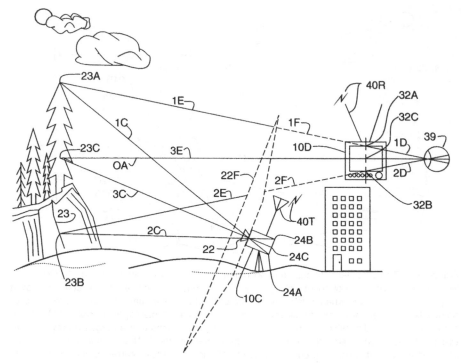

Figure 3.11 Subject matter confined to a single plane 23 may be collinearly imaged and displayed by using the same large fictional lens model. Imagine therefore that fictional lens 22F captures eyeward bound rays such as 1E and 2E when in fact rays 1C and 2C are captured. These rays are then samplings of fictional rays 1F and 2F that are resynthesized by the display (shown here as a television receiver) that produces rays 1D and 2D. Consider, for example, ray 1C, which forms an image at point 24A in the camera denoted as 10C. The image, transmitted by transmitter 40T, is received as 40R and displayed as pixel 32A on the television. Therefore, although this point is responsive to light along ray 1C, we can pretend that it was responsive to light along ray 1E. So the collinearity criterion is modeled by a fictionally large lens 22F.

Obviously subject matter moved closer to the apparatus will show as being not properly lined up. Clearly, a person standing right in front of the camera will not be behind the television yet will appear on the television. Likewise a person standing directly behind the television will not be seen by the camera which is located to the left of the television. Thus subject matter that exists at a variety of different depths, and not confined to a plane, may be impossible to line up in all areas, with its image on the screen. See, for example, Figure 3.13.

3.3.4   Exact Identity Mapping Over a Variety of Depth Planes

In order to better facilitate rapid switching back and forth between the mediated and unmediated worlds, particularly in the context of a partially mediated reality, it was desired to mediate part of the visual field without alteration in the identity configuration (e.g., when the computer was issued the identity map, equivalent to

(a)   (b)

Figure 3.12 Illusory transparency. Examples of a camera supplying a television with an image of subject matter blocked by the television. (a) A television camera on a tripod at left supplies an Apple "Studio" television display with an image of the lower portion of Niagara Falls blocked by the television display (resting on an easel to the right of the camera tripod). The camera and display were carefully arranged by the author, along with a second camera to capture this picture of the apparatus. Only when viewed from the special location of the second camera, does the illusion of transparency exist. (b) Various still cameras set up on a hill capture pictures of trees on a more distant hillside on Christian Island. One of the still cameras having an NTSC output displays an image on the television display.

a direct connection from camera to viewfinder), over a variety of different depth planes.

This was accomplished with a two-sided mirror. In many embodiments a pellicle was used, while sometimes a glass silvered on one or both sides was used, as illustrated in Figure 3.14.

In this way a portion of the wearer's visual field of view may be replaced by the exact same subject matter, in perfect spatial register with the real world. The image could, in principle, also be registered in tonal range. This is done using the *quantigraphic imaging* framework for estimating the unknown nonlinear response of the camera, and also estimating the response of the display, and compensating for both [64]. So far focus has been ignored, and infinite depth-of-field has been assumed. In practice, a viewfinder with a focus adjustment is used for the computer screen, and the focus adjustment is driven by a servomechanism controlled by an autofocus camera. Thus the camera automatically focuses on the subject matter of interest, and controls the focus of the viewfinder so that the apparent distance to the object is the same when seen through the apparatus as with the apparatus removed.

Figure 3.13 Various cameras with television outputs are set up on the walkway, but none of them can recreate the subject matter behind the television display in a manner that conveys a perfect illusion of transparency, because the subject matter does not exist in a single depth plane. There exists no choice of camera orientation, zoom setting, and viewer location that creates an exact illusion of transparency for the portion of the Brooklyn Bridge blocked by the television screen. Notice how the railings don't quite line up correctly as they vary in depth with respect to the first support tower of the bridge.

It is desirable that embodiments of the personal imaging system with manual focus cameras also have the focus of the camera linked to the focus of the viewfinder. Through this linkage both may be adjusted together with a single knob. Moreover a camera with zoom lens may be used together with a viewfinder having zoom lens. The zoom mechanisms are linked in such a way that the viewfinder image magnification is reduced as the camera magnification is increased. This appropriate linkage allows any increase in magnification by the camera to be negated exactly by decreasing the apparent size of the viewfinder image. As mentioned previously, this procedure may seem counterintuitive, given traditional cameras, but it was found to assist greatly in elimination of undesirable long-term effects caused by wearing a camera not implementing the virtual light collinearity principle.

The calibration of the autofocus zoom camera and the zoom viewfinder was done by temporarily removing the double-sided mirror and adjusting the focus and zoom of the viewfinder to maximize video feedback. This must be done for each zoom and focus setting so that the zoom and focus of the viewfinder will properly track the zoom and focus of the camera. In using video feedback as a calibration tool, a computer system can be made to monitor the video output of the camera, adjust the viewfinder, and generate a lookup table for the viewfinder settings corresponding to each camera setting. In this way calibration can be automated during the manufacture of the personal imaging system. Some similar

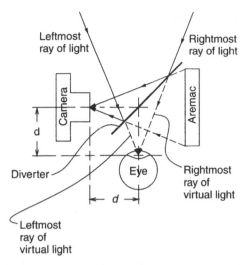

Figure 3.14 The orthoscopic reality mediator. A double-sided mirror diverts incoming rays of light to a camera while providing the eye with a view of a display screen connected to the wearable computer system. The display screen appears backward to the eye. But, since the computer captures a backward stream of images (the camera's view of the world is also through a mirror), display of that video stream will create an illusion of transparency. Thus the leftmost ray of light diverted by the mirror, into the camera, may be quantified, and that quantity becomes processed and resynthesized by virtue of the computer's display output. This way it appears to emerge from the same direction as if the apparatus were absent. Likewise for the rightmost ray of light, as well as any in between. This principle of "virtual light" generalizes to three dimensions, though the drawing has simplified it to two dimensions. Typically such an apparatus may operate with orthoquantigraphic capability through the use of quantigraphic image processing [63].

embodiments of the personal imaging system have used two cameras and two viewfinders. In some embodiments the vergence of the viewfinders was linked to the focus mechanism of the viewfinders and the focus setting of cameras. The result was a single automatic or manual focus adjustment for viewfinder vergence, camera vergence, viewfinder focus, and camera focus. However, a number of these embodiments became too cumbersome for unobtrusive implementation, rendering them unacceptable for ordinary day-to-day usage. Therefore most of what follows will describe other variations of single-eyed (partially mediated) systems.

Partial Mediation within the Mediation Zone

Partially mediated reality typically involves a mediation zone (field of view of the viewfinder) over which visual reality can be completely reconfigured. However, a more moderate form of mediated reality is now described. In what follows, the mediation is partial in the sense that not only it affects only part of the field of view (e.g., one eye or part of one eye) but the mediation is partial *within* the mediation zone. The original reason for introducing this concept was to make the apparatus less obtrusive and allow others to see the wearer's eye(s) unobstructed by the mediation zone.

The apparatus of Figure 3.14 does not permit others to make full eye contact with the wearer. Therefore a similar apparatus was built using a beamsplitter instead of the double-sided mirror. In this case a partial reflection of the display is visible to the eye of the wearer by way of the beamsplitter. The leftmost ray of light of the partial view of the display is aligned with the direct view of the leftmost ray of light from the original scene, and likewise for the rightmost ray, or any ray within the field of view of the viewfinder. Thus the wearer sees a superposition of whatever real object is located in front of the apparatus and a displayed picture of the same real object at the same location. The degree of transparency of the beamsplitter affects the degree of mediation. For example, a half-silvered beamsplitter gives rise to a 50% mediation within the mediation zone.

In order to prevent video feedback, in which light from the display screen would shine into the camera, a polarizer was positioned in front of the camera. The polarization axis of the polarizer was aligned at right angles to the polarization axis of the polarizer inside the display screen, in situations where the display screen already had a built-in polarizer as is typical of small battery-powered LCD televisions, LCD camcorder viewfinders, and LCD computer displays. In embodiments of this form of partially mediated reality where the display screen did not have a built in polarizer, a polarizer was added in front of the display screen. Thus video feedback was prevented by virtue of the two crossed polarizers in the path between the display and the camera. If the display screen displays the exact same rays of light that come from the real world, the view presented to the eye is essentially the same as it might otherwise be.

In order that the viewfinder provide a distinct view of the world, it was found to be desirable that the virtual light from the display screen be made different in color from the real light from the scene. For example, simply using a black-and-white display, or a black-and-green display, gave rise to a unique appearance of the region of the visual field of the viewfinder by virtue of a difference in color between the displayed image and the real world upon which it is exactly superimposed. Even with such chromatic mediation of the displayed view of the world, it was still found to be far more difficult to discern whether or not video was correctly exposed, than when the double-sided mirror was used instead of the beamsplitter. Therefore, when using these partially see-through implementations of the apparatus, it was found to be necessary to use a pseudocolor image or unique patterns to indicate areas of overexposure or underexposure. Correct exposure and good composition are important, even if the video is only used for object recognition (e.g., if there is no desire to generate a picture as the final result). Thus even in tasks such as object recognition, a good viewfinder system is of great benefit.

In this see-through embodiment, calibration was done by temporarily removing the polarizer and adjusting for maximum video feedback. The apparatus may be concealed in eyeglass frames in which the beamsplitter is embedded in one or both lenses of the eyeglasses, or behind one or both lenses. In the case in which a monocular version of the apparatus is being used, the apparatus is built into one lens, and a dummy version of the beamsplitter portion of the apparatus may be positioned in the other lens for visual symmetry. It was found that such an arrangement tended to call less attention to itself than when only one beamsplitter was used.

These beamsplitters may be integrated into the lenses in such a manner to have the appearance of the lenses in ordinary bifocal eyeglasses. Moreover magnification may be unobtrusively introduced by virtue of the bifocal characteristics of such eyeglasses. Typically the entire eyeglass lens is tinted to match the density of the beamsplitter portion of the lens, so there is no visual discontinuity introduced by the beamsplitter. It is not uncommon for modern eyeglasses to have a light-sensitive tint so that a slight glazed appearance does not call attention to itself.

3.4 PROBLEMS WITH PREVIOUSLY KNOWN CAMERA VIEWFINDERS

Apart from large-view cameras upon which the image is observed on a ground glass, most viewfinders present an erect image. See, for example, U.S. Pat. 5095326 entitled "Keppler-type erect image viewfinder and erecting prism." In contrast to this fact, it is well known that one can become accustomed, through long-term psychophysical adaptation (as reported by George M. Stratton, in *Psychology Review*, in 1896 and 1897), to eyeglasses that present an upside-down image. After wearing upside-down glasses constantly, for eight days (keeping himself blindfolded when removing the glasses for bathing or sleeping), Stratton found that he could see normally through the glasses. More recent experiments, as conducted by and reported by Mann in an MIT technical report *Mediated Reality*, medialab vismod TR-260, (1994; the report is available in http://wearcam.org/mediated-reality/index.html), suggest that slight transformations such as rotation by a few degrees or small image displacements give rise to a reversed aftereffect that is more rapidly assimilated by the user of the device. Often more detrimental effects were found in performing other tasks through the camera as well as in flashbacks upon removal of the camera after it has been worn for many hours while doing tasks that require good hand-to-eye coordination, and the like. These findings suggest that merely mounting a conventional camera such as a small 35 mm rangefinder camera or a small video camcorder to a helmet, so that one can look through the viewfinder and use it hands-free while performing other tasks, will result in poor performance at doing those tasks while looking through the camera viewfinder.

Part of the reason for poor performance associated with simply attaching a conventional camera to a helmet is the induced parallax and the failure to provide an orthoscopic view. Even viewfinders that correct for parallax, as described in U.S. Pat. 5692227 in which a rangefinder is coupled to a parallax error compensating mechanism, only correct for parallax between the viewfinder and the camera lens that is taking the picture. They do not correct for parallax between the viewfinder and the image that would be observed with the naked eye while not looking through the camera.

Open-air viewfinders are often used on extremely low-cost cameras (e.g., disposable 35 mm cameras), as well as on some professional cameras for use at night when the light levels are too low to tolerate any optical loss in the viewfinder. Examples of open-air viewfinders used on professional cameras, in addition to regular viewfinders, include those used on the Grafflex press cameras of the 1940s (which had three different kinds of viewfinders: a regular optical viewfinder, a ground glass, and an open-air viewfinder), as well as those used on some twin-lens reflex cameras.

While such viewfinders, if used with a wearable camera system, have the advantage of not inducing the problems such as flashback effects described above, the edges of the open-air viewfinder are not in focus. They are too close to the eye for the eye to focus on, and they have no optics to make the viewfinder appear sharp. Moreover, although such open-air viewfinders induce no parallax error in subject matter viewed through such viewfinders, they fail to eliminate the offset between the camera's center of projection and the actual center of projection of the eye (to the extent that one cannot readily remove one's eye and locate the camera in the eye socket, exactly where the eye's normal center of projection resides).

Electronic Viewfinders

Many modern cameras use electronic viewfinders. They therefore provide an electronically mediated environment in which the visual perception of reality is altered, both geometrically (due to the same parallax errors found in optical viewfinders), because of tonal distortion (e.g., color distortion or complete loss of color) and reduced dynamic range, and because of reduced frame rate since the electronic viewfinder only updates images 30 or 60 times per second, and sometimes even less. (Many studies have been done on display update rates. Most of these studies come from the virtual reality community [62].)

Not all aspects of a viewfinder-altered visual perception are bad, though. One of the very reasons for having an electronic viewfinder is to alter the user's visual perception by introducing indicia (shutter speed, or other text and graphical overlays) or by actually mediating visual perception more substantively (e.g., by applying zebra-stripe banding to indicate areas of overexposure). This altered visual perception serves a very useful and important purpose.

Electronic information displays are well known. They have been used extensively in the military and industrial sectors [65], as well as in virtual reality (VR) systems [39]. Using any of these various information displays as a viewfinder gives rise to similar problems such as the offset between the camera's center of projection and the actual center of projection of the eye.

Augmented reality systems [40] use displays that are partially transparent. Augmented reality displays have many practical uses in industry [66]. When these displays are used as viewfinders, they function much like the open-air viewfinders. They provide sharp focus but still do not solve the discrepancy between the eye's center of projection and camera's center of projection.

Other kinds of information displays such as Microvision's scanning displays [67], or the Private Eye manufactured by Reflection Technologies, can also be used for virtual reality or augmented reality. Nevertheless, similar problems arise when an attempt is made to use them as camera viewfinders.

A so-called infinity sight [68], commonly used in telescopes, has also been used to superimpose crosshairs for a camera. However, the camera's center of projection would not line up with that of the eye looking through the device.

Another problem with all of the above-mentioned camera systems is the fixed focus of the viewfinders. Although the camera lens itself has depth of field control (automatic focus, automatic aperture, etc.), known viewfinders lack such control.

Focus Adjustments and Camera Viewfinders

The various optical camera viewfinders, electronic camera viewfinders, and information displays usually have a focus or diopter adjustment knob, or have a fixed focus or fixed diopter setting.

Many viewfinders have a focus adjustment. This is intended for those who would normally wear prescription eyeglasses but would remove their glasses while shooting. The focus adjustment is therefore designed to compensate for differences among users. Ordinarily, once a user sets the focus for his or her particular eyesight condition, that user will not change the focus unless another person who has a different prescription uses the camera.

The viewfinders provided by many 35 mm cameras do not have a focus adjustment. Older cameras that did not have a diopter adjustment were manufactured so that the point of focus in the viewfinder was infinity, regardless of where the camera lens was focused. More modern cameras that do not have a diopter adjustment tend to be manufactured so that the point of focus is 1 m regardless of where the camera lens is focused. Therefore photographers who wear strong corrective eyewear need to purchase special lenses to be installed into the camera viewfinder opening, when taking off the eyewear to use a camera that lacks a diopter adjustment knob.

Amateur photographers often close the eye that is not looking through the viewfinder, whereas more experienced photographers will often keep both eyes open. The camera eye (the one looking through the viewfinder) sets up the composition by aiming the camera, and composing the picture. The noncamera eye provides a general awareness of the scene beyond the extent that is covered by the camera or shown in the viewfinder.

Once the diopter setting knob is adjusted for an individual user, it is generally not changed. Therefore people such as professional cinematographers, who walk around looking through a viewfinder for many hours a day, often experience eyestrain because the viewfinder presents objects at a fixed distance, while their other eye sees objects at varying distances from the camera.

The purpose of the next section is to describe a device that causes the eye itself to function, in effect, as if it were both a camera and a viewfinder, and in which the subject matter viewed through the device is presented at the same focal distance as subject not viewed through the device. Thus the device operates in such a manner as to cause zero or near-zero eyestrain, while allowing the user of the device to capture video in a natural fashion. What is presented therefore is a more natural kind of camera that can function as a true extension of the mind and body, and in which the visual perception of reality may be computationally altered in a controlled way without causing eyestrain.

3.5   THE AREMAC

The device to be described has three main parts:

- A measurement system typically consisting of a camera system, or sensor array with appropriate optics.
- A diverter system, for diverting eyeward bound light into the measurement system and therefore causing the eye of the user of the device to behave, in effect, as if it were a camera.
- An aremac for reconstructing at least some of the diverted rays of eyeward bound light. Thus the aremac does the opposite of what the camera does, and is, in many ways, a camera in reverse. The etymology of the word "aremac" itself, arises from spelling the word "camera" backwards.

There are two embodiments of the aremac: (1) one in which a focuser (e.g., an electronically focusable lens) tracks the focus of the camera to reconstruct rays of diverted light in the same depth plane as imaged by the camera, and (2) another in which the aremac has extended or infinite depth of focus so that the eye itself can focus on different objects in a scene viewed through the apparatus.

3.5.1   The Focus-Tracking Aremac

The first embodiment of the aremac is one in which the aremac has focus linked to the measurement system (i.e., camera) focus so that objects seen depicted on the aremac of the device appear to be at the same distance from the user of the device as the real objects so depicted. In manual focus systems the user of the device is given a focus control that simultaneously adjusts both the aremac focus and the camera focus. In automatic focus embodiments, the camera focus also controls the aremac focus. Such a linked focus gives rise to a more natural viewfinder experience as well as reduced eyestrain. Reduced eyestrain is important because the device is intended to be worn continually.

The operation of the depth tracking aremac is shown in Figure 3.15. Because the eye's own lens L_3 experiences what it would have experienced in the absence of the apparatus, the apparatus, in effect, taps into and out of the eye, causing the eye to become both the camera and the viewfinder (display). Therefore the device is called an EyeTap device.

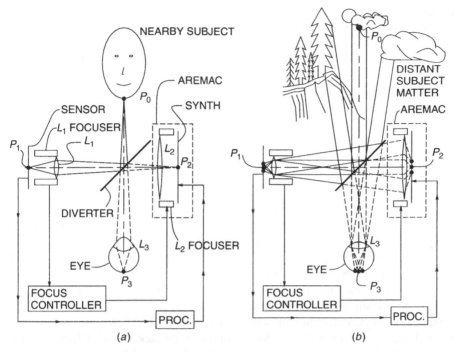

Figure 3.15 Focus tracking aremac. (*a*) With a NEARBY SUBJECT, a point P_0 that would otherwise be imaged at P_3 in the EYE of a user of the device is instead imaged to point P_1 on the image SENSOR, because the DIVERTER diverts EYEward bound light to lens L_1. When subject matter is nearby, the L_1 FOCUSER moves objective lens L_1 out away from the SENSOR automatically in much the same way as an automatic focus camera functions. A signal from the L_1 FOCUSER directs the L_2 FOCUSER, by way of the FOCUS CONTROLLER, to move lens L_2 outward away from the light SYNTHesizer. At the same time an image from the SENSOR is directed through an image PROCessor, into the light SYNTHesizer. Point P_2 of the display element is responsive to point P_1 of the SENSOR. Likewise other points on the light SYNTHesizer are each responsive to corresponding points on the SENSOR so that the SYNTHesizer produces a complete image for viewing through lens L_2 by the EYE, after reflection off of the back side of the DIVERTER. The position of L_2 is such that the EYE's own lens L_3 will focus to the same distance as it would have focused in the absence of the entire device. Therefore, when lens L_1 moves outward, the eye's lens muscles tense up and lens L_3 becomes thicker. (*b*) With DISTANT SUBJECT MATTER, rays of parallel light are diverted toward the SENSOR where lens L_1 automatically retracts to focus these rays at point P_1. When lens L_1 retracts, so does lens L_2. When lens L_2 retracts, the light SYNTHesizer ends up generating parallel rays of light that bounce off the backside of the DIVERTER. These parallel rays of light enter the EYE and cause its own lens L_3 to relax to infinity (L_3 gets thinner), as it would have done in the absence of the entire device. Rays denoted by solid lines are real light (diverging or parallel) from the subject matter, whereas rays denoted by dotted lines are virtual light (converging toward the eye) synthesized by the device.

Often lens L_1 is a varifocal lens, or otherwise has a variable field of view (i.e., zoom functionality). In this case it is desired that the aremac also have a variable field of view. In particular, field of view control mechanisms (whether mechanical, electronic, or hybrid) are linked in such a way that the aremac image magnification is reduced as the camera magnification is increased. Through this appropriate linkage, any increase in magnification by the camera is negated exactly by decreasing the apparent size of the viewfinder image.

The operation of the aremac focus and zoom tracking is shown in Figure 3.16. Stereo effects are well known in virtual reality systems [69] where two information channels are often found to create a better sense of realism. Likewise in stereo versions of the proposed device, there are two cameras or measurement systems and two aremacs that each regenerate the respective outputs of the camera or measurement systems.

3.5.2 The Aperture Stop Aremac

As was presented in the previous subsection, an aremac, by way of its focus tracking, gives a new purpose to focusable information displays. This embodiment of the aremac is well suited to most situations where there is subject matter of interest against a background of less interest, or there is only the background. However, subject matter of interest sometimes appears at a variety of depths, in a typical scene, such that there may be some desire for increased depth of field.

One important attribute of previously known viewfinders, as well as other kinds of displays, is the lack of depth of focus control. Although many of these prior devices have some kind of focus control, they lack *depth* of focus control.

Accordingly the author proposes an extended depth of focus aremac that is a device that works more like a camera in reverse than a typical display. The reason it is more like a camera in reverse is that it includes a lens having an aperture, iris, and the like, such that there is some *depth-of-field control* or extension (i.e., *depth-of-focus control*). Thus the aremac is endowed typically with two controls: one for focus, and another for *depth of focus*. Of course, one, the other, or both of these controls may be preset or automatically controlled so that they don't need to be adjusted by a user of the aremac.

An important difference between a camera and this aremac is that a camera can have a single lens group that has an aperture stop. In the limit, as the aperture size is reduced, the aperture stop becomes a pinhole camera. However, we cannot do the same for a display or viewfinder. Inserting aperture stops into the optics of viewfinders and headworn displays will cause reduction in field of view, unlike the effects observed in inserting aperture stops into the optics of cameras. This is because cameras collect light passing through a single point, called the center of projection (COP), whereas the aremac must produce rays of light through an external point, namely the eye. In particular, cameras may be modeled as a single point (the COP), whereas displays are better modeled as somewhat planar surfaces (more like a television screen). In order to get an aperture stop effect, we could put an aperture stop at the eye location (perhaps wear an opaque contact lens that had a small transparent hole in it), but this approach is often not convenient or practical.

Therefore one approach to creating an aremac with extended depth of focus is to use a plurality of lens groups. A simple design for such an aremac is illustrated

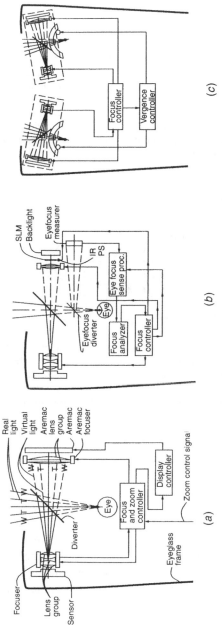

(a)

(b)

(c)

Figure 3.16 Aremac depth tracking in the EyeTap system is achieved by having the aremac and camera both focused together by a single focus control input, either manual or automatic. Solid lines denote real light from subject matter, and dashed lines denote virtual light synthesized by the aremac. (a) Aremac focus controlled by autofocus camera. When the camera focuses to infinity, the aremac focuses so that it presents subject matter that appears as if it is infinitely far. When the camera focuses close, the aremac presents subject matter that appears to be at the same close distance. A zoom input controls both the camera and aremac to negate any image magnification and thus maintain the EyeTap condition. Rays of light defining both the camera and aremac fields of view are denoted W. Rays of light defining the narrowest field of view are denoted T (for "Tele"). Note that the camera and aremac focus both controlled by eye focus. An eyefocus measurer obtains an approximate estimate of the focal distance of the eye. Both the camera and aremac then focus to approximately this same distance. (c) Focus of right camera and both aremacs (including vergence) controlled by autofocus camera on left side. In a two-eyed system it is preferable that both cameras and both aremacs focus to the same distance. Therefore one of the cameras is a focus master, and the other camera is a focus slave. Alternatively, a focus combiner is used to average the focus distance of both cameras and then make the two cameras focus at equal distance. The two aremacs, as well as the vergence of both systems, also track this same depth plane as defined by camera autofocus.

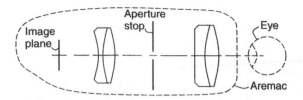

Figure 3.17 Aremac based on aperture stop between reversed petzval lens groups. The use of two lens groups in a viewfinder permit the insertion of an aperture stop in between. This results in a viewfinder having extended depth of focus. As a result no matter at what depth the eye of a user is focusing on, the image plane will appear sharp. The nonshooting eye (the eye not looking through the camera) can focus on subject matter at any distance, and the camera eye (the eye looking into the aremac) can assert its own focus without eyestrain. Clearly, in some sense, the aremac is a nonassertive viewfinder in that it does not impose a strong need for the user's eye to focus at any particular distance.

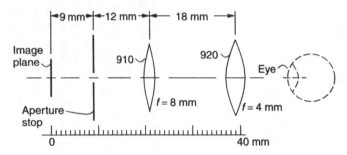

Figure 3.18 Aremac with distal aperture stop. As will be seen later in this chapter, an important first step toward making the apparatus covert is moving the aperture stop out from within the optics, and bringing it further back toward the image plane. The dimensions of the preferred embodiment are indicated in millimeters, and the focal lengths of each of the lenses are also so indicated. Again the eye is indicated in dashed lines, since it is not actually part of the aremac apparatus.

in Figure 3.17, where the eye is depicted in dashed lines, since it is not part of the aremac.

The author has found it preferable that the optics be concealed within what appear to be ordinary eyeglasses. The aperture stop, being dark (usually black), tends to be visible in the eyeglasses, and so should best be removed from where it can be seen. Figure 3.18 depicts an embodiment of the aremac invention in which the aperture stop is more distant from the eye, and is located further back toward the display element. In this way the aperture stop is conveniently made as part of the display element housing, which reduces cost and makes the system more easily manufacturable.

A Practical Embodiment of the Aperture Stop Aremac

Folded optical path designs are commonly used in virtual reality displays. A folded optical path may also be used in the device described in this paper (see

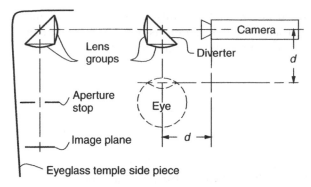

Figure 3.19 Aremac with distal aperture stop and folded optical path. Folding the optical path moves elements of the display system out of the way so that most of the elements can be concealed by the temple side piece of the eyeglasses. Moreover the folded design takes most of the aremac out of the way of the user's view of the world, such that less of the user's vision is obstructed. A camera that is concealed in the nosebridge of the eyeglasses can look across and obtain light reflected off the backside of the folding optics. The folding is by way of 45 degree mirrors or beamsplitters, the one closer to the eye being called a "diverter." This diverter diverts light that would otherwise have entered an eye of the user of the device, into the camera. The distance from the eye to the optical center of the diverter is called the "EyeTap" distance, and is denoted by the letter d. This distance is equal to the distance from the camera to the optical center of the diverter. Thus the camera provides an image of rays of light that would otherwise enter an eye of the user of the device. So the effective center of projection of the camera is located in the left eye of the user of the device. Since the camera and aremac can both have depth of focus controls, both can be in focus from four inches to infinity. In this way the apparatus can easily operate over the normal range of focusing for the healthiest of human eyes.

Fig. 3.19), where the folding has an additional purpose, namely one of the folds as the additional function of a diverter to divert light sideways into the eye. The purpose of the diverter is threefold:

- To get the optics, and display element out from in front of the eye and to allow portions of the apparatus to be moved closer to the user's head. This reduces the moment of inertia, for example, and makes the apparatus more covert and more comfortable to wear.
- To get more of the apparatus out of the user's field of view so that less of the user's vision is obstructed.
- To facilitate the insertion of a camera, in such a way that the camera can receive light that would otherwise pass through the center of projection of a lens of an eye of the user of the apparatus.

Ordinarily lenses and other vitreous or vitrionic elements embedded in the front glass portion of eyeglass lenses can be hidden, owing to the similar vitreous appearance of the eyeglass lens and the lens group to be concealed therein. However, the design can be further optimized so that the lens group closest to the eye is reduced in size and visibility at the expense of making the further lens group larger and otherwise more visible. Since the further lens group can be concealed at the edge of the eyeglass lens, by the frames of the eyeglasses, such a design provides a very useful trade-off.

An aperture stop, by its nature, is far more difficult to conceal in an eyeglass lens than transparent optics. Aperture stops are generally black. A large black disk, for example, with a small hole in it, would be hard to conceal in the main central portion of an eyeglass lens. Therefore the use of a distal aperture stop helps by getting the aperture stop back far enough that it can be concealed by the frames of the eyeglasses. Preferably the frames of the eyeglasses are black, so that the aperture stop which is also preferably black, along with a housing to prevent light leakage, will all blend in to be concealed within the eyeglass frames.

3.5.3 The Pinhole Aremac

With the aremac, depth of focus can be controlled, or enhanced, by the end-user (by adjusting an iris on the aremac), under computer program control (automatically adjusting the iris in response to information obtained by the camera's autofocus system and knowledge of the depth of field of the scene), or in manufacture (simply by including a small enough aperture stop that it does not need to be adjusted). A small aperture stop, installed during manufacture, can be so made that it provides depth of focus equal to the depth of focus of the eye (so that the aremac presents an image that appears sharp when the eye is focused anywhere from four inches to infinity, which is the normal range of a healthy eye).

Many modern miniature surveillance cameras have very small apertures, and thus provide essentially unlimited depth of focus. Pinhole cameras (which were traditionally only of historical or artistic interest for use with film) have made a comeback in the world of covert video surveillance. Pinhole cameras provide essentially infinite depth of focus. Because video resolution is so much lower than film resolution, the diffraction effects of the pinhole are less evident. Similarly, in applications where NTSC resolution is sufficient (e.g., for providing a viewfinder function for a covert camera, or for providing a computer mediated reality or partially mediated reality experience based on imagery that originated from NTSC resolution image capture), the author proposes the pinhole aremac.

The pinhole aremac (Fig. 3.20a) has infinite depth of focus and therefore provides no sense of focus and no assertion upon the eye of a user. Information displayed thereupon does not cause the eye of the user to focus to any particular distance it would not otherwise want to focus on.

One drawback of the pinhole aremac is periodic diffraction (see Fig. 3.20b) arising from the use of a spatial light modulator (SLM), having a periodic structure. Note that this form of diffraction is different from the general diffractive effects that make pinhole camera pictures not quite perfectly sharp (and likewise

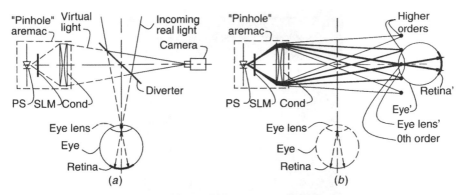

Figure 3.20 Laser EyeTap system. (*a*) RM based on the pinhole aremac. The pinhole aremac consists of a point source of light (PS), a spatial light modulator (SLM), and a condensing lens to convert real light into virtual light (COND). Incoming rays of real light from the scene are replaced (or augmented) with corresponding rays of virtual light from the pinhole aremac. The point source of light is derived from a solid state laser, along with a simple spatial filter and spreading optics. The pinhole aremac is a vitronic display system and is therefore prototyped through immersion in a xylene solution. (*b*) The diverter effectively locates the camera in the eye, or equivalently, it locates the eye (denoted EYE′, with its lens and retina denoted EYE LENS′ and RETINA′ respectively) at the camera. Here the original eye location is shown in dashed lines, and the effective eye location in solid lines, to show where various diffractive orders land on the eye. It is essential to design the apparatus so that only one diffractive order enters the lens of the eye.

for pinhole aremacs that present not perfectly sharp images). In the author's opinion, diffraction blurring is acceptable, but periodic diffraction is not. Periodic diffraction causes the appearance of ghosted replicas of subject matter, and is most evident when there is text displayed on the aremac.

Through the incorporation of a higher-order diffractive excluder, this problem can be resolved. The finished design (see Fig. 3.21) has no moving parts, and it can be economically manufactured.

The apparatus is preferably concealed in eyeglass frames in which the diverter is either embedded in one onto both lenses of the eyeglasses. In the case where a monocular version of the apparatus is being used, the apparatus is built into one lens, and a dummy version of the diverter portion of the apparatus is positioned in the other lens for visual symmetry. It was found that such an arrangement tended to call less attention to itself than when only one diverter was used for a monocular embodiment.

These diverters may be integrated into the lenses to have the appearance of the lenses in ordinary bifocal eyeglasses. Moreover magnification may be unobtrusively introduced by virtue of the bifocal characteristics of such eyeglasses. Typically the entire eyeglass lens is tinted to match the density of the beamsplitter portion of the lens, so there is no visual discontinuity introduced by the diverter. It is common for modern eyeglasses to have a light-sensitive tint so that a slight glazed appearance does not call attention to itself.

Figure 3.21 Covert prototype of camera and viewfinder having appearance of ordinary bifocal eyeglasses. This is a monocular left-eyed system, with a dummy lens in the right eye having the same physical appearance as the left-eye lens. The apparatus has essentially infinite depth of focus and therefore provides essentially zero eyestrain. This apparatus is useful for shooting documentary video, electronic newsgathering, as well as for mediated shared visual communications space.

3.5.4   The Diverter Constancy Phenomenon

When the diverter moves, the EyeTap point moves, but the collinearity condition remains. Each ray of virtual light synthesized by the aremac is still collinear with a corresponding ray of real light from subject matter. This situation shown in Figure 3.22 where the diverter is shown in two positions, denoted DIV and DIV′. Since moving the diverter moves the EyeTap point, the two examples being denoted EYE and EYE′, the diverter can be made to track the eye, so that the EyeTap effect is sustained over movement of the eye, or some degree of relative movement of the device with respect to the eye.

3.6   THE FOVEATED PERSONAL IMAGING SYSTEM

A more recent embodiment of the personal imaging system incorporates two display screens, as depicted in Figure 3.23. Incoming light is intercepted from the direct visual path and directed instead, by a double-sided mirror to a beamsplitter.

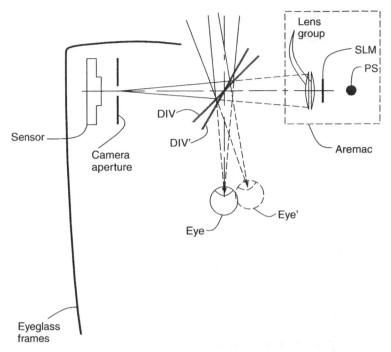

Figure 3.22 The diverter constancy phenomenon. Movement of the diverter does not affect the collinearity criterion but simply shifts the eyetap point. Therefore, the diverter position can be controlled by a device that tracks the eye's position to cause the eyetap point to follow the eye.

A portion of this light passes through the beamsplitter and is absorbed and quantified by a wide-camera. A portion of this incoming light is also reflected by the beamsplitter and directed to the tele-camera. The image from the wide-camera is displayed on a large screen, of size 0.7 inches (approx. 18 mm) on the diagonal, forming a widefield-of-view image of virtual light from the wide-camera. The image from the tele-camera is displayed on a small screen, typically of screen size $\frac{1}{4}$ inch (approx. 6 mm) on the diagonal, forming a virtual image of the tele-camera as virtual light. A smaller display screen is used to display the image from the tele-camera in order to negate the increased magnification that the tele-camera would otherwise provide. This way there is no magnification, and both images appear as if the rays of light are passing through the apparatus, as if the virtual light rays align with the real light rays were they not intercepted by the double-sided mirror. The large display screen is viewed as a reflection in the mirror, while the small display screen is viewed as a reflection in the beamsplitter. Note also that the distance between the two display screens, as measured along the optical axis of the wide-camera is set to be equal to the distance between the double-sided mirror and the beamsplitter as measured along the optical axis of the tele-camera. The apparent distance to both display screens is the same, so the

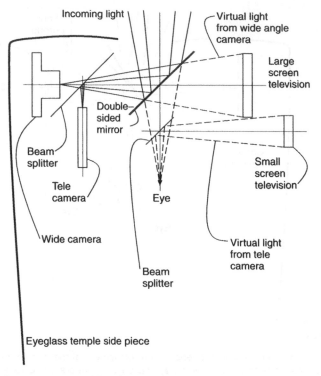

Figure 3.23 Foveated personal imaging system. A large display screen (0.7 inch diagonal) displays virtual light from a wide-camera, while a small display screen (0.25 inch diagonal) displays virtual light from a tele-camera. The wide-camera typically performs only head-tracking, as in the foveated system depicted earlier, but having a viewfinder for the head-tracker was still found to be of benefit in long-term adaptation.

wearer experiences a view of the two displays superimposed upon one another in the same depth plane.

In most embodiments the display screens were equipped with lenses to form an apparent image in the same depth plane as a central real object in the scene. Alternatively, the display screens may be equipped with lens assemblies of differing magnification to adjust their magnifications. Then the display screen displaying the image from the tele-camera would subtend a smaller visual angle than the display screen displaying the image from wide-camera, and so these visual angles would match the visual angles of the incoming rays of light. In this way two displays of equal size may be used to simplify manufacture of the apparatus.

3.7 TEACHING THE EYETAP PRINCIPLE

An important aspect of the author's research has been the teaching of students through simple examples. In order to teach the fundamentals, the author made

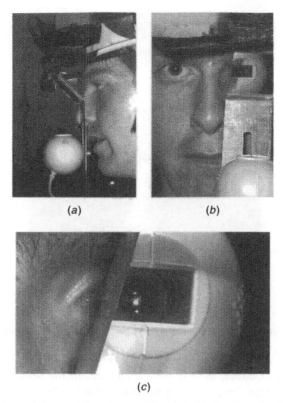

(a)   (b)

(c)

Figure 3.24 Deliberately large and crude examples of EyeTap systems for illustrative teaching purposes. (a) Side view of crude helmet-mounted device for teaching the principles of tapping the eye. Note the connectix QuickCam below the diverter and the aremac above the diverter. There is no need for focus controls because the apparatus has a very wide depth of field. (b) The eye is a camera. Front view showing the camera effectively located in the user's left eye. Note the elongated slot for adjustability of the EyeTap distance. (c) Close-up of left eye, as seen while wearing the EyeTap apparatus. These EyeTap devices cause the eye to behave as a camera in the sense that the camera replaces the eye, and the aremac replaces the subject matter that would otherwise be seen by the eye.

a crude embodiment of the EyeTap system on a bicycle helmet, with an aremac and a fixed focus camera that had sufficient depth of field (the author chose the connectix QuickCam because of low cost). Purchasing 20 quickcams, receiving donations of 20 Xybernaut wearable computers, and putting together 20 aremacs, the author provided students enrolled in his course with these items, along with the example system built by the author. This exercise was part of course number ECE1766 taught at the University of Toronto, Department of Electrical and Computer Engineering (http://wearcam.org/ece1766.htm), where each student has an opportunity to design and build an embodiment of the EyeTap system. Examples of systems put together by students, following instructions from the author, appear in Figure 3.24. These EyeTap devices cause the eye

Figure 3.25   Eyeglass-based EyeTap system (left eye tapped by camera and aremac).

itself to behave, in effect, as if it were a camera, in the sense that the camera replaces the eye. This "eye is a camera" concept is evident in Figure 3.24c.

The author also teaches the students how to build the apparatus onto and into eyeglasses, as shown in Fig 3.25 (in both covert and noncovert systems). The diverter is made from plexiglass mirror because of the ease with which it can be cut by students on a table, by scratching with a knive and ruler and breaking at the edge of the table. This material is also safer (free of fragments of glass that might get in the user's eye). Two pieces of mirror are glued back-to-back to make a two-sided mirror. The resulting ghosting helps teach the students the importance of first-surface mirrors, which are used later in the course.

This simple apparatus allows a portion of the user's visual field of view to be replaced by the exact same subject matter, in perfect spatial register with the real world. The image is also registered in tonal range, using the *quantigraphic imaging* framework for estimating the unknown nonlinear response of the camera, and also estimating the response of the aremac and compensating for both [64].

3.7.1 Calculating the Size and Shape of the Diverter

A diverter is based on the field of view determined from the aremac. The aremac is often mounted above the user's eye, facing down, and the camera is mounted below, facing up. Alternatively, the aremac may be to one side and the camera to the other side.

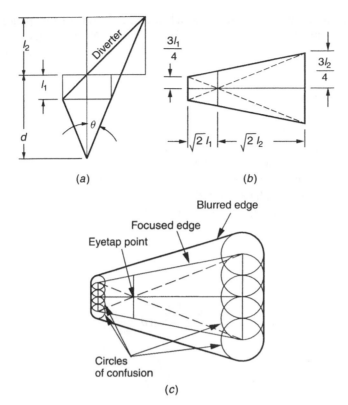

(a)   (b)

(c)

Figure 3.26 A simple planar diverter. (a) view showing the plane of the diverter as a line. (b) View perpendicular to plane of diverter. (c) Compensation for the fact that the diverter is not in sharp focus by either the eye or the camera.

Figure 3.26 depicts a close-up view of just the diverter where the dimensions of the diverter are indicated. These dimensions are indicated in Figure 3.26a with respect to the EyeTap point of the diverter, where a view is shown in which the plane of the diverter is seen as a line. The EyeTap point is defined as the point where the optical axis of the camera intersects the diverter. To calculate the dimensions, a square is drawn between the upper right end of the diverter and the EyeTap point, and a smaller square is drawn between the EyeTap point and the lower left end of the diverter.

It should be emphasized that the diverter should be the correct size. If it is too big, it will obstruct vision beyond that which is reconstructed as virtual light from the aremac. If it is too small, it will provide a smaller mediation zone than that which the apparatus is capable of producing.

Let the horizontal half-angle subtended by the camera be θ, as illustrated in Figure 3.26a.

Let d denote the distance from the center of projection of the eye's lens (i.e., the location of the pencil of rays corresponding to the reflection of the diverted light) to the point on the diverter at which the optical axis of this pencil of rays intersects the diverter, as illustrated in Figure 3.26a. Note that the optical axis of the camera is considered to intersect the optical axis of the eye, and this point at which the two optical axes intersect is called the EyeTap point. Also note that the distance from the center of projection of the eye to the EyeTap point is equal to the distance from the center of projection of the camera to the EyeTap Point. This distance is called the EyeTap distance, and is denoted by the letter d.

Let l_1 denote the length of the diverter to the left of this point as projected orthographically onto a plane parallel to the image plane. This distance l_1 is the edge length of the smaller square in Figure 3.26a.

Let l_2 denote the length of diverter to the right of this point as projected orthographically onto a plane parallel to the image plane. This distance l_2 is the edge length of the larger square in Figure 3.26a. Therefore

$$\tan \theta = \frac{l_1}{d - l_1} \tag{3.1}$$

and

$$l_1 = \frac{d \tan \theta}{1 + \tan \theta} \tag{3.2}$$

Similarly

$$\tan \theta = \frac{l_2}{d + l_2} \tag{3.3}$$

and

$$l_2 = \frac{d \tan \theta}{1 - \tan \theta} \tag{3.4}$$

The width of the diverter is thus the square root of two times the sum of these two lengths:

$$w = \sqrt{2}(l_1 + l_2) = \sqrt{2} \left(\frac{d \tan \theta}{1 + \tan \theta} + \frac{d \tan \theta}{1 - \tan \theta} \right) \tag{3.5}$$

Since one end of the diverter is closer to the camera than the other, the diverter will have a trapezoidal shape, as illustrated in Figure 3.26b. The side closer to the eye will be less tall than the side further from the eye. When oriented at a 45 degree angle inside a pair of eyeglasses, the diverter should subtend a solid rectangular cone 4 units wide and 3 units high, for a VGA or NTSC aspect ratio of 4 : 3. The left and right sides subtend the same angle, even though the right side is taller in reality. Dimensions of the diverter as viewed at a 0 degree angle (i.e., directly head-on) are illustrated in Figure 3.26b. We know that there will be no foreshortening of height (i.e., foreshortening in the vertical direction) because both the near and far edge of the diverter are parallel to the image plane in the eye.

The standard aspect ratio of video images (whether NTSC, VGA, SVGA, or DVGA) is 4 units wide and 3 units high, so we know that the total height at the EyeTap point (where the optical axis intersects the diverter) is $\frac{3}{4}\sqrt{2}(l_1 + l_2)$. Moreover the left half of the diverter is simply a perspective projection of the left half of an aremac image onto a 45 degree angle, and so $\frac{3}{2}l_1$ high at that point (i.e., in the plane defined along distance l_1, we would see the left side of the picture). It is easiest to think of the diverter in four quadrants. For this reason the diverter has been partitioned into four quadrants of projectively equal sizes (but of course the Euclidean sizes of the right quadrants are larger owing to the fact that they are farther from the camera). These quadrants are indicated by the centerlines that are drawn in Figure 3.26.

From this observation we have that the diverter is

$$\frac{3}{2}l_1 = \frac{3}{2}\frac{d\tan\theta}{1 + \tan\theta}$$

high at the left side and

$$\frac{3}{2}l_2 = \frac{3}{2}\frac{d\tan\theta}{1 - \tan\theta}$$

high at the right side, and has a width of

$$\sqrt{2}\left(\frac{d\tan\theta}{1 + \tan\theta} + \frac{d\tan\theta}{1 - \tan\theta}\right)$$

This is a simplification of the actual size of the diverter because the diverter will be slightly out of focus. There is a small increase in size to account for the circle of confusion of the camera lens. For this reason the diverter typically has a slightly larger trapezoidal size and the corners are slightly rounded. This increased size is depicted in Figure 3.26c.

Figure 3.26c depicts a frontal view of the diverter with corners rounded by a circle of projectively constant size. This is an approximation to the actual shape, since the circle of confusion will be projectively smaller further from the camera (toward the scene and thus toward better focus). The actual size of the blurring circle will be somewhere between constant projective size and constant Euclidean size. However, the important thing to note is the rounded corners and the fact that it is slightly larger than that calculated by way of focused "pinhole geometry" depicted in Figure 3.26a and Figure 3.26b.

3.8 CALIBRATION OF EYETAP SYSTEMS

EyeTap systems have unique point spread functions (PSFs) and modulation transfer functions (MTFs) for example, that can easily be measured and compensated for. Photoquantigraphic imaging is a new signal-processing methodology that is well suited to calibration and enhancement of EyeTap images [70]. This theory states that modification of the image material is best done in lightspace rather than imagespace, and it provides a methodology for treatment of the camera as a measurement instrument in which the camera reports the actual quantity of light arriving from each direction in space. Using this new mathematical theory results in much more natural appearances of the image material in an EyeTap system. The concept of photoquantigraphic imaging provides for a new kind of image restoration (see Fig. 3.27) quite suitable for EyeTap content.

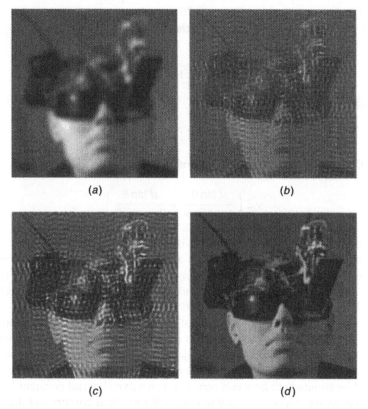

(a)   (b)

(c)   (d)

Figure 3.27 Photoquantigraphic Image restoration. (a) Images captured by EyeTap devices are often blurry and milky in appearance. (b) Traditional image restoration does a poor job of recovering the original image even when the point spread function (PSF) and modulation transfer function (MTF) are known or easily measured. (c) Attempts at inverse filtering and further tone scale adjustments fail to provide a clear image. Although no longer "milky" in appearance, the image still suffers from undesirable inverse filtering artifacts. (d) By recognizing that the degradation happens in lightspace [70], not in imagespace, photoquantigraphic restoration brings improved results. Since EyeTap systems operate in lightspace anyway, in the sense that images are converted into lightspace, modified (augmented, diminished, or otherwise altered), and then converted back to imagespace for display on the aremac, there is little additional computational burden in restoring them in lightspace. Such lightspace processing will be described in more detail in Chapters 4 and 5.

3.9 USING THE DEVICE AS A REALITY MEDIATOR

Because the device absorbs, quantifies, processes, and reconstructs light passing through it, there are extensive applications in mediated reality. Mediated reality differs from virtual reality in the sense that mediated reality allows the visual perception of reality to be augmented, deliberately diminished, or, more generally, computationally altered. Reality mediators have been demonstrated as useful for assisting the visually challenged [1], as well as for various other purposes such as filtering out unwanted advertising (as a filter for packets of light, as a photonic firewall for establishing forwarding rules on visual information, etc.).

Fully mediated reality, which typically involves a mediation zone (field of view of the camera and aremac) over which visual reality can be completely reconfigured, has been explored previously [1]. However, a more moderate form of mediated reality is possible using the apparatus of Figure 3.21. Mediation is often only partial in the sense that it affects only part of the field of view (e.g., one eye or part of one eye), but mediation can also be partial *within* the mediation zone. The original reason for introducing this concept was to make the apparatus less obtrusive so that others can see the user's eye(s) unobstructed by the mediation zone.

The author has built many devices for partially mediated reality, often using a beamsplitter instead of the double-sided mirror for the diverter. This allowed a partial reflection of the aremac to be visible to the eye of the user by way of the beamsplitter.

Thus the user sees a superposition of whatever real object is located in front of the apparatus and an aremac picture of the same real object at the same location. The degree of transparency of the beamsplitter affects the degree of mediation. For example, a half-silvered beamsplitter gives rise to a 50% mediation within the mediation zone.

To prevent video feedback, in which light from the aremac would shine into the camera, a polarizer was positioned in front of the camera. The polarization axis of the polarizer was aligned at right angles to the polarization axis of the polarization of the aremac (since most aremacs are polarized). Thus video feedback was prevented by the two crossed polarizers in the path between the display screen and the camera. If the aremac displays the exact same rays of light that come from the real world, the view presented to the eye is essentially the same. However, for the RM to provide a distinct view of the world, it was found that the virtual light from the aremac had to be made different in color from the real light of the scene. For example, simply using a black-and-white aremac, or a black-and-red aremac, gave rise to a unique appearance of the region of the mediation zone of the RM by virtue of a difference in color between the aremac image and the real world upon which it is exactly superimposed. Even with such chromatic mediation of the aremac view of the world, it was still found to be far more difficult to discern whether or not the video was correctly exposed than when the double-sided mirror was used instead of the beamsplitter. Therefore, when using these partially see-through implementations of the apparatus, it was found to be necessary to use a pseudocolor image or unique patterns to indicate areas of overexposure or underexposure. Correct exposure and good composition are important, even if the video is only used for object recognition (i.e., if there is no desire to generate a picture as the final result). Thus even in tasks such as object recognition, a good viewfinder system is of great benefit.

In this see-through embodiment, calibration (adjusting the camera and aremac positions, as well as adjusting fields of view and various optical elements) was done by temporarily removing the polarizer and adjusting for maximum video feedback.

3.10   USER STUDIES

Besides providing reduced eyestrain, the author has found that the EyeTap system allows the user to capture dynamic events, such as a volleyball game, from the perspective of a participant. To confirm the benefits of the new device, the author has done extensive performance evaluation testing of the device as compared to wearable camera systems. An example of one of the performance test results appears in Figure 3.28.

3.11   SUMMARY AND CONCLUSIONS

This chapter described a new device. The device includes a capability to measure a quantity of light in each ray that would otherwise enter an eye of the user, and a reconstruction capability to regenerate these rays of light. The measurement capability causes the eye itself to function as a camera. The reconstruction capability is by way of a device called an aremac. The aremac is a display

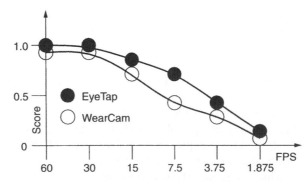

Figure 3.28   The sharp knee in the curve of frame rate versus ability to do many tasks. Many tasks require a certain minimum frame rate below which performance drops off rapidly. EyeTap systems work better than wearable camera systems at a given frame rate. EyeTap systems can be used at lower frame rates to obtain the same degree of performance as can be obtained with a wearable camera system operating at a higher frame rate.

technology that does not impose a sense of focus on the eye of a user looking into it. An aremac is essentially like a camera in reverse, providing depth of focus control for a display medium. Two embodiments were described, one in which the aremac has focus controlled by the camera portion of the device and the other in which the aremac has extended depth of focus. An extreme case of the latter, called the pinhole aremac, was also described. The pinhole aremac is implemented with solid state lasers, has no moving parts, and is cheap and simple to manufacture. It has infinite depth of field, and its use results in zero eyestrain.

The device using the aremac is well suited to augmented reality, mediated reality, or simply as an improved camera viewfinder. Some of the technical problems associated with EyeTap systems, such as the milky and blurred appearance of video shot with the apparatus, were also addressed. The end result is a lightweight comfortable device suitable for shooting lifelong documentary video.

3.12   EXERCISES, PROBLEM SETS, AND HOMEWORK

3.12.1   Diverter Embodiment of EyeTap

Draw a diagram depicting the 45 degree diverter embodiment of the WearCam invention. [Hint: There are three major components to the 45 degree diverter embodiment of WearCam. One of these is a two-sided mirror ("diverter") oriented at a 45 degree angle to the optical axes of two other components.] What are the two other components? Where are they located? The layout is depicted in Figure 3.29, where two of the three components have been deleted from the diagram. Complete the diagram.

3.12.2   Calculating the Size of the Diverter

Design a diverter based on the field of view you determined from the aremac (i.e., a simple head-mounted display) your group was assigned. Assume that the aremac is mounted above the user's eye, facing down, and that the camera is below, facing up.

3.12.3   Diverter Size

What size should the diverter be? What happens if it is too small? What happens if it is too big?

About how big does the diverter need to be? If it is too big, it will block out more of the field of view than needed. If it is too small, it will not divert (mediate) enough light. If it is the right size, it will provide a viewfinder that allows a portion of the field of view to be replaced by a displayed (computer rendered) image of exactly the same objects that would normally be seen there, and yet permit the wearer to see around it. It should roughly match the visual

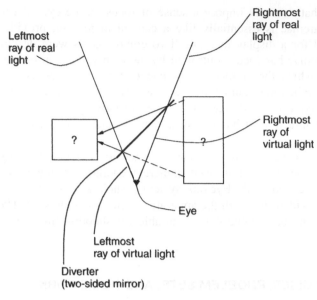

Figure 3.29 The "virtual light" principle of mediated reality implemented in the "diverter" embodiment of the WearCam invention. Two of the components have been removed from this diagram. What are they, and where should they go?

cone of view. What are the approximate dimensions of the diverter as a function of angle subtended by the mediation zone for this embodiment of the reality mediator (WearCam)? Assume that the mediation zone has an aspect ratio given by four units of width and three units of height.

3.12.4 Shape of Diverter

If you did the calculations for the previous question correctly, you should have ended up with a certain shape. Why isn't this shape of the diverter simply rectangular (or square)?

3.12.5 Compensating for Slight Aremac Camera Mismatch

What might you do to compensate for a camera with field of view that is close to matching the field of view of the aremac?

If you have to choose between a camera that is slightly too wide and one that is slightly too tele, which would you pick and why?

4

COMPARAMETRIC EQUATIONS, QUANTIGRAPHIC IMAGE PROCESSING, AND COMPARAGRAPHIC RENDERING

The EyeTap glasses of the previous chapter absorb and quantify rays of light, process these rays of light, and then resynthesize corresponding rays of light. Each synthesized ray of light is collinear with, and responsive to, a corresponding absorbed ray of light. The exact manner in which it is responsive is the subject of this chapter. In other words, this chapter provides meaning to the word "quantify" in the phrase "absorb and quantify."

It is argued that hidden within the flow of signals from typical cameras, through image processing, to display media, is a homomorphic filter. While homomorphic filtering is often desirable, there are some occasions when it is not. Thus cancellation of this implicit homomorphic filter is proposed, through the introduction of an antihomomorphic filter. This concept gives rise to the principle of photoquantigraphic image processing, wherein it is argued that most cameras can be modeled as an array of idealized light meters each linearly responsive to a semimonotonic function of the quantity of light received and integrated over a fixed spectral response profile. This quantity, called the "photoquantigraphic quantity," is neither radiometric nor photometric but rather depends only on the spectral response of the sensor elements in the camera. A particular class of functional equations, called "comparametric equations," is introduced as a basis for photoquantigraphic image processing. Comparametric equations are fundamental to the analysis and processing of multiple images differing only in exposure. The well-known gamma correction of an image is presented as a simple example of a comparametric equation, for which it is shown that the underlying photoquantigraphic function does not pass through the origin. For this reason it is argued that exposure adjustment by gamma correction is inherently flawed, and alternatives are provided. These alternatives, when applied to a plurality of images that differ only in exposure, give rise to a new kind of processing in the amplitude domain (as opposed to the time domain or the frequency domain). While the theoretical framework presented in this chapter originated within the field of wearable cybernetics (wearable photographic apparatus) in the 1970s and early 1980s, it is applicable to the processing of images from nearly all types of modern cameras, wearable or otherwise. This chapter follows roughly a 1992 unpublished report by the author entitled "Lightspace and the Wyckoff Principle."

4.1   HISTORICAL BACKGROUND

The theory of photoquantigraphic image processing, with comparametric equations, arose out of the field of wearable cybernetics, within the context of so-called mediated reality (MR) [19] and personal imaging [1], as described in previous chapters. However, this theory has potentially much more widespread applications in image processing than just the wearable photographic personal assistant for which it was developed. Accordingly a general formulation that does not necessarily involve a wearable photographic system will be given in this chapter. In this way, this chapter may be read and used independent of the specific application to which it pertains within the context of this book.

4.2   THE WYCKOFF PRINCIPLE AND THE RANGE OF LIGHT

The quantity of light falling on an image sensor array, or the like, is a real-valued function $q(x, y)$ of two real variables x and y. An image is typically a degraded measurement of this function, where degredations may be divided into two categories: those that act on the domain (x, y) and those that act on the range q. Sampling, aliasing, and blurring act on the domain, while noise (including quantization noise) and the nonlinear response function of the camera act on the range q.

Registering and combining multiple pictures of the same subject matter will often result in an improved image of greater definition. There are four classes of such improvement:

1. Increased spatial resolution (domain resolution)
2. Increased spatial extent (domain extent)
3. Increased tonal fidelity (range resolution)
4. Increased dynamic range (range extent)

4.2.1   What's Good for the Domain Is Good for the Range

The notion of producing a better picture by combining multiple input pictures has been well studied with regard to the domain (x, y) of these pictures. Horn and Schunk, for example, provide means of determining optical flow [71], and many researchers have then used this result to spatially *register* multiple images and provide a single image of increased spatial resolution and increased spatial extent. Subpixel registration methods such as those proposed by [72] attempt to increase *domain resolution*. These methods depend on slight (subpixel) shift from one image to the next. Image compositing (mosaicking) methods such as those proposed by [73,74] attempt to increase *domain extent*. These methods depend on large shifts from one image to the next.

Although methods that are aimed at increasing *domain resolution* and *domain extent* tend to also improve tonal fidelity by virtue of a signal-averaging and noise-reducing effect, we will see in what follows that images of different exposure can be combined to further improve upon tonal fidelity and dynamic range. Just as spatial shifts in the domain (x, y) improve the image, we will also see that exposure shifts (shifts in the range, q) also improve the image.

4.2.2 Extending Dynamic Range and Improvement of Range Resolution by Combining Differently Exposed Pictures of the Same Subject Matter

The principles of photoquantigraphic image processing and the notion of using differently exposed pictures of the same subject matter to make a picture composite of extended dynamic range was inspired by the pioneering work of Charles Wyckoff who invented so-called extended response film [75,76].

Before the days of digital image processing, Wyckoff formulated a multiple layer photographic emulsion [76,75]. The Wyckoff film had three layers that were identical in their spectral sensitivities (each was roughly equally sensitive to all wavelengths of light) and differed only in their overall sensitivities to light (e.g., the bottom layer was very *slow*, with an ISO rating of 2, while the top layer was very *fast* with an ISO rating of 600).

A picture taken on Wyckoff film can both record a high dynamic range (e.g., a hundred million to one) and capture very subtle differences in exposure. Furthermore the Wyckoff picture has very good spatial resolution, and thus *appears* to overcome the resolution to depth trade-off by using different color dyes in each layer that have a specular density as opposed the diffuse density of silver. Wyckoff printed his *grayscale* pictures on color paper, so the *fast* (yellow) layer would print blue, the *medium* (magenta) layer would print green, and the *slow* (cyan) layer would print red. His result was a *pseudocolor* image similar to those used now in data visualization systems to display floating point arrays on a computer screen of limited dynamic range.

Wyckoff's best-known pictures are perhaps his motion pictures of nuclear explosions in which one can clearly see the faint glow of a bomb just before it explodes (which appears blue, since it only exposed the fast top layer), as well as the details in the highlights of the explosion (which appear white, since they exposed all three layers whose details are discernible primarily on account of the slow bottom layer).

The idea of computationally combining differently exposed pictures of the same scene to obtain extended dynamic range (i.e., a similar effect to that embodied by the Wyckoff film) has been recently proposed [63]. In fact, most everyday scenes have a far greater dynamic range than can be recorded on a photographic film or electronic imaging apparatus. A set of pictures that appear identical except for their exposure collectively show us much more dynamic range than any single picture from a set, and this also allows the camera's response function to be estimated, to within a single constant unknown scalar [59,63,77].

A set of functions

$$f_i(\mathbf{x}) = f(k_i q(\mathbf{x})),$$ (4.1)

where k_i are scalar constants, is known as a Wyckoff set [63,77], so named because of the similarity with the layers of a Wyckoff film. A Wyckoff set of functions $f_i(\mathbf{x})$ describes a set of images differing only in exposure, when $\mathbf{x} = (x, y)$ is the continuous spatial coordinate of the focal plane of an electronic imaging array (or piece of film), q is the quantity of light falling on the array (or film), and f is the unknown nonlinearity of the camera's (or combined film's and scanner's) response function. Generally, f is assumed to be a pointwise function, that is, invariant to $\mathbf{x}$.

4.2.3   The Photoquantigraphic Quantity, *q*

The quantity q in (4.1) is called the *photoquantigraphic* quantity [2], or just the photoquantity (or photoq) for short. This quantity is neither radiometric (*radiance* or *irradiance*) nor photometric (*luminance* or *illuminance*). Notably, since the camera will not necessarily have the same spectral response as the human eye, or in particular, that of the photopic spectral luminous efficiency function as determined by the CIE and standardized in 1924, q is not brightness, lightness, luminance, nor illuminance. Instead, photoquantigraphic imaging measures the quantity of light integrated over the spectral response of the particular camera system,

$$q = \int_0^\infty q_s(\lambda)s(\lambda)\, d\lambda,$$ (4.2)

where $q_s(\lambda)$ is the actual light falling on the image sensor and s is the spectral sensitivity of an element of the sensor array. It is assumed that the spectral sensitivity does not vary across the sensor array.

4.2.4   The Camera as an Array of Light Meters

The quantity q reads in units that are quantifiable (i.e., linearized or logarithmic) in much the same way that a photographic light meter measures in quantifiable (linear or logarithmic) units. However, just as the photographic light meter imparts to the measurement its own spectral response (e.g., a light meter using a selenium cell will impart the spectral response of selenium cells to the measurement), photoquantigraphic imaging accepts that there will be a particular spectral response of the camera that will define the photoquantigraphic unit q.

Each camera will typically have its own photoquantigraphic unit. In this way the camera may be regarded as an array of light meters:

$$q(x, y) = \int_0^\infty q_{ss}(x, y, \lambda)s(\lambda)\,d\lambda, \tag{4.3}$$

where q_{ss} is the spatially varying spectral distribution of light falling on the image sensor. This light might, in principle, be captured by an ideal Lippman photography process that preserves the entire spectral response at every point on an ideal film plane, but more practically, it can only be captured in grayscale or tricolor (or a finite number of color) response at each point.

Thus varying numbers of photons of lesser or greater energy (frequency times Planck's constant) are absorbed by a given element of the sensor array and, over the temporal integration time of a single frame in the video sequence (or the picture taking time of a still image) will result in the photoquantigraphic quantity given by 4.3.

In a color camera, $q(x, y)$ is simply a vector quantity, such as $[q_r(x, y), q_g(x, y), q_b(x, y)]$, where each component is derived from a separate spectral sensitivity function. In this chapter the theory will be developed and explained for grayscale images, where it is understood that most images are color images for which the procedures are applied to the separate color channels. Thus in both grayscale and color cameras the continuous spectral information $q_s(\lambda)$ is lost through conversion to a single number q or to typically 3 numbers, q_r, q_g, and q_b.

Ordinarily cameras give rise to noise. That is, there is noise from the sensor elements and further noise within the camera (or equivalently noise due to film grain and subsequent scanning of a film, etc.). A goal of photoquantigraphic imaging is to estimate the photoquantity q in the presence of noise. Since $q_s(\lambda)$ is destroyed, the best we can do is to estimate q. Thus q is the fundamental or "atomic" unit of photoquantigraphic image processing.

4.2.5 The Accidentally Discovered Compander

Most cameras do not provide an output that varies linearly with light input. Instead, most cameras contain a dynamic range compressor, as illustrated in Figure 4.1. Historically the dynamic range compressor in video cameras arose because it was found that televisions did not produce a linear response to the video signal. In particular, it was found that early cathode ray screens provided a light output approximately equal to voltage raised to the exponent of 2.5. Rather than build a circuit into every television to compensate for this nonlinearity, a partial compensation (exponent of 1/2.22) was introduced into the television camera at much lesser cost, since there were far more televisions than television cameras in those days before widespread deployment of video surveillance cameras, and the like. Indeed, early television stations, with names such as "American Broadcasting Corporation" and "National Broadcasting Corporation" suggest this

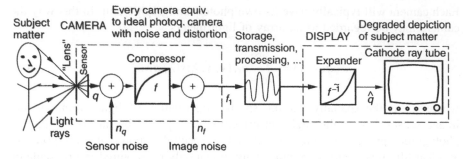

Figure 4.1 Typical camera and display. Light from subject matter passes through lens (approximated with simple algebraic projective geometry, or an idealized "pinhole") and is quantified in q units by a sensor array where noise n_q is also added to produce an output that is compressed in dynamic range by an unknown function f. Further noise n_f is introduced by the camera electronics, including quantization noise if the camera is a digital camera and compression noise if the camera produces a compressed output such as a jpeg image, giving rise to an output image $f_1(x, y)$. The apparatus that converts light rays into $f_1(x, y)$ is labeled CAMERA. The image f_1 is transmitted or recorded and played back into a DISPLAY system, where the dynamic range is expanded again. Most cathode ray tubes exhibit a nonlinear response to voltage, and this nonlinear response is the expander. The block labeled "expander" is therefore not usually a separate device. Typical print media also exhibit a nonlinear response that embodies an implicit expander.

one-to-many mapping (one camera to many televisions across a whole country). Clearly, it was easier to introduce an inverse mapping into the camera than to fix all televisions.[1]

Through a fortunate and amazing coincidence, the logarithmic response of human visual perception is approximately the same as the inverse of the response of a television tube (i.e., human visual response is approximately the same as the response of the television camera) [78,79]. For this reason, processing done on typical video signals could be on a perceptually relevant tone scale. Moreover any quantization on such a video signal (e.g., quantization into 8 bits) could be close to ideal in the sense that each step of the quantizer could have associated with it a roughly equal perceptual change in perceptual units.

Figure 4.2 shows plots of the compressor (and expander) used in video systems together with the corresponding logarithm $\log(q + 1)$, and antilogarithm $\exp(q) - 1$, plots of the human visual system and its inverse. (The plots have been normalized so that the scales match.) With images in print media, there is a similarly expansive effect in which the ink from the dots bleeds and spreads out on the printed paper, such that the midtones darken in the print. For this reason printed matter has a nonlinear response curve similar in shape to that of a cathode ray tube (i.e., the nonlinearity expands the dynamic range of the printed image). Thus cameras designed to capture images for display on video

---

[1] It should be noted that some cameras, such as many modern video surveillance cameras, operate linearly when operating at very low light levels.

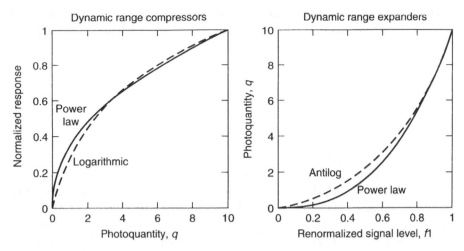

Figure 4.2 The power law dynamic range compression implemented inside most cameras showing approximately the same shape of curve as the logarithmic function, over the range of signals typically used in video and still photography. The power law response of typical cathode ray tubes, as well as that of typical print media, is quite similar to the antilog function. The act of doing conventional linear filtering operations on images obtained from typical video cameras, or from still cameras taking pictures intended for typical print media, is in effect homomorphic filtering with an approximately logarithmic nonlinearity.

screens have approximately the same kind of built-in dynamic range compression suitable for print media as well.

It is interesting to compare this naturally occurring (and somewhat accidental) development in video and print media with the deliberate introduction of companders (compressors and expanders) in audio. Both the accidentally occurring compression and expansion of picture signals and the deliberate use of logarithmic (or mu-law) compression and expansion of audio signals serve to allow 8 bits to be used to often encode these signals in a satisfactory manner. (Without dynamic range compression, 12 to 16 bits would be needed to obtain satisfactory reproduction.)

Most still cameras also provide dynamic range compression built into the camera. For example, the Kodak DCS-420 and DCS-460 cameras capture internally in 12 bits (per pixel per color) and then apply dynamic range compression, and finally output the range-compressed images in 8 bits (per pixel per color).

4.2.6 Why Stockham Was Wrong

When video signals are processed, using linear filters, there is an implicit homomorphic filtering operation on the photoquantity. As should be evident from Figure 4.1, operations of storage, transmission, and image processing take place between approximately reciprocal nonlinear functions of dynamic range compression and dynamic range expansion.

Many users of image-processing systems are unaware of this fact, because there is a common misconception that cameras produce a linear output, and that displays respond linearly. There is a common misconception that nonlinearities in cameras and displays arise from defects and poor-quality circuits, when in actual fact these nonlinearities are fortuitously present in display media and deliberately present in most cameras. Thus the effect of processing signals such as f_1 in Figure 4.1 with linear filtering is, whether one is aware of it or not, homomorphic filtering.

Tom Stockham advocated a kind of homomorphic filtering operation in which the logarithm of the input image is taken, followed by linear filtering (i.e., linear space invariant filters), and then by taking the antilogarithm [58].

In essence, what Stockham didn't appear to realize is that such homomorphic filtering is already manifest in simply doing ordinary linear filtering on ordinary picture signals (from video, film, or otherwise). In particular, the compressor gives an image $f_1 = f(q) = q^{1/2.22} = q^{0.45}$ (ignoring noise n_q and n_f) that has the approximate effect of $f_1 = f(q) = log(q + 1)$. This is roughly the same shape of curve and roughly the same effect (i.e., to brighten the midtones of the image prior to processing) as shown in Figure 4.2. Similarly a typical video display has the effect of undoing (approximately) the compression, and thus darkening the midtones of the image after processing with $\hat{q} = f^{-1}(f_1) = f_1^{2.5}$.

In some sense what Stockham did, without really realizing it, was to apply dynamic range compression to already range compressed images, and then do linear filtering, and then apply dynamic range expansion to images being fed to already expansive display media.

4.2.7 On the Value of Doing the Exact Opposite of What Stockham Advocated

There exist certain kinds of image processing for which it is preferable to operate linearly on the photoquantity q. Such operations include sharpening of an image to undo the effect of the point spread function (PSF) blur of a lens (see Fig. 3.27). Interestingly many textbooks and papers that describe image restoration (i.e., deblurring an image) fail to take into account the inherent nonlinearity deliberately built into most cameras.

What is needed to do this deblurring and other kinds of photoquantigraphic image processing is an *antihomomorphic filter*. The manner in which an antihomomorphic filter is inserted into the image processing path is shown in Figure 4.3.

Consider an image acquired through an imperfect lens that imparts a blurring to the image, with a blurring kernel B. The lens blurs the actual spatiospectral (spatially varying and spectrally varying) quantity of light $q_{ss}(x, y, \lambda)$, which is the quantity of light falling on the sensor array just prior to being *measured* by the sensor array:

$$\tilde{q}_{ss}(x, y, \lambda) = \iint B(x - u, y - v) q_{ss}(u, v, \lambda) \, du \, dv. \qquad (4.4)$$

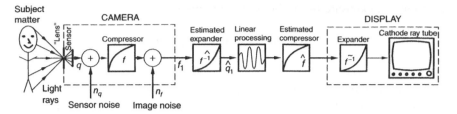

Figure 4.3 The antihomomorphic filter. Two new elements $\hat{f}^{-1}$ and $\hat{f}$ have been inserted, as compared to Figure 4.1. These are *estimates* of the inverse and forward nonlinear response function of the camera. Estimates are required because the exact nonlinear response of a camera is generally not part of the camera specifications. (Many camera vendors do not even disclose this information if asked.) Because of noise in the signal f_1, and also because of noise in the estimate of the camera nonlinearity f, what we have at the output of $\hat{f}^{-1}$ is not q but rather an estimate $\tilde{q}$. This signal is processed using linear filtering, and then the processed result is passed through the estimated camera response function $\hat{f}$, which returns it to a compressed tone scale suitable for viewing on a typical television, computer, and the like, or for further processing.

This blurred spatiospectral quantity of light $\tilde{q}_{ss}(x, y, \lambda)$ is then photoquantified by the sensor array:

$$
\begin{aligned}
q(x, y) &= \int_0^\infty \tilde{q}_{ss}(x, y, \lambda)s(\lambda)\, d\lambda \\
&= \int_0^\infty \int_{-\infty}^\infty \int_{-\infty}^\infty B(x - u, y - v)q_{ss}(u, v, \lambda)s(\lambda)\, du\, dv\, d\lambda \\
&= \int_{-\infty}^\infty \int_{-\infty}^\infty B(x - u, y - v)\left(\int_0^\infty q_{ss}(u, v, \lambda)s(\lambda)\, d\lambda\right) du\, dv \\
&= \int_{-\infty}^\infty \int_{-\infty}^\infty B(x - u, y - v)q(u, v)\, du\, dv,
\end{aligned}
\tag{4.5}
$$

which is just the blurred photoquantity q.

The antihomomorphic filter of Figure 4.3 can be used to better undo the effect of lens blur than traditional linear filtering, which simply applies linear operations to the signal f_1 and therefore operates homomorphically rather than linearly on the photoquantity q. So we see that in many practical situations there is an articulable basis for doing exactly the opposite of what Stockham advocated. Our expanding the dynamic range of the image before processing and compressing it afterward is opposed to what Stockham advocated, which was to compress the dynamic range before processing and expand it afterward.

4.2.8   Using Differently Exposed Pictures of the Same Subject Matter to Get a Better Estimate of q

Because of the effects of noise (quantization noise, sensor noise, etc.), in practical imaging situations, the Wyckoff set, which describes a plurality of pictures that differ only in exposure (4.1), should be rewritten

$$f_i(\mathbf{x}) = f(k_i q(\mathbf{x}) + n_{q_i}) + n_{f_i}, \tag{4.6}$$

where each image has, associated with it, a separate realization of a photoquanti-graphic noise process n_q and an image noise process n_f that includes noise introduced by the electronics of the dynamic range compressor f, and other electronics in the camera that affect the signal *after* its dynamic range has been compressed. In a digital camera, n_f also includes the two effects of finite word length, namely quantization noise (applied after the image has undergone dynamic range compression), and the clipping or saturation noise of limited dynamic range. In a camera that produces a data-compressed output, such as the Kodak DC260 which produces JPEG images, n_f also includes data-compression noise (JPEG artifacts, etc., which are also applied to the signal after it has undergone dynamic range compression). Refer again to Figure 4.1.

If it were not for noise, we could obtain the photoquantity q from any one of a plurality of differently exposed pictures of the same subject matter, for example, as

$$q = \frac{1}{k_i} f^{-1}(f_i), \tag{4.7}$$

where the existence of an inverse for f follows from the semimonotonicity assumption. Semimonotonicity follows from the fact that we expect pixel values to either increase or stay the same with increasing quantity of light falling on the image sensor.[2] However, because of noise, we obtain an advantage by capturing multiple pictures that differ only in exposure. The dark (underexposed) pictures show us highlight details of the scene that would have been overcome by noise (i.e., washed out) had the picture been "properly exposed." Similarly the light pictures show us some shadow detail that would not have appeared above the noise threshold had the picture been "properly exposed."

Each image thus provides us with an estimate of the actual photoquantity q:

$$q = \frac{1}{k_i}(f^{-1}(f_i - n_{f_i}) - n_{q_i}), \tag{4.8}$$

where n_{q_i} is the photoquantigraphic noise associated with image i, and n_{f_i} is the image noise for image i. This estimate of q, $\hat{q}$ may be written

$$\hat{q}_i = \frac{1}{\hat{k}_i} \hat{f}^{-1}(f_i), \tag{4.9}$$

where $\hat{q}_i$ is the estimate of q based on considering image i, and $\hat{k}_i$ is the estimate of the exposure of image i based on considering a plurality of differently exposed

---

[2] Except in rare instances where the illumination is so intense as to damage the imaging apparatus, for example, when the sun burns through photographic negative film and appears black in the final print or scan.

images. The estimated $\hat{q}_i$ is also typically based on an estimate of the camera response function f, which is also based on considering a plurality of differently exposed images. Although we could just assume a generic function $f(q) = q^{0.45}$, in practice, f varies from camera to camera. We can, however, make certain assumptions about f that are reasonable for most cameras, such as that f does not decrease when q is increased (that f is semimonotonic), that it is usually smooth, and that $f(0) = 0$.

In what follows, we will see how k and f are estimated from multiple differently exposed pictures. For the time being, let us suppose that they have been successfully estimated so that we can calculate $\hat{q}_i$ from each of the input images i. Such calculations, for each input image i, give rise to a plurality of estimates of q, which in theory would be identical, were it not for noise. However, in practice, because of noise, the estimates $\hat{q}_i$ are each corrupted *in different ways*. Therefore it has been suggested that multiple differently exposed images may be combined to provide a single estimate of q that can then be turned into an image of greater dynamic range, greater tonal resolution, and less noise [63,77]. The criteria under which collective processing of multiple differently exposed images of the same subject matter will give rise to an output image that is acceptable at every point (x, y) in the output image, are summarized below:

The Wyckoff Signal/Noise Criteria
$\forall (x_0, y_0) \in (x, y), \exists k_i q(x_0, y_0)$ such that

1. $k_i q(x_0, y_0) \gg n_{q_i}$, and
2. $c_i(q(x_0, y_0)) \gg c_i \left(\frac{1}{k_i} f^{-1}(n_{f_i}) \right)$.

The first criterion indicates that for every pixel in the output image, at least one of the input images provides sufficient exposure at that pixel location to overcome sensor noise, n_{q_i}. The second criterion states that of those at least one input image provides an exposure that falls favorably (i.e., is neither overexposed nor underexposed) on the response curve of the camera, so as not to be overcome by camera noise n_{f_i}. The manner in which differently exposed images of the same subject matter are combined is illustrated, by way of an example involving three input images, in Figure 4.4.

Moreover it has been shown [59] that the constants k_i as well as the unknown nonlinear response function of the camera can be determined, up to a single unknown scalar constant, given nothing more than two or more pictures of the same subject matter in which the pictures differ only in exposure. Thus the reciprocal exposures used to tonally register (tonally align) the multiple input images are estimates $1/\hat{k}_i$ in Figure 4.4. These exposure estimates are generally made by applying an estimation algorithm to the input images, either while simultaneously estimating f or as a separate estimation process (since f only has to be estimated once for each camera, but the exposure k_i is estimated for every picture i that is taken).

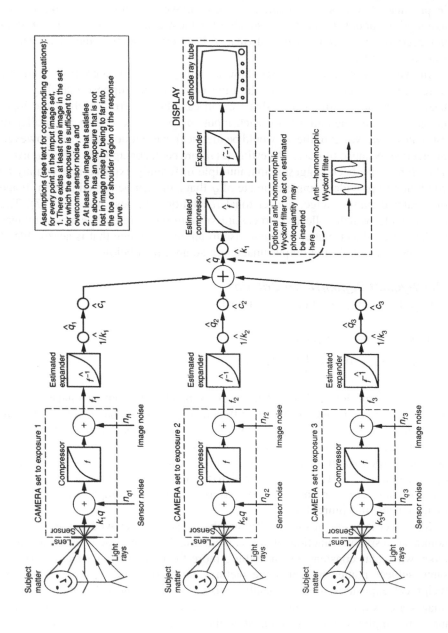

Assumptions (see text for corresponding equations): for every point in the input image set,
1. There exists at least one image in the set for which the exposure is sufficient to overcome sensor noise, and
2. At least one image has an exposure that is not lost in image noise by being to far into the toe or shoulder region of the response curve.

DISPLAY

Cathode ray tube

Expander
$\tilde{f}^{-1}$

Estimated compressor
$\hat{f}$

$\hat{k}_1$

$\hat{q}$

Optional anti–homomorphic Wyckoff filter to act on estimated photoquantity may be inserted here

Anti–homomorphic Wyckoff filter

$\hat{c}_1$
$\hat{q}_1$
$1/\hat{k}_1$

Estimated expander
$\hat{f}^{-1}$

f_1

CAMERA set to exposure 1

Compressor
f

$+$

n_{f1}

Image noise

"Lens"
Sensor

$+$

$k_1 q$

n_{q1}

Sensor noise

Subject matter

Light rays

$\hat{c}_2$
$\hat{q}_2$
$1/\hat{k}_2$

Estimated expander
$\hat{f}^{-1}$

f_2

CAMERA set to exposure 2

Compressor
f

$+$

n_{f2}

Image noise

"Lens"
Sensor

$+$

$k_2 q$

n_{q2}

Sensor noise

Subject matter

Light rays

$\hat{c}_3$
$\hat{q}_3$
$1/\hat{k}_3$

Estimated expander
$\hat{f}^{-1}$

f_3

CAMERA set to exposure 3

Compressor
f

$+$

n_{f3}

Image noise

"Lens"
Sensor

$+$

$k_3 q$

n_{q3}

Sensor noise

Subject matter

Light rays

Owing to the large dynamic range that some Wyckoff sets can cover, small errors in f tend to have adverse effects on the overall estimate $\hat{q}$. Thus it is preferable to estimate f as a separate process (i.e., by taking hundreds of exposures with the camera under computer program control). Once f is known (previously measured), then k_i can be estimated for a particular set of images.

The final estimate for q, depicted in Figure 4.4, is given by

$$\hat{q}(x, y) = \frac{\sum_i \hat{c}_i \hat{q}_i}{\sum_i \hat{c}_i} = \frac{\sum_i [\hat{c}_i(\hat{q}(x, y))/\hat{k}_i]\hat{f}^{-1}(f_i(x, y))}{\sum_i \hat{c}_i(\hat{q}(x, y))}, \qquad (4.10)$$

where $\hat{c}_i$ is given by

$$\hat{c}_i(\log(q(x, y))) = \frac{d f_i(x, y)}{d \log \hat{q}(x, y)} = \frac{d \hat{f}(\hat{k}_i \hat{q}(x, y))}{d \log \hat{q}(x, y)}. \qquad (4.11)$$

From this expression we can see that $c_i(\log(q))$ are just shifted versions of $c(\log(q))$, or dilated versions of $c(q)$.

The intuition behind the certainty function is that it captures the slope of the response function, which indicates how quickly the output (pixel value or the like) of the camera varies for given input. In the noisy camera, especially a digital camera where quantization noise is involved, generally the camera's

---

Figure 4.4 The Wyckoff principle. Multiple differently exposed images of the same subject matter are captured by a single camera. In this example there are three different exposures. The first exposure (CAMERA set to exposure 1) gives rise to an exposure $k_1 q$, the second to $k_2 q$, and the third to $k_3 q$. Each exposure has a different realization of the same noise process associated with it, and the three noisy pictures that the camera provides are denoted f_1, f_2, and f_3. These three differently exposed pictures comprise a noisy Wyckoff set. To combine them into a single estimate, the effect of f is undone with an estimate $\hat{f}$ that represents our best guess of what the function f is. While many video cameras use something close to the standard $f = kq^{0.45}$ function, it is preferable to attempt to estimate f for the specific camera in use. Generally, this estimate is made together with an estimate of the exposures k_i. After re-expanding the dynamic ranges with $\hat{f}^{-1}$, the inverse of the estimated exposures $1/\hat{k}_i$ is applied. In this way the darker images are made lighter and the lighter images are made darker, so they all (theoretically) match. At this point the images will all appear as if they were taken with identical exposure, except for the fact that the pictures that were brighter to start with will be noisy in lighter areas of the image and those that had been darker to start with will be noisy in dark areas of the image. Thus rather than simply applying ordinary *signal averaging*, a weighted average is taken. The weights are the spatially varying *certainty functions* $c_i(x, y)$. These certainty functions turn out to be the derivative of the camera response function shifted up or down by an amount k_i. In practice, since f is an estimate, so is c_i, and it is denoted $\hat{c}_i$ in the figure. The weighted sum is $\hat{q}(x, y)$, the estimate of the photoquantity $q(x, y)$. To view this quantity on a video display, it is first adjusted in exposure, and it may be adjusted to a different exposure level than any of the exposure levels used in taking the input images. In this figure, for illustrative purposes, it is set to the estimated exposure of the first image, $\hat{k}_1$. The result is then range-compressed with $\hat{f}$ for display on an expansive medium (DISPLAY).

output will be reliable where it is most sensitive to a fixed change in input light level. This point where the camera is most responsive to changes in input is at the peak of the certainty function c. The peak in c tends to be near the middle of the camera's exposure range. On the other hand, where the camera exposure input is extremely large or small (i.e., the sensor is very overexposed or very underexposed), the change in output for a given input is much less. Thus the output is not very responsive to the input and the change in output can be easily overcome by noise. Thus c tends to fall off toward zero on either side of its peak value.

The certainty functions are functions of q. We may also write the uncertainty functions, which are functions of pixel value in the image (i.e., functions of grayvalue in f_i), as

$$U(x, y) = \frac{dF^{-1}(f_i(x, y))}{df_i(x, y)}. \tag{4.12}$$

Its reciprocal is the certainty function C in the domain of the image (i.e., the certainty function in *pixel coordinates*):

$$C(x, y) = \frac{df_i(x, y)}{dF-1(f_i(x, y))}, \tag{4.13}$$

where $F = \log f$ and $F^{-1}() = log(f^{-1}())$. Note that C is the same for all images (i.e., for all values of image index i), whereas c_i was defined separately for each image. For any i the function c_i is a shifted (dilated) version of any other certainty function c_j, where the shift (dilation) depends on the log exposure K_i (the exposure k_i).

The final estimate of q (4.10) is simply a weighted sum of the estimates from q obtained from each of the input images, where each input image is weighted by the certainties in that image.

4.2.9 Exposure Interpolation and Extrapolation

The architecture of this process is shown in Figure 4.5, which depicts an image acquisition section (in this illustration, of three images), followed by an analysis section (to estimate q) and by a resynthesis section to generate an image again at the output (in this case four different possible output images are shown). The output image can look like any of the input images, but with improved signal-to-noise ratio, better tonal range, better color fidelity, and the like. Moreover an output image can be an interpolated or extrapolated version in which it is lighter or darker than any of the input images.

It should be noted that this process of interpolation or extrapolation provides a new way of adjusting the tonal range of an image, and this new method is called "comparadjustment." As illustrated in Figure 4.5, the image synthesis portion may also include various kinds of deblurring operations, and other kinds of image-sharpening and lateral inhibition filters to reduce the dynamic range of

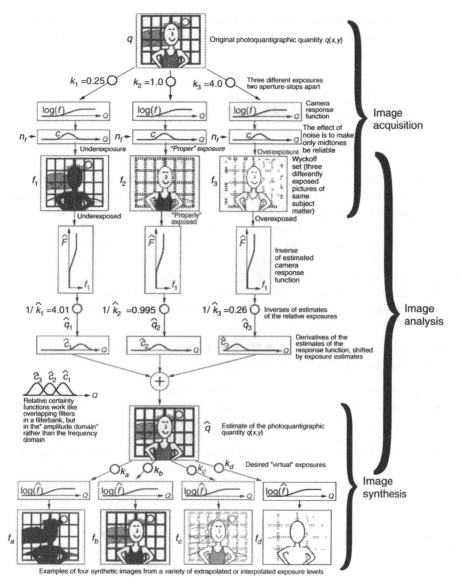

Figure 4.5 Comparadjustment (quantigraphic image exposure adjustment on a Wyckoff set). Multiple (in this example, 3) differently exposed (in this example by $K = 2$ f/stops) images are acquired. Estimates of q from each image are obtained. These are combined by weighted sum. The weights are the estimates of the certainty function shifted along the exposure axis by an amount given by the estimated exposure for each image. From the estimated photoquantity $\hat{q}$, one or more output images may be generated by multiplying by the desired synthetic exposure and passing the result through the estimated camera nonlinearity. In this example four synthetic pictures are generated, each being an extrapolated or interpolated exposure of the three input exposures. Thus we have a "virtual camera" [64] in which a exposure can be set retroactively.

the output image without loss of fine details. The result can be printed on paper or presented to an electronic display in such a way as to have optimal tonal definition.

4.3 COMPARAMETRIC IMAGE PROCESSING: COMPARING DIFFERENTLY EXPOSED IMAGES OF THE SAME SUBJECT MATTER

As previously mentioned, comparison of two or more differently exposed images may be done to determine q, or simply to tonally register the images without determining q. Also, as previously mentioned, tonal registration is more numerically stable than estimation of q, so there are some advantages to comparametric analysis and comparametric image processing in which one of the images is selected as a reference image, and others are expressed in terms of this reference image, rather than in terms of q. Typically the dark images are lightened, and/or the light images are darkened so that all the images match the selected reference image. Note that in such lightening and darkening operations, full precision is retained for further comparametric processing. Thus all but the reference image will be stored as an array of floating point numbers.

4.3.1 Misconceptions about Gamma Correction: Why Gamma Correction Is the Wrong Thing to Do!

So-called gamma correction (raising the pixel values in an image to an exponent) is often used to lighten or darken images. While gamma correction does have important uses, such as lightening or darkening images to compensate for incorrect display settings, it will now be shown that when one uses gamma correction to lighten or darken an image to compensate for incorrect exposure, one is making an unrealistic assumption about the camera response function whether or not one is aware of it.

Proposition 4.3.1 *Tonally registering differently exposed images of the same subject matter by gamma correcting them with exponent $\gamma = k^\Gamma$ is equivalent to assuming that the nonlinear response function of the camera is $f(q) = \exp(q^\Gamma)$.* □

Proof The process of gamma correcting an image f to obtain a gamma-corrected image $g = f^\gamma$ may be written

$$g(q) = f(kq) = (f(q))^\gamma, \tag{4.14}$$

where f is the original image, and g is the lightened or darkened image. Solving (4.14) for f, the camera response function, we obtain

$$f(q) = \exp(q^\Gamma) = \exp(q^{\log(\gamma)/\log(k)}). \quad □ \tag{4.15}$$

We can verify that (4.15) is a solution of (4.14) by noting that $g(q) = f(kq) = \exp\left((kq)^\Gamma\right) = \exp(k^\Gamma q^\Gamma) = \left(\exp(q^\Gamma)\right)^\gamma = f^\gamma$.

Example Two images, f_1 and f_2 differ only in exposure. Image f_2 was taken with twice as much exposure as f_1; that is, if $f_1 = f(q)$, then $f_2 = f(2q)$. Suppose that we wish to tonally align the two images by darkening f_2. If we darken f_2 by squaring all the pixel values of f_2 (normalized on the interval from 0 to 1, of course), then we have implicity assumed, whether we choose to admit it or not, that the camera response function must have been $f(q) = \exp(q^{\log_k(2)}) = \exp(q)$.

We see that the underlying solution of gamma correction, namely the camera response function (4.15), does not pass through the origin. In fact $f(0) = 1$. Since most cameras are designed so that they produce a signal level output of zero when the light input is zero, the function $f(q)$ does not correspond to a realistic or reasonable camera response function. Even a medium that does not itself fall to zero at zero exposure (e.g., film) is ordinarily scanned in such a way that the scanned output is zero for zero exposure, assuming that the $d_{\min}$ (minimum density for the particular emulsion being scanned) is properly set in the scanner. Therefore it is inappropriate and incorrect to use gamma correction to lighten or darken differently exposed images of the same subject matter, when the goal of this lightening or darkening is tonal registration (making them look the "same," apart from the effects of noise which is accentuated in the shadow detail of images that are lightened and the highlight detail of images that are darkened).

4.3.2 Comparametric Plots and Comparametric Equations

To understand the shortcomings of gamma correction, and to understand some alternatives, the concept of comparametric equations and comparametric plots will now be introduced. Equation 4.14 is an example of what is called a *comparametric equation* [64]. *Comparametric equations* are a special case of the more general class of equations called *functional equations* [80] and *comparametric plots* are a special case of the more general class of plots called *parametric plots*.

The notion of a parametric plot is well understood. For example, the parametric plot $(r\cos(q), r\sin(q))$ is a plot of a circle of radius r. Note that the circle can be expressed in a form that does not depend explicitly on q, and that the shape of the circle plotted is independent (assuming perfect precision in the sin and cos functions) of the extent q so long as the domain of q includes at least all points around the circle (i.e., an interval over 2π such as the interval from 0 to 2π).

Informally, a comparametric plot ("comparaplot" for short) is a special kind of parametric plot in which a function f is plotted against itself, and in which the parameterization of the ordinate is a linearly scaled parameterization of the abscissa. An intuitive understanding of a comparametric plot is provided by way of Figure 4.6. Illustrated is a hypothetical system that would generate a

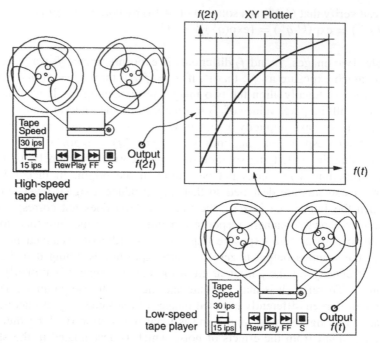

Figure 4.6 A system that generates comparametric plots. To gain a better intuitive understanding of what a comparametric plot is, consider two tape recorders that record identical copies of the same subject matter and then play it back at different speeds. The outputs of the two tape recorders are fed into an *XY* plotter, so that we have a plot of $f(t)$ on the *X* axis and a plot of $f(2t)$ on the *Y* axis. Plotting the function *f* against a contracted or dilated (stretched out) version of itself gives rise to a comparametric plot. If the two tapes start playing at the same time origin, a linear comparametric plot is generated.

comparametric plot by playing two tape recordings of the same subject matter (i.e., two copies of exactly the same tape recorded arbitrary signal) at two different speeds into an XY plotter. If the subject matter recorded on the tapes is simply a sinusoidal waveform, then the resulting comparametric plot is a Lissajous figure. Lissajous figures are comparametric plots where the function f is a sinusoid. However, for arbitrary signals recorded on the two tapes, the comparametric plot is a generalization of the well-known Lissajous figure.

Depending on when the tapes are started, and on the relative speeds of the two playbacks, the comparametric plot takes on the form $x = f(t)$ and $y = f(at + b)$, where t is time, f is the subject matter recorded on the tape, x is the output of the first tape machine, and y is the output of the second tape machine.

The plot $(f(t), f(at + b))$ will be called an *affine comparametric plot*. The special case when $b = 0$ will be called a *linear comparametric plot*, and corresponds to the situation when both tape machines begin playing back the subject matter at exactly the same time origin, although at possibly different speeds. Since the *linear comparametric plot* is of particular interest in this book, it will be assumed, when not otherwise specified, that $b = 0$ (we are referring to a *linear comparametric plot*).

More precisely, the linear comparametric plot is defined as follows:

Definition 4.3.1 *A plot along coordinates* $(f(q), f(kq))$ *is called a comparametric plot [64] of the function* $f(q)$. □

Here the quantity q is used, rather than time t, because it will not necessarily be time in all applications. In fact it will most often (in the rest of this book) be a quantity of light rather than an axis of time. The function $f()$ will also be an attribute of the recording device (camera), rather than an attribute of the input signal. Thus the response function of the camera will take on the role of the signal recorded on the tape in this analogy.

A function $f(q)$ has a family of comparametric plots, one for each value of the constant k, which is called the *comparametric ratio*.

Proposition 4.3.2 *When a function* $f(q)$ *is monotonic, the comparametric plot* $(f(q), f(kq))$ *can be expressed as a monotonic function* $g(f)$ *not involving* q. □

Thus the plot in Definition 4.3.1 may be rewritten as a plot $(f, g(f))$, not involving q. In this form the function g is called the *comparametric function*, and it expresses the range of the function $f(kq)$ as a function of the range of the function $f(q)$, independently of the domain q of the function f.

The plot g defines what is called a *comparametric equation*:

Definition 4.3.2 *Equations of the form* $g(f(q)) = f(kq)$ *are called comparametric equations [64].* □

A better understanding of comparametric equations may be had by referring to the following diagram:

$$
\begin{array}{ccc}
q & \xrightarrow{\;k\;} & kq \\
{\scriptstyle f}\downarrow & & \downarrow{\scriptstyle f} \\
f(g) & \xrightarrow[\;g\;]{} & f(kq)
\end{array}
\qquad (4.16)
$$

wherein it is evident that there are two equivalent paths to follow from q to $f(kq)$:

$$g \circ f = f \circ k. \qquad (4.17)$$

Equation (4.17) may be rewritten

$$g = f \circ k \circ f^{-1}, \qquad (4.18)$$

which provides an alternative definition of *comparametric equation* to that given in Definition 4.3.2.

Equation 4.14 is an example of a comparametric equation, and (4.15) is a solution of (4.14).

It is often preferable that comparametric equations be on the interval from zero to one in the range of f. Equivalently stated, we desire comparametric equations to be on the interval from zero to one in the domain of g and the range of g. In this case the corresponding plots and equations are said to be *unicomparametric*. (Actual images typically range from 0 to 255 and must thus be rescaled so that they range from 0 to 1, for unicomparametric image processing.)

Often we also impose further constraints that $f(0) = 0$, $g(0) = 0$, $g(1) = 1$, and differentiability at the origin. Solving a comparametric equation is equivalent to determining the unknown camera response function from a pair of images that differ only in exposure, when the comparametric equation represents the relationship between grayvalues in the two pictures, and the comparametric ratio k represents the ratio of exposures (i.e., if one picture was given taken with twice the exposure of the other, then $k = 2$).

4.3.3   Zeta Correction of Images

An alternative to *gamma correction* is proposed. This alternative, called *zeta correction* [70], will also serve as another example of a comparametric equation.

For zeta correction, we simply adjust the exponential solution (4.15) of the comparametric equation given by traditional gamma correction, $f(q) = \exp(q^\Gamma)$, so that the solution passes through the origin:

$$f(q) = \exp(q^\Gamma) - 1. \tag{4.19}$$

This camera response function passes through the origin (i.e., $f(0) = 0$, and is therefore much more realistic and reasonable than the response function implicit in gamma correction of images).

Using this camera response function (4.19), we define zeta correction as

$$g = (f + 1)^\gamma - 1, \tag{4.20}$$

which is the comparametric equation to which (4.19) is a solution. Thus (4.20) defines a recipe for darkening or lightening an image $f(q)$ to arrive at a corrected (comparadjusted) image $g(f(q))$ where the underlying response function $f(q)$ is zero for $q = 0$.

More generally, in applying this recipe for comparadjustment of images, the camera response function could be assumed to have been any of a family of curves defined by

$$f(q) = \exp(\beta q^\Gamma) - 1, \tag{4.21}$$

which are all solutions to (4.20).

As with gamma correction, the comparametric equation of zeta correction passes through the origin. To be unicomparametric, we would like to have it also pass through $(1, 1)$, meaning we would like $g(1) = 1$.

We can achieve this unicomparametric attribute by first applying a property of comparametric equations that will be shown later, namely that if we replace f with a function $h(f)$ and replace g with the same function $h(g)$ in a comparametric equation and its solution, the transformed solution is a solution to the transformed comparametric equation. Let us consider $h(f) = \kappa f$ and $h(g) = \kappa g$ (i.e., h serves to multiply by a constant κ). We therefore have that

$$f(q) = \frac{\exp(q^\Gamma) - 1}{\kappa} \qquad (4.22)$$

is a solution to the transformed comparametric equation:

$$g = \frac{(\kappa f + 1)^\gamma - 1}{\kappa}. \qquad (4.23)$$

Now, if we choose $\kappa = 2^\varsigma - 1$, we obtain a response function

$$f(q) = \frac{\exp(q^\Gamma) - 1}{2^\varsigma - 1}. \qquad (4.24)$$

The comparametric equation (4.23), with the denominator deleted, forms the basis for zeta correction of images:

$$g = \begin{cases} ((2^\varsigma - 1)f + 1)^{1/\varsigma} - 1, & \forall \varsigma \neq 0, \\ 2^f - 1 & \text{for } \varsigma = 0, \end{cases} \qquad (4.25)$$

where γ has been fixed to be equal to $1/\varsigma$ so that there is only one degree of freedom, ς.

Implicit in zeta correction of images is the assumption of an exponential camera response function, scaled. Although this is not realistic (given that the exponential function expands dynamic range, and most cameras have compressive response functions rather than expansive response functions), it is preferable to gamma correction because of the implicit notion of a response function for which $f(0) = 0$. With standard IEEE arithmetic, values of ς can range from approximately -50 to $+1000$.

4.3.4 Quadratic Approximation to Response Function

It is easier to derive a comparametric equation by working backward from a solution to a comparametric equation than it is to solve a comparametric equation. Thus we can build up a table of various comparametric equations and their solutions, and then use properties of comparametric equations, which will be described later, to rework entries from the table into desired formats. This procedure is similar to the way that Laplace transforms are inverted by using a table along with known properties.

Accordingly let us consider some other simple examples of comparametric equations and their solutions. Suppose, for example, that we have a solution

$$f(q) = aq^2 + bq + c \tag{4.26}$$

to a comparametric equation $g = g(f)$. To generate the comparametric equation to which (4.26) is a solution, we note that $g(f(q)) = f(kq) = a(kq)^2 + b(kq) + c$. Now we wish to find the relationship between g and f not involving q. The easiest way to do this is to eliminate q from each of f and g by noting (starting with f) that

$$\frac{1}{a}f = q^2 + \frac{b}{a}q + \frac{c}{a} \tag{4.27}$$

and completing the square

$$\frac{1}{a}f = \left(q + \frac{b}{2a}\right)^2 + \frac{c}{a} - \frac{b^2}{(2a)^2}. \tag{4.28}$$

This gives

$$q = \frac{-b \pm \sqrt{b^2 - 4a(c - f)}}{2a}. \tag{4.29}$$

Similarly, for g, we have

$$kq = \frac{-b \pm \sqrt{b^2 - 4a(c - g)}}{2a}. \tag{4.30}$$

So, setting k times (4.29) equal to (4.30), we have

$$k\frac{-b \pm \sqrt{b^2 - 4a(c - f)}}{2a} = \frac{-b \pm \sqrt{b^2 - 4a(c - g)}}{2a} \tag{4.31}$$

which gives us the desired relationship between f and g without involving q. Equation (4.31) is therefore a comparametric equation. It has the solution given by (4.26).

Equation (4.31) can be made explicit in g:

$$g = \frac{\begin{array}{c} -2b + b^2 + 4ac - 2b^2k \pm 2bk\sqrt{b^2 - 4a(c - f)} + 2b^2k^2 \\ - 4ack^2 + 4afk^2 \mp 2bk^2\sqrt{b^2 - 4a(c - f)} \end{array}}{4a}, \tag{4.32}$$

which can be written in a simpler form as

$$g = \frac{k^2d^2 \pm 2b(k - k^2)d + k^2b^2 - 2b^2k + 4ac + b^2 - 2b}{4a} \tag{4.33}$$

if we let the discriminant of (4.29) be $d = \sqrt{b^2 - 4a(c - f)}$. Equation 4.33, can be further understood in an even simpler form:

$$g = \alpha \pm \beta d + \gamma d^2, \qquad (4.34)$$

where $\alpha = (k^2 b^2 - 2b^2 k + 4ac + b^2 - 2b)/(4a)$, $\beta = (b(k - k^2))/(2a)$, and $\gamma = (k^2)/(4a)$.

From (4.34) the general shape of the curve contains a constant component, a primarily square root component, and a somewhat linear component, such that the equation captures the general shape of quadratic curves but scaled down halfway in powers. Thus (4.34) will be referred to as a "half-quadratic," or "biratic" model.

4.3.5 Practical Example: Verifying Comparametric Analysis

One of the important goals of comparametric analysis is to be able to determine a camera response function and the exposure settings from two or more differently exposed images [63,59,77]. Thus, even if we do not have the camera, we can determine the response function of the camera from only the differently exposed images.

Just as it is much easier to generate a comparametric equation from the solution of a comparametric equation, it is also much easier to work backward from the camera, if we have it available to us, than it is to solve the response function when we only have a collection of pictures of overlapping scene content to work with. Thus we will consider first the easier task of finding the response function when we have the camera.

Logarithmic Logistic Curve Unrolling (Logunrolling):
The Photocell Experiment
Suppose that we just want to measure the response function of one pixel of the camera, which we can regard as a light sensor, much like a photocell, cadmium sulphide (CDS) cell, or solar cell (i.e., like the selenium solar cell used in a light meter). To measure the response function of such a cell, all we really need is a small light source that we could move toward the cell while observing the cell's output. In a camera the output is usually a number that ranges from 0 to 255, or a set of three numbers that range from 0 to 255.

We next provide a light source of known relative output. We can do this by varying the voltage on a lamp, for example. We could use a light dimmer, but light dimmers produce a lot of flicker due to triac switching noise. Therefore it is better to use a variable autotransformer (a Variac(TM), Powerstat(TM), etc.) to adjust the voltage to a light bulb, and to use the well-known fact that the light output of most light bulbs varies as $q = v^{3.5}$ (the three and a halfth power law). We note that the color temperature of lights shifts when they are operated at different voltages, meaning that the light becomes more yellow as the voltage decreases.

A simpler and much more accurate and consistent way to vary the output of a light source is to move it further from or closer to the sensor, or to cover portions of it with black cardboard. So we begin with the light source far away, and move it toward the sensor (camera, cell, or whatever) until some small output f_1 is observable by the sensor. We associate this light output with the quantity of light q_1 produced by the light source. Then we cover half the light source, if it's a small lamp, with a round reflector; we cover exactly half the reflector output of the lamp with black paper, and this causes the quantity of light received at the sensor to decrease to $q_0 = q_1/2$. The measured quantity at the sensor is now $f_0 = f(q_0)$. Next we move the half-covered lamp toward the sensor until the quantity f_1 is observed. At this point, although the lamp is half covered up, it is closer to the sensor, so the same amount of light q_1 reaches the sensor as did when the lamp was further away and not half covered. Now, if we uncover the other half of the lamp, the quantity of light received at the sensor will increase to $q_2 = 2q_1$. Thus, whatever quantity we observe, call it f_2, it will be equal to $f(2q_1)$ which is equal to $f(4q_0)$, where f is the unknown response function of the camera. We continue this process, now covering half the lamp back up again to reduce its output back down to that of q_1, and then moving it still closer to the sensor until we observe an output of f_2 on the sensor. At this point we know that the lamp is providing a quantity of light q_2 to the sensor even though it is half covered. We can uncover the lamp in order to observe f_3 which we know will be $f_3 = f(2q_2) = f(4q_1) = f(8q_0)$. As we repeat the process, we are able to measure the response function of the sensor on a logarithmic scale where the base of the logarithm is 2.[3]

This process is called "log unrolling," and we will denote it by the function logunroll( ). Alternatively, we could use the inverse square law of light to determine the response function of the camera.

Unfortunately, both the log-unrolling method, and the inverse square law method suffer from various problems:

- Only one element (i.e., one pixel or one region of pixels) of the sensor array is used, so these methods are not very robust.

- Most cameras have some kind of automatic gain control or automatic exposure. Even cameras that claim to provide manual exposure settings often fail to provide truly nonimage-dependent settings. Thus most cameras, even when set to "manual," will exhibit a change in output at the one area of the sensor that depends on light incident on other areas of the sensor.

- The output scale is too widely spaced. We only get one reading per doubling of the exposure in the half covering method.

---

[3] This $\log_2$ spacing is quite wide; we only get to find f on a very coarse q axis that doubles each time. However, we could use a smaller interval, by covering the lamp in quarter sections, or smaller sections, such as varying the lamp in smaller output increments with pie-shaped octants of black paper.

• If we try to reduce the factor k from 2 to $4/3$ by quarter-covering, the cumulative error increases.

Measuring the Response Function f

Both the log-unrolling method and the inverse square law method are easy to implement with almost no special equipment other than the camera and other objects one can find in the average home or office, such as a lamp and some black cardboard.

However, if we have access to a test pattern, having regions of known transmissivity or reflectivity, we can measure the response function of the camera much more easily, and in a way that does not suffer from many of the problems with the log-unrolling method, and the inverse square law method. A CamAlign-CGH test pattern from DSC Laboratories, Toronto, Canada (Serial No. S009494), as shown in Figure 4.7 was used. The author cropped out the top graylevels test pattern portion of the picture, and averaged down columns, to obtain a mean plot as shown in Figure 4.8a. The author then differentiated the resulting list of numbers to find the transition regions, and took the median across each such region to obtain a robust estimate of $f(q)$ for each of the 11 steps, as well as the black regions of the test pattern. Using the known reflectivity of each of these 12 regions, a set of 12 ordered pairs $(q, f(q))$ results. These data are tabulated

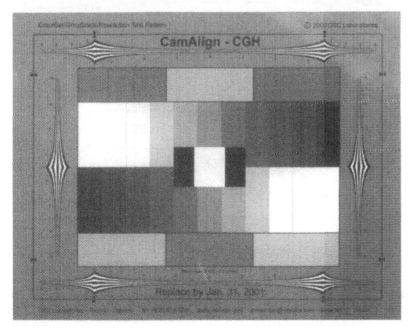

Figure 4.7   Picture of test pattern taken by author on Wednesday December 20, 2000, late afternoon, with imaging portion of wearable camera system mounted to tripod, for the purpose of determining the response function $f(q)$ of the imaging apparatus. Exposure was 1/30 s at f/16 (60 mm lens on a D1 sensor array). WearComp transmission index v115 (115th light vector of this transmission from a Xybernaut MA IV).

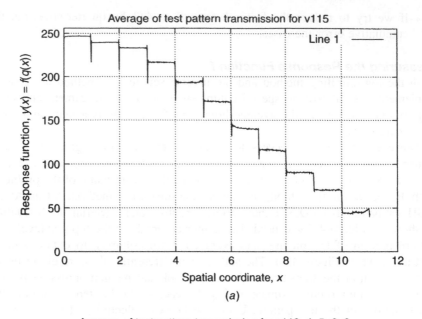

(a)

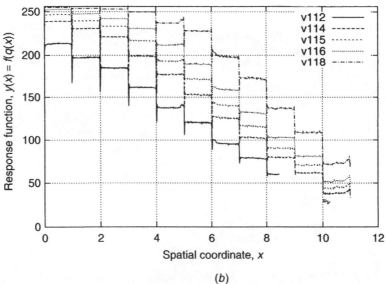

(b)

Figure 4.8 Test pattern plots generated by segmenting out bars and averaging down columns to average out noise and improve the estimate. (a) The greatest exposure for which the highest level on the chart was sufficiently below 255 that clipping would not bias the estimate was v115 (1/30 s exposure). (b) Plots shown for one-third stop below and above v115, as well as a full stop below and above v115. Exposures were 1/60 s for v112, 1/40 s for v114, 1/25 s for v116, and 1/15 s for v118.

Table 4.1 Samples of q and $f(q)$ Derived from the 11 Graybars Plus the Two Black Regions of the Test Pattern as Measured in Picture Transmission v115

Data Point	q	$255f(q)$
0	**0**	**0**
1	0.011	23.757634
2	0.021	44.856354
3	0.048	70.447514
4	0.079	90.480663
5	0.126	116.176796
6	0.185	140.685083
7	0.264	171.232044
8	0.358	193.215470
9	0.472	216.505525
10	0.622	233.182320
11	0.733	239.433702
12	0.893	246.718232

Note the inclusion of the data point at the origin. In the case where the origin is not known, a large number of images may be taken with the lens cap of the camera on in a darkroom, and averaged together to define a zero image to be subtracted from every subsequent input image.

in Table 4.1. Justification for choice of exposure (1/30 s which corresponds to test pattern transmission v115) to generate this table is evident from Figure 4.8b where an exposure of 1/25 s (one-third stop more) comes very close to 255 at the highest bar, such that statistical variation due to noise would cause a bias downward in the estimate. Other plots above and below the chosen exposure are shown in Figure 4.8b.

To fit the model $f = aq^2 + bq + c$ to the 12 observed data points (q_k, f_k), we minimize $\varepsilon = \sum_k (aq^2 + bq + c - f)^2$ and set the derivative to zero:

$$
\begin{bmatrix}
\sum_k q^4 & \sum_k q^3 & \sum_k q^2 \\
\sum_k q^3 & \sum_k q^2 & \sum_k q^1 \\
\sum_k q^2 & \sum_k q^1 & \sum_k q^0
\end{bmatrix}
\begin{bmatrix} a \\ b \\ c \end{bmatrix}
=
\begin{bmatrix}
\sum_k q^2 f \\
\sum_k qf \\
\sum_k f
\end{bmatrix}.
\tag{4.35}
$$

Alternatively, it was found to be simpler (using the "Octave" matrix manipulation program) to construct the leftmost three columns of a Vandermonde matrix $V = [v1 \quad v2 \quad v3]$, where $v1 = q \circ q$, $v2 = q$ and $v3$ is a vector of ones having the same size as q, and where q is a column vector of the 12 samples of q. (The symbol $\circ$ denotes Hadamard multiplication in which corresponding elements are multiplied, and is implemented in the Octave matrix program by

".*".) The coefficients a, b, and c were found to be $[a \quad b \quad c]^T = \text{pinv}(V)f$, ($a = -1.5636$, $b = 2.2624$, and $c = 0.15204$) where pinv denotes the Moore Penrose pseudoinverse.

The 12 ordered pairs from Table 4.1 (from analysis of transmission v115) are shown plotted in Figure 4.9 along with a best fit to the quadratic model of (4.26) in panel (a). Since we know that (or we create the system so that by design) $f(0) = 0$, we can let $\mathbf{V_0} = [v1 \quad v2]$ and solve $[a \quad b]^T = \text{pinv}(V_0)f$, where we then impose that $c = 0$, so that the curve passes through the known point at the origin (see Fig. 4.9b).

Higher-order polymomials (cubics, quartics, etc.) do not fit the data very well either as is evident in Figure 4.10. The half-quadratic (biratic) function (4.34), which is the comparametric equation corresponding to the quadratic equation, is simple, but the comparametric equation corresponding to the cubic or quartic function, is much more complicated. The comparametric equation will not even reasonably fit on the printed page to show in this book. Accordingly a better model is needed.

4.3.6 Inverse Quadratic Approximation to Response Function and its Squadratic Comparametric Equation

Equation (4.26) does not fit response curves very well because the response curves tend to be compressive, not expansive. Response curves are generally concave down, rather than concave up. In other words, response curves tend to look more like square root functions than like square functions. Thus it is helpful to consider an inverse quadratic model that fits response functions quite nicely:

$$f = \frac{-b \pm \sqrt{b^2 - 4a(c - q)}}{2a}. \tag{4.36}$$

Following the procedure of eliminating q from each of f and g, we use the inverse forms

$$q = af^2 + bf + c \tag{4.37}$$

and

$$kq = ag^2 + bf + c. \tag{4.38}$$

Substituting these into (4.36) gives rise to the comparametric equation:

$$g = \frac{-b \pm \sqrt{b^2 - 4a(c - kaf^2 + bf + c)}}{2a} \tag{4.39}$$

which will be called the "squadratic model" so-named because of its similarity to the square root of a quadratic formula.

Solving for the parameters a, b, and c, for the 12 data points of the WearCam system gives curves plotted in Figure 4.11a.

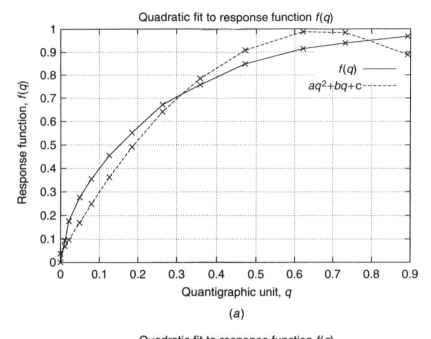

(a)

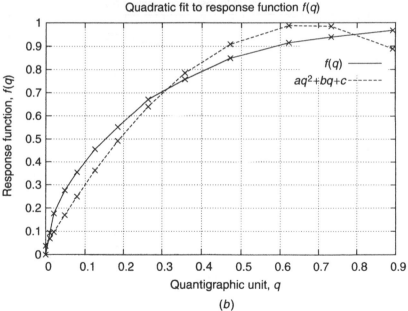

(b)

Figure 4.9 Plots of $f(q)$ together with best quadratic curve fits. The range f is normalized on the interval from 0 to 1. (a) Unfortunately, a quadratic fit comes far from passing through the origin, and (b) even if constrained to do so, the curve becomes concave upward in places. This is a very poor fit to the observed data.

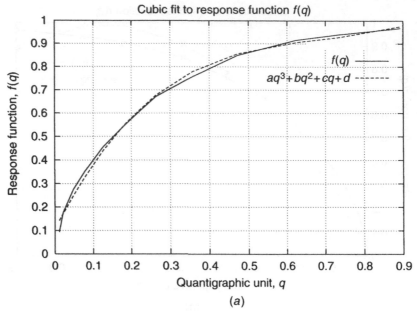

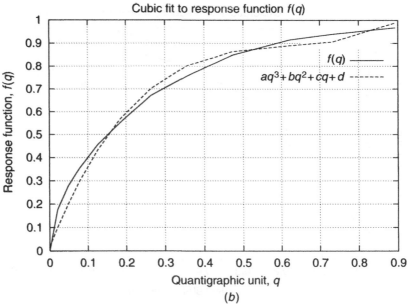

Figure 4.10 (a) Unfortunately, a cubic fit still comes far from passing through the origin, and (b) even if constrained to do so, the curve becomes concave upwards in places. This is a very poor fit to the observed data.

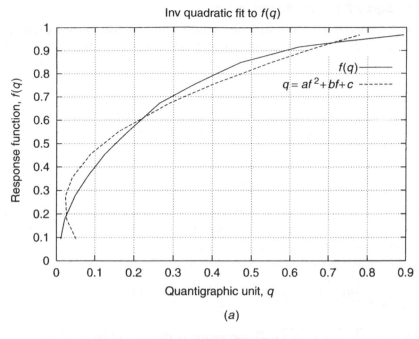

(a)

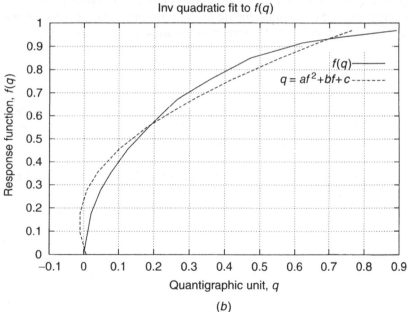

(b)

Figure 4.11 (a) The best-fit inverse quadratic for $f(q)$ turns out to not be a function. (b) Constraining it to pass through the origin does not help solve the problem.

4.3.7   Sqrtic Fit to the Function $f(q)$

A much better model that fits the general shape of the response curve is $f(q) = aq + b\sqrt{q} + c$ which will be called the sqrtic model. To fit this model to the 12 observed data points (q_k, f_k), we minimize $\varepsilon = \sum_k (aq + b\sqrt{q} + c - f)^2$ and set the derivative to zero:

$$
\begin{bmatrix}
\sum_k q^2 & \sum_k q^{3/2} & \sum_k q^1 \\
\sum_k q^{3/2} & \sum_k q^1 & \sum_k q^{1/2} \\
\sum_k q^1 & \sum_k q^{1/2} & \sum_k q^0
\end{bmatrix}
\begin{bmatrix}
a \\ b \\ c
\end{bmatrix}
=
\begin{bmatrix}
\sum_k qf \\
\sum_k q^{1/2} f \\
\sum_k f
\end{bmatrix}. \tag{4.40}
$$

This gives $a = -0.79539$, $b = 1.8984$, and $c = -0.10060$ unconstrained, and $a = -0.44849$, $b = 1.4940$, $c = 0$, constrained through the origin. The corresponding curves are plotted in Figure 4.12.

The comparametric equation corresponding to the sqrtic model is given by

$$
g = \frac{2ac - b^2 \sqrt{k} \pm bd\sqrt{k} + b^2 k - 2ack + 2afk \mp bdk}{2a}, \tag{4.41}
$$

where $d = \sqrt{b^2 - 4a(c - f)}$. This equation is plotted in Figure 4.13b.

A comparison of the comparametric plots for the quadratic $f(q)$ model and the sqrtic $f(q)$ model with $k = 2$ is shown in Figure 4.13. The plot of Figure 4.13a is unacceptable, because it is not monotonic. The plot of Figure 4.13b is far more preferable, and indicates that the sqrtic model is a much better fit than the quadratic model.

It is evident from the plot of Figure 4.13b that there is an almost linear portion, and then a clipped (highly nonlinear) portion where saturation occurs. In what follows, saturation models will be described, starting now with an affine model (i.e., the situation where the comparametric plot is a straight line).

Measurement of the True Camera Response Function with Multiple Differently Exposed Pictures of a Test Chart

An accurate measurement of true response function of an imaging apparatus is useful in order to verify that the new methods of finding the response function actually work. Although we assume this true response function is not known (e.g., we assume we do not have the camera available to us, in order to get pictures of a test chart), we will see the value in using a known case to verify the accuracy of the proposed methods.

Previously the author selected the best exposure of the CamAlign-CGH test chart as being transmitted image v115 (Fig. 4.7), based on looking at the plots in Figure 4.8a and concluding that v115 had the greatest exposure without being too close to saturation.

However, consistent with the hypothesis of this chapter, namely that we can do better by considering multiple differently exposed pictures of the same subject

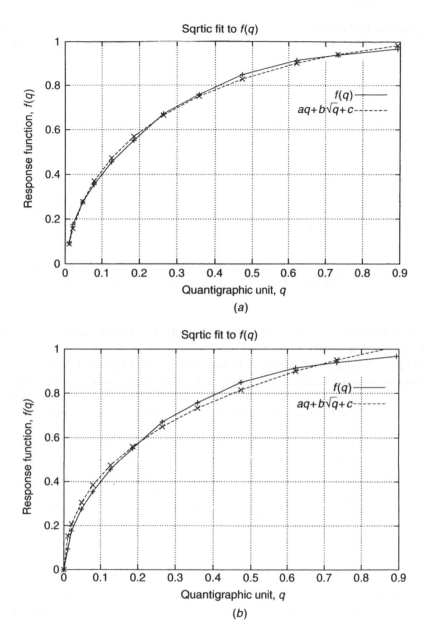

Figure 4.12 (a) The best-fit inverse quadratic for $f(q)$ turns out to not be a function. (b) Constraining it to pass through the origin does not help solve the problem.

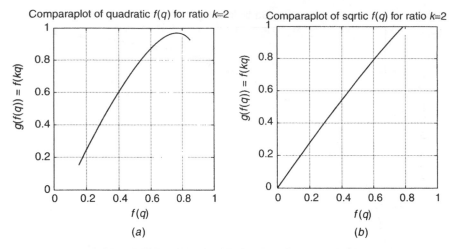

Figure 4.13 Comparison of the comparametric plots for the last two models, with $k = 2$: (a) Comparaplot for quadratic model of $f(q)$; (b) comparaplot for sqrtic model of $f(q)$.

matter, we can in fact apply this same philosophy to the way we obtain ground-truth measurement data.

Table 4.1 was generated from picture v115, and likewise Table 4.2 shows 19 sets of ordered pairs arising from each of 19 differently exposed pictures (numbered v100 to v118) of the test chart. The actual known quantity of light entering the wearable imaging system is the same for all of these, and is denoted q in the table.

Plotting the data in Table 4.2, we obtain the 19 plots shown in Figure 4.14a. Shifting these results appropriately (i.e., by the K_i values), to line them up, gives the ground-truth, known response function, f, shown in Figure 4.14b.

For simplicity, the base of the logarithm is chosen such that the shift in Q is by an integer quantity for each of the exposures. In this example, the base of the logarithm is $\sqrt[3]{2}$ since the pictures were all taken at third F-stop exposure intervals, by way of exposure times listed in Table 4.3.

4.3.8 Example Showing How to Solve a Comparametric Equation: The Affine Comparametric Equation and *Affine Correction* of Images

Solving a comparametric equation involves "reverse engineering" a comparametric plot to determine the underlying response function that gave rise to the comparametric plot. For example, one might ask: For what class of analytic functions is the comparametric plot a straight line? This question amounts to solving the following *comparametric equation*:

$$g(f(q)) = f(kq) = af(q) + b. \tag{4.42}$$

Table 4.2 Samples of q and $f(q)$ Derived from the 11 Graybars Plus the Two Black Regions of the Test Pattern as Measured in Each of 19 Images (v100–v118) Transmitted from the Wearable Imaging Apparatus

q	v100	v101	v102	v103	v104	v105	v106	v107	v108	v109	v110	v111	v112	v113	v114	v115	v116	v117	v118
0.011	1.7	1.7	1.8	2.2	2.6	3.1	3.6	4.4	5.5	7.1	8.7	10.3	12.9	16.1	19.7	23.8	28.7	34.0	41.9
0.021	2.6	2.7	3.1	3.8	4.6	5.8	7.1	8.9	11.5	15.3	18.1	21.6	26.9	32.5	38.5	44.9	52.4	60.4	72.6
0.048	4.3	4.8	5.5	7.1	8.7	11.2	13.8	17.1	21.7	28.2	32.5	37.9	45.3	53.2	61.5	70.4	80.9	92.3	108.8
0.079	6.1	7.0	8.2	10.5	13.0	16.5	20.1	24.8	30.9	38.8	44.1	50.8	59.8	69.7	79.6	90.5	103.1	117.0	137.2
0.126	9.2	10.6	12.6	15.9	19.4	24.4	29.6	35.2	43.0	52.7	59.2	67.7	78.8	90.8	102.9	116.2	131.9	148.7	172.5
0.185	12.9	14.7	17.3	21.7	26.6	32.4	38.4	45.5	54.6	65.9	73.5	83.8	95.9	109.6	125.7	140.7	159.0	175.0	198.3
0.264	18.3	20.6	24.4	30.0	35.6	42.9	50.2	58.6	69.6	83.4	92.6	104.0	120.6	136.9	152.8	171.2	189.2	207.9	227.7
0.358	23.0	26.1	30.3	36.7	43.4	51.7	60.1	69.9	82.2	97.5	107.3	121.5	137.7	156.3	176.7	193.2	211.7	223.3	236.9
0.472	29.4	32.7	37.6	45.2	52.6	62.3	72.1	83.1	97.0	114.6	126.3	141.6	161.5	181.1	199.0	216.5	230.5	239.8	249.8
0.622	36.2	40.2	46.1	54.5	63.3	74.4	85.5	98.0	113.7	133.8	146.9	164.2	184.5	203.6	221.0	233.2	242.0	249.2	253.0
0.733	40.7	45.0	51.2	60.3	70.0	81.9	93.9	107.2	124.2	145.8	159.7	177.3	197.3	216.4	230.5	239.4	247.5	253.0	254.0
0.893	46.7	51.2	58.0	68.2	78.8	91.7	105.0	119.5	138.0	161.4	176.0	193.1	213.3	228.8	238.9	246.7	252.7	254.0	255.0

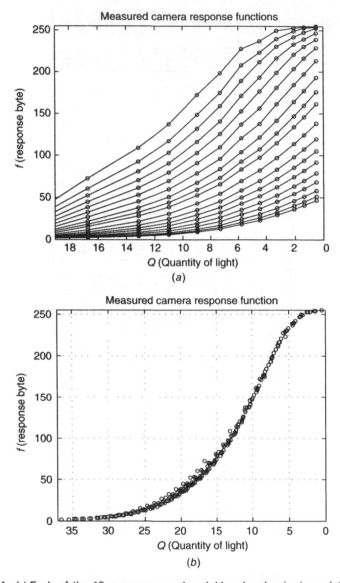

Figure 4.14 (a) Each of the 19 exposures produced 11 ordered pairs in a plot of $f(Q)$ as a function of $Q = \log(q)$. (The point at the origin is omitted since the data is plotted on a logarithmic scale). The data points are represented as circles, and are connected together by straight lines to make it more clear which of the points belongs to which exposure. Note that the known Q values (as provided by DSC Labs) are not uniformly spaced. (b) Shifting these 19 plots left or right by the appropriate exposure constant K_i allowed them all to line up to produce the ground truth known-response function $f(Q)$. The base of the logarithm is chosen as $\sqrt[3]{2}$ (the k_i ratios) so that the amount of left-right shift is equal to an integer for all plots.

Solving (4.42) means determining the general class of functions $f(q)$ for which (4.42) is true. Let $f(q)$ be expressed as a Laurent series:

$$f(q) = \ldots c_{-2}q^{-2} + c_{-1}q^{-1} + c_0 + c_1 q + c_2 q^2 + \ldots = \sum_{-\infty}^{\infty} c_n q^n. \qquad (4.43)$$

Similarly g may be expressed as a Laurent series:

$$g = f(kq) = \ldots c_{-2}k^{-2}q^{-2} + c_{-1}k^{-1}q^{-1} + c_0 + c_1 kq + c_2 k^2 q^2$$
$$+ \ldots = \sum_{-\infty}^{\infty} c_n k^n q^n. \qquad (4.44)$$

Differentiating (4.43) and (4.44), we have

$$\frac{df}{dq} = \sum_{-\infty}^{\infty} n c_n q^{n-1},$$
$$\frac{dg}{dq} = \sum_{-\infty}^{\infty} n c_n k^n q^{n-1}. \qquad (4.45)$$

Table 4.3 Approximate Exposure Times in Seconds

Image	Exposure Time (sec)
v100.jpg	1/1000
v101.jpg	1/800
v102.jpg	1/640
v103.jpg	1/500
v104.jpg	1/400
v105.jpg	1/320
v106.jpg	1/250
v107.jpg	1/200
v108.jpg	1/160
v109.jpg	1/125
v110.jpg	1/100
v111.jpg	1/80
v112.jpg	1/60
v113.jpg	1/50
v114.jpg	1/40
v115.jpg	1/30
v116.jpg	1/25
v117.jpg	1/20
v118.jpg	1/15

Note: Times are as displayed on imaging system (e.g. they are rounded off very crudely).

A straight line (4.42) has constant slope, or equivalently,

$$\frac{dg}{df} = a \tag{4.46}$$

so that

$$\frac{dg}{dq} = \frac{dg}{df}\frac{df}{dq} = a\frac{df}{dq}, \tag{4.47}$$

Combining (4.45) and (4.47) gives

$$\sum_{-\infty}^{\infty} nc_n k^n q^{n-1} = a\sum_{-\infty}^{\infty} nc_n q^{n-1}, \tag{4.48}$$

which can hold only if at most one of the coefficients c_n is nonzero. Let at most one nonzero coefficient be the mth coefficient c_m so that

$$\frac{df}{dq} = mc_m q^{m-1}. \tag{4.49}$$

Integrating (4.49), we obtain

$$f(q) = \begin{cases} \alpha + c_m q^m = \alpha + \beta q^\gamma & \forall m \neq 0, \\ B\log(\beta q) & \text{for } m = 0, \end{cases} \tag{4.50}$$

where continuous values of α, β, and γ are allowed, and the coefficient at the origin is not necessarily set to zero.

One of these solutions turns out, perhaps coincidentally, to be the familiar model

$$f(q) = \alpha + \beta q^\gamma \tag{4.51}$$

used by photographers to characterize the response of a variety of photographic emulsions, including so-called extended response film [75]. It is known that (4.51) becomes the equation of a straight line when expressed in logarithmic coordinates, if we subtract α (as many scanners such as PhotoCD attempt to do by prompting the user to scan a piece of blank film from the film trailer before scanning the rest of the roll of film):

$$\log(f(q) - \alpha) = \gamma \log(q) + \beta \tag{4.52}$$

It is an interesting coincidence that the comparametric plot of this function (4.51) is also a straight line:

Proposition 4.3.3 *The comparametric plot corresponding to the standard photographic response function (4.51) is a straight line. The slope is k^γ, and the intercept is $\alpha(1 - k^\gamma)$.* □

Proof $g(f(kq)) = f(kq) = \alpha + \beta(kq)^\gamma$ Rearranging to eliminate q gives $g = k^\gamma(\alpha + \beta q^\gamma) + \alpha(1 - k^\gamma)$ so that

$$g = k^\gamma f + \alpha(1 - k^\gamma) \qquad \square \qquad (4.53)$$

Note that the constant β does not appear in the comparametric equation. Thus we cannot determine β from the comparametric equation. The physical (intuitive) interpretation is that we can only determine the nonlinear response function of a camera up to a single unknown scalar constant.

Note that (4.14) looks quite similar in form to (4.51). It in fact is identical if we set $\alpha = 0$ and $\beta = 1$. However, one must recall that (4.14) is a comparametric equation and that (4.51) is a solution to a (different) comparametric equation. Thus we must be careful not to confuse the two. The first corresponds to gamma correction of an image, while the second corresponds to the camera response function that is implicit in applying (4.53) to lighten or darken the image. To make this distinction clear, applying (4.53) to lighten or darken an image will be called *affine correcting* (i.e., correcting by modeling the comparametric function with a straight line). The special case of *affine correction* when the intercept is equal to zero will be called *linear correction*.

Preferably *affine correction* of an image also includes a step of clipping values greater than one to one, and values less than zero to zero, in the output image:

$$g = \min(\max(k^\gamma f + \alpha(1 - k^\gamma), 0), 1). \qquad (4.54)$$

If the intercept is zero and the slope is greater than one, the effect, neglecting noise, of (4.54), is to lighten the image in a natural manner that properly simulates the effect of having taken the picture with greater exposure. In this case the effect is theoretically identical to that which would have been obtained by using a greater exposure on the camera, assuming that the response function of the camera follows the power law $f = q^\gamma$, as many cameras do in practice. Thus it has been shown that the correct way to lighten an image is to apply *linear correction*, not *gamma correction* (apart from correction of an image to match an incorrectly adjusted display device or the like, where gamma correction is still the correct operation to apply).

As before, we have worked forward, starting with the solution (4.51) and deriving the comparametric equation (4.53) of which (4.51) is a solution. It is much easier to generate comparametric equations from their solutions than it is to solve comparametric equations.

This comparametric equation is both useful and simple. The simplicity is in the ease with which it is solved, and by the fact that the solution happens to be the most commonly used camera response model in photography. As we will later see, when processing images, the comparametric function can be estimated by fitting a straight line through data points describing the comparametric relation between images. However, there are two shortcomings to *affine correction*:

1. It is not inherently unicomparametric, so it must be clipped to one when it exceeds one, and clipped to zero when it falls below zero, as shown in (4.54).

2. Its solution, $f(q)$, only describes the response of cameras within their normal operating regime. Since the art of photoquantigraphic image processing involves a great deal of image processing done on images that have been deliberately and grossly overexposed or underexposed, there is a need for a comparametric model that captures the essence of cameras at both extremes of exposure (i.e., both overexposure and underexposure).

The shortcomings of affine correction become apparent when we look at the fit to a typical camera response function (Fig. 4.15). A straight line fit to actual measured data from the response function is shown in Figure 4.15a. The power law fit is only valid over a very narrow range of exposure latitudes, as shown in Figure 4.15a. While this fit may be satisfactory for conventional photography it is not acceptable for cybernetic photography in which the deliberate exposure extremes arise from construction of Wyckoff sets.

4.3.9 Power of Root over Root Plus Constant Correction of Images

Although *affine correction* was an improvement over *zeta correction*, which itself was an improvement over *gamma correction*, *affine correction* still has the two shortcomings listed above. Therefore another form of image exposure correction is proposed, and it will be called *power of root over root plus constant correction*. This new exposure correction is unicomparametric (bounded in normalized units between 0 and 1) and also has a parameter to control the softness of the transition into the *toe* and *shoulder* regions of the response function, rather than the hard clipping introduced by (4.54).

As with affine correction, *power of root over root plus constant correction* will be introduced first by its solution, from which the comparametric equation will be derived. The solution is

$$f(q) = \left(\frac{e^b q^a}{e^b q^a + 1} \right)^c, \tag{4.55}$$

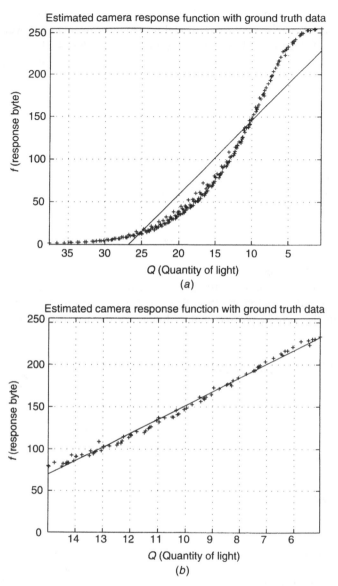

Figure 4.15 The standard power law photographic response function (4.51) can only fit the response of the imaging apparatus over a narrow region of exposure latitude. (*a*) Best fit over the full 37/3 F-stops is poor. (*b*) Best fit over an interval of ten thirds of a stop is satisfactory. Although this region of exposures is typical of conventional photography, a feature of cybernetic photography is the use of deliberate massive overexposure and underexposure. Indeed, the human eye has a much wider exposure latitude than is suggested by the narrow region over which the power law model is valid. Therefore a new model that captures the essence of the imaging system's response function in regions of extreme exposure is required.

which has only three parameters. Thus no extra unnecessary degrees of freedom (which might otherwise capture or model noise) have been added over and above the number of degrees of freedom in the previous model (4.51).

An intuitive understanding of (4.55) can be better had by rewriting it:

$$f = \begin{cases} \dfrac{1}{(1+e^{-(a\log(q)+b)})^c} & \forall q \neq 0, \\ 0 & \text{for } q = 0. \end{cases} \tag{4.56}$$

written in this form, the soft transition into the toe (region of underexposure) and shoulder (region of overexposure) regions is evident by the shape this curve has if plotted on a logarithmic exposure scale,

$$f = \frac{1}{(1+e^{-(aQ+b)})^c}, \tag{4.57}$$

where $Q = \log(q)$; see Figure 4.16.

The (4.57) model may, at first, only seem like a slight improvement over (4.51), given our common intuition that most exposure information is ordinarily captured in the central portion that is linear on the logarithmic exposure plot.

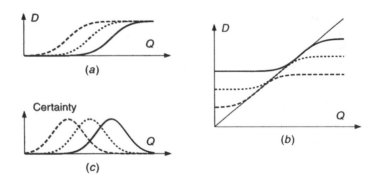

Figure 4.16 Example of response functions $1/(1+e^{-(a\log(q)+b)})^c$, which have soft transition into the toe region of underexposure and shoulder region of overexposure. Traditionally these responses would be on film, such as the Wyckoff film, having density 'D' as a function of log exposure (i.e., $Q = \log(q)$). (a) Response functions corresponding to three different exposures. In the Wyckoff film these would correspond to a coarse-grained (fast) layer, denoted by a dashed line, that responds to a small quantity of light, a medium-grained layer, denoted by a dotted line, that responds moderately, and a fine-grained layer, denoted by a solid line, that responds to a large quantity of light. Ideally, when the more sensitive layer saturates, the next most sensitive layer begins responding, so each layer covers one of a set of slightly overlapping amplitude bins. (b) Tonally aligning (i.e., tonally "registering" by comparadjustment), the images creates a situation where each image provides a portion of the overall response curve. (c) The amplitude bin over which each contributes is given by differentiating each of these response functions, to obtain the relative "certainty function." Regions of highest certainty are regions where the sensitivity (change in observable output with respect to a given change in input) is maximum.

However, it is important that we unlearn what we have been taught in traditional photography, where incorrectly exposed images are ordinarily thrown away rather than used to enhance the other images! It must be emphasized that comparametric image processing differs from traditional image processing in the sense that in comparametric image processing (using the Wyckoff principle, as illustrated in Fig. 4.4) the images typically include some that are *deliberately* underexposed and overexposed. This overexposure of some images and underexposure of other images is often deliberately taken to extremes. Therefore the additional sophistication of the model (4.55) is of great value in capturing the essence of a set of images where some extend to great extremes in the *toe* or *shoulder* regions of the response function.

Proposition 4.3.4 *The comparametric equation of which the proposed photographic response function (4.55) is a solution, is given by*

$$g(f) = \frac{fk^{ac}}{(\sqrt[c]{f}(k^a - 1) + 1)^c},$$

(4.58)

where $K = log(k)$.   □

Again, note that $g(f)$ does not depend on b, which is consistent with our knowledge that the comparametric equation captures the information of $f(q)$ up to a single unknown scalar proportionality constant.

Therefore we may rewrite (4.55) in a simplified form

$$f(q) = \left(\frac{q^a}{q^a + 1}\right)^c,$$

(4.59)

where b has been normalized to zero, and where it is understood that $q > 0$, since it is a quantity of light (therefore f is always real). Thus we have, for q,

$$q = \sqrt[a]{\frac{\sqrt[c]{f(q)}}{1 - \sqrt[c]{f(q)}}}.$$

(4.60)

From this simple form, we see that there are two degrees of freedom, given by the free parameters a and c. It is useful and intuitive to consider the slope of the corresponding comparametric equation (4.58),

$$\frac{dg}{df} = \frac{k^{ac}}{(\sqrt[c]{f}(k^a - 1) + 1)^{c+1}}$$

(4.61)

evaluated at the origin, which is k^{ac}.

If the exposure, k, is known we can resolve the two degrees of freedom of this function into a slope-at-the-origin term k^{ac}, and a sharpness term proportional to a/c. Thus we can vary the product ac to match the slope at the origin. Then, once the slope at the origin is fixed, we can replace a with $a*$ sharpness and replace c with $c*$ sharpness where sharpness typically varies from 1 to 200, depending on the nature of the camera or imaging system (e.g., 10 might be a typical value for sharpness for a typical camera system).

Once the values of a and c are determined for a particular camera, the response function of that camera is known by way of (4.60). Equation (4.60) provides a recipe for converting from imagespace to lightspace. It is thus implemented, for example, in the comparametric toolkit as function pnm2plm (from `http://wearcam.org/cement`), which converts images to portable lightspace maps.

It should also be emphasized that (4.60) never saturates. Only when q increases without bound, does f approach one (the maximum value). In an actual camera, such as one having 8 bits per pixel per channel, the value 255 would never quite be reached.

In practice, however, we know that cameras do saturate (i.e., there is usually a finite value of q for which the camera will give a maximum output). Thus the actual behavior of a camera is somewhere between the classic model (4.51) and that of (4.60). In particular, a saturated model turns out to be the best.

4.3.10 Saturated Power of Root over Root Plus Constant Correction of Images

Equation 4.55 may be rewritten

$$f(q) = s \left(\frac{e^b q^a}{e^b q^a + 1} \right)^c , \tag{4.62}$$

where s is a saturation parameter and operator that causes (4.62) to no longer remain on the interval from 0 to 1 unless $s = 1$. Saturation, s, operates linearly as a multiplicative constant when the operand is less than or equal to one, and it operates as a clipping operator, to clip the result to one, when the operand is greater than one. Thus s plays a dual role as a saturation parameter (saturation constant) for $s \leq 1$ and as an operator for $s > 1$.

Treating s linearly (assuming that the regime $s \leq 1$), we can work through, as follows:

$$q^a = \frac{\sqrt[c]{f}}{\sqrt[c]{s} - \sqrt[c]{f}} \tag{4.63}$$

and

$$k^a q^a = \frac{\sqrt[c]{g}}{\sqrt[c]{s} - \sqrt[c]{g}}. \tag{4.64}$$

This obtains

$$\sqrt[c]{g} = \frac{k^a \sqrt[c]{s} \sqrt[c]{f}}{\sqrt[c]{f}(k^a - 1) + \sqrt[c]{s}}, \tag{4.65}$$

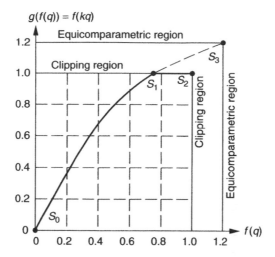

Figure 4.17 A scaling factor with saturation arithmetic to the power of root over root plus constant correction. The scaling factor allows for an equicomparametric function with equicomparametricity not necessarily equal to unity. A typical linear scaling saturation constant of equicomparametricity is 1.2, as shown in the figure. This model accounts for soft saturation toward a limit, followed by hard saturation right at the limit. Four points are shown in the illustration: the curve starts at s_0 (the origin) and moves toward s_1, where it is clipped, and then moves toward s_2. A fourth point, s_3 shows, where it would have gone (from s_2) if it were not for the saturation operator.

giving

$$g(f) = \frac{sfk^{ac}}{(\sqrt[c]{f}(k^a - 1) + \sqrt[c]{s})^c}. \tag{4.66}$$

Now we find it useful to rewrite (4.66) in terms of the quantity g/s:

$$g/s = \frac{(f/s)k^{ac}}{(\sqrt[c]{f/s}(k^a - 1) + 1)^c}, \tag{4.67}$$

where we can see the effect of the saturation parameter is simply to set forth a new scaling. This new scaling is shown in Figure 4.17. The result is a three-parameter model with parameters a, c, and s. This model accurately describes the relationships among sets of images coming from a very large number of different kinds of imaging systems.

4.3.11 Some Solutions to Some Comparametric Equations That Are Particularly Illustrative or Useful

Some examples of comparametric equations, with comparametric ratio k, and their solutions are summarized in Table 4.4.

Table 4.4 Illustrative or Useful Examples of Comparametric Equations and their Solutions

Comparametric Equations $g(f(q)) = f(kq)$	Solution (Camera Response Function) $f(q)$
$g = f^\gamma$	$f = \exp(q^\Gamma), \quad \gamma = k^\Gamma$
$g = k^\gamma f$	$f = q^\gamma$
$g = af + b \; \forall a \neq 1 \text{ or } b = 0$	$f = \alpha + \beta q^\gamma, \quad a = k^\gamma, b = \alpha(1 - k^\gamma)$
$g = f + a \log k$	$f = a \log(q) + b$
$g = (\sqrt{f} + \log k)^\gamma$	$f = \log^\gamma q$
$g = (f + 1)^\gamma - 1$	$f = \exp(\beta q^\Gamma) - 1, \quad \gamma = k^\Gamma$
$g = e^b f^a = e^{\alpha(1 - k^\gamma)} f^{(k^\gamma)}$	$\log f = \alpha + \beta q^\gamma$
$g = \exp((\log f)^{(k^b)})$	$f = \exp(a^{(q^b)})$
$g = \exp(\log^k f)$	$f = \exp(a^{bq})$
$g = \alpha \pm \beta d + \gamma d^2$, where	$f = aq^2 + bq + c$
$d = \sqrt{b^2 - 4a(c - f)}$,	
$\alpha = \dfrac{k^2 b^2 - 2b^2 k + 4ac + b^2 - 2b}{4a}$,	
$\beta = \dfrac{b(k - k^2)}{2a}$, and $\gamma = \dfrac{k^2}{4a}$	

$$g = \frac{-b \pm \sqrt{b^2 - 4a(c - kaf^2 + bf + c)}}{2a}$$

$$f = \frac{-b \pm \sqrt{b^2 - 4a(c - q)}}{2a}$$

$$g = \frac{2ac - b^2\sqrt{k} \pm bd\sqrt{k} + b^2k - 2ack + 2afk \mp bdk}{2a},$$

$$f = aq + b\sqrt{q} + c$$

$$d = \sqrt{b^2 - 4a(c - f)}$$

$$g = \frac{2}{\pi}\arctan\left(k\tan\left(\frac{\pi}{2}f\right)\right)$$

$$f = \frac{2}{\pi}\arctan(q)$$

$$g = \frac{1}{\pi}\arctan\left(b\pi\log k + \tan\left(\left(f - \frac{1}{2}\right)\pi\right)\right) + \frac{1}{2}$$

$$f = \begin{cases} \dfrac{1}{\pi}\arctan(b\pi\log q) + \dfrac{1}{2} & \forall q \neq 0 \\[2mm] 0 & \text{for } q = 0 \end{cases}$$

$$g = \left(\frac{\sqrt[c]{f}k^a}{\sqrt[c]{f}(k^a - 1) + 1}\right)^c$$

$$f = \left(\frac{e^b q^a}{e^b q^a + 1}\right)^c = \begin{cases} \left(\dfrac{1}{1 + e^{-(a\log q + b)}}\right)^c & \forall q \neq 0 \\[2mm] 0 & \text{for } q = 0 \end{cases}$$

$$g = \exp\left(\left(\frac{\sqrt[c]{\log f}\,k^a}{\sqrt[c]{\log f}(k^a - 1) + 1}\right)^c\right)$$

$$f = \exp\left(\left(\frac{e^b q^a}{e^b q^a + 1}\right)^c\right) = \begin{cases} \exp\left(\left(\dfrac{1}{1 + e^{-(a\log q + b)}}\right)^c\right) & \forall q \neq 0 \\[2mm] 0 & \text{for } q = 0 \end{cases}$$

Note: The third equation from the top and second from the bottom were found to describe a large variety of cameras and have been used in a wide variety of photoquantigraphic image-processing applications. The second equation from the bottom is the one that is most commonly used by the author. The bottom entry in the table is for use when camera output is logarithmic, that is, when scanning film in units of *density*.

4.3.12   Properties of Comparametric Equations

As stated previously, the comparametric equation only provides information about the actual photoquantity up to a single unknown scalar quantity. That is, if $f(q)$ is a solution of comparametric equation g, then so is $f(\beta q)$. We can think of this as a coordinate transformation from q to βq, in the domain of f. In general, the comparametric plot $(f(q), g(f(q)))$ has the same shape as the comparametric plot $(f(h(q)), g(f(h(q))))$ for all bijective h.

Thus, if we replace f with a function $h(f)$ and replace g with the same function $h(g)$ in a comparametric equation and in its solution, the transformed solution is a solution to the transformed comparametric equation. From this fact we can construct a property of comparametric equations.

Proposition 4.3.5 *A comparametric equation* $\breve{g}(f(q)) = g(f(h(q))) = g(\breve{f}(q))$ *has solution* $\breve{f}(q) = f(h(q))$ *for any bijective function h.*   □

Likewise, we can also consider coordinate transformations in the range of comparametric equations, and their effects on the solutions:

Proposition 4.3.6 *A comparametric equation* $g(f) = h(\breve{g})$, *has solution* $f = h(\breve{f})$, *where* $\breve{g}(q) = \breve{f}(kq)$ *is a comparametric equation with solution* $\breve{f}(q)$.   □

Properties of comparametric equations related to their coordinate transformations are presented in Table 4.5. Some simple examples of using coordinate transformation properties to solve comparametric equations are now provided:

Example 1 Let $\breve{g} = a\breve{f} + b$, which we know has the solution $\breve{f} = \alpha + \beta q^{\gamma}$, with $a = k^{\gamma}$ and $b = \alpha(1 - a)$. Let $h(\ ) = (\ ) + n_f$, where h is a transformation that consists of simply adding noise. Thus $g(f) = h(\breve{g}) = \breve{g} + n_f = a\breve{f} + b + n_f$, so that $g = a(f - n_f) + b + n_f$ has solution $f = h(\breve{f}) = \alpha + \beta q^{\gamma} + n_f$.

Example 2 From Table 4.2, observe that the comparametric equation $\breve{g} = a\breve{f} + b$ has the solution $\breve{f} = \alpha + \beta q^{\gamma}$. Let $h(\ ) = \exp(\ )$. We can thus solve $g(f) = h(\breve{g}) = \exp(a\breve{f} + b) = \exp(a\log(f) + b) = e^b f^a$ by noting that $f = h(\breve{f}) = \exp(\breve{f}) = \exp(\alpha + \beta q^{\gamma})$.

This solution also appears in Table 4.4. We may also use this solution to seed the solution of the comparametric equation second from the bottom of Table 4.4, by using $h(x) = x/(x + 1)$. The equation second from the bottom of Table 4.4 may then be further coordinate transformed into the equation at the bottom of Table 4.4 by using $h(x) = \exp(x)$. Thus properties of comparametric equations, such as those summarized in Table 4.5, can be used to help solve comparametric equations, such as those listed in Table 4.4.

Table 4.5 Properties of Comparametric Equations

Comparametric Equations $g(f(q)) = f(kq)$	Solutions (Camera Response Function) $f(q)$
$\breve{g}(f) = g(\breve{f})$, where $\breve{g}(f(q)) = g(f(h(q)))$	$\breve{f}(q) = f(h(q))$ $\forall$ bijective h
$g(f) = \breve{g}(f)$, where $\breve{g}(f(q)) = \breve{f}(\beta q)$	$f(q) = \breve{f}(\beta q)$
$g(f) = g(h(\breve{f})) = h(\breve{g})$, where $\breve{g}(q) = \breve{f}(kq)$	$f = h(\breve{f})$
$h^{-1}(g) = \breve{g}(\breve{f})$	$f = h(\breve{f})$

4.4 THE COMPARAGRAM: PRACTICAL IMPLEMENTATIONS OF COMPARANALYSIS

This section pertains to the practical implementation of the theory presented in previous sections.

4.4.1 Comparing Two Images That Differ Only in Exposure

Consider a plurality of pictures, $f_1 = f(q_1)$, $f_2 = f(q_2)$, $f_3 = f(q_3)$, and so on, where $q_1 = k_1 q$, $q_2 = k_2 q$, $q_3 = k_3 q$, etc., are the quantities of light in each of the exposures of identical subject matter, q is the true quantity of light in which exposure constants k_1, k_2, k_3, etc., are normalized out, and f is the unknown response function of the imaging system. Now, without loss of generality, consider any two such differently exposed pictures of the same subject matter, $f_1(\mathbf{x}) = f(k_1 q(\mathbf{x}))$ and $f_2(\mathbf{x}) = f(k_2 q(\mathbf{x}))$, and recognize that in the absence of noise, the relationship between the two images, f_1, and f_2, would be

$$\frac{1}{k_1} f^{-1}(f_1) = q = \frac{1}{k_2} f^{-1}(f_2) \tag{4.68}$$

so that

$$f_2 = f\left(\frac{k_2}{k_1} f^{-1}(f_1)\right) = f(k f^{-1}(f_1)) \tag{4.69}$$

where $k = k_2/k_1$.

Equation (4.69) provides a recipe for comparadjustment (tonally registering one image with respect to the other). The comparadjustment procedure comprises of three steps:

- Convert the first image f_1 into a quantity of light estimate $k_1 q$.
- Convert this quantity of light estimate $k_1 q$ into a scaled quantity of light estimate $(k_2/k_1)(k_1 q) = k_2 q$.
- Convert this quantity of light back to a picture by evaluating it with f to give $f_2 = f(k_2 q)$.

It is evident then that (4.69) is a comparametric equation.

The (4.69) process of "registering" the second image with the first differs from the image registration procedure commonly used in much of machine vision [81–84] and image resolution enhancement [72–73] because it operates on the *range* $f(q(\mathbf{x}))$ (tonal range) of the image $f_i(\mathbf{x})$ as opposed to its *domain* (spatial coordinates) $\mathbf{x} = (x, y)$.

4.4.2 The Comparagram

The comparagram between two images is a matrix of size M by N, where M is the number of gray levels in the first image and N is the number of gray levels in the second image [59,77]. The comparagram, which is assumed to be taken over differently exposed pictures of the same subject matter, is a generalization of the concept of a histogram to a joint histogram bin count of corresponding pixels in each of the two images. The convention is to have each pixel value from the first image plotted on the first (i.e., "x") axis, against the second corresponding pixel (e.g., at the same coordinates) of the second image being plotted on the second axis (i.e., the "y" axis). Since the number of gray levels in both images is usually the same (i.e., 256), the comparagram is usually a square matrix (i.e., of dimensions 256 by 256).

Comparagrams of Color Images
In the multichannel (color input images, complex-valued input images, etc.), the comparagram is an array of dimensions K by L by M by N, where K is the number of channels in the first image and L is the number of channels in the second image. Thus color RGB unsigned character images will have a comparagram that is 3 by 3 by 256 by 256. Usually this is displayed as a 768 by 768 block matrix:

```
RR[256,256]   RG[256,256]   RB[256,256]
GR[256,256]   GG[256,256]   GB[256,256]
BR[256,256]   BG[256,256]   BB[256,256]
```

Alternatively, since the diagonal blocks (the joint-comparagrams) are of greatest interest, the cross-comparagrams are often omitted so that the comparagram of a color image can be stored and displayed as a color image itself, where the red channel is the red–red comparagram RR[256,256], the green channel is the green–green comparagram GG[256,256], and the blue channel is the blue–blue comparagram BB[256,256]. These are often fitted into an unsigned character by clipping values beyond 255 to 255, or by displaying on a square root or thresholded logarithmic scale.

4.4.3 Understanding the Comparagram

To better understand the comparagram, let us consider the comparametric relationship between an image, and a modified version of that same image, where the modification may be done by the Modify Curves function of any of a variety of image manipulation programs such as the Gnu Image Manipulation Program, or John Bradley's XV, or another similar image-editing program, as shown in Figure 4.18. Here we can see that if we are given an original image and a modified image, we can recover the modification by computing the comparagram between the original and the modified image. In other words, the comparagram captures the essence of the relationship between the tone scale of the original image and the tone scale of the modified image.

4.4.4 Recovering the Response Function from the Comparagram

It can be seen from (4.69) that the general problem of solving (4.69) can be done directly on the comparagram instead of the original pair of images. The comparagram captures what we need to know about the tonal differences in the two images. In particular, in (4.69) we have known images f_1, f_2, etc., but the response function of the camera, f, and the exposure ratio, k, are the unknowns we wish to solve for. We could solve this by choosing $\hat{f}^{-1}$, the estimate of the inverse of the response function of the camera, so that the degree to which this equation (4.69) is untrue is minimized. In particular, we wish to minimize the quantity $f_2 - f(kf^{-1}(f_1))$ over all the observable data. That is, since the comparagram $J[m, n]$ provides high bin counts where the equation is obeyed to a greater degree, we wish to minimize

$$\varepsilon = \sum_{m=0}^{255} \sum_{n=0}^{255} \left(\frac{n}{255} - \hat{f}\left(k\hat{f}^{-1}\left(\frac{m}{255} \right) \right) \right)^2 J[m, n],\qquad (4.70)$$

This comparagram is a representation of $f_1 = x = m/255$ against $f_2 = y = n/255$. Equivalently, we simply choose $\hat{f}^{-1}$ that minimizes

$$\varepsilon = \sum_{m=0}^{255} \sum_{n=0}^{255} (\hat{f}^{-1}(y) - k\hat{f}^{-1}(x))^2 J[m, n]$$

$$= \sum_{m=0}^{255} \sum_{n=0}^{255} \left(\hat{f}^{-1}\left(\frac{n}{255} \right) - k\hat{f}^{-1}\left(\frac{m}{255} \right) \right)^2 J[m, n],\qquad (4.71)$$

or equivalently, that minimizes the logarithm of the degree to which this equation (4.69) is untrue. This is obtained by minimizing

$$\varepsilon = \sum_{m=0}^{255} \sum_{n=0}^{255} \left(\hat{F}^{-1}\left(\frac{n}{255} \right) - \hat{F}^{-1}\left(\frac{m}{255} - K \right) \right)^2 J[m, n],\qquad (4.72)$$

which may be further simplified by using a base k logarithm so that $K = 1$. This summation may be taken over any number of pairwise comparagrammed images by further summing over $L - 1$ such comparagrams arising from a sequence of L images. The result is a better estimate of F^{-1}, which is simply a LookUp

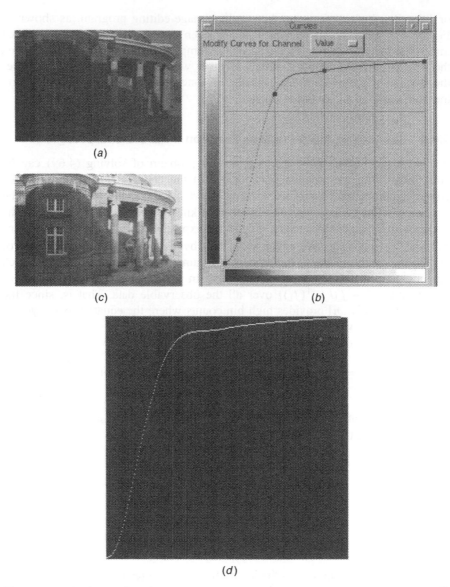

(a)

(c)   *(b)*

(d)

Figure 4.18 Understanding the comparagram by using it to recover the curve in Modify Curves (*a*) Original image. (*b*) The Modify Curves function of GIMP menu item Curves is applied to the original image. (*c*) Modified image resulting from this Modify Curves operation being applied to the original image. (*d*) The comparagram of the original image and the modified image. Notice how the modification is recovered. The comparagram allows us to recover, from just the two images (original and modified), the curve that was applied by the Modify Curves function. Completely black areas of the comparagram indicate bin counts of zero, whereas lighter areas indicate high bin counts. From here on, however, comparagrams will be shown in a reversed tone scale to conserve ink or toner.

Table (LUT) for converting from an image such as a Portable PixMap (PPM) format to a Portable LightspaceMap (PLM), as is implemented by the pnm2plm program.

Additionally the estimate $\hat{f}^{-1}$ (or equivalently, F^{-1}) is generally constrained to be semimonotonic (and preferably smooth as well). Semimonotonicity is forced by preventing its derivative from going negative, and this is usually done using a quadratic programming system such as "qp.m," An example of such programs is Octave or Matlab, which follows:

```
%  Solves for Finv, given that matrix is in J
%  assumes comparagram is in matrix J
%  Use: J = comparagram(v0,v1)
%       testqp
%       plot(Finv)
%
%  matlab help syntax is x=qp(H,f,A,b)
%                        F=qp(A,Kvector,-D,zero);
%                        F=qp(A,y,C,zero); % C also includes
%                           F(0)>=0

[A,y]=comparunroll(J);  % unrolls comparagram; can also apply
       robust statistics

% diff(F) given by D*F
D=[-eye(255) zeros(255,1)]  +  [zeros(255,1) eye(255)];

% constraint matrix is for C*F negative, e.g. <=zeros, ...
                                             C=-D;
% add in F(0)>0:
C=[[-1  zeros(1,255)]; -D];

zero=zeros(256,1); % 255 zeros for diff; 1 zero for F(0)>=0

H=A.'*A;
b=A.'*y;

% determine range of light given domain of image
F0=(4/128)*cumsum(hanning(256)); % assuming 0..4 stops range
   of light
F=qp(H,b,C,zero,zeros(256,1),10*ones(256,1),F0); % limit to
   max 10 stop range
```

We now see how well this method works on a typical dataset comprised of pictures differing only in exposure. The sequence of pictures is from a dark interior looking out into bright sunlight, with bright sky in the background. The dynamic range of the original subject matter is far in excess of what can be captured in any one of the constituent pictures. Such an image sequence is shown in Figure 4.19. From the comparagrams, the response function is determined

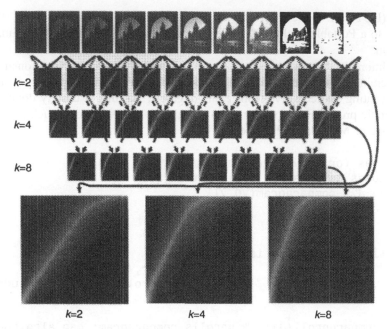

Figure 4.19 A sequence of differently exposed pictures of the same subject matter. Such variable gain sequences give rise to a family of comparagrams. In this sequence the gain happens to have increased from left to right. The square matrix J (called a comparagram) is shown for each pair of images under the image pairs themselves, for $k = 2^1 = 2$. The next row shows pairwise comparagrams for skip $= 2$ (e.g., $k = 2^2 = 4$), and then for skip $= 3$ (e.g., $k = 2^3 = 8$). Various skip values give rise to families of comparagrams that capture all the necessary exposure difference information. Each skip value provides a family of comparagrams. Comparagrams of the same skip value are added together and displayed at the bottom, for $k = 2$, $k = 4$, and $k = 8$.

using the least squares method, with monotonicity and smoothness constraints, to obtain the recovered response function shown in Figure 4.20a.

Although it is constrained by smoothness and monotonicity, the model as fitted in Figure 4.20a has 256 degrees of freedom. In fact there are simpler models that have fewer degrees of freedom (and therefore better noise immunity). So, rather than trying to estimate the 256 sample values of the LUT directly from the comparagrams, we can use any of the various models previously presented, in order to break the problem down into two separate simpler (and better constrained) steps:

1. *Comparametric regression:*   Finding a smooth semimonotonic function g that passes through most of the highest bins in the comparagram.
2. *Solving the comparametric equation:*   Unrolling this function, $g(f(q)) = f(kq)$, into $f(q/q_0)$ by regarding it an *iterative map* onto itself (see Figure 4.21). The iterative map (*logistic map*) is familiar in chaos theory [85,86], but here the result is a deterministic function since the map

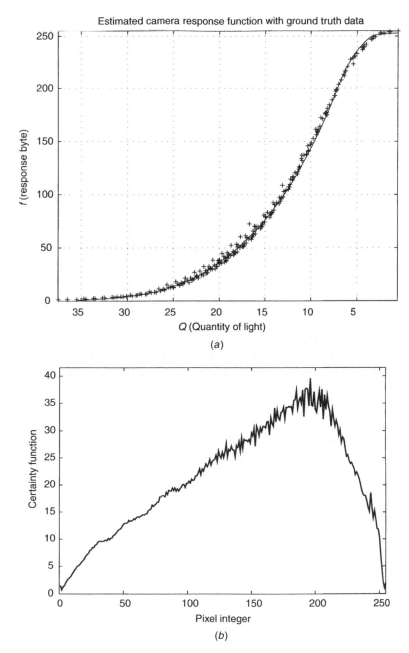

Figure 4.20 (*a*) A least squares solution to the data shown in Figure 4.19, using a novel multiscale smoothing algorithm, is shown as a solid line. The plus signs denote known ground truth data measured from the camera using the test chart. We can see that the least squares solution recovered from the data in Figure 4.19 is in close agreement with the data recovered from the test chart. (*b*) The derivative of the computed response function is the certainty function. Note that despite the excellent fit to the known data, the certainty function allows us to see slight roughness in the curve which is accentuated by the process of taking the derivative.

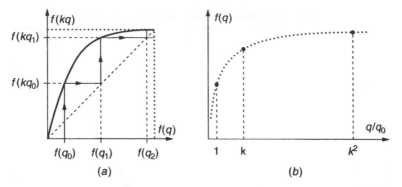

Figure 4.21 Log unrolling. Logarithmic logistic unrolling procedure for finding the pointwise nonlinearity of an image sensor from the comparametric equation that describes the relationship between two pictures differing only in their exposures. (a) Comparametric plot: Plot of pixel values in one image against corresponding pixel values in the other. (b) Response curve: Points on the response curve, found from only the two pictures, without any knowledge about the characteristics of the image sensor. These discrete points are only for illustrative purposes. If a logarithmic exposure scale is used (which is what most photographers use), then the points fall uniformly on the $Q = \log(q/q_0)$ axis.

is monotonic. The unrolling process of is a robust way of processing the entire aggregate information from a large dataset. It produces a similar result to the logistic curve unrolling (photocell experiment) described earlier, but without the obvious problem of only considering one element of the sensor array.

Separating the estimation process into two stages allows us a more direct route to "registering" the image domains if, for example, we do not need to know f but only require g, which is the recipe for expressing the range of $f(kq)$ in the units of $f(q)$. In particular, we can lighten or darken images to match one another without ever having to solve for q. The comparadjustment process of tonally adjusting (i.e., registering) images using comparagraphic information and the corresponding program function name appear on the WWW site that accompanies this text as "comparadj()."

The first part of this two-step process allows us to determine the relationship between two pictures that differ only in exposure. So we can directly perform operations like image exposure interpolation and extrapolation as in Figure 4.5 and skip the intermediate step of computing q. Not all image processing applications require determining q, so there is great value in understanding the simple relationship between differently exposed pictures of the same subject matter.

At the very least, even when we do not need to find $f(q)$, we may wish to find $g(f)$. One simple algorithm for estimating the comparametric equation $g(f)$ from actual comparagrams is to find the peaks (indexes of the highest bin count) along each row of the comparagram, or along each column. This way lookup tables may be used to convert an image from the tone scale of the first image from which the comparagram was computed, to the second image from which the comparagram was computed, and vice versa (depending on whether one is computing along rows or along columns of the comparagram). However, this simplistic approach is undesirable for various reasons. Obviously only integer values will result, so converting one image to the tone scale of the another image will result in loss of precision (i.e, likely differing pixel values will end up being converted to identical pixel values). If we regard the comparagram as a joint probability distribution (i.e., joint histogram), the interpretation of selecting highest bin counts corresponds to a maximum likelihood estimate (MLE).

We may regard the process of selecting the maximum bin count across each row or column as just one example of a moment calculation, and then consider other moments. The first moment (center of gravity along each row or down each column) typically gives us a noninteger value for each entry of this lookup table. If the comparagram were regarded as a joint probability distribution function (i.e., cross-histogram), this method of selecting first moments across rows or down columns would amount to a Bayes least error (BLE) least squares formulation (Bayes least squares).

Calculating moments across rows or down columns is somewhat successful in "slenderizing" the comparagram into a comparametric plot. However, it still does not enforce monotonicity or smoothness. Although smoothness is an arbitrary imposition, we do know for certain that the phenomenon should be monotonic. Therefore, even if not imposing smoothness (i.e., making no assumptions about the data), we should at least impose monotonicity.

To impose the monotonicity constraint, we proceed as follows:

1. Establish an upper bounding curve, g_u, using a "ratchet effect" of four steps:
   a. Define $g_u(0) = 0$.
   b. Compute moments along each row or column (depending on whether the mapping is from range $f(q)$ to range $f(kq)$, and vice versa). Without loss of generality, the algorithm is described for columns (i.e., to determine g that takes us from $f(q)$ to $f(kq)$ as opposed to g^{-1} that takes us the other way). Call the moment of the nth column m_n.
   c. Set $g_u(1) = \max(g_u(0), m_1)$.
   d. Proceed recursively, setting $g_u(n) = \max(g_u(n-1), m_n)$ as n is increased, then going left to right across columns of the joint-histogram until the maximum value of n is reached.
2. Establish a lower bounding curve, g_l, using a similar "ratchet effect," but starting at N, the maximum value of n, and initializing $g_l(N) = M$, where M is the maximum possible pixel value (typically 255). This is done by decreasing n, moving us from right to left on the cross-histogram, and it is done by selecting $\min(g_l(n), m_{n-1})$.
3. The final result, $g(f(q))$, is computed from the average: $g = (g_u + g_l)/2$.

A simple practical test case is now presented. The object is to find comparametric plots of the sensor array inside one of the personal imaging rigs designed and built (as described in Chapters 1 and 2) by the author. To generate the comparagrams, the author captured images differing only in exposure, the exposure being changed by adjusting the integration time ("shutter" speed) of the sensor array. Rather than just using two differently exposed images, the author used a total of five differently exposed images[4] (see Fig. 4.22).

The duration of the exposures was known (1/4000, 1/2000, 1/1000, 1/500, and 1/250 of a second), and comparagrams were generated for each possible combination of these image pairs. Knowing that some curves were redundant (e.g., there were four curves for $k = 2$, three for $k = 4$, two for $k = 8$, but only one for $k = 16$), we could average together the comparagrams in cases where there are more than one. The averaged comparagram was then slenderized, using the proposed algorithm presented in the previous subsection. The slenderized comparagrams (i.e., the comparametric plots) are shown as a family of curves in Figure 4.23a. From the five images, four curves were generated above the diagonal, and four more below the diagonal, the latter being generated by reversing the order of the image sequence. The diagonal, which represents any image compared against itself, is known to be the identity function $g(f) = f$. Thus there are nine curves in Figure 4.23a. Through the process of interpolating (and extrapolating) between (and beyond) these curves, a function $g(f(q)) = f(kq)$ may be returned for any desired value of k. Thus we now have a complete nonparametric recipe for comparadjusting (tonally adjusting an image to be lighter or darker as if a greater or lesser exposure had been provided). This recipe characterizes the response function of the particular sensor array and digitization hardware. In this sense we say that the camera system is *calibrated*.

Some alternatives to direct estimation of g from the comparagrams involve fitting to some parametric curve, such as a spline. In the next subsection, examples of such parametric choice for g are described.

4.4.5 Comparametric Regression and the Comparagram

In situations where the image data are extremely noisy, and/or where a closed-form solution for $f(q)$ is desired, a parameterized form of the comparametric function is used, in which a function $g(f)$ corresponding to a suitably parameterized response function $f(q)$ is selected. The method amounts to a *curve-fitting* problem in which the parameters of g are selected so that g best fits

---

[4] Each of these images was gathered by signal averaging (capturing 16 times, and then averaging the images together) to reduce noise. This step is probably not necessary with most full-sized cameras, but noise from the EyeTap sensor array was very high because a very small sensor array was used and built into an ordinary pair of sunglasses, in such a way that the opening through which light entered was very small. Primarily because the device needed to be covert, the image quality was very poor. However, as we will see in subsequent chapters, this poor image quality can be mitigated by various new image-processing techniques.

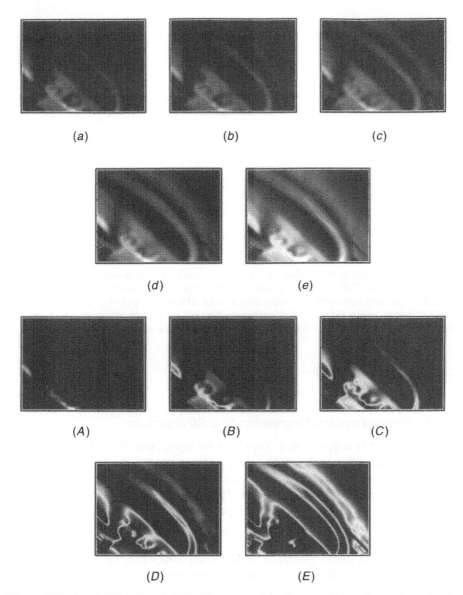

Figure 4.22 (*a–e*) Collection of differently exposed images used to calibrate the author's eyeglass-based personal imaging system. These images differ only in exposure. (*A–E*) Certainty images corresponding to each image. The certainty images, $c(f(x, y))$, are calculated by evaluating f with the derivative of the estimated response function. Areas of higher certainty are white and correspond to the midtones, while areas of low certainty are black and correspond to highlights and shadows, which are clipped or saturated at the extrema (toe or shoulder of the response curve) of possible exposures. Another interpretation of the proposed method of combining multiple images of different exposure is to think of the result as a weighted sum of exposure adjusted images (adjusted to the same range), where the weights are the certainty images.

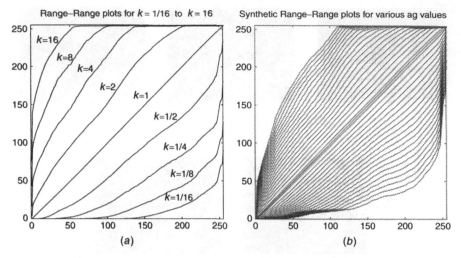

Figure 4.23 Comparametric plots, $g(f(q(x, y))) = f(kq(x, y))$, characterizing the specific eyeglass-mounted CCD sensor array and wearable digitizer combination designed and built by author. (a) Plots estimated from comparagrams of differently exposed pictures of the same subject matter, using the proposed nonparametric self-calibration algorithm. (b) Family of curves generated for various values of k, by interpolating between the nine curves in (a).

one or more comparagrams constructed from two or more differently exposed images under analysis.

4.4.6 Comparametric Regression to a Straight Line

The result (4.53) suggests that $f(q)$ can be determined from two differently exposed images by applying linear regression to the comparagram jointly expressed of at least two images J, treating each entry as a data point and weighting by the number of bin counts $J(m, n)$ at each point. Often this is done by weighting with $(J(m, n))^\lambda$. For example, $\lambda = 0$ (assuming that empty bins are not counted) provides the classic linear regression problem in which all nonempty bins are weighted equally and the slope and intercept of the best-fit line through nonempty bins is found. Generally, λ is chosen somewhere between $\frac{1}{4}$ and 2.

A simple example is presented, that of reverse-engineering the standard Kodak PhotoCD scanner issued to most major photographic processing and scanning houses. In most situations a human operator runs the machine and decides, by visual inspection, what "brightness" level to scan the image at (there is also an automatic exposure feature that allows the operator to preview the scanned image and decide whether or not the chosen "brightness" level needs to be overridden). By scanning the same image at different "brightness" settings, a Wyckoff set results. This allows the scanner to capture nearly the entire dynamic range of the film, which is of great utility since typical photographic negative film captures far greater dynamic range than possible with the scanner as it is ordinarily used. A photographic negative taken from a scene of extremely high contrast (a sculpture on exhibit at the List Visual Arts Center, MIT, in a completely darkened room, illuminated with a bare flash lamp from one side only) was selected because of its great dynamic range that could not be captured in any single scan. A Wyckoff set was constructed by scanning the same negative at five different "brightness" settings (Fig. 4.24). The settings were controlled by a slider that was calibrated in arbitrary units from -99 to $+99$, while running Kodak's proprietary scanning software. Kodak provides no information about what these units mean. Accordingly the goal of the experiment was to find a closed-form mathematical equation describing the effects of the "brightness" slider on the scans, and to recover the unknown nonlinearity of the scanner. In order to make the problem a little more challenging and, more important, to better illustrate the principles of comparametric image processing, the d_{min} procedure of scanning a blank film at the beginning of the roll was overridden.

Jointly (pairwise) comparagrams J_{01}, J_{12}, J_{23}, and J_{34} were computed from the five images (v_0 through v_4) of Figure 4.24. They are displayed as density plots (i.e., treated as images of dimension 256 by 256 pixels, where the darkness of the image is proportional to the number of counts—darkness rather than

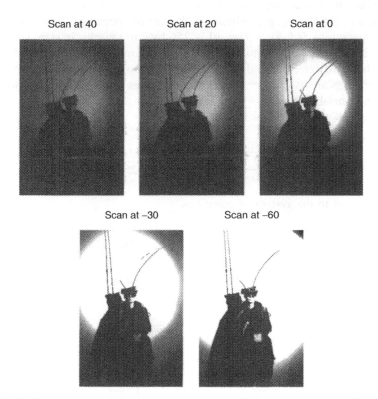

Figure 4.24 These scans from a photographic negative differ only in the choice of "brightness" setting selected using the slider provided on the X-windows screen by the proprietary Kodak PhotoCD scanning software. The slider is calibrated in arbitrary units from -99 to $+99$. Five scans were done and the setting of the slider is noted above each scan.

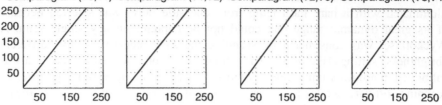

Figure 4.25 Pairwise comparagrams of the images in Figure 4.25. It is evident that the data are well fitted by a straight line, which suggests that Kodak must have used the standard nonlinear response function $f(q) = \alpha + \beta q^\gamma$ in the design of their PhotoCD scanner.

lightness to make it easier to see the pattern) in Figure 4.25. Affine regression (often incorrectly referred to as "linear regression") was applied to the data, and the best-fit straight line is shown passing through the data points. The best-fit straight line

$$g = af + b \qquad (4.73)$$

is computed by minimizing the sum of squares of the error $e = (af_k + b - g_k)$ over the data points (f_k, g_k), which are the sample points of the comparagram. The comparagram $J(f, g) = J[m, n]$ is 256 by 256 samples in size, so we have $f = m/255$ and $g = n/255$ to set the comparagram $J( )$ on the closed interval from 0 to 1, where $J[\ ]$ is defined on the interval from 0 to 255. (Note that square brackets are used to denote discrete variables and round brackets to denote continuous variables.)

The sum of squared errors is denoted

$$\varepsilon = \sum\sum(e^2) = \sum_{m=0}^{255}\sum_{n=0}^{255}\left(a\frac{m}{255} + b - \frac{n}{255}\right)^2 J[m, n]. \qquad (4.74)$$

This gives rise to the system of equations

$$\frac{d\varepsilon}{da} = 2\sum(af + b - g)\, fJ(f, g), \qquad (4.75)$$

$$\frac{d\varepsilon}{db} = 2\sum(af + b - g)\, J(f, g), \qquad (4.76)$$

with the solution

$$\begin{bmatrix} \sum\limits_{m,n} f^2 J[m, n] & \sum\limits_{m,n} fJ[m, n] \\ \sum\limits_{m,n} fJ[m, n] & \sum\limits_{m,n} J[m, n] \end{bmatrix} \begin{bmatrix} a \\ b \end{bmatrix} = \begin{bmatrix} \sum\limits_{m,n} gJ[m, n] \\ \sum\limits_{m,n} J[m, n] \end{bmatrix}. \qquad (4.77)$$

Because the $d_{\min}$ procedure was overridden, notice that the plots do not pass through the origin. The two leftmost plots had nearly identical slopes and intercepts, and likewise for the two rightmost, which indicates that the arbitrary Kodak units of "brightness" are self-consistent (i.e., J_{01}, which describes the relationship between a scan at a "brightness" of 40 units and one of 20 units as essentially the same as J_{12}, which describes the relationship between a scan at a "brightness" of 20 units and one of 0 units). Since there are three parameters in (4.51), k, α, and γ, which describe only two degrees of freedom (slope and intercept), γ may be chosen so that $k = \sqrt[\gamma]{a}$ works out to be linearly proportional to arbitrary Kodak units. Thus setting $(\sqrt[\gamma]{a_{\text{left}}})/(\sqrt[\gamma]{a_{\text{right}}}) = 20/30$ (where a_{left} is the average slope of the two leftmost plots and a_{right} the average slope of the two rightmost plots) results in the value $\gamma = 0.2254$ From this we obtain $\alpha = b/(1 - a) = 23.88$. Thus we have that

$$f(k_i q) = 23.88 + (kq)^{0.2254}, \tag{4.78}$$

where k_i is in arbitrary Kodak units ($k_0 = 40$ for the leftmost image, $k_1 = 20$ for the next image, $k_2 = 0$ for the middle image, $k_3 = -30$, and $k_4 = -60$). Thus (4.78) gives us a closed–form solution that describes the response curve associated with each of the five exposures $f(k_i q)$, $i \in \mathbb{Z}$, $0 \le i \le 4$. The curves $f(k_i q)$ may be differentiated, and if these derivatives are evaluated at

$$q_i = \frac{1}{k_i} \sqrt[\alpha]{f_i(x, y) - \alpha},$$

the so-called certainty images, shown in Figure 4.26 are obtained.

In the next section an example of the use of the certainty functions to construct an optimal estimate $\hat{q}(x, y)$ will be demonstrated.

4.4.7 Comparametric Regression to the *Exponent over Inverse Exponent of Exponent Plus Constant* Model

For the second example, the comparametric model proposed in (4.58) will be used.

In many practical situations, real-world images are very noisy. Accordingly, an example of noisy images that comprise a Wyckoff set (Fig. 4.27), in which an extremely poor scan was deliberately used to scan images from a publication [59], is now considered.

Clearly, the images in Figure 4.27 are of very poor quality. This is confirmed by their joint-comparagram (Fig. 4.28a). Using the regression of (4.58) to the comparagram combined with the knowledge (from the publication from which the images were obtained [59]) that $K = 2$, we find that $a = 0.0017$ and $c = -3.01$. These data provide a closed-form solution for the response function. The two effective response functions, which are shifted versions of this one response function, where the relative shift is K, are plotted in Figure 4.29, together with their derivatives. (Recall that the derivatives of the response functions are the certainty functions.) Since a closed-form solution has been obtained, it may be easily

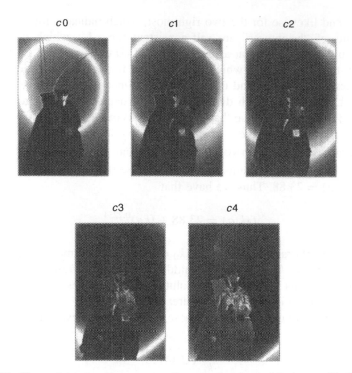

Figure 4.26   The *certainty functions* express the rate of change of $f(q(x, y))$ with $Q(x, y)$. The certainty functions may be used to compute the *certainty images*, $f(c_i)$. White areas in one of the certainty images indicate that pixel values $f(q)$ change fastest with a corresponding change in the photoquantity, Q. When using the camera as a lightmeter (a photoquantigraphic instrument to estimate q), it will be most sensitive where the certainty images are white. White areas of these certainty images correspond to midgray values (*midtones*) of the corresponding original images in Figure 4.24, while dark areas correspond to extreme pixel values (either highlights or shadows) of the original images in Figure 4.24. Black areas of the *certainty image* indicate that Q changes drastically with small changes in pixel value, and thus an estimate of Q in these areas will be overcome by image noise n_{f_i}.

differentiated without the further increase in the noise that usually accompanies differentiation. Otherwise, when determining the certainty functions from poor estimates of f, the certainty functions would be even more noisy than the poor estimate of f itself. The resulting certainty images, denoted by $c(f_i)$, are shown in Figure 4.30. Each of the images, $f_i(x, y)$, gives rise to an actual estimate of the quantity of light arriving at the image sensor (4.9). These estimates were combined by way of (4.10), resulting in the composite image appears shown in Figure 4.31. Note that the resulting image $\hat{I}_1$ looks very similar to f_1, except that it is a floating point image array of much greater tonal range and image quality.

Furthermore, given a Wyckoff set, a composite image may be rendered at any in-between exposure from the set (exposure interpolation), as well as somewhat beyond the exposures given (exposure extrapolation). This result suggests the "VirtualCamera" [64], which allows images to be rendered at any desired exposure once q is computed.

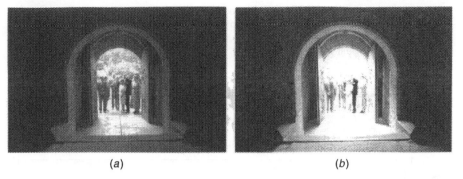

(*a*)   (*b*)

Figure 4.27 Noisy images badly scanned from a publication. These images are identical except for exposure and a good deal of quantization noise, additive noise, scanning noise, and the like. (*a*) Darker image shows clearly the eight people standing outside the doorway but shows little of the architectural details of the dimly lit interior. (*b*) Lighter image shows the architecture of the interior, but it is not possible to determine how many people are standing outside, let alone recognize any of them.

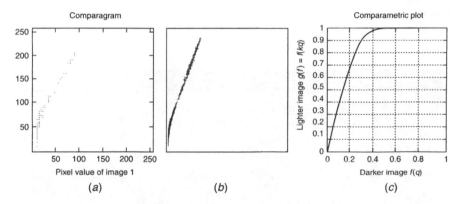

(*a*)   (*b*)   (*c*)

Figure 4.28 Comparametric regression. (*a*) Joint comparagram. Note that because the images were extremely noisy, the comparagram is spread out over a fat ridge. Gaps appear in the comparagram owing to the poor quality of the scanning process. (*b*) Even the comparagram of the images prior to the deliberately poor scan of them is spread out, indicating that the images were quite noisy to begin with. (*c*) Comparametric regression is used to solve for the parameters of the comparametric function. The resulting comparametric plot is a noise-removed version of the joint-comparagram; it provides a smoothly constrained comparametric relationship between the two differently exposed images.

This capability is somewhat similar to QuickTime VR and other image-based rendering systems, except that it operates in the range of the images $\hat{f}_i$ rather than their domain.

Another example, running a simple nonlinear optimization package[1] on the wearable computer system to fit the three comparagrams in Figure 4.19, gave

---

[1] A variant similar to BFGS, written by M. Adnan Ali, Corey Manders, and Steve Mann.

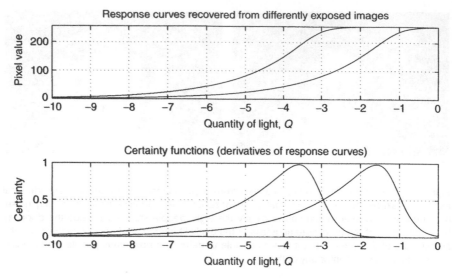

Figure 4.29   Relative response functions $F(Q + K_i)$ recovered from the images in Figure 4.27, plotted with their derivatives. The derivatives of these response functions suggests a degree of confidence in the estimate $\hat{Q}_i = F^{-1}(f_i) - K_i$ derived from each input image.

(a)   (b)

Figure 4.30   Certainty images that are used as weights when the weighted sum of estimates of the actual quantity of light is computed. Bright areas correspond to large degrees of certainty.

the values $a = 4.0462$ and $c = 0.1448$. The response curve for these values is shown in Figure 4.32, together with known ground-truth data. Since a closed-form solution has been obtained, it may be easily differentiated without the further increase in noise that usually accompanies differentiation. (Compare to Figure 4.20b.)

Once the response function is found a modified version shifted over slightly for each possible exposure value can be formulated (see Fig. 4.33a). Each of these will have a corresponding certainty function (Fig. 4.33b). Together, the certainty functions form a bank of amplitude domain filters decomposing the image into various tonal bands. Thus, the quantity of light for each frame of

Figure 4.31 Composite image made by simultaneously estimating the unknown nonlinearity of the camera as well as the true quantity of light incident on the camera's sensor array, given two input images from Figure 4.27. The combined optimal estimate of $\hat{q}$ is expressed here in the coordinates of the lighter (rightmost) image. Nothing was done to appreciably enhance this image (i.e., the procedure of estimating q and then just converting it back into a picture again may seem pointless). Still we can note that while the image appears much like the rightmost input image, the clipping of the highlight details has been softened somewhat. Later we will see methods of actual image enhancement done by processing $\hat{q}$ prior to converting it back to an image again. © Steve Mann, 1993.

the sequence can optimally contribute to the output rendition of the wearable imaging system, so that, the quantity of light sent into the eye of the wearer is appropriately optimal and free of noise. Such a system actually allows the wearer to see more than could be ordinarily seen (e.g., to see into deep dark shadows while simultaneously looking straight into the bright sun or the flame of an arc welder's rig without eye damage). The apparatus also allows the wearer to see in nearly total darkness.

4.5   SPATIOTONAL PHOTOQUANTIGRAPHIC FILTERS

Most print and display media have limited dynamic range. Thus one might be tempted to argue against the utility of the Wyckoff principle based on this fact. One could ask, for example, why bother building a Wyckoff camera that can capture such dynamic ranges if televisions and print media cannot display more than a very limited dynamic range? Why bother capturing the photoquantity q with more accuracy than is needed for display?

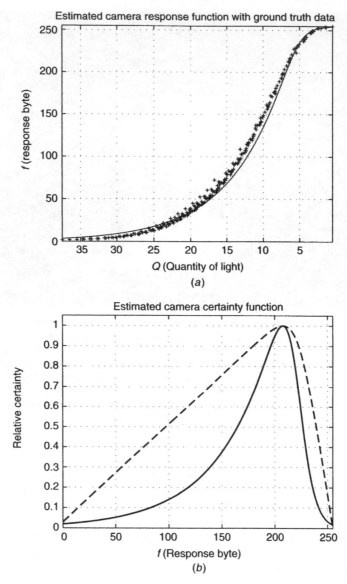

Figure 4.32 The author's simple two parameter model fits the response curve almost as well as the much more complicated 256 parameter model (e.g., the lookup table) of Figure 4.20a, and in some areas (e.g., near the top of the response curve) the fit is actually better. This method of using comparametric equations is far more efficient than the least squares method that produced the data in Figure 4.20a. Moreover, the result provides a closed-form solution rather than merely a lookup table. (b) This method also results in a very smooth response function, as we can see by taking its derivative to obtain the certainty function. Here the relative certainty function is shown on both a linear scale (solid line) and log scale (dashed line). Compare this certainty function to that of Figure 4.20b to note the improved smoothing effect of the simple two parameter model.

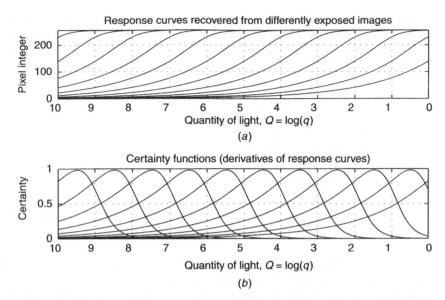

Figure 4.33 Response curves and their certainty functions: (a) Response functions shifted for each possible K (e.g., each exposure that the imaging apparatus is capable of making). (b) Amplitude domain filterbanks arise from the overlapping shifted certainty functions.

Some possible answers to this question are:

1. Estimates of q are still useful for machine vision and other applications that do not involve direct viewing of a final picture. An example is the wearable face recognizer [14] that determines the identity of an individual from a plurality of differently exposed pictures of that person, and then presents the identity in the form of a text label (virtual name tag) on the retina of an eye of the wearer of the eyeglass–based apparatus. Since $\hat{q}$ need not be displayed, the problem of output dynamic range, and the like, of the display (i.e., number of distinct intensity levels of the laser beam shining into a lens of the eye of the wearer) is of no consequence.

2. Although the ordinary dynamic range and the range resolution (typically 8 bits) is sufficient for print media (given the deliberately introduced nonlinearities that best use the limited range resolution), when performing operations such as deblurring, noise artifacts become more evident. In general, sharpening involves high-pass filtering, and thus sharpening will often tend to uncover noise artifacts that would normally exist below the perceptual threshold when viewed through ordinary display media. In particular, sharpening often uncovers noise in the shadow areas, making

dark areas of the image appear noisy in the final print or display. Thus in addition to the benefits of performing sharpening photoquantigraphically by applying an antihomomorphic filter as in Figure 4.3 to undo the blur of (4.5), there is also further benefit from doing the generalized antihomomorphic filtering operation at the point $\hat{q}$ in Figure 4.4, rather than just that depicted in Figure 4.3.

3. A third benefit from capturing a true and accurate measurement of the photoquantity, even if all that is desired is a nice picture (i.e., even if what is desired is not necessarily a true or accurate depiction of reality), is that additional processing may be done to produce a picture in which the limited dynamic range of the display or print medium shows a much greater dynamic range of input signal, through the use of further image processing on the photoquantity prior to display or printing.

It is this third benefit that will be further described, as well as illustrated through a very compelling example, in this section.

Ordinarily humans cannot directly perceive the "signal" we process numerically but rather we perceive the effects of the "signal" on perceptible media such as television screens. In particular, in order to display $\hat{q}(x, y)$, it is typically converted into an image $f(\hat{q}(x, y))$ and displayed, for example, on a television screen.

Figure 4.31 is an attempt to display, on the printed page, a signal that contains much greater dynamic range than can be directly represented in print. To obtain this display, the estimate $\hat{q}$ was converted into an image by evaluating $\hat{f}(\hat{k}_2 \hat{q})$. Even though we see some slight benefit, over f_2 (one of the input images) the benefit has not been made fully visible in this print.

4.5.1   Spatiotonal Processing of Photoquantities

To fully appreciate the benefits of photoquantigraphic image processing, in Chapter 6 we will consider seemingly impossible scenes to photograph reasonably (in a natural way without bringing in lighting equipment of any kind). There it will be shown how a strong high-pass (sharpening) filter can be applied to $\hat{q}$ and sharpen the photoquantity $\hat{q}$ as well as provide lateral inhibition similar to the way in which the human eye functions.

Because of this filtering operation we will see that there no longer needs to be a monotonic relationship between input photoquantity q and output level on the printed page. The dynamic range of the image will be reduced to that of printed media, while still revealing details over an extreme range of light quantities in the scene. This will answer the question, "Why capture more dynamic range than you can display?"

4.6 GLOSSARY OF FUNCTIONS

comparagram( )

> Takes two grayscale pictures and returns an M by N array, where M is the number of gray values in the first picture and N is the number of grayvalues in the second picture. If the pictures are multichannel, a hypermatrix of dimensions K by L by M by N is returned, where K is the number of channels in the first image and L is the number of channels in the second image and block (k, l) is the comparagram between channel k of the first image and channel l of the second image.

comparagramrgb( )

> Returns the diagonal blocks of the above function, but arranged as layers of a red–green–blue (RGB) image. Thus the red channel of the returned comparagram will be the comparagram (often denoted comparagramrr) of the red channels of the two input images, while the green channel of the returned comparagram (comparagramgg) will be the comparagram of the green channels of the two images, and the blue channel (comparagrambb) will be the comparagram of the blue channels of the input image.

comparadj( )

> Adjusts (tonally registers) an image based on a supplied comparagram.

comparafit( )

> Fits a specified closed form function to a comparagram.

comparalut( )

> Slenderizes a comparagram using Bayes least error (BLE) formulation to provide a nonparametric reciple (lookup table) from a comparagram.

comparasum( )

> Takes a sequence of images and computes the pairwise comparagrams, and then sums the results to provide an aggregate comparagram for the whole set. This function is intended for use when the sequence of images is a Wyckoff set of logarithmically spaced exposure intervals.

logunroll( )

> Unrolls the inherent response function, as if a *log*istic curve, into a response function sampled on *log*arithmically spaced exposure intervals.

comparunroll( )

> Unrolls a comparagram to obtain the underlying response function evaluated on a logarithmically spaced set of points.

comparasolve( )

> Provides a closed form solution for the response function, given a comparagram as input.

certaint( )   *Taints* images with un*certainty* by adding a certainty channel to the image. If the certainted image is to be saved, the output image file format is png, since this format will support certainty channels. Often a single certainty channel is used for all input channels; for example, a color image goes from RGB to RGBC, where C is certainty

cement( )   Computer-enhanced multiple exposure numerical technique combines multiple images by various means, the default (if no other law of composition is specified) being to certaint( ) them, convert them to lightspace, weight them by the relative exposures (if known, or determined from the pairwise comparagrams), and then compute a weighted sum where the weights are the blurred certainty layers of the respective input images. Output is a PLM (portable lightspace map).

4.7 EXERCISES, PROBLEM SETS, AND HOMEWORK

4.7.1 Parametric Plots

Construct the parametric plot of $(\cos t, \sin t)$ for 100 points of the parameter t ranging from 0 to 6. This can be done, using the Octave program, as follows:

```
octave:5> t=linspace(0,6);
octave:6> plot(cos(t),sin(t))
```

What do you observe about the shape of the plot? Is the shape complete? If not, what must be done to make the shape complete?

Now construct the same parametric plot for 100 points of the parameter t ranging from 0 to 6000. This can be done using the Octave commands:

```
octave:7> t=linspace(0,6000);
octave:8> plot(cos(t),sin(t))
```

What do you observe? Why is the shape not that of a smooth relation?

4.7.2 Comparaplots and Processing "Virtual Light"

The reality mediator (WearCam) absorbs and quantifies light, processes these numerical quantities, and then re-synthesizes the result.

Recall from Chapter 3 that this process is as follows:

1. Light enters the apparatus and is converted into numbers.
2. The numbers pass through the computer.
3. The numbers are turned back into light that enters the eye.

This might seem like a rather expensive and complicated "window," and one might ask, Why go to such trouble just to make a transparent viewing window? The reason is that this creates a visual "reality stream" that allows one to modify, or to allow others to modify, one's visual perception of reality. To do this, step 2 above is changed from just passing through to modifying light, while it is in numerical form.

In this chapter we saw that these numbers are referred to as "photoquanta." It is desired that the "photoquanta" be calculated from ordinary digitized pictures. To understand photoquanta, consider two images that differ only in exposure. These two images may be matched to a so-called comparaplot (comparametric plot).

Recall the following definition: The *comparametric plot* of a function $f(q)$ is defined as the parametric plot of $f(q)$ versus $f(kq)$, where k is a scalar constant and q is the real-valued *comparameter*.

Proposition 4.7.1 *When a function $f(q)$ is monotonic, the comparametric plot $(f(q), f(kq))$ can be expressed as a function $g(f)$ not involving q.* □

Consider the function $f(q) = q^{1/3}$. Construct a comparametric plot for a fixed value of the comparametric ratio $k = 2$. In other words, construct a plot of $f(q)$ versus $f(2q)$. What do you notice about this comparametric plot?

4.7.3 A Simple Exercise in Comparametric Plots

What class of semimonotonic functions $f(q)$ is such that the comparametric plot of $f(q)$ versus $f(2q)$ is a straight line? Consider only $q \geq 0$, $q \in \mathbb{R}$ (this corresponds to real quantities of light greater than or equal to zero). Identify the most general (broadest) class of functions whose comparametric plots are straight lines.

4.7.4 A Simple Example with Actual Pictures

Obtain two images that differ only in exposure. You can do this using the WearComp and QuickCam by varying the brightness (anchor the QuickCam fixed on a tripod or mount pointing at a fixed scene rather than wearing it — the wearable version of the Wyckoff principle will be taught in Chapter 6; for now just fix the camera on a tripod). Alternatively, you could use the standard "mannfamily" image sequence, for example, one image called "Dark exposure" from http://wearcam.org/mannfamily_dark.pgm and "Light exposure" from `http://wearcam.org/mannfamily_light.pgm` Full-size color images in higher resolution are in `http://wearcam.org/mannfamily_dark.jpg` and `http://wearcam.org/mannfamily_light.jpg`.

Compute the histograms of each of the two images as well as the comparagram jointly across both of these two images. What do you notice about the comparagram? Explain the physical intuitive interpretation of the comparagram, as compared with the two histograms.

Don't use the gif files on the www page, use the pgm version of the files, because the C-code provided there doesn't work with gif files. We're trying to phase out the use of gif because of the proprietary (Unisys) nonfree nature of this file format. If disk space is an issue, you can save in the lossless png (Portable Network Graphics) format, which has largely replaced the gif format.

4.7.5 Unconstrained Comparafit

Regard the comparagram as a set of bin counts on ordered pairs (x, y) where $x = m/255$ and $y = n/255$. Find a function $f^{-1}(q)$ such that $f^{-1}(y) - kf^{-1}(x)$ is minimized when weighted by the bin counts of the comparagram $J[m, n]$; that is, determine $f^{-1}(q)$ that minimizes $\varepsilon = \sum_{m=0}^{255} \sum_{n=0}^{255} (f^{-1}(y) - kf^{-1}(x))^2 J[m, n]$, or equivalently, determine F^{-1} that minimizes $\varepsilon = \sum_{m=0}^{255} \sum_{n=0}^{255} (F^{-1}(y) - F^{-1}(x) - K)^2 J[m, n]$. In the example of Section 4.7.4 the value of k is 4 ($K = \log_2(k) = 2$).

What are some of the problems with this "solution"?

4.7.6 Weakly Constrained Comparafit

Find a function $f^{-1}(q)$ such that $f^{-1}(y) - 4f^{-1}(x)$ is minimized when weighted by the bin counts of the comparagram $J[m, n]$, as in the previous question, but this time further add the constraint that f^{-1} be semimonotonic. [Hint: Constrain the first difference (as given by the Octave "diff" command) of the desired solution to be nonnegative. Additional hint: This problem is a quick one-liner if you set it up right and then use a package called qp.m (quadratic programming).]

Is this solution better than the previous solution, and if so, in what ways? What are some of the problems with this "solution"?

Bonus question: Try imposing some smoothness constraints, and describe your results.

4.7.7 Properly Constrained Comparafit

Select a function from the left column of Table 4.4, and fit this function to the comparagram. Explain your reasons for choosing whichever function you select. Now since you know the solutions of the entries in this table (from the right side of the table), report on $f(q)$ recovered from the comparagram. Assume that $k = 4$ (i.e., $K = 2$). You have now solved for the nonlinear response function of the camera given only two differently exposed images.

4.7.8   Combining Differently Exposed Images

Combine the two images together to render a single image of improved dynamic range and tonal fidelity, as described in this previous chapter. A rough outline, consisting of skeletal example C-code may be found at `http://wearcam.org/wyckoff.html`.

Experiment with different ways of combining these (or your own) images. Try first applying f^{-1} to the two images to obtain two estimates of the quantity of light q. Multiplying the first by four (to lighten it up enough to tonally "register" it with the second) and then try adding the two; for example, $4a + b$ where a is the first and b is the second. Don't forget to pass the result back through f and scale the result back down, or you will overrun the 0 to 255 image interval. When you scale down, what you're doing is a weighted average: $(4a + 1b)/(4 + 1)$, where the weights are 4 and 1. If you are using your own images, the number will not necessarily be 4, but you can easily find what your number is, either by experiment or measurement.

Explain your results; don't just submit the finished pictures without an explanation. Also feel free to try other laws of composition to combine the two (or more) differently exposed pictures to obtain a single image of greater dynamic range.

4.7.9   Certainty Functions

Now try using weights that depend on the image pixel value. The weighting should be higher for pixel values near 127, and lower for pixel values near 0 or 255. This can be done by defining a Gaussian certainty function, c, such that $c = \exp(-x^2)$, or $c = \mathrm{pow}(e, \mathrm{pow}(x, 2))$ in "C," where e is the Naperian base $(2.718\ldots)$ and $x = 6 * (\text{pixelvalue}/255) - 3$ makes it roll off nicely at "3 sigma" either side. (So pixel value 0 has very small certainty as does pixel value 255, but pixel value 127 has a high certainty value.)

Moderate pixels are favored so that extreme pixel values (which are under- or overexposed) are weighted less while properly or moderate exposed values more. Implement the "certainty" function as a function call. Test it to see if you get certainty $(0) = 1.2341 * 10^{-4}$, and certainty $(127) = 0.9999$. So now try calculating the weighted sum $(4 * c(a) * a + c(b) * b)/(4 * c(a) + c(b))$

You might also find useful the program "certaint.c" from `http://wearcam.org/orbits/`. This program taints an image with uncertainty. A certainted image can be loaded into GIMP (Gnu image manipulation program) or further processed (combined with other certainted images) using the CEMENT (computer-enhanced multiple exposure numerical technique) program, as an alternative to writing your own programs for combining the images.

4.7.10   Preprocessing (Blurring the Certainty Functions) and Postprocessing

Try blurring the certainty functions prior to using them as weights to do the weighted average that combines the images in lightspace. Experiment with various blur radii, and comment on your results. Also try sharpening the final resulting image. Experiment with a combination of blurring the certainty functions and sharpening the final resultant combined image.

In addition to submitting the final pictures, explain your results. Feel free to try other laws of composition to combine the two (or more) differently exposed pictures to obtain a single image of greater dynamic range.

5

LIGHTSPACE AND ANTIHOMOMORPHIC VECTOR SPACES

The research described in this chapter arises from the author's work in designing and building a wearable graphics production facility used to create a new kind of visual art over the past 15 or 20 years. This work bridges the gap between computer graphics, photographic imaging, and painting with powerful yet portable electronic flashlamps. Beyond being of historical significance (the invention of the wearable computer, mediated reality, etc.), this background can lead to broader and more useful applications.

The work described in this chapter follows on the work of Chapter 4, where it was argued that hidden within the flow of signals from a camera, through image processing, to display, is a homomorphic filter. While homomorphic filtering is often desirable, there are occasions when it is not. The cancellation of this implicit homomorphic filter, as introduced in Chapter 4, through the introduction of an antihomomorphic filter, will lead us, in this chapter, to the concept of antihomomorphic superposition and antihomomorphic vector spaces. This chapter follows roughly a 1992 unpublished report by the author, entitled "Lightspace and the Wyckoff Principle," and describes a new genre of visual art that the author developed in the 1970s and early 1980s.

The theory of antihomomorphic vector spaces arose out of a desire to create a new kind of visual art combining elements of imaging, photography, and graphics, within the context of personal imaging.

Personal imaging is an attempt to:

1. resituate the camera in a new way — as a true extension of the mind and body rather than merely a tool we might carry with us; and
2. allow us to capture a personal account of reality, with a goal toward:
   a. personal documentary; and

179

b. an expressive (artistic and creative) form of imaging arising from the ability to capture a rich multidimensional description of a scene, and then "render" an image from this description at a later time.

The last goal is not to alter the scene content, as is the goal of much in the way of digital photography [87] — through such programs as GIMP or its weaker work-alikes such as Adobe's PhotoShop. Instead, a goal of personal imaging is to manipulate the tonal range and apparent scene illumination, with the goal of faithfully, but expressively, capturing an image of objects actually present in the scene.

In much the same way that Leonardo da Vinci's or Jan Vermeer's paintings portray realistic scenes, but with inexplicable light and shade (i.e., the shadows often appear to correspond to no single possible light source), a goal of personal imaging is to take a first step toward a new direction in imaging to attain a mastery over tonal range, light-and-shadow, and so on.

Accordingly, a general framework for understanding some simple but important properties of light, in the context of a personal imaging system, is put forth.

5.1 LIGHTSPACE

A mathematical framework that describes a model of the way that light interacts with a scene or object is put forth in this chapter. This framework is called "lightspace." It is first shown how any of a variety of typical light sources (including those found in the home, office, and photography studio) can be mathematically represented in terms of a collection of primitive elements called "spotflashes." Due to the photoquantigraphic (linearity and superposition) properties of light, it is then shown that any lighting situation (combination of sunlight, fluorescent light, etc.) can be expressed as a collection of spotflashes. Lightspace captures everything that can be known about how a scene will respond to each of all possible spotflashes and, by this decomposition, to any possible light source.

5.2 THE LIGHTSPACE ANALYSIS FUNCTION

We begin by asking what potentially can be learned from measurements of all the light rays present in a particular region of space. Adelson asks this question:

> What information about the world is contained in the light filling a region of space? Space is filled with a dense array of light rays of various intensities. The set of rays passing through any point in space is mathematically termed a *pencil*. Leonardo da Vinci refers to this set of rays as a "radiant pyramid." [88]

Leonardo expressed essentially the same idea, realizing the significance of this complete visual description:

The body of the air is full of an infinite number of radiant pyramids caused by the objects located in it.[1] These pyramids intersect and interweave without interfering with each other during their independent passage throughout the air in which they are infused. [89]

We can also ask how we might benefit from being able to capture, analyze, and resynthesize these light rays. In particular, *black-and-white* (*grayscale*) photography captures the pencil of light at a particular point in space time (x, y, z, t) integrated over all wavelengths (or integrated together with the spectral sensitivity curve of the film). Color photography captures three readings of this wavelength-integrated pencil of light each with a different spectral sensitivity (color). An earlier form of color photography, known as *Lippman photography* [90,91] decomposes the light into an infinite[2] number of spectral bands, providing a record of the true spectral content of the light at each point on the film.

A long-exposure photograph captures a time-integrated pencil of light. Thus a black-and-white photograph captures the pencil of light at a specific spatial location (x, y, z), integrated over all (or a particular range of) time, and over all (or a particular range of) wavelengths. Thus the idealized (conceptual) analog camera is a means of making uncountably many measurements at the same time (i.e., measuring many of these light rays at once).

5.2.1   The Spot-Flash-Spectrometer

For the moment, let us suppose that we can measure (and record) the energy in a single one of these rays of light, at a particular wavelength, at a particular instant in time.[3] We select a point in space (x, y, z) and place a flashmeter at the end of a collimator (Fig. 5.1) at that location. We select the wavelength of interest by adjusting the prism[4] which is part of the collimator. We select the time period of interest by activating the trigger input of the flashmeter. In practice, a flashmeter integrates the total quantity of light over a short time period, such as 1/500 of a second, but we can envision an apparatus where this time interval can be made arbitrarily short, while the instrument is made more and more sensitive.[5] Note that the collimator and prism serve to restrict our measurement to light traveling in a particular direction, at a particular wavelength, λ.

---

[1] Perhaps more correctly, by the interaction of light with the objects located in it.

[2] While we might argue about infinities, in the context of quantum (i.e., discretization) effects of light, and the like, the term "infinite" is used in the same conceptual spirit as Leonardo used it, that is, without regard to practical implementation, or actual information content.

[3] Neglecting any uncertainty effects due to the wavelike nature of light, and any precision effects due to the particle-like nature of light.

[4] In practice, a blazed grating (diffraction grating built into a curved mirror) might be used, since it selects a particular wavelength of light more efficiently than a prism, though the familiar triangular icon is used to denote this splitting up of the white light into a rainbow of wavelengths.

[5] Neglecting the theoretical limitations of both sensor noise and the quantum (photon) nature of light.

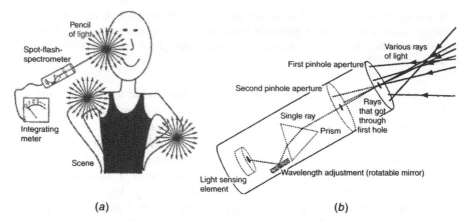

(a)   *(b)*

Figure 5.1 Every point in an illuminated 3-D scene radiates light. Conceptually, at least, we can characterize the scene, and the way it is illuminated, by measuring these rays in all directions of the surrounding space. At each point in space, we measure the amount of light traveling in every possible direction (direction being characterized by a unit vector that has two degrees of freedom). Since objects have various colors and, more generally, various spectral properties, so too will the rays of light reflected by them, so that wavelength is also a quantity that we wish to measure. (a) Measurement of one of these rays of light. (b) Detail of measuring apparatus comprising omnidirectional point sensor in collimating apparatus. We will call this apparatus a "spot-flash-spectrometer."

There are seven degrees of freedom in this measuring apparatus.[6] These are denoted by $\theta, \phi, \lambda, t, x, y$, and z, where the first two degrees of freedom are derived from a unit vector that indicates the direction we are aiming the apparatus, and the last three denote the location of the apparatus in space (or the last four denote the location in 4-space, if one prefers to think that way). At each point in this seven-dimensional analysis space we obtain a reading that indicates the quantity of light at that point in the space. This quantity of light might be found, for example, by observing an integrating voltmeter connected to the light-sensing element at the end of the collimator tube. The entire apparatus, called a "spot-flash-spectrometer" or "spot-spectrometer," is similar to the flash spotmeter that photographers use to measure light bouncing off a single spot in the image. Typically this is over a narrow (one degree or so) beam spread and short (about 1/500) time interval.

Suppose that we obtain a complete set of these measurements of the uncountably[7] many rays of light present in the space around the scene.

---

[6] Note that in a transparent medium one can move along a ray of light with no change. So measuring the lightspace along a plane will suffice, making the measurement of it throughout the entire volume redundant. In many ways, of course, the lightspace representation is conceptual rather than practical.

[7] Again, the term "uncountable" is used in a conceptual spirit. If the reader prefers to visualize the rationals — dense in the reals but countable — or prefers to visualize a countably infinite discrete lattice, or a sufficiently dense finite sampling lattice, this will still convey the general spirit of light theorized by Leonardo.

The complete description is a real-valued function of seven real variables. It completely characterizes the scene to the extent that we are able to later synthesize all possible natural-light (i.e., no flash or other artificially imposed light sources allowed) pictures (still pictures or motion pictures) that are taken of the scene. This function is called the lightspace analysis function (LAF).[8] It explains what was meant by the numerical description produced by the lightspace analysis glass of Chapter 4.

Say, that we now know the lightspace analysis function defined over the setting[9] of Dallas, November 22, 1963. From this lightspace analysis function we would be able to synthesize all possible natural-light pictures of the presidential entourage with unlimited accuracy and resolution. We could synthesize motion pictures of the grassy knoll at the time that the president was shot, and we could know everything about this event that could be obtained by visual means (i.e., by the rays of light present in this setting). In a sense we could extract more information than if we had been there, for we could synthesize extreme close-up pictures of the gunman on the grassy knoll, and magnify them even more to show the serial number on his gun, without any risk of being shot by him. We could generate a movie at any desired frame rate, such as 10,000 frames per second, and watch the bullet come out the barrel of the gun, examining it in slow motion to see what markings it might have on it while it is traveling through the air, even though this information might not have been of interest (or even thought of) at the time that the lightspace analysis function had been measured, acquired, and stored.

To speed up the measurement of a LAF, we consider a collection of measuring instruments combined into a single unit. Some examples might include:

- A spot-spectrometer that has many light sensing elements placed inside, around the prism, so that each one measures a particular wavelength. This instrument could simultaneously measure many wavelengths over a discrete lattice.
- A number of spot-spectrometers operating in parallel at the same time, to simultaneously measure more than one ray of light. Rather than placing them in a row (simple linear array), there is a nice conceptual interpretation that results if the collimators are placed so that they all measure light rays passing through the same point (Fig. 5.2). With this arrangement, all the information gathered from the various light-sensing elements pertains to the same pencil of light.

In our present case we are interested in an instrument that would simultaneously measure an uncountable number of light rays coming in from an uncountable number of different directions, and measure the spectral content (i.e., make measurements at an uncountable number of wavelengths) of each ray. Though

---

[8] Adelson calls this function the "plenoptic function" [88].

[9] A *setting* is a time-span and space-span, or, if you prefer, a region of (x, y, z, t) 4-space.

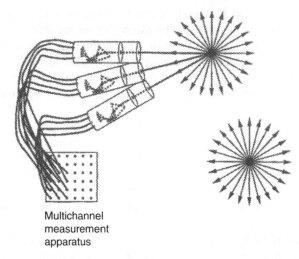

Multichannel
measurement
apparatus

Figure 5.2   A number of spotmeters arranged to simultaneously measure multiple rays of light. Here the instruments measure rays at four different wavelengths, traveling in three different directions, but the rays all pass through the same point in space. If we had uncountably many measurements over all possible wavelengths and directions at one point, we would have an apparatus capable of capturing a complete description of the pencil of light at that point in space.

this is impossible in practice, the human eye comes very close, with its 100 million or so light-sensitive elements. Thus we will denote this collection of spot-flash-spectrometers by the human-eye icon ("eyecon") depicted in Figure 5.3. However, the important difference to keep in mind when making this analogy is that the human eye only captures three spectral bands (i.e., represents all spectral readings as three real numbers denoting the spectrum integrated with each of the three spectral sensitivities), whereas the proposed collection of spot-spectrometers captures all spectral information of each light ray passing through the particular point where it is positioned, at every instant in time, so that a multichannel recording apparatus could be used to capture this information.

5.3   THE "SPOTFLASH" PRIMITIVE

So far a great deal has been said about rays of light. Now let us consider an apparatus for generating one. If we take the light-measuring instrument depicted in Figure 5.1 and replace the light sensor with a flashtube (a device capable of creating a brief burst of white light that radiates in all directions), we obtain a similar unit that functions in reverse. The flashtube emits white light in all directions (Fig. 5.4), and the prism (or diffraction grating) causes these rays of white light to break up into their component wavelengths. Only the ray of light that has a certain specific wavelength will make it out through the holes in the two apertures. The result is a single ray of light that is localized in space (by virtue

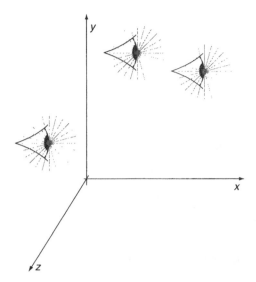

Figure 5.3 An uncountable number of spot-spectrometers arranged (as in Fig. 5.2) to simultaneously measure multiple rays of light is denoted by the human eye icon ("eyecon") because of the similarity to the human visual system. An important difference, though, is that in the human visual system there are only three spectral bands (colors), whereas in our version there are an uncountable number of spectral bands. Another important difference is that our collection of spot-spectrometers can "see" in all directions simultaneously, whereas the human visual system does not allow one to see rays coming from behind. Each eyecon represents an apparatus that records a real-valued function of four real variables, $f(\theta, \phi, \lambda, t)$, so that if the 3-D space were packed with uncountably many of these, the result would be a recording of the lightspace analysis function, $f(\theta, \phi, \lambda, t, x, y, z)$.

of the selection of its location), in time (by virtue of the instantaneous nature of electronic flash), in wavelength (by virtue of the prism), and in direction (azimuth and elevation).

Perhaps the closest actual realization of a spotflash would be a pulsed variable wavelength dye-laser[10] which can create short bursts of light of selectable wavelength, confined to a narrow beam.

As with the spotmeter, there are seven degrees of freedom associated with this light source: azimuth, θ_l; elevation, ϕ_l; wavelength, λ_l; time, t_l; and spatial position (x_l, y_l, z_l).

5.3.1 Building a Conceptual Lighting Toolbox: Using the Spotflash to Synthesize Other Light Sources

The spotflash is a primitive form upon which other light sources may be built. We will construct a hypothetical toolbox containing various lights built up from a number of spotflashes.

---

[10] Though lasers are well known for their coherency, in this chapter we ignore the coherency properties of light, and use lasers as examples of shining rays of monochromatic light along a single direction.

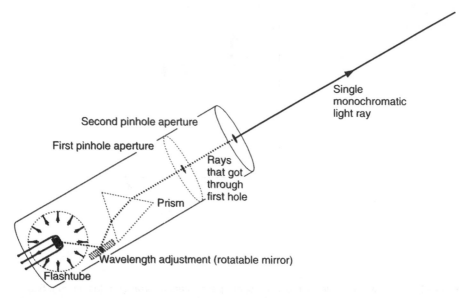

Figure 5.4 Monochromatic flash spotlight source of adjustable wavelength. This light source is referred to as a "spotflash" because it is similar to a colored spotlight that is flashed for a brief duration. (Note the integrating sphere around the flashlamp; it is reflective inside, and has a small hole through which light can emerge.)

White Spotflash

The ideal spotflash is infinitesimally[11] small, so we can pack arbitrarily many of them into as small a space as desired. If we pack uncountably many spotflashes close enough together, and have them all shine in the same direction, we can set each one at a slightly different wavelength. The spotflashes will act collectively to produce a single ray of light that contains all wavelengths. Now imagine that we connect all of the trigger inputs together so that they all flash simultaneously at each of the uncountably many component wavelengths. We will call this light source the "white-spotflash." The white-spotflash produces a brief burst of white light confined to a narrow beam. Now that we have built a white-spotflash, we put it into our conceptual toolbox for future use.

Fan Beam (Pencil of White Light)

Say we pack uncountably many white-spotflashes together into the same space so that they fan out in different directions. The light rays all exist in the same plane, and all pass through the same point. Then, we fire all of the white-spotflashes at the same time to obtain a sheet of directed light that all emanates from a single point. We call this light source the "fan beam," and place it into our conceptual toolbox for future use. This arrangement of white-spotflashes resembles the arrangement of flash spotmeters in Figure 5.2.

---

[11] Again, the same caveat applies to "infinitesimal" as to "infinite" and "uncountable."

Flash Point Source (Bundle of White Light)

Now we pack uncountably many white-spotflashes together into the same space so that they fan out in all possible directions but pass through the same point. We obtain a "flash point source" of light. Having constructed a "flash point source," we place it in our conceptual toolbox for future use. Light sources that approximate this ideal flash point source are particularly common. A good example is Harold Edgerton's *microflash point source* which is a small spark gap that produces a flash of white light, radiating in all directions, and lasting approximately a third of a microsecond. Any bare electronic flashtube (i.e., with no reflector) is a reasonably close approximation to a flash point source.

Point Source

Say we take a flash point source and fire it repeatedly[12] to obtain a flashing light. If we allow the time period between flashes to approach zero, the light stays on continuously. We have now constructed a continuous source of white light that radiates in all directions. We place this point source in the conceptual toolbox for future use.

In practice, if we could use a microflash point source that lasts a third of a microsecond, and flash it with a 3 Mhz trigger signal (three million flashes per second) it would light up continuously.[13]

The point source is much like a bare light bulb, or a household lamp with the shade removed, continuously radiating white light in all directions, but from a single point in (x, y, z) space.

Linelight

We can take uncountably many point sources and arrange them along a line in 3-space (x, y, z), or we can take a lineflash and flash it repeatedly so that it stays on. Either way we obtain a linear source of light called the "linelight," which we place in the conceptual toolbox for future use. This light source is similar to the long fluorescent tubes that are used in office buildings.

Sheetlight

A sheetflash fired repetitively, so that it stays on, produces a continuous light source called a "sheetlight." Videographers often use a light bulb placed behind a white cloth to create a light source similar to the "sheetlight." Likewise we "construct" a sheetlight and place it in our conceptual lighting toolbox for future use.

Volume Light

Uncountably many sheetlights stacked on top of one another form a "volume light," which we now place into our conceptual toolbox. Some practical examples

---

[12] Alternatively, we can think of this arrangement as a row of flash point sources arranged along the time axis and fired together in (x, y, z, t) 4-space.

[13] Of course, this "practical" example is actually hypothetical. The flash takes time to "recycle" itself to be ready for the next flash. In this thought experiment, recycle time is neglected. Alternatively, imagine a xenon arc lamp that stays on continuously.

of volumetric light sources include the light from luminous gas like the sun, or a flame. Note that we have made the nonrealistic assumption that each of these constituent sheetlights is transparent.

Integration of Light to Achieve Otherwise Unrealizable Light Sources

This assumption that rays of light can pass through the sheetlight instrument is no small assumption. Photographer's softboxes, which are the practical closest approximation to sheetlight are far from transparent. Typically a large cavity behind the sheet is needed to house a more conventional light source.

Now suppose that a picture is illuminated by a sheetlight located between the camera and the object being photographed. That is, what we desire is a picture of an object as it appears while we look through the sheetlight. One way of obtaining such a picture is to average over the light intensity falling on an image sensor (i.e., through a long-exposure photograph, or through making a video and then photoquantigraphically averaging all the frames together, as was described in Chapter 4), while moving a linelight across directly in front of the object. The linelight is moved (e.g., from left to right), directly in front of the camera, but because it is in motion, it is not seen by the camera — so the object itself gets averaged out over time. A picture taken in this manner is shown in Figure 5.5. As indicated in the figure, the light source may be constructed to radiate in some directions more than others, and this radiation pattern may even change (evolve) as the light source is moved from left to right. An approximate (i.e., discrete) realization of a linelight that can evolve as it moves from left to right was created by the author in the 1970s; it is depicted in Figure 5.6a.

An example of the use of the linelight is provided in Figure 5.7. The information captured from this process is parameterized on two planes, a light plane and an image plane. The light plane parameterizes the direction from which rays of light enter into the scene, while the image plane parameterizes directions from which rays of light leave the scene. This four-dimensional space is enough to synthesize a picture of the scene as it would appear if it were illuminated by any desired shape of light source that lies in the light plane or other manifold (i.e., the plane or other manifold through which the linelight passed during the data acquisition). For example, a picture of how the scene would look under a long slender-shaped light source (like that produced by a long straight fluorescent light tube) may be obtained by using the approach of Chapter 4 for lightspace measurements. Recall that we determined q, then integrated over the desired light shape (i.e., integrating the four-dimensional space down to a two-dimensional image), and last undid the linearization process by evaluating $f(q)$. In reality, these measurements are made over a discrete sampling lattice (finite number of lamps, finite number of pixels in each photometrically linearized camera). The Wyckoff principle allows us to neglect the effects of finite word length (quantization in the quantity of light reported at each sensor element). Thus the measurement space depicted in Figure 5.7 may be regarded as a continuous

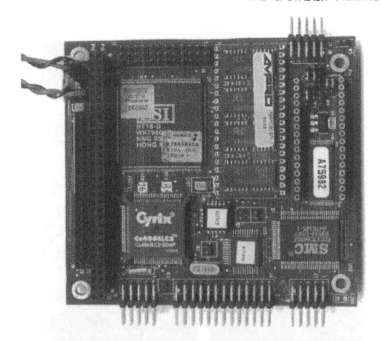

Figure 5.5 "For now we see through a glass, lightly." Imagine that there is a plane of light (i.e., a glass or sheet that produces light itself). Imagine now that this light source is totally transparent and that it is placed between you and some object. The resulting light is very soft upon the object, providing a uniform illumination without distinct shadows. Such a light source does not exist in practice but may be simulated by photoquantigraphically combining multiple pictures (as was described in Chapter 4), each taken with a linear source of light ("linelight"). Here a linelight was moved from left to right. Note that the linelight need not radiate equally in all directions. If it is constructed so that it will radiate more to the right than to the left, a nice and subtle shading will result, giving the kind of light we might expect to find in a Vermeer painting (very soft yet distinctly coming from the left). The lightspace framework provides a means of synthesizing such otherwise impossible light sources — light sources that could never exist in reality. Having a "toolbox" containing such light sources affords one with great artistic and creative potential.

real-valued function of four integer variables. Rather than integrating over the desired light shape, we would proceed to sum (antihomomorphically) over the desired light vector subspace. This summation corresponds to taking a weighted sum of the images themselves. Examples of these summations are depicted in Figure 5.8.

It should also be noted that the linelight, which is made from uncountably many point sources (or a finite approximation), may also have fine structure. Each of these point sources may be such that it radiates unequally in various directions. A simple example of a picture that was illuminated with an approximation to a

(a) (b)

Figure 5.6 Early embodiments of the author's original "photographer's assistant" application of personal imaging. (a) 1970s "painting with light vectors' pushbroom" system and 1980 CRT display. The linear array of lamps, controlled by a body-worn processor (WearComp), was operated much like a dot-matrix printer to sweep out spatial patterns of structured light. (b) Jacket and clothing based computing. As this project evolved in the 1970s and into the early 1980s, the components became spread out on clothing rather than located in a backpack. Separate 0.6 inch cathode ray tubes attachable/detachable to/from ordinary safetyglasses, as well as waist-worn television sets replaced the earlier and more cumbersome helmet-based screens of the 1970s. Notice the change from the two antennas in (a) to the single antenna in (b), which provided wireless communication of video, voice, and data to and from a remote base station.

linelight appears in Figure 5.9.[14] Here the linelight is used as a light source to indirectly illuminate subject matter of interest. In certain situations the linelight may appear directly in the image as shown in Figure 5.10.

---

[14] As we learn how the image is generated, it will become quite obvious why the *directionality* arises. Here the author set up the three models in a rail boxcar, open at both sides, but stationary on a set of railway tracks. On an adjacent railway track, a train with headlamps moved across behind the models, during a long exposure which was integrated over time. However, the thought exercise — thinking of this process as a single static long slender light source, composed of uncountably many point sources that each radiate over some fixed solid angle to the right — helps us to better understand the principle of lightspace.

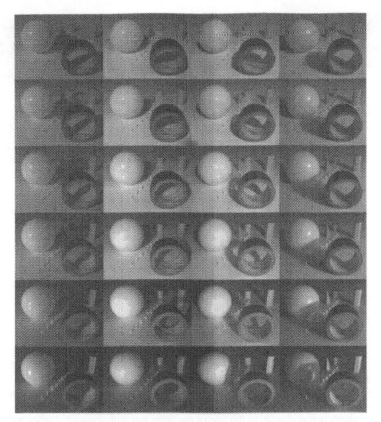

Figure 5.7 Partial lightspace acquired from a system similar to that depicted in Figure 5.6*a*. (Pictured here is a white glass ball, a roll of cloth tape, wooden blocks, and white plastic letters.) As the row of lamps is swept across (sequenced), it traces out a plane of light ("sheetlight"). The resulting measurement space is a four-dimensional array, parameterized by two index (azimuth and elevation) describing rays of incoming light, and two indexes (azimuth and elevation) describing rays of outgoing light. Here this information is displayed as a block matrix, where each block is an image. The indexes of the block indicate the light vector, while the indexes within the block are pixel coordinates.

Dimensions of Light

Figure 5.11 illustrates some of these light sources, categorized by the number of dimensions (degrees of freedom) that they have in both 4-space (t, z, y, z), and 7-space $(\theta, \phi, \lambda, t, x, y, z)$.

The Aremac and Controllable Light Sources

We now have, in our conceptual toolbox, various hypothetical light sources, such as a point source of white light, an infinitely long slender lamp (a line that produces light), an infinite sheet of light (a plane that produces light, from which there could be, but only conceptually due to self-occlusion, constructed an infinite 3-D volume that produces light). We have already seen pictures taken using some

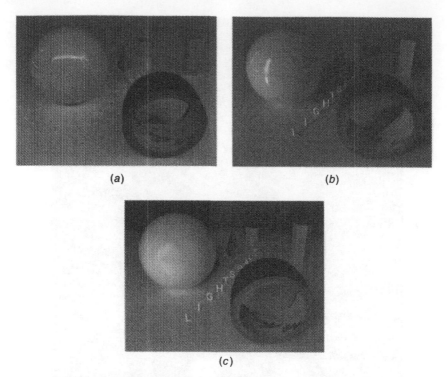

Figure 5.8 Antihomomorphic superposition over various surfaces in lightspace. (a) Here the author synthesized the effect of a scene illuminated with long horizontal slender light source (i.e., as would be visible if it were lit with a bare fluorescent light tube), reconstructing shadows that appear sharp perpendicular to the line of the lamp but soft across it. Notice the slender line highlight in the specular sphere. (b) Here the effect of a vertical slender light source is synthesized. (c) Here the effect of two light sources is synthesized so that the scene appears as if lit by a vertical line source, as well as a star-shaped source to the right of it. Both sources coming from the left of the camera. The soft yet highly directional light is in some way reminiscent of a Vermeer painting, yet all of the input images were taken by the harsh but moving light source of the pushbroom apparatus.

practical approximations to these light sources. These pictures allowed us to expand our creative horizons by manipulating otherwise impossible light sources (i.e., light sources that do not exist in reality). Through the integration of these light sources over lightspace, we are able to synthesize a picture as it would have appeared had it been taken with such a light source.

We now imagine that we have full control of each light source. In particular, the light volume (volumetric light source) is composed of uncountably many spotflashes (infinitesimal rays of light). If, as we construct the various light sources, we retain control of the individual spotflashes, rather than connecting them together to fire in unison, we obtain a "controllable light source."

Figure 5.9 Subject matter illuminated, from behind, by linelight. This picture is particularly illustrative because the light source itself (the two thick bands, and two thinner bands in the background which are the linelights) is visible in the picture. However, we see that the three people standing in the open doorway, illuminated by the linelight, are lit on their left side more than on their right side. Also notice how the doorway is lit more on the right side of the picture than on the left side. This *directionality* of the light source is owing from the fact that the picture is effectively composed of point sources that each radiate mostly to the right. (©) Steve Mann, 1984.

Say we assemble a number of spotflashes of different wavelength, as we did to form the white spotflash, but this time we retain control (i.e., we have a voltage on each spotflash). We should be able to select any desired spectral distribution (i.e., color). We call the resulting source a "controllable spotflash." The controllable spotflash takes a real-valued function of one real variable as its input, and from this input, produces, for a brief instant, a ray of light that has a spectral distribution corresponding to that input function.

The controllable spotflash subsumes the white spotflash as a special case. The white spotflash corresponds to a controllable spotflash driven with a wavelength function that is constant. Assembling a number of controllable spotflashes at

Figure 5.10 Painting with linelight. Ordinarily the linelight is used to illuminate subject matter. It is therefore seldom itself directly seen in a picture. However, to illustrate the principle of the linelight, it may be improperly used to shine light directly into the camera rather than for illuminating subject matter. (a) In integrating over a lattice of light vectors, any shape or pattern of light can be created. Here light shaped like text, HELLO, is created. The author appears with linelight at the end of letter "H." (b) Different integration over lightspace produces text shaped like WORLD. The author with linelight appears near the letter "W." (c) The noise-gated version is only responsive to light due to the pushbroom itself. The author does not appear anywhere in the picture. Various interweaved patterns of graphics and text may intermingle. Here we see text HELLO WORLD.

the same location but pointing in all possible directions in a given plane, and maintaining separate control of each spotflash, provides us with a source that can produce any pencil of light, varying in intensity and spectral distribution, as a function of angle. This apparatus is called the "controllable flashpencil," and it takes as input, a real-valued function of two real variables.

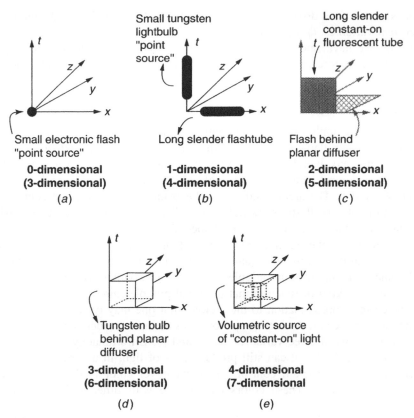

Figure 5.11 A taxonomy of light sources in 4-space. The dimensionality in the 4-space (x, y, z, t) is indicated below each set of examples, while the dimensionality in the new 7-space is indicated in parentheses. (a) A flash point source located at the origin gives a brief flash of white light that radiates in all directions (θ, ϕ) over all wavelengths, λ, and is therefore characterized as having 3 degrees of freedom. A fat dot is used to denote a practical real-world approximation to the point flash source, which has a nonzero flash duration and a nonzero spatial extent. (b) Both the point source and the lineflash have 4 degrees of freedom. Here the point source is located at the spatial (x, y, z) origin and extends out along the t axis, while the lineflash is aligned along the x axis. A fat line of finite length is used to denote a typical real-world approximation to the ideal source. (c) A flash behind a planar diffuser, and a long slender fluorescent tube are both approximations to these light sources that have 5 degrees of freedom. (d) Here a tungsten bulb behind a white sheet gives a dense planar array of point sources that is confined to the plane $z = 0$ but spreads out over the 6 remaining degrees of freedom. (e) A volumetric source, such as might be generated by light striking particles suspended in the air, radiates white light from all points in space and in all directions. It is denoted as a *hypercube* in 4-space, and exhibits all 7 degrees of freedom in 7-space.

Assembling a number of controllable spotflashes at the same location but pointing in all possible directions in 3D space, and maintaining separate control of each of them, provides us with a source that can produce any pattern of flash emanating from a given location. This light source is called a "controllable flash point source." It is driven by a control signal that is a real-valued function of three real variables, θ_l, ϕ_l, and λ_l.

So far we have said that a flashtube can be activated to flash or to stay on constantly, but more generally, its output can be varied rapidly and continuously, through the application of a time-varying voltage.[15]

The Aremac

Similarly, if we apply time-varying control to the controllable flash point source, we obtain a controllable point source which is the aremac. The aremac is capable of producing any bundle of light rays that pass through a given point. It is driven by a control signal that is a real-valued function of four real variables, θ_l, ϕ_l, λ_l, and t_l. The aremac subsumes the controllable flash point source, and the controllable spotflash as special cases. Clearly, it also subsumes the white spotflash, and the flash point source as special cases.

The aremac is the exact reverse concept of the pinhole camera. The ideal pinhole camera[16] absorbs and quantifies incoming rays of light and produces a real-valued function of four variables (x, y, t, λ) as output. The aremac takes as input the same kind of function that the ideal pinhole camera gives as output.

The closest approximation to the aremac that one may typically come across is the video projector. A video projector takes as input a video signal (three real-valued functions of three variables, x, y, and t). Unfortunately, its wavelength is not controllable, but it can still produce rays of light in a variety of different directions, under program control, to be whatever color is desired within its limited color gamut. These colors can evolve with time, at least up to the frame/field rate.

A linear array of separately addressable aremacs produces a controllable line source. Stacking these one above the other (and maintaining separate control of each) produces a controllable sheet source. Now, if we take uncountably many controllable sheet sources and place them one above the other, maintaining separate control of each, we arrive at a light source that is controlled by a real-valued function of seven real variables, θ_l, ϕ_l, λ_l, t_l, x_l, y_l, and z_l. We call this light source the "lightspace aremac."

The lightspace aremac subsumes all of the light sources that we have mentioned so far. In this sense it is the most general light source — the only one we really need in our conceptual lighting toolbox.

An interesting subset of the lightspace aremac is the computer screen. Computer screens typically comprise over a million small light sources spread out

---

[15] An ordinary tungsten-filament lightbulb can also be driven with a time-varying voltage. But it responds quite sluggishly to the control voltage because of the time required to heat or cool the filament. The electronic flash is much more in keeping with the spirit of the ideal time-varying lightsource. Indeed, visual artist Joe Davis has shown that the output intensity of an electronic flash can be modulated at video rates so that it can be used to transmit video to a photoreceptor at some remote location.

[16] The ideal pinhole camera of course does not exist in practice. The closest approximation would be a motion picture camera that implements the Lippman photography process.

over a time-varying 2D lattice; we may think of it as a 3-D lattice in (t_l, x_l, y_l). Each light source can be separately adjusted in its light output. A grayscale computer screen is driven by a signal that is an integer-valued function of three integer variables: t_l, x_l, and y_l, but the number of values that the function can assume (typically 256) and the fine-grained nature of the lattice (typically over 1000 pixels in the spatial direction, and 72 frames per second in the temporal direction) make it behave almost indistinguishably from a hypothetical device driven by a real-valued function of three real variables. Using the computer screen as a light source, we can, for example, synthesize the light from a particular north-facing window (or cloudy-day window) by displaying the light pattern of that window. This light pattern might be an image array as depicted in Figure 5.12. When taking a picture in a darkened room, where the only source of light is the computer screen displaying the image of Figure 5.12, we will obtain a picture similar to the effect of using a real window as a light source, when the sky outside is completely overcast. Because the light from each point on the screen radiates in all directions, we cannot synthesize the light as we can the sunlight streaming in through a window. This is because the screen cannot send out a ray that is confined to a particular direction of travel. Thus we cannot use the computer screen to take a picture of a scene as it would appear illuminated by light coming through a window on a sunny day (i.e., with parallel rays of light illuminating the scene or object being photographed).

Figure 5.12 Using a computer screen to simulate the light from a window on a cloudy day. All of the regions on the screen that are shaded correspond to areas that should be set to the largest numerical value (typically 255), while the solid (black) areas denote regions of the screen that should be set to the lowest numerical value (0). The light coming from the screen would then light up the room in the same way as a window of this shape and size. This trivial example illustrates the way in which the computer screen can be used as a controllable light source.

5.4   LAF × LSF IMAGING ("LIGHTSPACE")

So far we have considered the camera as a mechanism for simultaneously measuring many rays of light passing through a single point, that is, measuring a portion of the lightspace analysis function. As mentioned from time to time, knowing the lightspace analysis function allows us to reconstruct natural-light pictures of a scene, but not pictures taken by our choice of lighting. For example, with the lightspace analysis function of the setting of Dallas, November 22, 1963, we cannot construct a picture equivalent to one that was taken with a *fill-flash*.[17] The reason for this limitation lies in the structure of the LAF.

Though the lightspace analysis function provides an information-rich scene description, and seems to give us far more visual information than we could ever hope to use, an even more complete scene characterization, called "lightspace," is now described.

Lightspace attempts to characterize everything that can be known about the way that light can interact with a scene. Knowing the lightspace of the setting of Dallas, November 22, 1963, for example, would allow us to synthesize a picture that had been taken with flash, or to synthesize a picture taken on a completely overcast day (despite the fact that the weather was quite clear that day), obtaining, for example, a completely shadow-free picture of the gunman on the grassy knoll (though he had been standing there in bright sunlight, with strong shadows).

We define lightspace as the set of all lightspace analysis functions measured while shining onto the scene each possible ray of light. Thus the lightspace consists of a lightspace analysis function located at every point in the 7 dimensional space $(\theta_l, \phi_l, \lambda_l, t_l, x_l, y_l, z_l)$. In this way, lightspace is the vector outer product (tensor product) of the LAF with the LSF. Equivalently, then, the lightspace is a real-valued function of 14 real variables. The lightspace may be evaluated at a single point in this 14-D space using a spot-flash-spectrometer and spotflash, as shown in Figure 5.13.

5.4.1   Upper-Triangular Nature of Lightspace along Two Dimensions: Fluorescent and Phosphorescent Objects

Not all light rays sent out will return. Some may pass by the scene and travel off into 3-space. The lightspace corresponding to these rays will thus be zero. Therefore it should be clear that a ray of light sent out at a particular point in 7-space, $(\theta_l, \phi_l, \lambda_l, t_l, x_l, y_l, z_l)$ does not arrive back at the location of the sensor in 7-space, $(\theta, \phi, \lambda, t, x, y, z)$.

A good practical example of zero-valued regions of lightspace arises when the light reading is taken before the ray is sent out. This situation is depicted mathematically as $t < t_l$ (see also Fig. 5.14a). Similarly, if we shine red light ($\lambda = 700$ nm) on the scene, and look through a blue filter ($\lambda = 400$ nm), we

---

[17] On bright sunny days, a small flash helps to fill in some of the shadows, which results in a much improved picture. Such a flash is called a *fill-flash*.

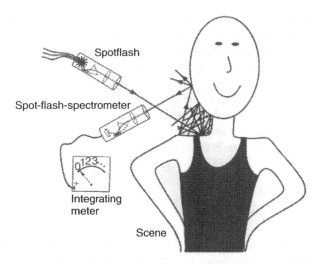

Figure 5.13 Measuring one point in the lightspace around a particular scene, using a spot-flash-spectrometer and a spotflash. The measurement provides a real-valued quantity that indicates how much light comes back along the direction (θ, ϕ), at the wavelength λ, and time t, to location (x, y, z), as a result of flashing a monochromatic ray of light in the direction (θ_l, ϕ_l), having a wavelength of λ_l, at time t_l, from location (x_l, y_l, z_l).

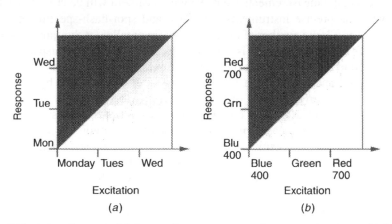

Figure 5.14 In practice, not all light rays that are sent out will return to the sensor. (a) If we try to measure the response before the excitation, we would expect a zero result. (b) Many natural objects will radiate red light as a result of blue excitation, but the reverse is not generally true. (These are "density plot," where black indicates a boolean true for causality (i.e., response comes after excitation).

would not expect to see any response. In general, then, the lightspace will be zero whenever $t < t_l$ or $\lambda < \lambda_l$.

Now, if we flash a ray of light at the scene, and then look a few seconds later, we may still pick up a nonzero reading. Consider, for example, a glow-in-the-dark toy (or clock), a computer screen, or a TV screen. Even though it might be turned off, it will glow for a short time after it is excited by an external source of light, due to the presence of phosfluorescent materials. Thus the objects can absorb light at one time, and reradiate it at another.

Similarly some objects will absorb light at short wavelengths (e.g., ultraviolet or blue light) and reradiate at longer wavelengths. Such materials are said to be *fluorescent*. A fluorescent red object might, for example, provide a nonzero return to a sensor tuned to $\lambda = 700$ nm (red), even though it is illuminated only by a source at $\lambda = 400$ nm (blue). Thus, along the time and wavelength axes, lightspace is upper triangular[18] (Fig. 5.14*b*).

5.5 LIGHTSPACE SUBSPACES

In practice, the lightspace is too unwieldy to work with directly. It is, instead, only useful as a conceptual framework in which to pose other practical problems. As was mentioned earlier, rather than using a spotflash and spot-flash-spectrometer to measure lightspace, we will most likely use a camera. A videocamera, for example, can be used to capture an information-rich description of the world, so in a sense it provides many measurements of the lightspace.

In practice, the measurements we make with a camera will be cruder than those made with the precise instruments (spotflash and spot-flash-spectrometer). The camera makes a large number of measurements in parallel (at the same time). The crudeness of each measurement is expressed by integrating the lightspace together with some kind of 14-D blurring function. For example, a single grayscale picture, taken with a camera having an image sensor of dimension 480 by 640 pixels, and taken with a particular kind of illumination, may be expressed as a collection of $480 \times 640 = 307,200$ crude measurements of the light rays passing through a particular point. Each measurement corresponds to a certain sensing element of the image array that is sensitive to a range of azimuthal angles, θ and elevational angles, ϕ. Each reading is also sensitive to a very broad range of wavelengths, and the shutter speed dictates the range of time to which the measurements are sensitive.

Thus the blurring kernel will completely blur the λ axis, sample the time axis at a single point, and somewhat blur the other axes. A color image of the same dimensions will provide three times as many readings, each one blurred quite severely along the wavelength axis, but not so severely as the grayscale image readings. A color motion picture will represent a blurring and repetitive sampling of the time axis. A one second (30 frames per second) movie then provides us with $3 \times 30 \times 480 \times 640 = 27,648,000$ measurements (i.e., 27,000 K of data), each blurred by the nature of the measurement device (camera).

---

[18] The term is borrowed from linear algebra and denotes matrices with entries of zero below the main diagonal.

We can trade some resolution in the camera parameters for resolution in the excitation parameters, for example, by having a flash activated every second frame so that half of the frames are naturally lit and the other half are flash-lit. Using multiple sources of illumination in this way, we could attempt to crudely characterize the lightspace of the scene. Each of the measurements is given by

$$q_k = \int \int \int \int \int \int \int \int \int \int \int \int \int$$

$$\mathcal{L}(\theta_l, \phi_l, \lambda_l, t_l, x_l, y_l, z_l, \theta, \phi, \lambda, t, x, y, z)$$

$$\mathcal{B}_k(\theta_l, \phi_l, \lambda_l, t_l, x_l, y_l, z_l, \theta, \phi, \lambda, t, x, y, z)$$

$$d\theta_l d\phi_l d\lambda_l dt_l dx_l dy_l dz_l d\theta d\phi d\lambda dt dx dy dz, \tag{5.1}$$

where $\mathcal{L}$ is the lightspace and $\mathcal{B}_k$ is the blurring kernel of the kth measurement apparatus (incorporating both excitation and response).

We may rewrite this measurement (in the Lebesgue sense rather than the Reimann sense and avoid writing out all the integral signs):

$$q_k = \int \mathcal{L}(\theta_l, \phi_l, \lambda_l, t_l, x_l, y_l, z_l, \theta, \phi, \lambda, t, x, y, z) d\mu_k, \tag{5.2}$$

where μ_k is the measure associated with the blurring kernel of the kth measuring apparatus.

We will refer to a collection of such blurred measurements as a "lightspace subspace," for it fails to capture the entire lightspace. The lightspace subspace, rather, slices through portions of lightspace (decimates or samples it) and blurs those slices.

5.6 "LIGHTVECTOR" SUBSPACE

One such subspace is the lightvector subspace arising from multiple differently exposed images. In Chapter 4 we combined multiple pictures together to arrive at a single floating point image that captured both the great dynamic range and the subtle differences in intensities of the light on the image plane. This was due to a particular fixed lighting of the subject matter that did no vary other than by overall exposure. In this chapter we extend this concept to multiple dimensions.

A vector, v, of length L, may be regarded as a single point in a multidimensional space, $\mathbb{R}^L$. Similarly a real-valued grayscale picture defined on a discrete lattice of dimensions M (height) by N (width) may also be regarded as a single point in $R^{M \times N}$, a space called "imagespace." Any image can be represented as a point in imagespace because the picture may be unraveled into one long vector, row by row.[19] Thus, if we linearize, using the procedure of Chapter 4,

---

[19] This is the way that a picture (or any 2-D array) is typically stored in a file on a computer. The two-dimensional picture array is stored sequentially as an array in one dimension.

then, in the ideal noise-free world, all of the linearized elements of a Wyckoff set, $q_n(x, y) = f^{-1}(f_n(x, y))$, are linearly related to each other through a simple scale factor:

$$q_n = k_n q_0, \tag{5.3}$$

where q_0 is the linearized reference exposure. In practice, image noise prevents this from being the case, but theoretically, the camera and Wyckoff film provide us with a means of obtaining the one-dimensional subspace of the imagespace.

Let us first begin with the simplest special case in which all of the lightvectors are collinear.

5.6.1   One-Dimensional Lightvector Subspace

The manner in which differently exposed images of the same subject matter are combined was illustrated in Figure 4.4 by way of an example involving three input exposures. In the context of Chapter 4, these three different exposures were obtained by adjustment of the camera. Equivalently, if only one light source is present in the picture, and this only source of light can be adjusted, an equivalent effect is observed, which is illustrated in Figure 5.15.

As shown in Chapter 4, the constants k_i, as well as the unknown nonlinear response function of the camera, can be determined up to a single unknown scalar constant, from multiple pictures of the same subject matter in which the pictures differ only in exposure. Thus the reciprocal exposures used to tonally register (tonally align) the multiple input images are estimates, $1/\hat{k}_i$, in Figure 5.15, and these estimates are generally made by applying an estimation algorithm to the input images, either while simultaneously estimating f or as a separate estimation process (since f only has to be estimated once for each camera, but the exposure is estimated for every picture that is taken).

It is important to determine f accurately because the numerical stability of the processing depends heavily on f. In particular, owing to the large dynamic range that some Wyckoff sets can cover, small errors in f tend to have adverse effects on the overall estimate $\hat{q}$. Thus it may be preferable to estimate f as a separate process (i.e, by taking hundreds of exposures with the camera under computer program control). Once f is known (previously measured), then k_i can be estimated for a particular set of images.

5.6.2   Lightvector Interpolation and Extrapolation

The architecture of Figure 5.15 involves an image acquisition section (in this illustration, three images assumed to belong to the same Wyckoff set and therefore collectively defining a single lightvector), followed by an analysis section (to estimate q) and then by a resynthesis section (to generate an image again at the output). The output image can look like any of the input images, but with improved signal-to-noise ratio, better tonal range, better color fidelity, and so on. Moreover an output image can be an interpolated or extrapolated version in which it is lighter or darker than any of the input images. It can thus capture the

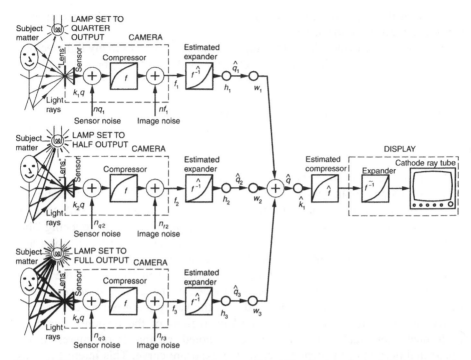

Figure 5.15 Multiple exposures to varying quantity of illumination. A single light source is activated multiple times from the same fixed location to obtain multiple images differing only in exposure. In this example there are three different exposures. The first exposure with LAMP SET TO QUARTER OUTPUT gives rise to an exposure k_{1q}, the second, with LAMP SET TO HALF OUTPUT, to k_{2q}, and the third, with LAMP SET TO FULL OUTPUT, to k_{3q}. Each exposure gives rise to a different realization of the same noise process, and the three noisy pictures that the camera provides are denoted f_1, f_2, and f_3. These three differently exposed pictures comprise a noisy Wyckoff set (i.e., a set of approximately collinear lightvectors in the antihomomorphic vector space). To combine them into a single estimate of the lightvector they collectively define, the effect of f is undone with an estimate $\hat{f}$ that represents our best guess of the function f, which varies from camera to camera. Linear filters h_i are next applied in an attempt to filter out sensor noise n_{q_i}. Generally, the f estimate is made together with an estimate of the exposures k_i. After reexpanding the dynamic ranges with $\hat{f}^{-1}$, the inverse of the estimated exposures $1/\hat{k}_i$ are applied. In this way the darker images are made lighter and the lighter images are made darker so that they all (theoretically) match. At this point the images will all appear as if they were taken with identical exposure to light, except for the fact that the pictures with higher lamp output will be noisy in lighter areas of the image and those taken with lower lamp output will be noisy in dark areas of the image. Thus, rather than simply applying ordinary *signal averaging*, a weighted average is taken by applying weights w_i, which include the estimated global exposures k_i and the spatially varying *certainty functions* $c_i(x, y)$. These certainty functions turn out to be the derivative of the camera response function shifted up or down by an amount k_i. The weighted sum is $\hat{q}(x, y)$, and the estimate of the photoquantity is $q(x, y)$. To view this quantity on a video display, it is first adjusted in exposure; it may be adjusted to a different exposure level not present in any of the input images. In this case it is set to the estimated exposure of the first image, $\hat{k}_1$. The result is then range-compressed with $\hat{f}$ for display on an expansive medium (DISPLAY).

response of the scene or object to any quantity of the light, as directed from a particular location in the scene.

As will become evident later, the output image is just one of many lightvectors, each of which describe the same subject matter but with the light source placed at a different location. To the extent that the output image is a lightvector, one can dial up or down the illumination of that particular lightvector. For example, through this interpolation process, one can increase or decrease a particular skyscraper in the cityscape in virtual effective light output, as seen in the computerized eyeglasses, while viewing the lightvector painting being generated.

It should be noted that the process of interpolation or extrapolation of the output of a single light source (or more generally, of a lightvector contribution to an image) is isomorphic to the process of Chapter 4. Recall that in comparadjusting, the tonal range of an image that corresponds to being able to adjust the picture is equivalent to one that would have been taken using any desired exposure. (This process was illustrated in Fig. 4.5.)

Of the various comparametric functions introduced in Chapter 4, the *power of root over root plus constant correction* model, or the *saturated power of root over root plus constant correction* model, is the vastly preferred model because it accurately portrays the *toe* and *shoulder* regions of the response curve. In traditional photography these regions are ignored; all that is of interest is the linear mid portion of the density versus log exposure curve. This interest in only the midtones is because, in traditional photography, areas outside this region are considered to be incorrectly exposed. However, many of the images in a Wyckoff set are *deliberately* underexposed and overexposed. In fact this deliberate overexposure of some images and underexposure of other images is often taken to extremes. Therefore the additional sophistication of the model (4.55) is of great value in capturing the essence of these extreme exposures, in which exposure into both the *toe* and *shoulder* regions are the norm rather than an aberration when practicing the art of painting with lightvectors.

5.6.3 Processing Differently Illuminated Wyckoff Sets of the Same Subject Matter

The concept of a single lightvector may be extended to a plurality of lightvectors. Let us first consider a situation where we have two lightvectors, each defined by a Wyckoff set. For simplicity of the example, suppose that we have two lightvectors, each defined by three exposures, as illustrated in Figure 5.16.

In particular, say we capture a collection f_1, f_2, f_3 of differently exposed images of subject matter while it is illuminated by a light source coming from the left, and generate a corresponding estimate $\hat{q}_L$ of the response of the subject matter to that first light source location. Then we illuminate the same subject matter from a second light source location, for example, with light coming from the right, to capture a collection f_4, f_5, f_6, and obtain an estimate $\hat{q}_R$ of the response of the subject matter to the second light source location (again, see

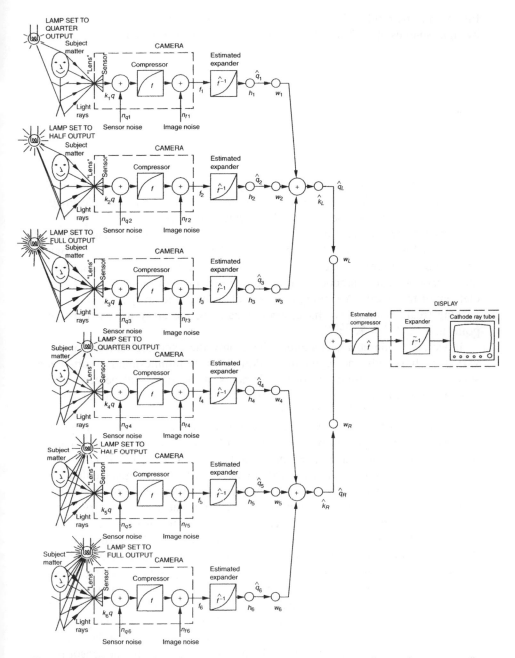

Figure 5.16 The generation of two lightvectors q_L and q_R corresponding to the scene as lit from the left and right respectively. Each lightvector is generated from three different exposures. The first lightvector is generated from the Wyckoff set f_1, f_2, f_3, and the second lightvector is generated from the Wyckoff set f_4, f_5, f_6.

Fig. 5.16). The result will be an image of the scene as it would appear illuminated by light sources at both locations. This image can be estimated as

$$\hat{f}_{\text{out}} = \hat{f}(\hat{k}_L \hat{q}_L(\mathbf{x}) + \hat{k}_R \hat{q}_R(\mathbf{x})). \tag{5.4}$$

Additionally, because each of the lightvectors q_L and q_R embodies a tremendous dynamic range, any desired combination of synthetic lightvectors can be created, by applying arbitrary weights, w_L and w_R to these two lightvectors:

$$\hat{f}_{\text{out}} = \hat{f}(w_L \hat{k}_L \hat{q}_L(\mathbf{x}) + w_R \hat{k}_R \hat{q}_R(\mathbf{x})). \tag{5.5}$$

The Wyckoff principle is based on linearity properties of light. Therefore it also embodies and includes superposition properties of light. Thus we could imagine any arbitrarily high number of such lightvectors, not just two.

Consider now a number of lightvectors coming from a discrete image sensor of dimension 480 by 640 (pixels). Suppose, that the images that this sensor provides are 480 by 640 arrays, and each element of the array responds with an output that is monotonically proportional to the quantity of light falling on a particular element of the sensor. Assuming that each element of the array is a continuously varying (real) quantity, we have, after linearizing the array for each image, a point in $\mathbb{R}^{480 \times 640} = \mathbb{R}^{307,200}$.

If we take a number of pictures where only the exposure (shutter speed) is varied, we have only one degree of freedom. With an infinitesimally short shutter speed (i.e., zero exposure), all of the elements of the array will be zero, and so this image will lie at the origin of the 307,200-D space. An arbitrary picture, v_1, will define an axis of the lightvector space.

Another picture, say, v_2, will define another axis of the lightvector space. If lightvector v_1 and lightvector v_2 arise from different illumination situations (not merely different light outputs), then these lightvectors v_1 and v_2 will not necessarily be collinear. Lightvectors v_1 and v_2 will not necessarily be orthogonal either.

Suppose that lightvector v_2 arises from taking an exposure of one second under natural lighting conditions. Lightvector v_2 will land at some arbitrary point in the 307,200-D space. A picture taken with an exposure of two seconds to the same natural lighting condition will define a lightvector that lies further out along the same axis defined by the first exposure v_2. More generally, any number of images that belong to a Wyckoff set (differ only in exposure) lie along the same axis (Fig. 5.17). Thus the set v_2, v_3, v_4 denotes photoquantities associated with three pictures that differ only in exposure. These three pictures therefore define an antihomomorphic vector space, as described in Chapter 4. Similarly a picture of the same scene, with the same camera location, but taken with a flash (using a short enough exposure that the only light arriving back at the image sensor is that due to the flash), produces an image array with different numerical values. This array of different numerical values lies somewhere else in $\mathbb{R}^{307,200}$. A picture taken with more or less flash illumination lies along the same coordinate axis as the first flash picture. Thus a Wyckoff set, such as v_6, v_7, v_8, also depicted in the figure, defines a second axis.

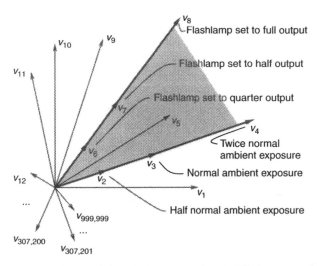

Figure 5.17 A picture sampled on a discrete 480 by 640 lattice may be regarded as a single point in $\mathbb{R}^{480 \times 640} = \mathbb{R}^{307,200}$. These lightvectors are not necessarily orthogonal, and thus there may be more than 307,200 such vectors present, depicted $v_1, v_2, \ldots, v_{999,999}$. Typically, however, the number of lightvectors is much less than the dimensionality of the space, 307,200. Some of the lightvectors are typically collinear, and the sets of collinear lightvectors are called "Wyckoff sets." A Wyckoff set formed by three pictures, differing only in exposure, is depicted as 3 collinear arrows coming out from the origin, v_2, v_3, v_4. Suppose that these three pictures were taken with no flash (just the natural light present in the scene). Suppose that another three pictures, v_6, v_7, v_8, are taken with a flash, and with such a high shutter speed that they are representative of the scene as lit by only the flash (i.e., the shutter speed is high enough to neglect contribution from the v_2, v_3, v_4 axis). These three pictures define a second Wyckoff set v_6, v_7, v_8, also depicted as three collinear arrows from the origin. The 2-D subspace formed from these two Wyckoff sets (natural light set and flash set) is depicted as a shaded gray planar region spanned by the two Wyckoff sets.

Why use more than a single pixture to define each of these axes? In particular, from just two images, such as $f_1 = v_2$ and $f_2 = v_6$, of differently illuminated subject matter, a single picture of any desired effective combination of the illuminants may be estimated:

$$\hat{f}_{12} = \hat{f}(k_1 \hat{f}^{-1}(f_1(\mathbf{x})) + k_2 \hat{f}^{-1}(f_2(\mathbf{x}))). \tag{5.6}$$

The answer is that in extreme situations we may wish to process the resulting images in lightspace, performing arithmetic that uses extended dynamic range. In such situations as noise arises, the use of multiple exposures to each lightvector is preferred to overcome the noise.

Thus the estimate is improved if we use multiple (i.e., two or three elements) of each of the two Wyckoff sets, that is, derive f_1 from the set v_2, v_3, v_4 and derive f_2 from the set v_6, v_7, v_8 as described in Chapter 4.

Because light quantities are additive, if we take a picture with a combination of natural light and flash light (i.e., if we leave the shutter open for an extended

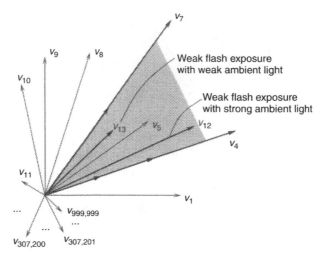

Figure 5.18 The 2-D subspace formed from various pictures, each taken with different combinations of the two light sources (natural and flash). Lightvectors denoted as bold lines exist as points in $\mathbb{R}^{307,200}$ that lie within the planar (2-D) subspace defined by these two light sources. Note that since the light intensity cannot be negative, that this subspace is confined to the portion of the plane bounded by the two pure lightvectors (natural light and flash).

period of time, and fire the flash sometime during that exposure), we obtain a point in $\mathbb{R}^{307,200}$ that lies on the plane defined by the two (natural light and flash) pure lightvectors v_2, v_3, v_4 and v_6, v_7, v_8. Various combinations of natural light with flash are depicted in this way in Figure 5.18. Enforcement of lightvectors being nonnegative can be made by introducing an arbitrary complex valued wavefunction ψ such that the lightvector is equal to $\langle \psi | \psi \rangle$.

5.6.4   "Practical" Example: 2-D Lightvector Subspace

Suppose that we take pictures of a particular static scene, with a fixed camera position (on a tripod), but vary only the lighting. Suppose that we further restrict the light sources to not change in shape, position, orientation, or color but allow them to only vary in intensity.

For the moment consider two light sources, each of adjustable intensity. The common practical example of two light sources arises when a photographer uses an on-camera flash to supplement the natural light in the scene. In our example we could vary the effective natural light intensity by adjusting the exposure time (i.e., by making one exposure for one second, and another for two seconds, we've doubled the amount of light arriving at the image sensor). We can vary the flash intensity (by its main capacitor or thyristor control). Since we have two degrees of freedom (shutter speed and flash output), we can obtain images from various linear combinations of the two light sources (Fig. 5.19).

For all practical purposes the flash duration is infinitesimally short. So, if a picture of the scene, as illuminated by only the flash, is desired, then we can obtain it by using a very short exposure (i.e., short enough that no natural light will affect

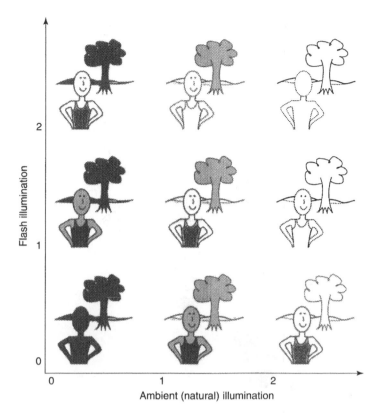

Figure 5.19 Hypothetical collection of pictures taken with different amounts of ambient (natural) light and flash. One axis denotes the quantity of natural light present (exposure), and the other denotes the quantity of flash, activated during the exposure. The flash adds to the total illumination of the scene, and affects primarily the foreground objects in the scene, while the natural light exposure affects the whole scene. These pictures form a 2-D image subspace, which may be regarded as being formed from the dimensions defined by two lightvectors. For argument's sake we might define the two lightvectors as being the image at coordinates (1, 0) and the image at (0, 1). These two images can form a basis set that may be used to generate all nine depicted here in this figure, as well as any other linear combination of the two lightvectors.

the image). However, to the extent that this might not be possible,[20] we may apply a coordinate transformation that shears the lightvector subspace. In particular, we effectively, subtract out the natural light, and obtain a "total-illumination" axis so that the images of Figure 5.19 move to new locations (Fig. 5.20) in the image space.

In Real Practice
In practice, the coordinate transformation depicted in these hypothetical situations may not be directly applied to pictures because the pictures have undergone some

---

[20] In practice, this happens with large studio flash systems because the capacitors are so big that the flash duration starts getting a little long, on the order of 1/60 second or so.

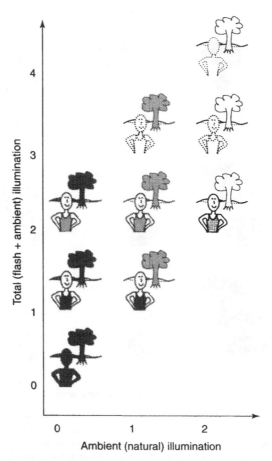

Figure 5.20 A coordinate-transformed 2-D image subspace formed from the dimensions of two lightvectors (natural light and on-camera flash). The new axes, natural light and total light, define respectively the light levels of the background and foreground objects in the scene.

unknown nonlinearity. Actual pictures typically do not represent the quantity of light falling on the image sensor, and the like, but rather represent some unknown (but typically monotonic) function of this light quantity. The human visual system is forgiving of distortion in the grayscale levels of images. Unlike sound recordings where nonlinear level distortion is objectionable, nonlinear level distortion in pictures is quite acceptable, even desirable. As was described in Chapter 4, typically pictures look better when nonlinear level distortion is applied to them, and they look particularly good when highlight details are clipped and shadow details are similarly lost. Photographers often describe images where the contrast is too low as lacking "punch" or "kick," even though they may contain more information about the scene than the pictures they have come to prefer.

What we desire therefore, for the purposes of this chapter, is a means of capturing from ordinary pictures as closely as possible the manner in which the scene responds to various light sources. We will see how this is accomplished through the process of using ordinary cameras as measuring instruments to determine, up to a single unknown scale factor, the quantity of light falling on the image sensor, due to a particular source of illumination. Even when the scene has an extremely high dynamic range (as most scenes do), we will still be able to determine the response to light.

If we only desire a nice looking picture in the end, the picture may be generated by suitable deliberate degradation and nonlinear distortion of the final measurement space, once we have done the processing in the linearized measurement space. Recall from Chapter 4 that such processing (i.e., processing on a calculated value of the quantity of light falling on the image sensor, followed by returning to a normal picture) is photoquantigraphic processing.

Equation (5.6) suggests a new form of virtual camera for retroactively synthesizing any desired quantity of exposure to flash and to natural ambient light.

Imagine now a camera that rapidly takes one or more pictures with the flash on, then rapidly takes one or more pictures without flash, so that the apparent amount of flash desired can be selected, retroactively, after the basis pictures (lightvectors) are taken.

An example of such a virtual camera in which two pictures, one taken with flash (a very short exposure so as to record primarily only that response which is due to the flash) and the other taken with natural light (over a long exposure) are combined to give the effect of a mixture of long exposure with flash, for any desired value of k_1 and k_2, is shown in Figure 5.21.

More generally, (5.6) defines a two-dimensional antihomomorphic lightvector space. The concept of the antihomomorphic lightvector space is illustrated in Figure 5.22. Furthermore it is preferable to work with multiple pictures rather than just two. Samples from the lightvector space of three differently illuminated pictures appears in Figure 5.23.

5.7 PAINTING WITH LIGHTVECTORS: PHOTOGRAPHIC/VIDEOGRAPHIC ORIGINS AND APPLICATIONS OF WEARCOMP-BASED MEDIATED REALITY

The author often used lamps such as those pictured in Figure 5.28 to walk around and illuminate different portions of subject matter, "painting in" various portions of scenes or objects. The resulting photoquantigraphic image composites, such as depicted in Figure 5.24, are at the boundary between painting, photography, and computer-generated imagery.

Using antihomomorphic vector spaces, pictures of extremely high tonal fidelity and very low noise, in all areas of the image from the darkest

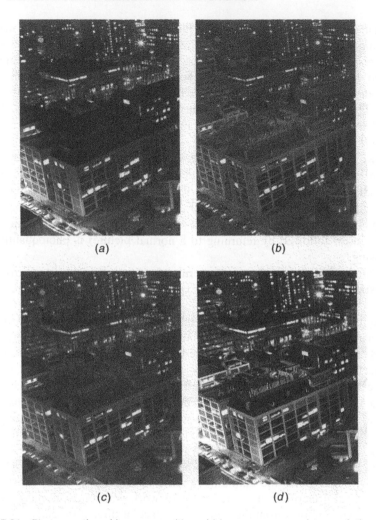

Figure 5.21 Photoquantigraphic superposition. (a) Long exposure picture of the city of Cambridge (Massachusetts). This picture of the large cityscape was taken under its natural (ambient) light. (b) Short exposure image taken with electronic flash (FT-623 flash tube operating at 4000 volts main, 30 kV trigger, and 16 kJ energy, in 30 inch highly polished chrome reflector, as shown in Fig. 5.28a) shows more detail on the rooftops of the buildings where very little of the city's various light sources are shining. Note the thin sliver of shadow to left of each building, as the flash was to the right of the camera. Notice how some portions of the picture in (a) are better represented while other portions in (b) are better. (c) Linear combination of the two images. Notice undesirable "muted" highlights. (d) Photoquantigraphic estimate provides an image with much better contrast and tonal fidelity. (©) Steve Mann, 1994.

shadows to the brightest highlights can be rendered. Many of these images are rendered from hundreds of input images, under a variety of illumination conditions. The system architecture for a large number of inputs is shown in Figure 5.25.

Two-Dimensional Lightspace (from two pictures of same scene)

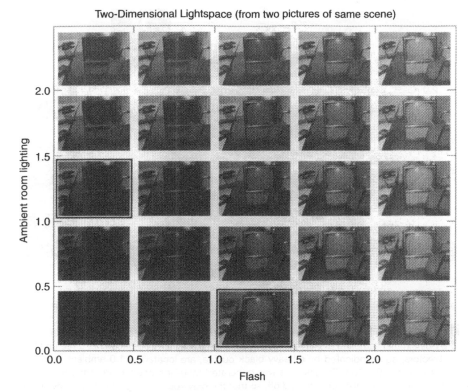

Figure 5.22 Two-dimensional antihomomorphic vector space formed from two input lightvectors (denoted by thick outlines). One lightvector represents the response of the subject matter to natural ambient light. The other lightvector represents the response of the subject matter to a flash lamp. From these two "basis" lightvectors, the response of the scene to any combination of natural ambient illumination and flash lamp can be synthesized. This two-dimensional lightvector space is a generalization of the one-dimensional lightvector synthesis that was depicted in Figure 4.5.

5.7.1 Photographic Origins of Wearable Computing and Augmented/Mediated Reality in the 1970s and 1980s

Personal imaging was originally motivated by the creation of a new genre of imaging. The idea was to create a system that could allow reality to be experienced with greater intensity and enjoyment than might otherwise be the case [1].

The effort at creating such a system also facilitated a new form of visual art called lightspace imaging (or lightspace rendering). The author chose a fixed point of view for the camera and then, once the camera was secured on a tripod, walked around and used various sources of illumination to sequentially build up an image, layer-upon-layer, in a manner analogous to paint brushed on canvas. Two early 1980s attempts, by the author, at creating expressive images using the personal imaging system developed by the author in the 1970s and early 1980s

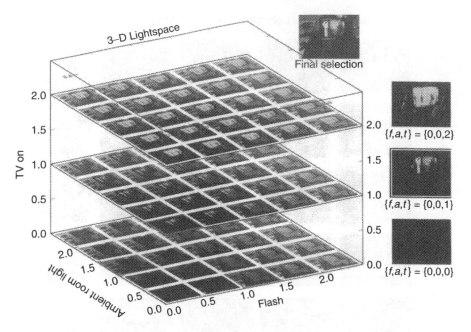

Figure 5.23 A 3-D antihomomorphic lightvector space. Each of the 75 pictures corresponds to a point in this sampling of the lightvector space on a 3 by 5 by 5 lattice. The three unit basis lightvectors, again indicated by a heavy black outline, are located at 1.0 ambient room light, 1.0 flash, and 1.0 TV on. The last axis was generated by taking one picture with no flash, and also with the lamp in the room turned off, so that the only source of light was the television set itself. The new axis (TV on) is depicted by itself to the right of this 3-D space, where there are three points along this axis. The origin at the bottom is all black, while the middle picture is the unit (input image) lightvector, and the top image is synthesized by calculating $f(2q_2)$, where $q_2(x, y)$ is the quantity of light falling on the image sensor due to the television set being turned on. Near the top of the figure, the final selection is indicated, which is the picture selected according to personal taste, from among all possible points in this 3-D lightvector space.

are depicted in Figure 5.26. Throughout the 1980s a small number of other artists also used the author's apparatus to create various lightvector paintings. However, due to the cumbersome nature of the early WearComp hardware, and to the fact that much of the apparatus was custom fit to the author, it was not widely used, over any extended periods of time, by others. However, the personal imaging system proved to be a new and useful invention for a variety of photographic imaging tasks.

To the extent that the artist's light sources were made far more powerful than the natural ambient light levels, the artist had a tremendous degree of control over the illumination in the scene. The resulting image was therefore a depiction of what was actually present in the scene, together with a potentially visually rich illumination sculpture surrounding it. Typically the illumination sources that the artist carried were powered by batteries. (Gasoline-powered light sources were found to be unsuitable in many environments such as indoor spaces where noise, exhaust, etc., were undesirable.) Therefore, owing to limitations on the output

Figure 5.24 Output of antihomomorphic lightvector image processing. This picture was mathematically generated from a number of differently illuminated pictures of the same subject matter, in which the subject matter was illuminated by walking around with a bank of flash lamps controlled by a wearable computer system in wireless communication with another computer controlling a camera at a fixed base station. (©) Steve Mann, 1985 .

capabilities of these light sources, the art was practiced in spaces that could be darkened sufficiently or, in the case of outdoor scenes, at times when the natural light levels were lowest.

In a typical application the user positioned the camera on a hillside, or the roof of a building, overlooking a city. Usually an assistant oversaw the operation of the camera. The user would roam about the city, walking down various streets, and use the light sources to illuminate buildings one at a time. Typically, for the wearable or portable light sources be of sufficient strength compared to the natural light in the scene (so that it was not necessary to shut off the electricity to the entire city to darken it sufficiently that the artist's light source be of greater relative brightness), some form of electronic flash is used as the light source. In some embodiments of the personal imaging invention, an FT-623 lamp (the most powerful lamp in the world, with output of 40 kJ, and housed in a lightweight 30 inch highly polished reflector, with a handle that allowed it to be easily held in one hand and aimed as shown in Figure 5.28a), was used to illuminate various buildings such as tall skyscrapers throughout a city. The viewfinder on the helmet displayed material from a remotely mounted camera with computer-generated text and graphics overlaid in the context of a collaborative telepresence environment. The assistant at the remote site wore a similar apparatus with a similar body-worn backpack-based processing system.

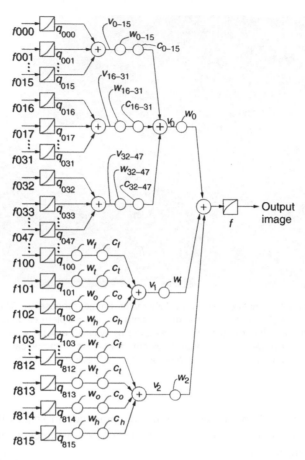

Figure 5.25 Antihomomorphic vector spaces. Arbitrarily many (typically 1000 or more) differently exposed images of the same subject matter are captured by a single camera. Typically pictures are signal averaged in sets of 16 for each of three exposures to obtain a background (ambient) illumination estimate $\hat{q}_q$. These lightvectors are denoted q_{000} through q_{047}. After applying appropriate weights and certainty functions, the computer calculates the ambient illumination lightvector v_0. Then, using the apparatus depicted in Figure 5.28, exposures are made in sets of four (four lamps, two lamps, one lamp, half). These give rise to estimates of q_{100} through q_{103}, and so on. After weighting and application of certainty functions, lightvector v_1 is calculated as the response of the subject matter to this source of illumination. The wearer of the computer system then moves to a new location and exposes the subject matter to another rapid burst of four flashes of light, producing an estimate of the subject matter's response to lightvector v_2. The lightvectors are then added, and the output image is calculated as $f(v_0 + v_1 + v_2 + \ldots)$.

5.7.2 Lightvector Amplification

The communications infrastructure was established such that the camera was only sensitive to light for a short time period (typically approximately 1/500 of a second), during the instant that the flash lamp produced light.

(a)   (b)

Figure 5.26 The camera used as a sketch pad or artist's canvas. A goal of personal imaging [1] is to create something more than the camera in its usual context. The images produced as artifacts of Personal Imaging are somewhere at the intersection of painting, computer graphics, and photography. (a) Notice how the broom appears to be its own light source (e.g. self-illuminated), while the open doorway appears to contain a light source emanating from within. The rich tonal range and details of the door itself, although only visible at a grazing viewing angle, are indicative of the affordances of the Lightspace Rendering [92,93] method. (b) hallways offer a unique perspective, which can also be illuminated expressively. (C) Steve Mann, sometime in the mid-1980s.

In using the personal imaging invention to selectively and sequentially illuminate portions of a scene or object, the user typically pointed the source at some object in the scene in front of the camera, and issued a command through the wearable computer system. A simplified diagram of the architecture is provided in Figure 5.27. The receiver at the camera is embodied in a communications protocol, which in newer embodiments of the invention runs over amateur packet radio, using a terminal node controller in KISS mode (TCP/IP). In the simple example illustrated here, the RECEIVER activates shutter solenoid S; what is depicted in this drawing is approximately typical of a 1940s press camera fitted with the standard 6 volt solenoid shutter release. Presently there are no moving parts in the camera, and the shutter is implemented electronically. The camera was sometimes designed so that it provided a sync signal in advance of becoming sensitive to light. This way pulse compression was used for the synchronization signal.

The wearable computer is mostly contained in a heavy black jacket. The artist typically wears black pants with the jacket and holds the light source with a black glove, as shown in Figure 5.27a. The black attire is not necessary, of course. Additionally, the housing of the lamp head is often painted a flat black color.

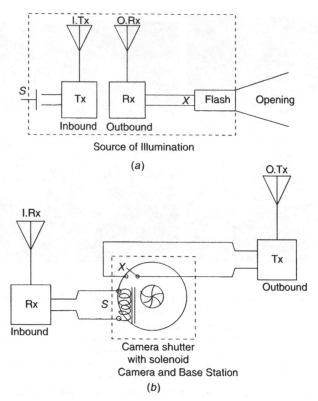

Figure 5.27 Artist's "paintbrush" for computer-supported collaborative photography. The artist issues commands to a remote camera using a data entry device while monitoring the resulting pictures and overlaid text + graphics on a head-mounted display. Here a simplified diagram is used to illustrate signal routing. (a) When the artist issues a command by switch closures (S), a signal is sent through an inbound communications channel, depicted as INBOUND transmitter Tx, to the central base station (b) and is received by the inbound receiver, denoted INBOUND Rx. This initiates frame capture (depicted by solenoid S) with a computer system located at the base station. At the correct instant during frame capture, a signal (depicted by flash sync contacts X) is sent back by the camera's outbound transmit channel depicted OUTBOUND Tx, to the artist (a) and received by the artist's light source synchronization receiver, depicted OUTBOUND Rx. This activates FLASH through its synchronization contacts denoted X. Light then emerges through the OPENING and illuminates the scene at the exact instant during which the camera's sensor array is sensitive to light. A short time later, the image from the camera base station (b) is sent via the OUTBOUND channel to the artist (a) and is displayed on the artist's head-mounted display, overlaid with a calculated summation of previous differently illuminated images of the same scene and appropriate graphics for manipulation of the summation coefficients.

A comparatively small lamp (small since the lamp and housing must be held in one hand) can illuminate a tall skyscraper or an office tower and yet appear, in the final image, to be the dominant light source, compared to interior fluorescent lights that are left turned on in a multistory building, or compared to moonlight or the light from streetlamps.

The artist's wearable computer system comprises a visual display that is capable of displaying the image from the camera (sent wirelessly over a data communications link from the computer that controls the camera). This display is updated with each new exposure. The wearable computer is often controlled by the artist through a chording keyboard mounted into the handle of the light source so that he does not need to carry a separate keyboard. This way, whatever light source the artist plugs into the body-worn system becomes the device for controlling the process.

In the early days the author experimented with a graphics-enabled computer system and power source that could be worn. He would walk through the city streets after dark, illuminating various buildings with powerful yet portable hand-held arrays of flash lamps. These systems, with proper signal processing, allowed the author to light up entire cities, or to capture other large urban structures such as the Brooklyn Bridge in a new and expressive light. The wearable photographic system turns the body into a measurement apparatus that collects data on how the subject responds to light. This process of creating visual art in a computer-mediated reality environment becomes a collaborative process in which one person (in this case, the author) can walk around and illuminate the picture subjects in various ways (see Fig. 5.28) while being in wireless communication with at least one other person operating a fixed base station (see Fig. 5.29). Each time the roaming member moves to a new location to take aim to light up subject, a new light vector is generated using the dataset from that particular lamp location and lamp orientation. Each such lightvector provides a description of how the subject responds to light from that particular location. Each lightvector is like a brushstroke of a painting; it is the collection of a large number of such lightvectors that makes up the completed lightvector painting.

Some examples of lightvector images from a lightvector painting of Times Square are shown in Figure 5.30. Another example of a lightvector painting is shown in Figure 6.31. Typically the exposures are maintained as separate image files overlaid on the artist's screen (head-mounted display) by the current view through the camera. The separate image files allow the artist to selectively delete the most recent exposure, or any of the other exposures previously combined into the running "sum" on the head-mounted display ("sum" is used in quotes here because the actual law of composition is the photoquantigraphic summation depicted in Fig 5.16). Additional graphic information is also overlaid to assist the artist in the choice of weighting for manipulation of this "sum." This capability makes this a more facile process than painting on canvas, where one must paint over mistakes rather than simply remove brushstrokes or adjust the intensity of brushstrokes after they are made. Furthermore exposures to light can be adjusted during the shooting or afterward, and then recombined. The capability of doing this during the shooting is an important aspect of the personal imaging invention, because it allows the artist to capture additional exposures if necessary, and thus to remain at the site until a desired picture is produced. The final picture as well as the underlying dataset of separately adjustable exposures can be sent wirelessly

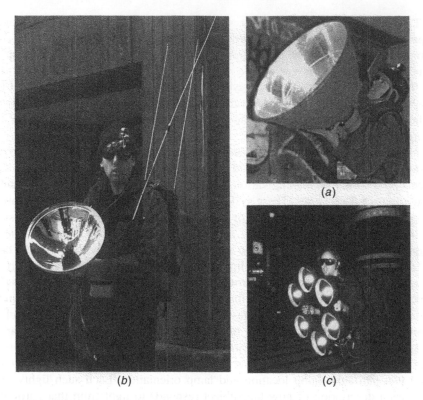

Figure 5.28 Early cybernetic photography systems for painting with lightvectors. A powerful handheld and wearable photographic lighting studio system with wearable multimedia computer is used to illuminate various subjects at different locations in space. The portable nature of the apparatus allows the wearer to move around and collaborate in a computer-mediated space. (a) A backpack-based wearable computer system that was completed in 1981 was used in conjunction with a 40 kJ flash lamp in a 30 inch (762 mm) reflector. (b) A jacket-based computer system that was completed in the summer of 1985 and used in conjunction with a 2.4 kJ flash lamp in a 14 inch (356 mm) reflector. Three separate long communications antennas are visible, two from the backpack and one from the jacket-based computer. (c) The backpack-based rig used to light up various skyscrapers in Times Square produces approximately 12 kJ of light into six separate lamp housings, providing better energy localization in each lamp, and giving a 100 ISO Guide Number of about 2000. The two antennae on the author's eyeglasses wirelessly link the eyeglasses to the base station shown in Figure 5.29.

to other sites when other collaborators like art directors must be involved in manipulating and combining the exposures and sending their comments to the artist by email, or in overlaying graphics onto the artist's head-mounted display, which then becomes a collaborative space. In the most recent embodiments of the 1990s this was facilitated through the World Wide Web. The additional communication facilitates the collection of additional exposures if it turns out that certain areas of the scene or object could be better served if they were more accurately described in the dataset.

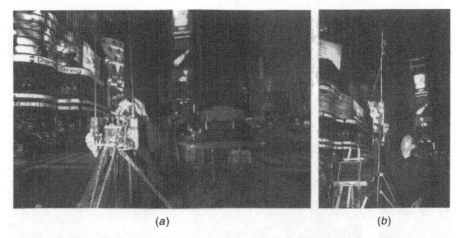

(a)   (b)

Figure 5.29 Setting up the base station in Times Square. (a) A portable graphics computer and image capture camera are set up on a tripod, from the base station (facing approximately south–southwest: Broadway is to the left; Seventh Avenue is to the right) with antennas for wireless communication to the wearable graphics processor and portable rig. Various other apparatus are visible on the table to the right of and behind the imager tripod. (b) One of the items on the table is an additional antenna stand. To the left of the antenna stand (on the easel) is a television that displays the "lightvector painting" as it is being generated. This television allows the person operating the base station to see the output of the author's wearable graphics processor while the author is walking through Times Square illuminating various skyscrapers with the handheld flash lamp.

5.7.3 Lightstrokes and Lightvectors

Each of a collection of differently illuminated exposures of the same scene or object is called a lightstroke. In personal imaging, a lightstroke is analogous to an artist's brushstroke, and it is the plurality of lightstrokes that are combined together that give the invention described here its unique ability to capture the way that a scene or object responds to various forms of light. From each exposure, an estimate can be made of the quantity of light falling on the image sensor, by applying the inverse transfer function of the camera. Such an estimate is called a lightvector [92].

Furthermore, a particular lightstroke may be repeated (i.e., the same exposure may be repeated in almost the same way, holding the light in the same position, each time a new lightstroke is acquired). The seemingly identical lightstrokes may collectively be used to obtain a better estimate of a lightvector, by averaging each lightvector together to obtain a single lightvector of improved signal-to-noise ratio. This signal-averaging technique may also be generalized to the extent that the lamp may be activated at various strengths, but otherwise held in the same position and pointed in the same direction at the scene. The result is to produce a lightvector that captures a broad dynamic range by using separate images that differ only in exposure level [59,63,77], and thus to apply the methodology described in Chapter 4 (the Wyckoff principle).

Figure 5.30 Lightvector paintings of Times Square. (a) Author illuminated the foreground in a single exposure. (b) Author illuminated some of the skyscrapers to the left in five exposures. (c) Author illuminated the central tower with the huge screen Panasonic television in three exposures. The six lamp rig puts out enough light to overpower the bright lights of Times Square, and becomes the dominant source of light in the lightvector painting. (d) Author illuminated the skyscrapers to the right in six exposures. (e) Author generated the final lightvector painting from approximately one hundred such exposures (lightvectors) while interactively adjusting their coefficients.

Figure 5.31 Lightvector paintings of the Brooklyn Bridge. (*a*) Natural ambient light captured in a single exposure. (*b*) The first tower of the bridge captured in 4 exposures to electronic flash. (*c*) The cabling of the bridge captured in 10 exposures. (*d*) Foreground to convey a dynamic sense of activity on the busy footpath walkway and bicycle route along the bridge, captured in 22 exposures. (*e*) Linear image processing (signal averaging). Note the muted highlights (areas of the image that are clipped at a gray value less than the dynamic range of the output medium), which cannot be fixed simply by histogram stretching. Linear signal processing (signal averaging) fails to create a natural-looking lightvector summation. (*f*) Antihomomorphic image processing using the methodology proposed in this chapter. Note the natural-looking bright highlights.

5.7.4 Other Practical Issues of Painting with Lightvectors

Another aspect of the invention is that the photographer does not need to work in total darkness as is typically the case with ordinary lightpainting. With an electronic flash, and even with a mechanical shutter (as is used with photographic film), the shutter is open for only about 1/500 for each "lightstroke." Thus the lightpainting can be done under normal lighting conditions (e.g., the room lights may often be left on). This aspect of the invention pertains to both traditional lightpainting (where the invention allows multiple flash-synched exposures to be made on the same piece of film, as well as to the use of separate recording media (separate film frames, electronic image captures etc.,) for each lightstroke. The invention makes use of innovative communications protocols and a user-interface that maintain the illusion that the system is immune to ambient light, while requiring no new skills beyond that of traditional lightpainting. The communications protocols typically include a full-duplex radio communications link so that a button on the flash sends a signal to the camera to make the shutter open, and at the same time, a radio wired to the flash sync contacts of the camera is already "listening" for when the shutter opens. The fact that the button is right on the flash gives the user the illusion that he or she is just pushing the lamp test button of a flash as in normal lightpainting, and the fact that there is really any communications link at all is hidden by this ergonomic user interface.

The invention also includes a variety of options for making the lightpainting task easier and more controlled. These innovations include such means as the photographer to determine if he or she can be "seen" by the camera (e.g., indicates extent of camera's coverage), various compositional aids, means of providing workspace-illumination that has no effect on the picture, and some innovative light sources.

5.7.5 Computer-Supported Collaborative Art (CSCA)

It may, at times, be desirable to have a real or virtual assistant at the camera to direct or advise the artist. In this case the artist's viewfinder, which presents an image from the perspective of the fixed camera, also affords the artist a view of what the assistant sees. Similarly it is advantageous at times that the assistant have a view from the perspective of the artist. To accomplish this, the artist has a second camera of a wearable form. Through this second camera, the artist allows the assistant to observe the scene from the artist's perspective. Thus the artist and assistant can collaborate by exchange of viewpoints, as if each had the eyes of the other. (Such a form of collaboration based on exchanged viewpoint is called seeing eye to eye [17].) Moreover through the use of shared cursors overlaid on this exchanged viewpoint, a useful form of computer supported collaborative photography has resulted.

The artist's camera is sometimes alternatively attached to and integrated with the light source (e.g., flash) in such a way that it provides a preview of the coverage of the flash. When this camera output is sent to the artist's own wearable computer screen, a flash viewfinder results. The flash viewfinder allows the artist to aim the flash, and allows the artist to see what is included within the cone of light that the flash will produce. Furthermore, when viewpoints are exchanged, the assistant at the main camera can see what the flash is pointed at prior to activation of the flash.

Typically there is a command that may be entered to switch between local mode (where the artist sees the flash viewfinder) and exchanged mode (where the artist sees out through the main camera and the assistant at the main camera sees out through the artist's eyes/flash viewfinder).

The personal imaging systems were used over a period of many years, for the production of visual art of this genre. Within the course context, this method was taught recently to a 1998 class (Fig. 5.32). Here students shared a common but altered perception of reality. All participants share the same perception of a visual reality that any one of the participants can alter.

5.8 COLLABORATIVE MEDIATED REALITY FIELD TRIALS

Typically the artist's wearable computer system comprises a visual display that is capable of displaying the image from the base station camera (typically sent wirelessly over a 2 megabit per second data communications link from the computer that controls the camera). Typically also this display is updated with each new lightstroke (exposure).

A number of participants may each carry a light source and point it to shoot at objects in the scene (or at each other), while having the effect of the light source persist in the mediated reality space even after the light source has finished producing light.

The display update is typically switchable between a mode that shows only the new exposure, and a cumulative mode that shows a photoquantigraphic summation over time that includes the new exposure photoquantigraphically added to previous exposures. This temporally cumulative display makes the device useful to the artist because it helps in the envisioning of a completed lightmodule painting.

5.8.1 Lightpaintball

The temporally cumulative display is useful in certain applications of the apparatus to gaming. For example, a game can be devised in which two players compete against each other. One player may try to paint the subject matter before the camera red, and the other will try to paint the subject matter blue. When the subject matter is an entire cityscape as seen from a camera located on the roof of a tall building, the game can be quite competitive and interesting. Additionally players can work either cooperatively on the same team or competitively, as when two teams each try to paint the city a different color, and "claim" territory with their color.

In some embodiments of the game the players can also shoot at each other with the flashguns. For example, if a player from the red team "paints" a blue-team photoborg red, he may disable or "kill" the blue-team photoborg, shutting

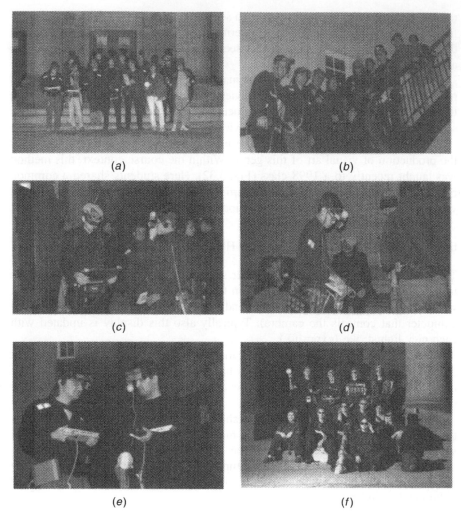

Figure 5.32 Mediated reality field trials. Each participant has the opportunity to aim various light sources at real subject matter in the scene. Within the "painting with lightvectors" paradigm, each lightvector alters the visual perception of reality for the entire group. All participants share a common perception of reality that any one of the participants can alter. (a) A series of field trials in 1998 demonstrated the capabilities of mediated reality for WearComp-supported collaboration. (b) The field trial takes place both indoors as well as outdoors, in a wide variety of settings. In collecting image data, the subject matter is illuminated inside and out. (c) Instruction and training is provided in real use scenarios. (d) Students learn how to program the apparatus in the field, and thus learn the importance of advance preparation (e.g. learning how to deal with typical problems that require debugging in the field). (e) Students collaborate and help each other with various unexpected problems that might arise. (f) In subsequent years field trials may be repeated, applying what was learned from previous years. Note the increased proportion of eyeglass-based rigs, and covert rigs.

down his flashgun. In other embodiments, the "kill" and "shoot" aspects can be removed, in which case the game is similar to a game like squash where the opponents work in a collegial fashion, getting out of each other's way while each side takes turns shooting. The red-team flashgun(s) and blue-team flashgun(s) can be fired alternately by a free-running base-station camera, or they can all fire together. When they fire alternately there is no problem disambiguating them. When they fire together, there is preferably a blue filter over each of the flashguns of the blue team, and a red filter over each of the flashguns of the red team, so that flashes of light from each team can be disambiguated in the same machine cycle.

5.8.2 Reality-Based EyeTap Video Games

A variety of different kinds of reality based EyeTap video games are possible, especially with real-time hardware implementations of the lightvector processing engine.

5.9 CONCLUSIONS

A new kind of imaging based on a wearable illumination system with an illumination rendering computer was described. Lightvector interpolation and extrapolation methods were included. These lightvector interpolations and extrapolations form the basis for the wearer being able to adjust the coefficients of any of the lightvectors in the scene.

The concept of antihomomorphic vector spaces was introduced within the context of linearity and superposition properties of light, for the synthesis and processing of differently illuminated images.

5.10 EXERCISES, PROBLEM SETS, AND HOMEWORK

5.10.1 Photoquantigraphic Image Processing

Consider two pictures that differ only in lighting. Use, for example, images from the `http://wearcam.org/ece1766/pnmpwadd/index.html` or `http://wearcam.org/ece1766/lightspace/` directories. A good choice is the image pair:

1. `day.jpg` (or take instead daysmall.jpg initially for debugging, since it will use less processing power), which was taken Nov 7 15:36, at f/2.8 for 1/125 s; and

2. `night.jpg` (or `nightsmall.jpg`) which was taken Nov 7 17:53, f/2.8 for 1/4 s.

The object is to combine these pictures and arrive at a single picture that renders the scene as it might have appeared if the sensor had responded to both sources of illumination (daytime natural light plus night-time building lights).

Begin by adding the two pictures together. You might do this with the GNU Image Manipulation Program (GIMP) by loading one image, say "gimp day.jpg," and then clicking on "open" to obtain a second image, say "night.jpg," in the same session of gimp. Then you can press control A in one window (to select all), then control C (to cut), and then control V to paste into the other window on top of the "day.jpg" image. Now the two images will appear as two layers in the same window. You can adjust the "transparency" of the top layer to about 50% and flatten the result to a single image to save it.

Alternatively, you could write a simple program to operate on two image arrays. Use a simple for-next loop through all pixels, and scale each total back down. [Hint: Since pixels go from 0 to 255, the total will go from 0 to 510, so you need to scale back down by a factor of 255/510.]

Whether you use the gimp or write your own program, describe the picture that results from adding the day.jpg and night.jpg images together.

5.10.2 Lightspace Processing

Now add the quantities of light arriving at the sensor array due to each picture. Then render a picture that would have resulted from this total quantity of light. Note how adding lightspaces of the pictures is different than just adding the pictures. You can do this by converting to lightspace, adding, and then converting back to imagespace.

Assume that the camera reports $f(q) = q^{0.45}$. [Hint: Compute the quantity of light falling on the image sensor due to the daytime natural light as $q_1 = f_1^{2.22}$, where f_1 is the first image, and the quantity of light falling on the image sensor due to the building lights at night as $q_2 = f_2^{2.22}$, where f_2 is the second image.] After computing the total, $q_1 + q_2$, compute the image $f(q_1 + q_2)$ that would have resulted from both light sources being on at the same time. Be sure to clip values that are greater than 255 to be equal to 255 before casting to unsigned character at the output.

Alternatively, you could find the Computer-Enhanced Multiple Exposure Technique (CEMENT) programs useful.

5.10.3 Varying the Weights

Consider the two pictures of Problem 5.10.1. Experiment with different weightings, by rendering $f((aq_1 + bq_2)/(a + b))$, as well as $\min(f(aq_1 + bq_2), 255)$. For example, the image $f((q1 + 8q2)/(1 + 8))$ is illustrated in day_125w1_night_4w8.jpg (small version is in day_125w1_night_4w8small.jpg) in the same WWW directory.

This image has a very similar appearance to an image that was actually taken Nov 9 at 17:12 while there was still a good amount of light left in the sky, but after the exterior building lights came on: dusk.jpg (small version in dusks.jpg).

Describe the difference you observe between adding the images and adding the lightspace, that is, in doing the addition operation in lightspace rather than imagespace.

The following program may be useful for these exercises: `http://wearcam.org/ece1766/pnmpwadd/pnmpwadd.c`, where this program assumes the images are of type ppm. So you will want to convert the jpeg programs to ppm, using, for example, djpeg.

Alternatively, you could use the entire set of CEMENT programs: `http://wearcam.org/cement` which will work for jpeg, pnm, or gzipped pnm files.

5.10.4 Linearly Adding Lightvectors is the Wrong Thing to Do

Using images you obtained from your own dusting or some of the stock lightvectors from last year, which may be found in `http://www.wearcam.org/ece1766/lightspace/dusting/` or from among other datasets in `http://wearcam.org/dusting/`, add various combinations of the images and describe the result for cases where the light sources do not overlap, and for cases where the light sources do overlap (i.e., the same pixel coordinates in more than one image are illuminated by the light sources associated with each of these images). Despite the fact that much of the image-processing literature is based on linear image processing, why is linear image processing the wrong thing to do?

5.10.5 Photoquantigraphically Adding Lightvectors

Combine the same images photoquantigraphically (i.e., in lightspace instead of image space), just as you did in the day + night picture of last assignment. Describe the differences between:

- adding multiple differently illuminated images, and
- adding their lightspaces and then converting back to image space.

5.10.6 CEMENT

Experiment with different weightings for rendering different light sources with different intensity. Arrive at a selected set of weights that provides what you feel is the most expressive image. This is an artistic choice that could be exhibited as a class project (i.e., an image or images from each participant in the class). Your image should be 2048 pixels down by 3072 pixels across, and ppm or jpeg compressed with at least jpeg quality 90.

A convenient way of experimenting with the lightvectors in this directory is to use the "cementinit," "cementi," etc., programs called by the "trowel.pl" script. These programs should be installed as `/usr/local/bin/trowel` on systems used in teaching this course.

A program such as "cementi" (cement in) typically takes one double (type P8) image and cements in one uchar (P6) image. First, you need to decide what lightvector will be the starting image into which others will be cemented. Suppose that we select "day.jpg" as the basis.

1. Convert "day.jpg" to ppm, as follows:

```
djpeg day.jpg > day.ppm
```

2. Verify this is a valid ppm file by looking at the beginning:

```
head day.ppm | less
you should see
P6
3072 2048
255
...
```

3. Convert it to pdm (portable doubleprecision map), as follows:

```
pnmuchar2doubleday.ppm -o day.pdm
```

Verify that this is a valid pdm file by looking at the beginning:

```
head day.pdm | less
you should see
P8
3072 2048
255
...
```

You may want to work with smaller images, for example, using pnmscale -xsize 640 -ysize 480 .... Alternatively, you could convert it to plm (portable lightspace map), as follows:

```
pnm2plm day.ppm -o day.plm
```

Next verify that this is a valid plm file by looking at the beginning:

```
head day.pdm | less
you should see
PA
3072 2048
255
...
```

You could also use the program "cementinit" to convert directly from pnm to plm and introduce an RGB weight as part of the conversion process.

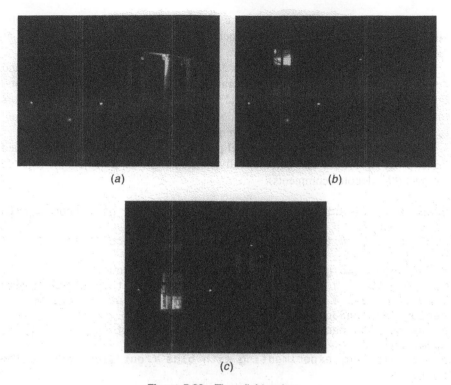

(a)   (b)

(c)

Figure 5.33   Three lightvectors.

Figure 5.34   Result of cementing these three lightvectors together.

Now try

```
gcc pnmcement_nocolour.c -lm -o pnmcement_nocolour
pnmcement_nocolour day.pdm vO35.pdm > total35.pdm
```

Observe and describe the result. To view the image, you need to convert it back
to uchar: pnmdouble2uchar total35.pdm -o total35.ppm and then use a program
like gimp or xv to view it: pnmcement_nocolor is missing the color weightings.

Another program called pnmcement.c has the color weightings. Alternatively, you could use the program "cementi" which should be installed as /usr/local/bin/cementi on systems used in this course.

Try pnmcement day.pdm v035.pdm .9 .7 .1 > total35.pdm, and observe and describe the resulting image. Try several different weightings and lightvectors. For example, once you have the total35.pdm file, cement other lightvectors into that file: pnmcement total35.pdm v030.ppm > total.pdm. Try cementing in several lightvectors with different weights and describe the result.

You could use the perl script trowel.pl, which reads an ascii text file called "cement.txt" and does this automatically. An example of a cement.txt text file follows ("#" denotes comments):

```
v035 .9 .8 .1 # that gives a very nice yellow glow from within
lower window
v030 .9 .5 0  # that brings out nice appearance at top of
window
# the above two give a good sense of the window
v025 0 0 .9   # ***great*** for top part of the second column
v029 .7 0 .8  # ***great*** for mid part of second column;
really cool shadow
# the magenta backlight above is unnatural but looks really
hyperreal
# i'll also try experimenting with blue front light and yellow
backlight
...
```

The "trowel.pl" script is a convenient wrapper that lets you cement together pnm images and jpeg images with a cement.txt file. It should be installed as /usr/local/bin/trowel.

Three lightvectors, as shown in Figure 5.33, were combined using CEMENT, and the result is shown in Figure 5.34.

There is a tendency for students to come up with interesting images but to forget to save the cement.txt file that produced them. For every image you generate *always save the CEMENT file that made it* (e.g., cement.txt). That way you can reproduce or modify it slightly. The CEMENT file is like the source code, and the image is like the executable. Don't save the image unless you also save the source cement.txt.

6

VIDEOORBITS: THE PROJECTIVE GEOMETRY RENAISSANCE

In the early days of personal imaging, a specific location was selected from which a measurement space or the like was constructed. From this single vantage point, a collection of differently illuminated/exposed images was constructed using the wearable computer and associated illumination apparatus. However, this approach was often facilitated by transmitting images from a specific location (base station) back to the wearable computer, and vice versa. Thus, when the author developed the eyeglass-based computer display/camera system, it was natural to exchange viewpoints with another person (i.e., the person operating the base station). This mode of operation ("seeing eye-to-eye") made the notion of perspective a critical factor, with projective geometry at the heart of personal imaging.

Personal imaging situates the camera such that it provides a unique first-person perspective. In the case of the eyeglass-mounted camera, the machine captures the world from the same perspective as its host (human).

In this chapter we will consider results of a new algorithm of projective geometry invented for such applications as "painting" environmental maps by looking around, wearable tetherless computer-mediated reality, the new genre of personal documentary that arises from this mediated reality, and the creation of a collective adiabatic intelligence arising from shared mediated-reality environments.

6.1 VIDEOORBITS

Direct featureless methods are presented for estimating the 8 parameters of an "exact" projective (homographic) coordinate transformation to register pairs of images, together with the application of seamlessly combining a plurality of images of the same scene. The result is a single image (or new image sequence)

233

of greater resolution or spatial extent. The approach is "exact" for two cases of static scenes: (1) images taken from the same location of an arbitrary 3-D scene, with a camera that is free to pan, tilt, rotate about its optical axis, and zoom and (2) images of a flat scene taken from arbitrary locations. The featureless projective approach generalizes interframe camera motion estimation methods that have previously used an *affine* model (which lacks the degrees of freedom to "exactly" characterize such phenomena as camera pan and tilt) and/or that have relied upon finding points of correspondence between the image frames. The featureless projective approach, which operates directly on the image pixels, is shown to be superior in accuracy and ability to enhance resolution. The proposed methods work well on image data collected from both good-quality and poor-quality video under a wide variety of conditions (sunny, cloudy, day, night). These new fully automatic methods are also shown to be robust to deviations from the assumptions of static scene and to exhibit no parallax.

Many problems require finding the coordinate transformation between two images of the same scene or object. In order to recover camera motion between video frames, to stabilize video images, to relate or recognize photographs taken from two different cameras, to compute depth within a 3-D scene, or for image registration and resolution enhancement, it is important to have a precise description of the coordinate transformation between a pair of images or video frames and some indication as to its accuracy.

Traditional *block matching* (as used in *motion estimation*) is really a special case of a more general *coordinate transformation*. In this chapter a new solution to the *motion estimation* problem is demonstrated, using a more general estimation of a coordinate transformation, and techniques for automatically finding the 8-parameter projective coordinate transformation that relates two frames taken of the same static scene are proposed. It is shown, both by theory and example, how the new approach is more accurate and robust than previous approaches that relied upon affine coordinate transformations, approximations to projective coordinate transformations, and/or the finding of point correspondences between the images. The new techniques take as input two frames, and automatically output the 8 parameters of the "exact" model, to properly register the frames. They do not require the tracking or correspondence of explicit features, yet they are computationally easy to implement.

Although the theory presented makes the typical assumptions of static scene and no parallax, It is shown that the new estimation techniques are robust to deviations from these assumptions. In particular, a direct featureless projective parameter estimation approach to image resolution enhancement and compositing is applied, and its success on a variety of practical and difficult cases, including some that violate the nonparallax and static scene assumptions, is illustrated.

An example image composite, made with featureless projective parameter estimation, is reproduced in Figure 6.1 where the spatial extent of the image is increased by panning the camera while compositing (e.g., by making a *panorama*), and the spatial resolution is increased by zooming the camera and by combining overlapping frames from different viewpoints.

Figure 6.1 Image composite made from three image regions (author moving between two different locations) in a large room: one image taken looking straight ahead (outlined in a solid line); one image taken panning to the left (outlined in a dashed line); one image taken panning to the right with substantial zoom-in (outlined in a dot-dash line). The second two have undergone a coordinate transformation to put them into the same coordinates as the first outlined in a solid line (the *reference frame*). This composite, made from NTSC-resolution images, occupies about 2000 pixels across and shows good detail down to the pixel level. Note the increased sharpness in regions visited by the zooming-in, compared to other areas. (See magnified portions of composite at the sides.) This composite only shows the result of combining three images, but in the final production, many more images can be used, resulting in a high-resolution full-color composite showing most of the large room. (Figure reproduced from [63], courtesy of IS&T.)

6.2 BACKGROUND

Hundreds of papers have been published on the problems of motion estimation and frame alignment (for review and comparison, see [94]). In this section the basic differences between coordinate transformations is reviewed and the importance of using the "exact" 8-parameter projective coordinate transformation is emphasized.

6.2.1 Coordinate Transformations

A coordinate transformation maps the image coordinates, $\mathbf{x} = [x,\ y]^T$ to a new set of coordinates, $\mathbf{x}' = [x',\ y']^T$. The approach to "finding the coordinate transformation" depends on assuming it will take one of the forms in Table 6.1, and then estimating the parameters (2 to 12 parameters depending on the model) in the chosen form. An illustration showing the effects possible with each of these forms is shown in Figure 6.3.

A common assumption (especially in motion estimation for coding, and optical flow for computer vision) is that the coordinate transformation between frames is translation. Tekalp, Ozkan, and Sezan [95] have applied this assumption to high-resolution image reconstruction. Although translation is the least constraining and simplest to implement of the seven coordinate transformations in Table 6.1, it is poor at handling large changes due to camera zoom, rotation, pan, and tilt.

Zheng and Chellappa [96] considered the image registration problem using a subset of the affine model — translation, rotation, and scale. Other researchers

Table 6.1   Image Coordinate Transformations

Model	Coordinate Transformation from $\mathbf{x}$ to $\mathbf{x}'$	Parameters
Translation	$\mathbf{x}' = \mathbf{x} + \mathbf{b}$	$\mathbf{b} \in \mathbb{R}^2$
Affine	$\mathbf{x}' = \mathbf{A}\mathbf{x} + \mathbf{b}$	$\mathbf{A} \in \mathbb{R}^{2\times2}, \mathbf{b} \in \mathbb{R}^2$
Bilinear	$x' = q_{x'xy}xy + q_{x'x}x + q_{x'y}y + q_{x'}$ $y' = q_{y'xy}xy + q_{y'x}x + q_{y'y}y + q_{y'}$	$q_* \in \mathbb{R}$
Projective	$\mathbf{x}' = \dfrac{\mathbf{A}\mathbf{x} + \mathbf{b}}{\mathbf{c}^T\mathbf{x} + 1}$	$\mathbf{A} \in \mathbb{R}^{2\times2}, \mathbf{b}, \mathbf{c} \in \mathbb{R}^2$
Relative-projective	$\mathbf{x}' = \dfrac{\mathbf{A}\mathbf{x} + \mathbf{b}}{\mathbf{c}^T\mathbf{x} + 1} + \mathbf{x}$	$\mathbf{A} \in \mathbb{R}^{2\times2}, \mathbf{b}, \mathbf{c} \in \mathbb{R}^2$
Pseudoperspective	$x' = q_{x'x}x + q_{x'y}y + q_{x'} + q_\alpha x^2 + q_\beta xy$ $y' = q_{y'x}x + q_{y'y}y + q_{y'} + q_\alpha xy + q_\beta y^2$	$q_* \in \mathbb{R}$
Biquadratic	$x' = q_{x'x^2}x^2 + q_{x'xy}xy + q_{x'y^2}y^2 + q_{x'x}x$ $\quad + q_{x'y}y + q_{x'}$ $y' = q_{y'x^2}x^2 + q_{y'xy}xy + q_{y'y^2}y^2 + q_{y'x}x$ $\quad + q_{y'y}y + q_{y'}$	$q_* \in \mathbb{R}$

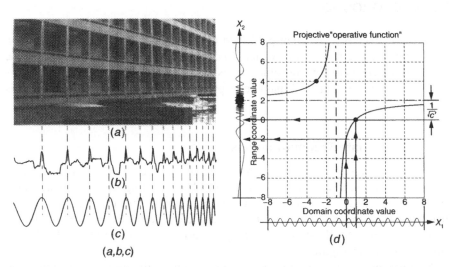

(a,b,c)

Figure 6.2 The projective chirping phenomenon. (a) A real-world object that exhibits periodicity generates a projection (image) with "chirping" — periodicity in perspective. (b) Center raster of image. (c) Best-fit projective chirp of form $\sin[2\pi((ax+b)/(cx+1))]$. (d) Graphical depiction of exemplar 1-D projective coordinate transformation of $\sin(2\pi x_1)$ into a projective chirp function, $\sin(2\pi x_2) = \sin[2\pi((2x_1 - 2)/(x_1 + 1))]$. The range coordinate as a function of the domain coordinate forms a rectangular hyperbola with asymptotes shifted to center at the *vanishing point*, $x_1 = -1/c = -1$, and exploding point, $x_2 = a/c = 2$; the chirpiness is $c' = c^2/(bc - a) = -\frac{1}{4}$.

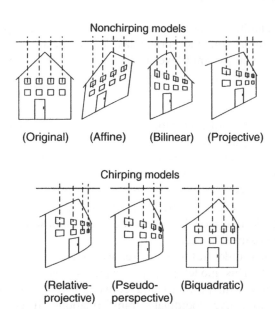

Figure 6.3 Pictorial effects of the six coordinate transformations of Table 6.1, arranged left to right by number of parameters. Note that translation leaves the ORIGINAL house figure unchanged, except in its location. Most important, all but the AFFINE coordinate transformation affect the periodicity of the window spacing (inducing the desired "chirping," which corresponds to what we see in the real world). Of these five, only the PROJECTIVE coordinate transformation preserves straight lines. The 8-parameter PROJECTIVE coordinate transformation "exactly" describes the possible image motions ("exact" meaning under the idealized zero-parallax conditions).

[72,97] have assumed affine motion (six parameters) between frames. For the assumptions of static scene and no parallax, the affine model exactly describes rotation about the optical axis of the camera, zoom of the camera, and pure shear, which the camera does not do, except in the limit as the lens focal length approaches infinity. The affine model cannot capture camera pan and tilt, and therefore cannot properly express the "keystoning" (projections of a rectangular shape to a wedge shape) and "chirping" we see in the real world. (By "chirping" what is meant is the effect of increasing or decreasing spatial frequency with respect to spatial location, as illustrated in Fig. 6.2) Consequently the affine model attempts to fit the wrong parameters to these effects. Although it has fewer parameters, the affine model is more susceptible to noise because it lacks the correct degrees of freedom needed to properly track the actual image motion.

The 8-parameter *projective* model gives the desired 8 parameters that exactly account for all possible zero-parallax camera motions; hence there is an important need for a featureless estimator of these parameters. The only algorithms proposed to date for such an estimator are [63] and, shortly after, [98]. In both algorithms a computationally expensive nonlinear optimization method was presented. In the earlier publication [63] a direct method was also proposed. This direct method uses simple linear algebra, and it is noniterative insofar as methods such as

Levenberg–Marquardt, and the like, are in no way required. The proposed method instead uses repetition with the correct law of composition on the projective group, going from one pyramid level to the next by application of the group's law of composition. The term "repetitive" rather than "iterative" is used, in particular, when it is desired to distinguish the proposed method from less preferable iterative methods, in the sense that the proposed method is direct *at each stage* of computation. In other words, the proposed method does not require a nonlinear optimization package at each stage.

Because the parameters of the projective coordinate transformation had traditionally been thought to be mathematically and computationally too difficult to solve, most researchers have used the simpler affine model or other approximations to the projective model. Before the featureless estimation of the parameters of the "exact" projective model is proposed and demonstrated, it is helpful to discuss some approximate models.

Going from first order (affine), to second order, gives the 12-parameter biquadratic model. This model properly captures both the chirping (change in spatial frequency with position) and converging lines (keystoning) effects associated with projective coordinate transformations. It does not constrain chirping and converging to work together (the example in Fig. 6.3 being chosen with zero convergence yet substantial chirping, illustrates this point). Despite its larger number of parameters, there is still considerable discrepancy between a projective coordinate transformation and the best-fit biquadratic coordinate transformation. Why stop at second order? Why not use a 20-parameter bicubic model? While an increase in the number of model parameters will result in a better fit, there is a trade-off where the model begins to fit noise. The physical camera model fits exactly in the 8-parameter projective group; therefore we know that eight are sufficient. Hence it seems reasonable to have a preference for approximate models with exactly eight parameters.

The 8-parameter bilinear model seems to be the most widely used model [99] in image processing, medical imaging, remote sensing, and computer graphics. This model is easily obtained from the biquadratic model by removing the four x^2 and y^2 terms. Although the resulting bilinear model captures the effect of converging lines, it completely fails to capture the effect of chirping.

The 8-parameter *pseudoperspective* model [100] and an 8-parameter relative-projective model both capture the converging lines and the chirping of a projective coordinate transformation. The pseudoperspective model, for example, may be thought of as first a means of removal of two of the quadratic terms $(q_{x'y^2} = q_{y'x^2} = 0)$, which results in a 10- parameter model (the q-chirp of [101]) and then of constraining the four remaining quadratic parameters to have two degrees of freedom. These constraints force the chirping effect (captured by $q_{x'x^2}$ and $q_{y'y^2}$) and the converging effect (captured by $q_{x'xy}$ and $q_{y'xy}$) to work together to match as closely as possible the effect of a projective coordinate transformation. In setting $q_\alpha = q_{x'x^2} = q_{y'xy}$, the chirping in the x-direction is forced to correspond with the converging of parallel lines in the x-direction (and likewise for the y-direction).

Of course, the desired "exact" 8 parameters come from the projective model, but they have been perceived as being notoriously difficult to estimate. The parameters for this model have been solved by Tsai and Huang [102], but their solution assumed that features had been identified in the two frames, along with their correspondences. The main contribution of this chapter is a simple featureless means of automatically solving for these 8 parameters.

Other researchers have looked at projective estimation in the context of obtaining 3-D models. Faugeras and Lustman [83], Shashua and Navab [103], and Sawhney [104] have considered the problem of estimating the projective parameters while computing the motion of a rigid planar patch, as part of a larger problem of finding 3-D motion and structure using parallax relative to an arbitrary plane in the scene. Kumar et al. [105] have also suggested registering frames of video by computing the flow along the *epipolar* lines, for which there is also an initial step of calculating the gross camera movement assuming no parallax. However, these methods have relied on feature correspondences and were aimed at 3-D scene modeling. My focus is not on recovering the 3-D scene model, but on aligning 2-D images of 3-D scenes. Feature correspondences greatly simplify the problem; however, they also have many problems. The focus of this chapter is simple featureless approaches to estimating the projective coordinate transformation between image pairs.

6.2.2   Camera Motion: Common Assumptions and Terminology

Two assumptions are typically made in this area of research. The first is that the scene is constant — changes of scene content and lighting are small between frames. The second is that of an ideal pinhole camera — implying unlimited depth of field with everything in focus (infinite resolution) and implying that straight lines map to straight lines.[1] Consequently the camera has three degrees of freedom in 2-D space and eight degrees of freedom in 3-D space: translation (X, Y, Z), zoom (scale in each of the image coordinates x and y), and rotation (rotation about the optical axis), pan, and tilt. These two assumptions are also made in this chapter.

In this chapter an "uncalibrated camera" refers to one in which the principal point[2] is not necessarily at the center (origin) of the image and the scale is not necessarily isotropic[3] It is assumed that the zoom is continually adjusted by the camera user, and that we do not know the zoom setting, or whether it was changed between recording frames of the image sequence. It is also assumed that each element in the camera sensor array returns a quantity that is linearly proportional

---

[1] When using low-cost wide-angle lenses, there is usually some barrel distortion, which we correct using the method of [106].

[2] The principal point is where the optical axis intersects the film.

[3] Isotropic means that magnification in the x and y directions is the same. Our assumption facilitates aligning frames taken from different cameras.

Table 6.2   Two No Parallax Cases for a Static Scene

	Scene Assumptions	Camera Assumptions
Case 1	Arbitrary 3-D	Free to zoom, rotate, pan, and tilt, fixed COP
Case 2	Planar	Free to zoom, rotate, pan, and tilt, free to translate

Note: The first situation has 7 degrees of freedom (yaw, pitch, roll, translation in each of the 3 spatial axes, and zoom), while the second has 4 degrees of freedom (pan, tilt, rotate, and zoom). Both, however, are represented within the 8 scalar parameters of the projective group of coordinate transformations.

to the quantity of light received.[4] With these assumptions, the exact camera motion that can be recovered is summarized in Table 6.2.

6.2.3   Orbits

Tsai and Huang [102] pointed out that the elements of the projective *group* give the true camera motions with respect to a planar surface. They explored the group structure associated with images of a 3-D rigid planar patch, as well as the associated *Lie algebra*, although they assume that the correspondence problem has been solved. The solution presented in this chapter (which does not require prior solution of correspondence) also depends on projective group theory. The basics of this theory are reviewed, before presenting the new solution in the next section.

Projective Group in 1-D Coordinates
A group is a set upon which there is defined an associative law of composition (*closure, associativity*), which contains at least one element (*identity*) whose composition with another element leaves it unchanged, and for which every element of the set has an *inverse*.

A *group* of operators together with a *set* of operands form a *group operation*.[5]

In this chapter coordinate transformations are the operators (group) and images are the operands (set). When the coordinate transformations form a group, then two such coordinate transformations, p_1 and p_2, acting in succession, on an image (e.g., p_1 acting on the image by doing a coordinate transformation, followed by a further coordinate transformation corresponding to p_2, acting on that result) can be replaced by a single coordinate transformation. That single coordinate transformation is given by the *law of composition* in the group.

The *orbit* of a particular element of the set, under the group operation [107], is the new set formed by applying to it all possible operators from the group.

---

[4] This condition can be enforced over a wide range of light intensity levels, by using the Wyckoff principle [75,59].

[5] Also known as a *group action* or *G-set* [107].

6.2.4   VideoOrbits

Here the orbit of particular interest is the collection of pictures arising from one picture through applying all possible projective coordinate transformations to that picture. This set is referred to as the VideoOrbit of the picture in question. Image sequences generated by zero-parallax camera motion on a static scene contain images that all lie in the same VideoOrbit.

The VideoOrbit of a given frame of a video sequence is defined to be the set of all images that can be produced by applying operators from the projective group to the given image. Hence the coordinate transformation problem may be restated: Given a set of images that lie in the same orbit of the group, it is desired to find for each image pair, that operator in the group which takes one image to the other image.

If two frames, f_1 and f_2, are in the same orbit, then there is an group operation, $\mathbf{p}$, such that the mean-squared error (MSE) between f_1 and $f_2' = \mathbf{p} \circ f_2$ is zero. In practice, however, the goal is to find which element of the group takes one image "nearest" the other, for there will be a certain amount of parallax, noise, interpolation error, edge effects, changes in lighting, depth of focus, and so on. Figure 6.4 illustrates the operator $\mathbf{p}$ acting on frame f_2 to move it nearest to frame f_1. (This figure does not, however, reveal the precise shape of the orbit, which occupies a 3-D parameter space for 1-D images or an 8-D parameter space for 2-D images.) For simplicity the theory is reviewed first for the projective coordinate transformation in one dimension.[6]

Suppose that we take two pictures, using the same exposure, of the same scene from fixed common location (e.g., where the camera is free to pan, tilt, and zoom between taking the two pictures). Both of the two pictures capture the

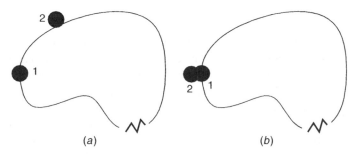

(a)   *(b)*

Figure 6.4   Video orbits. (*a*) The orbit of frame 1 is the set of all images that can be produced by acting on frame 1 with any element of the operator group. Assuming that frames 1 and 2 are from the same scene, frame 2 will be close to one of the possible projective coordinate transformations of frame 1. In other words, frame 2 "lies near the orbit of" frame 1. (*b*) By bringing frame 2 along its orbit, we can determine how closely the two orbits come together at frame 1.

---

[6] In this 2-D world, the "camera" consists of a center of projection (pinhole "lens") and a line (1-D sensor array or 1-D "film").

same pencil of light,[7] but each projects this information differently onto the film or image sensor. Neglecting that which falls beyond the borders of the pictures, each picture captures the same information about the scene but records it in a different way. The same object might, for example, appear larger in one image than in the other, or might appear more squashed at the left and stretched at the right than in the other. Thus we would expect to be able to construct one image from the other, so that only one picture should need to be taken (assuming that its field of view covers all the objects of interest) in order to synthesize all the others. We first explore this idea in a make-believe "Flatland" where objects exist on the 2-D page, rather than the 3-D world in which we live, and where pictures are real-valued functions of one real variable, rather than the more familiar real-valued functions of two real-variables.

For the two pictures of the same pencil of light in Flatland, a common COP is defined at the origin of our coordinate system in the plane. In Figure 6.5 a single camera that takes two pictures in succession is depicted as two cameras shown together in the same figure. Let Z_k, $k \in \{1, 2\}$ represent the distances, along each optical axis, to an arbitrary point in the scene, P, and let X_k represent the distances from P to each of the optical axes. The principal distances are denoted z_k. In the example of Figure 6.5, we are *zooming in* (increased magnification) as we go from frame 1 to frame 2.

Considering an arbitrary point P in the scene, subtending in a first picture an angle $\alpha = \arctan(x_1/z_1) = \arctan(x_1/z_1)$, the geometry of Figure 6.5 defines a mapping from x_1 to x_2, based on a camera rotating through an angle of θ between the taking of two pictures [108,17]:

$$x_2 = z_2 \tan(\arctan\left(\frac{x_1}{z_1}\right) - \theta) \qquad \forall x_1 \neq o_1, \tag{6.1}$$

where $o_1 = z_1 \tan(\pi/2 + \theta)$ is the location of the singularity in the domain x_1. This singularity is known as the "appearing point" [17]. The mapping (6.1) defines the coordinate transformation between any two pictures of the same subject matter, where the camera is free to pan, and zoom, between the taking of these two pictures. Noise (movement of subject matter, change in illumination, or circuit noise) is neglected in this simple model. There are three degrees of freedom, namely the relative angle θ, through which the camera rotated between taking of the two pictures, and the zoom settings, z_1 and z_2.

Unfortunately, this mapping (6.1) involves the evaluation of trigonometric functions at every point x_1 in the image domain. However, (6.1) can be rearranged in a form that only involves trigonometric calculations once per image pair, for the constants defining the relation between a particular pair of images.

---

[7] We neglect the boundaries (edges or ends of the sensor) and assume that both pictures have sufficient field of view to capture all of the objects of interest.

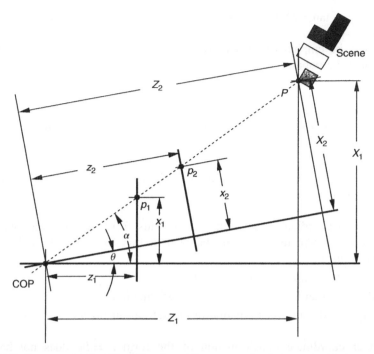

Figure 6.5 Camera at a fixed location. An arbitrary scene is photographed twice, each time with a different camera orientation and a different principal distance (zoom setting). In both cases the camera is located at the same place (COP) and thus captures the same pencil of light. The dotted line denotes a ray of light traveling from an arbitrary point **P** in the scene to the **COP**. Heavy lines denote both camera optical axes in each of the two orientations as well as the image sensor in each of its two pan and zoom positions. The two image sensors (or films) are in front of the camera to simplify mathematical derivations.

First, note the well-known trigonometric identity for the difference of two angles:

$$\tan(\alpha - \theta) = \frac{\tan(\alpha) - \tan(\theta)}{1 + \tan(\alpha)\tan(\theta)}. \tag{6.2}$$

Substitute into the equation $\tan(\alpha) = x_1/z_1$. Thus

$$x_2 = z_2 \frac{x_1/z_1 - \tan(\theta)}{1 + (x_1/z_1)\tan(\theta)} \tag{6.3}$$

Letting constants $a = z_2/z_1$, $b = -z_2\tan(\theta)$, and $c = \tan(\theta)/z_1$, the trigonometric computations are removed from the independent variable, so that

$$x_2 = \frac{ax_1 + b}{cx_1 + 1} \qquad \forall x_1 \neq o_1, \tag{6.4}$$

where $o_1 = z_1 \tan(\pi/2 + \theta) = -1/c$, is the location of the singularity in the domain.

It should be emphasized that if we set $c = 0$, we arrive at the affine group, upon which the popular wavelet transform is based. Recall that c, the degree of perspective, has been given the interpretation of a chirp rate [108] and forms the basis for the p-chirplet transform.

Let $\mathbf{p} \in \mathbf{P}$ denote a particular mapping from x_1 to x_2, governed by the three parameters (three degrees of freedom) of this mapping, $\mathbf{p}' = [z_1, z_2, \theta]$, or equivalently by a, b, and c from (6.4).

Now, within the context of the VideoOrbits theory [2], it is desired that the set of coordinate transformations set forth in (6.4) form a group of coordinate transformations. Thus it is desired that:

- any two coordinate transformations of this form, when composed, form another coordinate transformation also of this form, which is the *law of composition*;
- the law of composition be associative;
- there exists an identity coordinate transformation;
- every coordinate transformation in the set has an inverse.

A singular coordinate transformation of the form $a = bc$ does not have an inverse. However, we do not need to worry about such a singularity because this situation corresponds to $\tan^2(\theta) = -1$ for which θ is ComplexInfinity. Thus such a situation will not happen in practice.

However, a more likely problem is the situation for which θ is 90 degrees, giving values for b and c that are ComplexInfinity (since $\tan(\pi/2)$ is Complex-Infinity). This situation can easily happen, if we take a picture, and then swing the camera through a 90 degree angle and then take another picture, as shown in Figure 6.6. Thus a picture of a sinusoidally varying surface in the first camera would appear as a function of the form $\sin(1/x)$ in the second camera, and the coordinate transformation of this special case is given by $x_2 = 1/x_1$. More generally, coordinate transformations of the form $x_2 = a_1/x_1 + b_1$ cannot be expressed by (6.4).

Accordingly, in order to form a group representation, coordinate transformations may be expressed as $x_2 = (a_1 x_1 + b_1)/(c_1 x_1 + d_1)$, $\forall a_1 d_1 \neq b_1 c_1$. Elements of this group of coordinate transformations are denoted by p_{a_1, b_1, c_1, d_1}, where each has inverse $p_{-d_1, b_1, c_1, -a_1}$. The law of composition is given by $p_{e,f,g,h} \circ p_{a,b,c,d} = p_{ae+cf, be+df, ag+cd, bg+d^2}$.

In a sequence of video images, each frame of video is very similar to the one before it, or after it, and thus the coordinate transformation is very close to the neighborhood of the identity; that is, a is very close to 1, and b and c are very close to 0. Therefore the camera will certainly not be likely to swing through a 90 degree angle in 1/30 or 1/60 of a second (the time between frames), and even if it did, most lenses do not have a wide enough field of view that one would be able to register such images (as depicted in Fig. 6.6) anyway.

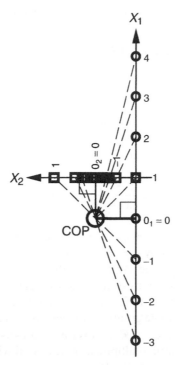

Figure 6.6 Cameras at 90 degree angles. In this situation $o_1 = 0$ and $o_2 = 0$. If we had in the domain x_1 a function such as $\sin(x_1)$, we would have the chirp function $\sin(1/x_1)$ in the range, as defined by the mapping $x_2 = 1/x_1$.

In almost all practical engineering applications, $d \neq 0$, so we are able to divide through by d, and denote the coordinate transformation $x_2 = (ax_1 + b)/(cx_1 + 1)$ by $x_2 = p_{a,b,c} \circ x_1$. When $a \neq 0$ and $c = 0$, the projective group becomes the affine group of coordinate transformations, and when $a = 1$ and $c = 0$, it becomes the group of translations.

To formalize this very subtle difference between the set of coordinate transformations p_{a_1,b_1,c_1,d_1}, and the set of coordinate transformations $p_{a,b,c}$, the first will be referred to as the projective group, whereas the second will be referred to as the projective group_(which is not, mathematically speaking, a true group, but behaves as a group over the range of parameters encountered in VideoOrbits applications. The two differ only over a set of measure zero in the parameter space.)

Proposition 6.2.1 *The set of all possible coordinate transformation operators,* $\mathbf{P}_1$*, given by the coordinate transformations (6.4),* $\forall a \neq bc$*, acting on a set of 1-D images, forms a group_-operation.* $\square$

Proof A pair of images produced by a particular camera rotation and change in principal distance (depicted in Fig. 6.5) corresponds to an operator from the group_that takes any function g on image line 1, to a function, h on image line 2:

$$h(x_2) = g(x_1) = \left(\frac{g - x_2 + b}{cx_2 - a} \right) \qquad \forall x_2 \neq o_2$$

$$= g \circ x_1 = g \circ \mathbf{p}^{-1} \circ x_2,$$

(6.5)

where $\mathbf{p} \circ x = (ax + b)/(cx + 1)$ and $o_2 = a/c$. As long as $a \neq bc$, each operator in the group_, $\mathbf{p}$, has an inverse. The inverse is given by composing the inverse coordinate transformation:

$$x_1 = \frac{b - x_2}{cx_2 - a} \qquad \forall x_2 \neq o_2$$

(6.6)

with the function $h()$ to obtain $g = h \circ \mathbf{p}$. The identity operation is given by $g = g \circ e$, where e is given by $a = 1$, $b = 0$, and $c = 0$.

In complex analysis (e.g., see Ahlfors [109]) the form $(az + b)/(cz + d)$ is known as a linear fractional transformation. Although our mapping is from $\mathbb{R}$ to $\mathbb{R}$ (as opposed to theirs from $\mathbb{C}$ to $\mathbb{C}$), we can still borrow the concepts of complex analysis. In particular, a simple group_-representation is provided using the 2×2 matrices, $\mathbf{p} = [a, b; c, 1] \in \mathbb{R}^2 \times \mathbb{R}^2$. Closure[8] and associativity are obtained by using the usual laws of matrix multiplication followed with dividing the resulting vector's first element by its second element. □

Proposition 1 says that an element of the $(ax + b)/(cx + 1)$ group_can be used to align any two frames of the 1-D image sequence provided that the COP remains fixed.

Proposition 6.2.2 *The set of operators that take nondegenerate nonsingular projections of a straight object to one another form a group_, $\mathbf{P}_2$.* □

A "straight" object is one that lies on a straight line in Flatland.[9]

Proof Consider a geometric argument. The mapping from the first (1-D) frame of an image sequence, $g(x_1)$ to the next frame, $h(x_2)$ is parameterized by the following: camera translation perpendicular to the object, t_z; camera translation parallel to the object, t_x; pan of frame 1, θ_1; pan of frame 2, θ_2; zoom of frame 1, z_1; and zoom of frame 2, z_2 (see Fig. 6.7). We want to obtain the mapping from

---

[8] Also know as the *law of composition* [107].

[9] An important difference to keep in mind, with respect to pictures of a flat object, is that in Flatland a picture taken of a picture is equivalent to a single picture for an equivalent camera orientation and position. However, with 2-D pictures in a 3-D world, a picture of a picture is, in general, not necessarily a simple perspective projection (you could continue taking pictures but not get anything new beyond the second picture). The 2-D version of the group representation contains both cases.

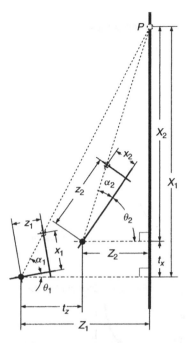

Figure 6.7 Two pictures of a flat (straight) object. The point P is imaged twice, each time with a different camera orientation, a different principal distance (zoom setting), and different camera location (resolved into components parallel and perpendicular to the object).

x_1 to x_2. Let us begin with the mapping from X_2 to x_2:

$$x_2 = z_2 \tan\left(\arctan\left(\frac{X_2}{Z_2}\right) - \theta_2\right) = \frac{a_2 X_2 + b_2}{c_2 X_2 + 1}, \tag{6.7}$$

which can be represented by the matrix $\mathbf{p}_2 = [a_2, b_2; c_2, 1]$ so that $x_2 = \mathbf{p}_2 \circ X_2$. Now $X_2 = X_1 - t_x$, and it is clear that this coordinate transformation is inside the group_, for there exists the choice of $a = 1$, $b = -t_x$, and $c = 0$ that describe it: $X_2 = \mathbf{p}_t \circ X_1$, where $\mathbf{p}_t = [1, -t_x; 0, 1]$. Finally, $x_1 = z_1 \tan(\arctan(X_1/Z_1) - \theta) = \mathbf{p}_1 \circ X_1$. Let $\mathbf{p}_1 = [a_1, b_1; c_1, 1]$. Then $\mathbf{p} = \mathbf{p}_2 \circ \mathbf{p}_t \circ \mathbf{p}_1^{-1}$ is in the group_ by the law of composition. Hence the operators that take one frame into another, $x_2 = \mathbf{p} \circ x_1$, form a group_. □

Proposition 6.2.2 says that an element of the $(ax + b)/(cx + 1)$ group_ can be used to align any two images of linear objects in flatland regardless of camera movement.

Proposition 6.2.3 *Each group_ of $\mathbf{P}_1$ and $\mathbf{P}_2$ are isomorphic; a group-representation for both is given by the 2×2 square matrix $[a, b; c, 1]$.* □

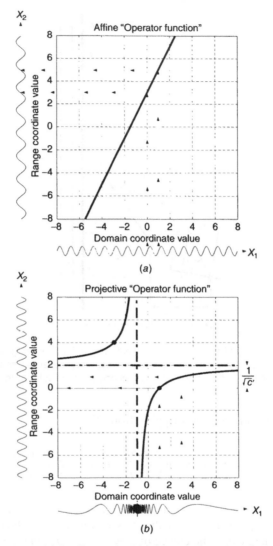

Figure 6.8   Comparison of 1-D affine and projective coordinate transformations, in terms of their operator functions, acting on a sinusoidal image. (a) Orthographic projection is equivalent to affine coordinate transformation, $y = ax + b$. Slope $a = 2$ and intercept $b = 3$. The operator function is a straight line in which the intercept is related to phase shift (delay), and the slope to dilation (which affects the frequency of the sinusoid). For any function $g(t)$ in the range, this operator maps functions $g \in G(\mathbb{R}_{\neq o_1})$ to functions $h \in H(\mathbb{R}_{\neq o_2})$ that are dilated by a factor of 2 and translated by 3. Fixing g and allowing slope $a \neq 0$ and intercept b to vary produces a family of *wavelets* where the original function g is known as the *mother wavelet*. (b) Perspective projection for a particular fixed value of $\mathbf{p}' = \{1, 2, 45°\}$. Note that the plot is a rectangular hyperbola like $x_2 = 1/(c'x_1)$ but with asymptotes at the shifted origin $(-1, 2)$. Here $h = \sin(2\pi x_2)$ is "dechirped" to g. The arrows indicate how a chosen cycle of chirp g is mapped to the corresponding cycle of the sinusoid h. Fixing g and allowing $a \neq 0$, b, and c to vary produces a class of functions, in the range, known as *P-chirps*. Note the singularity in the domain at $x_1 = -1$ and the singularity in the range at $x_2 = a/c = 2$. These singularities correspond to the *exploding point* and *vanishing point*, respectively.

Isomorphism follows because $\mathbf{P}_1$ and $\mathbf{P}_2$ have the same group_representation.[10] The $(ax + b)/(cx + 1)$ operators in the above propositions form the *projective group_* $\mathbf{P}$ in Flatland. □

The affine operator that takes a function space $\mathcal{G}$ to a function space $\mathcal{H}$ may itself be viewed as a function. Let us now construct a similar plot for a member of the group_of operators, $\mathbf{p} \in \mathbf{P}$, in particular, the operator $\mathbf{p} = [2, -2; 1, 1]$ that corresponds to $\mathbf{p}' = \{1, 2, 45°\} \in \mathbf{P}_1$ (zoom from 1 to 2, and angle of 45 degrees). We have also depicted the result of dechirping $g(x_2) = \sin(2\pi x_1)$ to $g(x_1)$. When H is the space of Fourier analysis functions (harmonic oscillations), then G is a family of functions known as P-chirps [108], adapted to a particular *exploding point*, o_1, and "normalized chirp-rate," $c' = c^2/(bc - a)$ [17]. Figure 6.8*b* is a *rectangular hyperbola* (e.g., $x_2 = 1/(c'x_1)$) (i.e., $x_2 = 1/c'x_1$) with an origin that has been shifted from $(0, 0)$ to (o_1, o_2). Operator functions that cause chirping are thus similar in form to those that perform dechirping. (Compare Fig. 6.8*b* with Fig. 6.2*d*.)

The geometry of the situation depicted in Figure 6.8*b* and Figure 6.2*d* is shown in Figure 6.9.

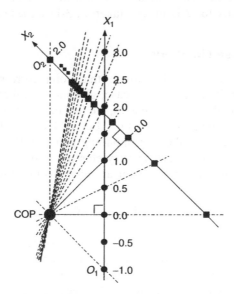

Figure 6.9 Graphical depiction of a situation where two pictures are related by a zoom from 1 to 2, and a 45 degree angle between the two camera positions. The geometry of this situation corresponds, in particular, to the operator $\mathbf{p} = [2, -2; 1, 1]$ which corresponds to $\mathbf{p}' = \{1, 2, 45°\}$, that is, zoom from 1 to 2, and an angle of 45 degrees between the optical axes of the camera positions This geometry corresponds to the operator functions plotted in Figure 6.8*b* and Figure 6.2*d*.

---

[10] For 2-D images in a 3-D world, the isomorphism no longer holds. However, the projective group_still *contains* and therefore represents both cases.

6.3   FRAMEWORK: MOTION PARAMETER ESTIMATION AND OPTICAL FLOW

To lay the framework for the new results, existing methods of parameter estimation for coordinate transformations will be reviewed. This framework will apply to existing methods as well as to new methods. The purpose of this review is to bring together a variety of methods that appear quite different but actually can be described in a more unified framework as is presented here.

The framework given breaks existing methods into two categories: feature-based, and featureless. Of the featureless methods, consider two subcategories: methods based on minimizing MSE (generalized correlation, direct nonlinear optimization) and methods based on spatiotemporal derivatives and optical flow. Variations such as *multiscale* have been omitted from these categories, since multiscale analysis can be applied to any of them. The new algorithms proposed in this chapter (with final form given in Section 6.4) are featureless, and based on (multiscale if desired) spatiotemporal derivatives.

Some of the descriptions of methods will be presented for hypothetical 1-D images taken of 2-D "scenes" or "objects." This simplification yields a clearer comparison of the estimation methods. The new theory and applications will be presented subsequently for 2-D images taken of 3-D scenes or objects.

6.3.1   Feature-Based Methods

Feature-based methods [110,111] assume that point correspondences in both images are available. In the projective case, given at least three correspondences between point pairs in the two 1-D images, we find the element, $\mathbf{p} = \{a, b, c\} \in \mathbf{P}$ that maps the second image into the first. Let $x_k, k = 1, 2, 3, \ldots$ be the points in one image, and let x'_k be the corresponding points in the other image. Then $x'_k = (ax_k + b)/(cx_k + 1)$. Re-arranging yields $ax_k + b - x_k x'_k c = x'_k$, so a, b, and c can be found by solving $k \geq 3$ linear equations in 3 unknowns:

$$\begin{bmatrix} x_k & 1 & -x'_k x_k \end{bmatrix} \begin{bmatrix} a & b & c \end{bmatrix}^T = \begin{bmatrix} x'_k \end{bmatrix}, \tag{6.8}$$

using least squares if there are more than three correspondence points. The extension from 1-D "images" to 2-D images is conceptually identical. For the affine and projective models, the minimum number of correspondence points needed in 2-D is three and four, respectively, because the number of degrees of freedom in 2-D is six for the affine model and eight for the projective model. Each point correspondence anchors two degrees of freedom because it is in 2-D.

A major difficulty with feature-based methods is finding the features. Good features are often hand-selected, or computed, possibly with some degree of human intervention [112]. A second problem with features is their sensitivity to noise and occlusion. Even if reliable features exist between frames (e.g., line markings on a playing field in a football video; see Section 6.5.2), these features may be subject to signal noise and occlusion (e.g., running football players blocking a feature). The emphasis in the rest of this chapter will be on robust featureless methods.

6.3.2 Featureless Methods Based on Generalized Cross-correlation

For completenes we will consider first what is perhaps the most obvious approach — generalized cross-correlation in 8-D parameter space — in order to motivate a different approach provided in Section 6.3.3. The motivation arises from ease of implemention and simplicity of computation.

Cross-correlation of two frames is a featureless method of recovering translation model parameters. Affine and projective parameters can also be recovered using generalized forms of cross-correlation.

Generalized cross-correlation is based on an inner-product formulation that establishes a similarity metric between two functions, say g and h, where $h \approx \mathbf{p} \circ g$ is an approximately coordinate-transformed version of g, but the parameters of the coordinate transformation, $\mathbf{p}$ are unknown.[11] We can find, by exhaustive search (applying all possible operators, $\mathbf{p}$, to h), the "best" $\mathbf{p}$ as the one that maximizes the inner product:

$$\int_{-\infty}^{\infty} g(x) \frac{\mathbf{p}^{-1} \circ h(x)}{\int_{-\infty}^{\infty} \mathbf{p}^{-1} \circ h(x)\, dx}\, dx, \tag{6.9}$$

where the energy of each coordinate-transformed h has been normalized before making the comparison. Equivalently, instead of maximizing a similarity metric, we can minimize some distance metric, such as MSE, given by $\int_{-\infty}^{\infty} (g(x) - \mathbf{p}^{-1} \circ h(x))^2 - Dx$. Solving (6.9) has an advantage over finding MSE when one image is not only a coordinate-transformed version of the other but also an amplitude-scaled version. Thus generally happens when there is an automatic gain control or an automatic iris in the camera.

In 1-D the orbit of an image under the affine group operation is a family of *wavelets* (assuming that the image is that of the desired "mother wavelet," in the sense that a wavelet family is generated by 1-D affine coordinate transformations of a single function), while the orbit of an image under the projective group of coordinate transformations is a family of projective chirplets [35],[12] the objective function (6.9) being the cross-chirplet transform. A computationally efficient algorithm for the cross-wavelet transform has previously been presented [116]. (See [117] for a good review on wavelet-based estimation of affine coordinate transformations.)

Adaptive variants of the chirplet transforms have been previously reported in the literature [118]. However, there are still many problems with the adaptive

---

[11] In the presence of additive white Gaussian noise, this method, also known as "matched filtering," leads to a maximum likelihood estimate of the parameters [113].

[12] Symplectomorphisms of the time–frequency plane [114, 115] have been applied to signal analysis [35], giving rise to the so-called q-chirplet [35], which differs from the projective chirplet discussed here.

chirplet approach; thus, for the remainder of this chapter, we consider featureless methods based on spatiotemporal derivatives.

6.3.3 Featureless Methods Based on Spatiotemporal Derivatives

Optical Flow ("Translation Flow")

When the change from one image to another is small, optical flow [71] may be used. In 1-D the traditional optical flow formulation assumes each point x in frame t is a translated version of the corresponding point in frame $t + \Delta t$, and that Δx, and Δt are chosen in the ratio $\Delta x / \Delta t = u_f$, the translational flow velocity of the point in question. The image brightness[13] $E(x, t)$ is described by

$$E(x, t) = E(x + \Delta x, t + \Delta t), \quad \forall (x, t), \tag{6.10}$$

where u_f is the translational flow velocity of the point in the case of pure translation; u_f is constant across the entire image. More generally, though, a pair of 1-D images are related by a quantity $u_f(x)$ at each point in one of the images.

Expanding the right-hand side of (6.10) in a Taylor series, and canceling 0th-order terms gives the well-known optical flow equation: $u_{f E_x} + E_t + \text{h.o.t.} = 0$, where $E_x = dE(x, t)/dx$ and $E_t = dE(x, t)/dt$ are the spatial and temporal derivatives, respectively, and h.o.t. denotes higher-order terms. Typically the higher-order terms are neglected, giving the expression for the optical flow at each point in one of the two images:

$$u_f E_x + E_t \approx 0. \tag{6.11}$$

Weighing the Difference between Affine Fit and Affine Flow

A comparison between two similar approaches is presented, in the familiar and obvious realm of linear regression versus direct affine estimation, highlighting the obvious differences between the two approaches. This difference, in weighting, motivates new weighting changes that will later simplify implementations pertaining to the new methods.

It is often desired to determine the coordinate transformation required to spatially register (align) two images, by performing a coordinate transformation on at least one of the two images to register it with the other. Without loss of generality, let us apply the coordinate transformation to the second image to register it with the first. Registration is often based on computing the optical flow between two images, g and h, and then using this calculated optical flow to find the coordinate transformation to apply to h to register it with g. We consider two approaches based on the affine model:[14] finding the optical flow at every point,

---

[13] While one may choose to debate whether or not this quantity is actually in units of brightness, this is the term used by Horn [71]. It is denoted by Horn using the letter E. Variables E, F, G, and H will be used to denote this quantity throughout this book, where, for example, $F(x, t) = f(q(x, t))$ is a typically unknown nonlinear function of the actual quantity of light falling on the image sensor.

[14] The 1-D affine model is a simple yet sufficiently interesting (non-Abelian) example selected to illustrate differences in weighting.

and then globally fitting this flow with an affine model (*affine fit*), and rewriting the optical flow equation in terms of a single global affine (not translation) motion model (*affine flow*).

Affine Fit

Wang and Adelson [119] proposed fitting an affine model to the optical flow field between two 2-D images. Their approach with 1-D images is briefly examined. The reduction in dimensions simplifies analysis and comparison to affine flow. Denote coordinates in the original image, g, by x, and in the new image, h, by x'. Suppose that h is a dilated and translated version of g so that $x' = ax + b$ for every corresponding pair (x', x). Equivalently the affine model of velocity (normalizing $\Delta t = 1$), $u_m = x' - x$, is given by $u_m = (a - 1)x + b$. We can expect a discrepancy between the flow velocity, u_f, and the model velocity, u_m, due either to errors in the flow calculation or to errors in the affine model assumption. Therefore we apply linear regression to get the best least-squares fit by minimizing

$$\varepsilon_{fit} = \sum_x (u_m - u_f)^2 = \sum_x \left(u_m + \frac{E_t}{E_x} \right)^2 = \sum_x \left((a-1)x + b + \frac{E_t}{E_x} \right)^2.$$

(6.12)

The constants a and b that minimize ε_{fit} over the entire patch are found by differentiating (6.12), with respect to a and b, and setting the derivatives to zero. This results in what are called the affine fit equations:

$$\begin{bmatrix} \sum_x x^2, & \sum_x x \\ \sum_x x, & \sum_x 1 \end{bmatrix} \begin{bmatrix} a-1 \\ b \end{bmatrix} = - \begin{bmatrix} \sum_x xE_t/E_x \\ \sum_x E_t/E_x \end{bmatrix}.$$

(6.13)

Affine Flow

Alternatively, the affine coordinate transformation may be directly incorporated into the brightness change constraint equation (6.10). Bergen et al. [120] proposed this method, affine flow, to distinguish it from the affine fit model of Wang and Adelson (6.13). Let us see how affine flow and affine fit are related. Substituting $u_m = (ax + b) - x$ directly into (6.11) in place of u_f and summing the squared error, we have

$$\varepsilon_{flow} = \sum_x (u_m E_x + E_t)^2 = \sum_x (((a-1)x + b)E_x + E_t)^2$$

(6.14)

over the whole image. Then differentiating, and equating the result to zero gives us a linear solution for both $a - 1$ and b:

$$\begin{bmatrix} \sum_x x^2 E_x^2, \sum_x x E_x^2 \\ \sum_x x E_x^2, \sum_x E_x^2 \end{bmatrix} \begin{bmatrix} a - 1 \\ b \end{bmatrix} = - \begin{bmatrix} \sum_x x E_x E_t \\ \sum_x E_x E_t \end{bmatrix} \qquad (6.15)$$

To see how result (6.15) compares to the affine fit, we rewrite (6.12):

$$\varepsilon_{fit} = \sum_x \left(\frac{u_m E_x + E_t}{E_x} \right)^2 \qquad (6.16)$$

and observe, comparing (6.14) and (6.16), that affine flow is equivalent to a weighted least-squares fit (i.e., a weighted *affine fit*), where the weighting is given by E_x^2. Thus the affine flow method tends to put more emphasis on areas of the image that are spatially varying than does the affine fit method. Of course, one is free to separately choose the weighting for each method in such a way that affine fit and affine flow methods give the same result.

Both intuition and practical experience tends to favor the affine flow weighting. More generally, perhaps we should ask "What is the best weighting?" Lucas and Kanade [121], among others, considered weighting issues, but the rather obvious difference in weighting between fit and flow did not enter into their analysis nor anywhere in the literature. The fact that the two approaches provide similar results, and yet drastically different weightings, suggests that we can exploit the choice of weighting. In particular, we will observe in Section 6.3.3 that we can select a weighting that makes the implementation, of rider orbit easier.

Another approach to the affine fit involves computation of the optical flow field using the multiscale iterative method of Lucas and Kanade, and *then* fitting to the affine model. An analogous variant of the affine flow method involves multiscale iteration as well, but in this case the iteration and multiscale hierarchy are incorporated directly into the affine estimator [120]. With the addition of multiscale analysis, the fit and flow methods differ in additional respects beyond just the weighting. My intuition and experience indicates that the direct multiscale affine flow performs better than the affine fit to the multiscale flow. Multiscale optical flow makes the assumption that blocks of the image are moving with pure translational motion and then paradoxically, that the affine fit refutes this pure-translation assumption. However, fit provides some utility over flow when it is desired to segment the image into regions undergoing different motions [122], or to gain robustness by rejecting portions of the image not obeying the assumed model.

Projective Fit and Projective Flow: New Techniques

Two new methods are proposed analogous to affine fit and affine flow: projective fit and projective flow. For the 1-D affine coordinate transformation, the graph of the range coordinate as a function of the domain coordinate is a straight line; for the projective coordinate transformation, the graph of the range coordinate as a function of the domain coordinate is a rectangular hyperbola (Fig. 6.2d). The affine fit case used linear regression, but in the projective case, hyperbolic regression is used. Consider the flow velocity given by (6.11) and the model velocity

$$u_m = x' - x = \frac{ax + b}{cx + 1} - x, \tag{6.17}$$

and minimize the sum of the squared difference as was done in (6.12):

$$\varepsilon = \sum_x \left(\frac{ax + b}{cx + 1} - x + \frac{E_t}{E_x}\right)^2. \tag{6.18}$$

As discussed earlier, the calculation can be simplified by judicious alteration of the weighting, in particular, multiplying each term of the summation (6.18) by $(cx + 1)$ before differentiating and solving. This gives

$$\left(\sum_x \phi\phi^T\right)[a, b, c]^T = \sum_x \left(x - \frac{E_t}{E_x}\right)\phi(x), \tag{6.19}$$

where the *regressor* is $\phi = \phi(x) = [x, 1, xE_t/E_x - x^2]^T$.

Projective Flow
For projective-flow (p-flow), substitute $u_m = (ax + b)/(cx + 1) - x$ into (6.14). Again, weighting by $(cx + 1)$ gives

$$\varepsilon_w = \sum(axE_x + bE_x + c(xE_t - x^2E_x) + E_t - xE_x)^2 \tag{6.20}$$

(the subscript w denotes weighting has taken place). The result is a linear system of equations for the parameters:

$$\left(\sum \phi_w\phi_w^T\right)[a, b, c]^T = \sum(xE_x - E_t)\phi_w, \tag{6.21}$$

where $\phi_w = [xE_x, E_x, xE_t - x^2E_x]^T$. Again, to show the difference in the weighting between projective flow and projective fit, we can rewrite (6.21):

$$\left(\sum E_x^2\phi\phi^T\right)[a, b, c]^T = \sum E_x^2(xE_x - E_t)\phi, \tag{6.22}$$

where ϕ is that defined in (6.19).

The Unweighted Projectivity Estimator
If we do not wish to apply the ad hoc weighting scheme, we may still estimate the parameters of projectivity in a simple manner, based on solving a linear system

of equations. To do this, we write the Taylor series of u_m,

$$u_m + x = b + (a - bc)x + (bc - a)cx^2 + (a - bc)c^2x^3 + \cdots, \qquad (6.23)$$

and use the first three terms, obtaining enough degrees of freedom to account for the three parameters being estimated. Letting the squared error due to higher-order terms in the Taylor series approximation be $\varepsilon = \sum(-h.o.t.)^2 = \sum((b + (a - bc - 1)x + (bc - a)cx^2)E_x + E_t)^2$, $\mathbf{q_2} = (bc - a)c$, $\mathbf{q_1} = a - bc - 1$, and $\mathbf{q_0} = b$, and differentiating with respect to each of the 3 parameters of $\mathbf{q}$, setting the derivatives equal to zero, and solving, gives the linear system of equations for unweighted projective flow:

$$\begin{bmatrix} \sum x^4 E_x^2 & \sum x^3 E_x^2 & \sum x^2 E_x^2 \\ \sum x^3 E_x^2 & \sum x^2 E_x^2 & \sum x E_x^2 \\ \sum x^2 E_x^2 & \sum x E_x^2 & \sum E_x^2 \end{bmatrix} \begin{bmatrix} q_2 \\ q_1 \\ q_0 \end{bmatrix} = - \begin{bmatrix} \sum x^2 E_x E_t \\ \sum x E_x E_t \\ \sum E_x E_t \end{bmatrix}. \qquad (6.24)$$

In Section 6.4 this derivation will be extended to 2-D images.

6.4   MULTISCALE IMPLEMENTATIONS IN 2-D

In the previous section two new techniques, projective-fit and projective-flow, were proposed. Now these algorithms are described for 2-D images. The brightness constancy constraint equation for 2-D images [71], which gives the flow velocity components in the x and y directions, analogous to (6.11) is

$$\mathbf{u_f}^T \mathbf{E_x} + E_t \approx 0. \qquad (6.25)$$

As is well known [71] the optical flow field in 2-D is underconstrained.[15] The model of *pure translation* at every point has two parameters, but there is only one equation (6.25) to solve. So it is common practice to compute the optical flow over some neighborhood, which must be at least two pixels, but is generally taken over a small block, 3×3, 5×5, or sometimes larger (including the entire image as in this chapter).

Our task is not to deal with the 2-D translational flow, but with the 2-D projective flow, estimating the eight parameters in the coordinate transformation:

$$\mathbf{x'} = \begin{bmatrix} x' \\ y' \end{bmatrix} = \frac{\mathbf{A}[x, y]^T + \mathbf{b}}{\mathbf{c}^T[x, y]^T + 1} = \frac{\mathbf{Ax} + \mathbf{b}}{\mathbf{c}^T \mathbf{x} + 1}. \qquad (6.26)$$

The desired eight scalar parameters are denoted by $\mathbf{p} = [\mathbf{A}, \mathbf{b}; \mathbf{c}, 1]$, $\mathbf{A} \in \mathbb{R}^{2 \times 2}$, $\mathbf{b} \in \mathbb{R}^{2 \times 1}$, and $\mathbf{c} \in \mathbb{R}^{2 \times 1}$.

---

[15] Optical flow in 1-D did not suffer from this problem.

For projective flow, we have, in the 2-D case

$$\varepsilon_{\text{flow}} = \sum \left(\mathbf{u}_m^T \mathbf{E}_x + E_t\right)^2 = \sum \left(\left(\frac{\mathbf{A}\mathbf{x} + \mathbf{b}}{\mathbf{c}^T\mathbf{x} + 1} - \mathbf{x}\right)^T \mathbf{E}_x + E_t\right)^2. \qquad (6.27)$$

Here the sum can be weighted as it was in the 1-D case:

$$\varepsilon_w = \sum \left((\mathbf{A}\mathbf{x} + \mathbf{b} - (\mathbf{c}^T\mathbf{x} + 1)\mathbf{x})^T \mathbf{E}_x + (\mathbf{c}^T\mathbf{x} + 1)E_t\right)^2. \qquad (6.28)$$

Differentiating with respect to the free parameters $\mathbf{A}$, $\mathbf{b}$, and $\mathbf{c}$, and setting the result to zero gives a linear solution:

$$\left(\sum \phi\phi^T\right)[a_{11}, a_{12}, b_1, a_{21}, a_{22}, b_2, c_1, c_2]^T = \sum (\mathbf{x}^T \mathbf{E}_x - E_t)\phi, \qquad (6.29)$$

where $\phi^T = [E_x(x, y, 1), E_y(x, y, 1), xE_t - x^2E_x - xyE_y, yE_t - xyE_x - y^2E_y]$.

6.4.1 Unweighted Projective Flow

As with the 1-D images, we make similar assumptions in expanding (6.26) in its own Taylor series, analogous to (6.23). If we take the Taylor series up to second-order terms, we obtain the biquadratic model mentioned in Section 6.2.1 (Fig. 6.3). As mentioned in Section 6.2.1, by appropriately constraining the 12 parameters of the biquadratic model, we obtain a variety of 8 parameter approximate models. In the algorithms for estimating the exact unweighted projective group parameters, these approximate models are used in an intermediate step.[16]

Recall, for example, that the Taylor series for the bilinear case gives

$$\begin{aligned}
u_m + x &= q_{x'xy}xy + (q_{x'x} + 1)x + q_{x'y}y + q_{x'}, \\
v_m + y &= q_{y'xy}xy + q_{y'x}x + (q_{y'y} + 1)y + q_{y'}.
\end{aligned} \qquad (6.30)$$

Incorporating these into the flow criteria yields a simple set of eight linear equations in eight unknowns:

$$\left(\sum_{x,y} (\phi(x, y)\phi^T(x, y))\right) q = E_{x,y}E_t\phi(x, y), \qquad (6.31)$$

where $\phi^T = [E_x(xy, x, y, 1), E_y(xy, x, y, 1)]$.
For the relative-projective model, ϕ is given by

$$\phi^T = [E_x(x, y, 1), E_y(x, y, 1), E_t(x, y)], \qquad (6.32)$$

---

[16] Use of an approximate model that doesn't capture chirping or preserve straight lines can still lead to the true projective parameters as long as the model captures at least eight degrees of freedom.

and for the pseudoperspective model, ϕ is given by

$$\phi^T = [E_x(x, y, 1), E_y(x, y, 1), (x^2 E_x + xy E_y, xy E_x + y^2 E_y)]. \qquad (6.33)$$

To see how well the model describes the coordinate transformation between two images, say, g and h, one might *warp*[17] h to g, using the estimated motion model, and then compute some quantity that indicates how different the resampled version of h is from g. The MSE between the reference image and the warped image might serve as a good measure of similarity. However, since we are really interested in how the *exact model* describes the coordinate transformation, we assess the goodness of fit by first relating the parameters of the approximate model to the exact model, and then find the MSE between the reference image and the comparison image after applying the coordinate transformation of the exact model. A method of finding the parameters of the exact model, given the approximate model, is presented in Section 6.4.1.

Four-Point Method for Relating Approximate Model to Exact Model

Any of the approximations above, after being related to the exact projective model, tend to behave well in the neighborhood of the identity, $\mathbf{A} = \mathbf{I}$, $\mathbf{b} = \mathbf{0}$, $\mathbf{c} = \mathbf{0}$. In 1-D, the model is explicitly expanded in a Taylor series about the identity; here, although this is not done explicitly, we will assume that the terms of the Taylor series of the model correspond to those taken about the identity. In the 1-D case we solve the three linear equations in three unknowns to estimate the parameters of the approximate motion model, and then relate the terms in this Taylor series to the exact parameters a, b, and c (which involves solving another set of three equations in three unknowns, the second set being nonlinear, although very easy to solve).

In the extension to 2-D, the estimate step is straightforward, but the relate step is more difficult, because we now have eight nonlinear equations in eight unknowns, relating the terms in the Taylor series of the approximate model to the desired exact model parameters. Instead of solving these equations directly, a simple procedure for relating the parameters of the approximate model to those of the exact model is proposed. This method is called the "four point method:"

1. Select four ordered pairs (the four corners of the bounding box containing the region under analysis, the four corners of the image if the whole image is under analysis, etc.). Here, for simplicity, suppose that these points are the corners of the unit square: $\mathbf{s} = [s_1, s_2, s_3, s_4] = [(0, 0)^T, (0, 1)^T, (1, 0)^T, (1, 1)^T]$.

2. Apply the coordinate transformation using the Taylor series for the approximate model, such as (6.30), to these points: $\mathbf{r} = \mathbf{u}_m(\mathbf{s})$.

---

[17] The term *warp* is appropriate here, since the approximate model does not preserve straight lines.

3. Treat, the correspondences between **r** and **s** just like features to produce four easy to solve linear equations:

$$
\begin{bmatrix} x_k' \\ y_k' \end{bmatrix} = \begin{bmatrix} x_k, y_k, 1, 0, 0, 0, & -x_k x_k', -y_k x_k' \\ 0, 0, 0, x_k, y_k, 1, & -x_k y_k', -y_k y_k' \end{bmatrix}
$$

$$
\left[a_{x'x}, a_{x'y}, b_{x'}, a_{y'x}, a_{y'y}, b_{y'}, c_x, c_y \right]^T , \tag{6.34}
$$

where $1 \leq k \leq 4$. This results in the exact eight parameters, **p**.

We remind the reader that the four corners are *not* feature correspondences as used in the feature-based methods of Section 6.3.1 but are used so that the two featureless models (approximate and exact) can be related to one another.

It is important to realize the full benefit of finding the exact parameters. While the "approximate model" is sufficient for small deviations from the identity, it is not adequate to describe large changes in perspective. However, if we use it to track small changes incrementally, and each time relate these small changes to the exact model (6.26), then we can accumulate these small changes using the *law of composition* afforded by the group structure. This is an especially favorable contribution of the group framework. For example, with a video sequence, we can accommodate very large accumulated changes in perspective in this manner. The problems with cumulative error can be eliminated, for the most part, by constantly propagating forward the true values, computing the residual using the approximate model, and each time relating this to the exact model to obtain a goodness-of-fit estimate.

Algorithm for Unweighted Projective Flow: Overview

Below is an outline of the algorithm; details of each step are in subsequent sections. Frames from an image sequence are compared pairwise to test whether or not they lie in the same orbit:

1. A Gaussian pyramid of three or four levels is constructed for each frame in the sequence.
2. The parameters **p** are estimated at the top of the pyramid, between the two lowest-resolution images of a frame pair, *g* and *h*, using the repetitive method depicted in Figure 6.10.
3. The estimated **p** is applied to the next higher-resolution (finer) image in the pyramid, **p** ∘ *g*, to make the two images at that level of the pyramid nearly congruent before estimating the **p** between them.
4. The process continues down the pyramid until the highest-resolution image in the pyramid is reached.

6.4.2   Multiscale Repetitive Implementation

The Taylor series formulations used implicitly assume smoothness; the performance is improved if the images are blurred before estimation. To accomplish this, we downsample less than critically after low-pass filtering in the pyramid. However, after estimation, we use the original (unblurred) images when applying the final coordinate transformation.

The strategy presented differs from the multiscale iterative (affine) strategy of Bergen et al. [120] in one important respect beyond simply an increase from six to eight parameters. The difference is the fact that we have two motion models; the exact motion model (6.26) and the approximate motion model, which is the Taylor series approximation to the motion model itself. The approximate motion model is used to repetitively converge to the exact motion model, by the algebraic *law of composition* which is afforded by the exact projective group model. In this strategy, the exact parameters are determined at each level of the pyramid, and passed to the next level. The steps involved are summarized schematically in Figure 6.10, and described below:

1. Initialize: Set $h_0 = h$ and set $\mathbf{p}_{0,0}$ to the identity operator.
2. Repeat (for $k = 1 \ldots K$).
    a. *Estimate*: Estimate the eight or more terms of the approximate model between two image frames, g and h_{k-1}. This results in approximate model parameters $\mathbf{q}_k$.
    b. *Relate*. Relate the approximate parameters $\mathbf{q}_k$ to the exact parameters using the four point method. The resulting exact parameters are $\mathbf{p}_k$.
    c. *Resample*. Apply the *law of composition* to accumulate the effect of the $\mathbf{p}_k$'s. Denote these composite parameters by $\mathbf{p}_{0,k} = \mathbf{p}_k \circ \mathbf{p}_{0,k-1}$. Then set $h_k = \mathbf{p}_{0,k} \circ h$. (This should have nearly the same effect as applying $\mathbf{p}_k$ to h_{k-1}, except that it will avoid additional interpolation and anti-aliasing errors you would get by resampling an already resampled image [99].)

Repeat until either the error between h_k and g falls below a threshold, or until some maximum number of repetitions is achieved. After the first repetition, the parameters $\mathbf{q}_2$ tend to be near the identity, since they account for the residual between the "perspective-corrected" image h_1 and the "true" image g. We find

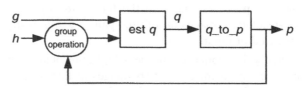

Figure 6.10 Method of computation of eight parameters **p** between two images from the same pyramid level, g and h. The approximate model parameters **q** are related to the exact model parameters **p** in a feedback system.

that only two or three repetitions are usually needed for frames from nearly the same orbit.

A rectangular image assumes the shape of an arbitrary quadrilateral when it undergoes a projective coordinate transformation. In coding the algorithm, the undefined portions are padded with the quantity NaN, a standard IEEE arithmetic value, so that any calculations involving these values automatically inherit NaN without slowing down the computations. The algorithm runs at a few frames per second on a typical WearComp.

6.4.3 VideoOrbits Head-Tracker

The VideoOrbits algorithm (repeated the multiscale estimate, relate, and resample approach) of the previous subsection gives rise to a new method of head-tracking based on the use of a video camera [1]. The VideoOrbits algorithm performs head-tracking visually, based on a natural environment, and works without the need for object recognition. Instead, it is based on algebraic projective geometry, and provides a featureless means of estimating the change in spatial coordinates arising from movement of the wearer's head, as illustrated in Figure 6.11.

6.4.4 Exploiting Commutativity for Parameter Estimation

There is a fundamental uncertainty [123] involved in the simultaneous estimation of parameters of a noncommutative group, akin to the Heisenberg uncertainty relation of quantum mechanics. In contrast, for a commutative[18] group (in the absence of noise), we can obtain the exact coordinate transformation.

Segman [124] considered the problem of estimating the parameters of a commutative group of coordinate transformations, in particular, the parameters of the affine group [125]. His work also deals with noncommutative groups, in particular, in the incorporation of scale in the Heisenberg group[19] [126].

Estimating the parameters of a commutative group is computationally efficient, such as through the use of Fourier cross-spectra [127]. This commutativity is exploited for estimating the parameters of the noncommutative 2-D projective group by first estimating the parameters that commute. For example, we improve performance if we first estimate the two parameters of translation, correct for the translation, and then proceed to estimate the eight projective parameters. We can also simultaneously estimate both the isotropic-zoom and the rotation about the optical axis by applying a log-polar coordinate transformation followed by a translation estimator. This process may also be achieved by a direct application of the Fourier-Mellin transform [128]. Similarly, if the only difference between g and h is a camera pan, then the pan may be estimated through a

---

[18] A commutative (or *Abelian*) group is one in which elements of the group commute, for example, translation along the x-axis commutes with translation along the y-axis, so the 2-D translation group is commutative.

[19] While the Heisenberg group deals with translation and frequency-translation (modulation), some of the concepts could be carried over to other more relevant group structures.

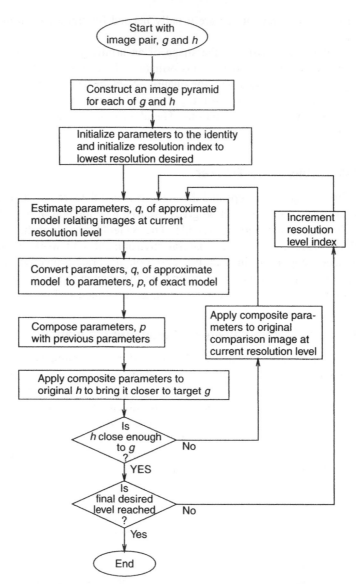

Figure 6.11 The VideoOrbits head-tracking algorithm. The new head-tracking algorithm requires no special devices installed in the environment. The camera in the personal imaging system (or the EyeTap) simply tracks itself based on its view of objects in the environment. The algorithm is based on algebraic projective geometry. It provides an estimate of the true projective coordinate transformation, which, for successive image pairs is composed using the projective group_. Successive pairs of images may be estimated in the neighborhood of the identity coordinate transformation (using an approximate representation), while absolute head-tracking is done using the exact group_ by relating the approximate parameters q to the exact parameters p in the innermost loop of the process. The algorithm typically runs at 5 to 10 frames per second on a general-purpose computer, but the simple structure of the algorithm makes it easy to implement in hardware for the higher frame rates needed for full-motion video.

coordinate transformation to cylindrical coordinates, followed by a translation estimator.

In practice, we run through the following commutative initialization before estimating the parameters of the projective group of coordinate transformations:

1. Assume that h is merely a translated version of g.
   a. Estimate this translation using the method of Girod [127].
   b. Shift h by the amount indicated by this estimate.
   c. Compute the *MSE* between the shifted h and g, and compare to the original MSE before shifting.
   d. If an improvement has resulted, use the shifted h from now on.
2. Assume that h is merely a rotated and isotropically zoomed version of g.
   a. Estimate the two parameters of this coordinate transformation.
   b. Apply these parameters to h.
   c. If an improvement has resulted, use the coordinate-transformed (rotated and scaled) h from now on.
3. Assume that h is merely an "x-chirped" (panned) version of g, and similarly, x-dechirp h. If an improvement results, use the x-dechirped h from now on. Repeat for y (tilt).

Compensating for one step may cause a change in choice of an earlier step. Thus it might seem desirable to run through the commutative estimates iteratively. However, experience on a large number of video sequences indicates that a single pass usually suffices, and in particular, will catch frequent situations where there is a pure zoom, a pure pan, a pure tilt, and so forth, both saving the rest of the algorithm computational effort, as well as accounting for simple coordinate transformations such as when one image is an upside-down version of the other. (Any of these pure cases corresponds to a single parameter group, which is commutative.) Without the commutative initialization step, these parameter estimation algorithms are prone to get caught in local optima, and thus never converge to the global optimum.

6.5 PERFORMANCE AND APPLICATIONS

Figure 6.12 shows some frames from a typical image sequence. Figure 6.13 shows the same frames brought into the coordinate system of frame (c), that is, the middle frame was chosen as the *reference frame*.

Given that we have established a means of estimating the projective coordinate transformation between any pair of images, there are two basic methods we use for finding the coordinate transformations between all pairs of a longer image sequence. Because of the group structure of the projective coordinate transformations, it suffices to arbitrarily select one frame and find the coordinate transformation between every other frame and this frame. The two basic methods are:

Figure 6.12 Frames from original image orbit, sent from author's personal imaging apparatus. The camera is mounted sideways so that it can "paint" out the image canvas with a wider "brush," when sweeping across for a panorama. Thus the visual field of view that the author experienced was rotated through 90 degrees. Much like George Stratton did with his upside-down glasses, the author adapted, over an extended period of time, to experiencing the world rotated 90 degrees. (Adaptation experiments were covered in Chapter 3.)

1. *Differential parameter estimation.* The coordinate transformations between successive pairs of images, $p_{0,1}$, $p_{1,2}$, $p_{2,3}$, ..., are estimated.
2. *Cumulative parameter estimation.* The coordinate transformation between each image and the reference image is estimated directly. Without loss of generality, select frame zero (E_0) as the reference frame and denote these coordinate transformations as $p_{0,1}$, $p_{0,2}$, $p_{0,3}$, ...

Theoretically the two methods are equivalent:

$$E_0 = p_{0,1} \circ p_{1,2} \circ \ldots \circ p_{n-1,n} E_n \qquad \text{differential method,}$$

$$E_0 = p_{0,n} E_n \qquad \text{cumulative method.} \tag{6.35}$$

(a)   (b)   (c)

(d)   (e)

Figure 6.13 Frames from original image video orbit after a coordinate transformation to move them along the orbit to the reference frame (c). The coordinate-transformed images are alike except for the region over which they are defined. The regions are not parallelograms; thus methods based on the affine model fail.

However, in practice, the two methods differ for two reasons:

1. *Cumulative error.* In practice, the estimated coordinate transformations between pairs of images register them only approximately, due to violations of the assumptions (objects moving in the scene, center of projection not fixed, camera swings around to bright window and automatic iris closes, etc.). When a large number of estimated parameters are composed, cumulative error sets in.

2. *Finite spatial extent of image plane.* Theoretically the images extend infinitely in all directions, but in practice, images are cropped to a rectangular bounding box. Therefore a given pair of images (especially if they are far from adjacent in the orbit) may not overlap at all; hence it is not possible to estimate the parameters of the coordinate transformation using those two frames.

The frames of Figure 6.12 were brought into register using the differential parameter estimation, and "cemented" together seamlessly on a common canvas.

Projective/projective   Affine/projective

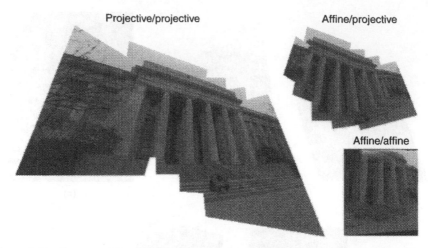

Affine/affine

Figure 6.14   Frames of Figure 6.13 "cemented," together on single image "canvas," with comparison of affine and projective models. Good registration of the projective/projective image is possible despite the noise in the amateur television receiver, wind-blown trees, and the fact that the rotation of the camera was not actually about its center of projection. The affine model fails to properly estimate the motion parameters (affine/affine), and even if the "exact" projective model is used to *estimate* the affine parameters, there is no affine coordinate transformation that will properly register all of the image frames.

"Cementing" involves piecing the frames together, for example, by median, mean, or trimmed mean, or combining on a subpixel grid [129]. (The trimmed mean was used here, but the particular method made little visible difference.) Figure 6.14 shows this result (projective/projective), with a comparison to two nonprojective cases. The first comparison is to affine/affine where affine parameters were estimated (also multiscale) and used for the coordinate transformation. The second comparison, affine/projective, uses the six affine parameters found by estimating the eight projective parameters and ignoring the two chirp parameters **c** (which capture the essence of tilt and pan). These six parameters **A, b** are more accurate than those obtained using the affine estimation, as the affine estimation tries to fit its shear parameters to the camera pan and tilt. In other words, the affine estimation does worse than the six affine parameters within the projective estimation. The affine coordinate transform is finally applied, giving the image shown. Note that the coordinate-transformed frames in the affine case are parallelograms.

6.5.1   Subcomposites and the Support Matrix

Two situations have so far been dealt with:

1. The camera movement is small, so any pair of frames chosen from the VideoOrbit have a substantial amount of overlap when expressed in a common coordinate system. (Use differential parameter estimation.)

2. The camera movement is monotonic, so any errors that accumulate along the registered sequence are not particularly noticeable. (Use cumulative parameter estimation.)

In the example of Figure 6.14, any cumulative errors are not particularly noticeable because the camera motion is progressive; that is, it does not reverse direction or loop around on itself. Now let us look at an example where the camera motion loops back on itself and small errors, because of violations of the assumptions (fixed camera location and static scene) accumulate.

Consider the image sequence shown in Figure 6.15. The composite arising from bringing these 16 image frames into the coordinates of the first frame exhibited somewhat poor registration due to cumulative error; this sequence is used to illustrate the importance of subcomposites.

The differential support matrix[20] appears in Figure 6.16. The entry $q_{m,n}$ tells us how much frame n overlaps with frame m in the matrix when expressed in the coordinates of frame m, for the sequence of Figure 6.15.

Examining the support matrix, and the mean-squared error estimates, the local maxima of the support matrix correspond to the local minima of the mean-squared error estimates, suggesting the subcomposites:[21] $\{7, 8, 9, 10, 6, 5\}$, $\{1, 2, 3, 4\}$, and $\{15, 14, 13, 12\}$. It is important to note that when the error is low, if the support is also low, the error estimate might not be valid. For example, if the two images overlap in only one pixel, then even if the error estimate is zero (i.e., the pixel has a value of 255 in both images), the alignment is not likely good.

The selected subcomposites appear in Figure 6.17. Estimating the coordinate transformation between these subcomposites, and putting them together into a common frame of reference results in a composite (Fig. 6.17) about 1200 pixels across. The image is sharp despite the fact that the person in the picture was moving slightly and the camera operator was also moving (violating the assumptions of both static scene and fixed center of projection).

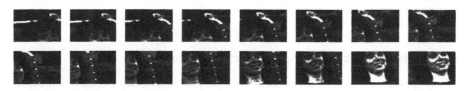

Figure 6.15 The Hewlett Packard "Claire" image sequence, which violates the assumptions of the model (the camera location was not fixed, and the scene was not completely static). Images appear in TV raster-scan order.

---

[20] The differential support matrix is not necessarily symmetric, while the cumulative support matrix for which the entry $q_{m,n}$ tells us how much frame n overlaps with frame m when expressed in the coordinates of frame 0 (reference frame) is symmetric.

[21] Researchers at Sarnoff also consider the use of subcomposites; they refer to them as *tiles* [130,131]

subPIC, frames 0 to 4

1.00	0.91	0.80	0.68	0.54	0.41	0.30	0.23	0.19	0.17	0.17	0.18	0.19	0.20	0.21	0.23
0.91	1.00	0.89	0.76	0.62	0.49	0.37	0.30	0.25	0.22	0.21	0.22	0.22	0.23	0.24	0.26
0.80	0.89	1.00	0.87	0.72	0.58	0.47	0.38	0.33	0.29	0.27	0.27	0.27	0.27	0.28	0.25
0.68	0.76	0.87	1.00	0.85	0.70	0.58	0.48	0.42	0.37	0.34	0.33	0.33	0.33	0.29	0.23
0.53	0.61	0.72	0.84	1.00	0.85	0.71	0.61	0.53	0.47	0.44	0.42	0.41	0.35	0.28	0.22
0.40	0.48	0.58	0.70	0.85	1.00	0.85	0.74	0.66	0.59	0.55	0.53	0.44	0.34	0.26	0.20
0.29	0.37	0.46	0.57	0.71	0.86	1.00	0.88	0.79	0.71	0.67	0.56	0.44	0.35	0.26	0.19
0.22	0.29	0.38	0.48	0.61	0.75	0.88	1.00	0.91	0.82	0.71	0.58	0.46	0.36	0.27	0.19
0.19	0.25	0.32	0.42	0.54	0.66	0.79	0.90	1.00	0.91	0.78	0.65	0.52	0.41	0.31	0.21
0.16	0.22	0.28	0.37	0.47	0.59	0.70	0.81	0.90	1.00	0.87	0.73	0.60	0.48	0.36	0.25
0.16	0.21	0.27	0.34	0.44	0.54	0.65	0.69	0.76	0.86	1.00	0.85	0.71	0.57	0.45	0.33
0.18	0.21	0.27	0.33	0.42	0.52	0.54	0.56	0.63	0.71	0.84	1.00	0.85	0.71	0.57	0.44
0.19	0.22	0.27	0.33	0.41	0.43	0.43	0.45	0.50	0.58	0.69	0.84	1.00	0.85	0.70	0.57
0.20	0.23	0.27	0.33	0.35	0.34	0.34	0.35	0.40	0.46	0.57	0.70	0.85	1.00	0.85	0.71
0.22	0.25	0.29	0.30	0.28	0.27	0.26	0.27	0.30	0.36	0.45	0.57	0.71	0.85	1.00	0.85
0.24	0.27	0.26	0.24	0.22	0.21	0.19	0.19	0.22	0.26	0.33	0.45	0.57	0.71	0.85	1.00

subPIC, frames 5 to 11

subPIC, frames 12 to 15

(*a*)

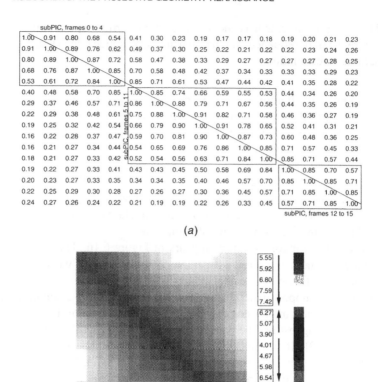

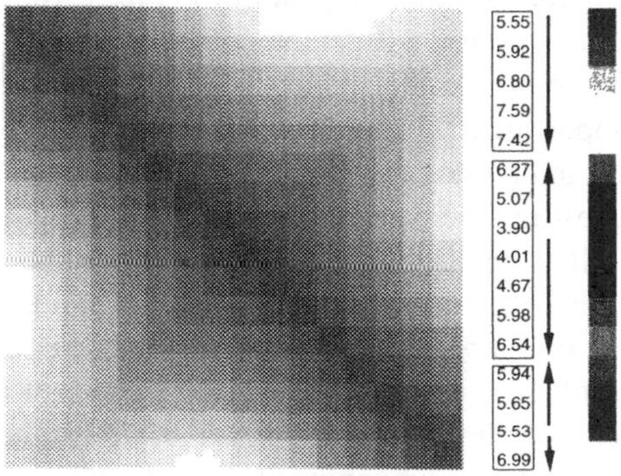
5.55
5.92
6.80
7.59
7.42
6.27
5.07
3.90
4.01
4.67
5.98
6.54
5.94
5.65
5.53
6.99

(*b*) (*c*) (*d*)

Figure 6.16 Support matrix and mean-squared registration error defined by image sequence in Figure 6.15 and the estimated coordinate transformations between images. (*a*) Entries in table. The diagonals are one, since every frame is fully supported in itself. The entries just above (or below) the diagonal give the amount of pairwise support. For example, frames 0 and 1 share high mutual support (0.91). Frames 7, 8, and 9 also share high mutual support (again 0.91). (*b*) Corresponding *density plot* (more dense ink indicates higher values). (*c*) Mean-square registration error; (*d*) corresponding density plot.

6.5.2 Flat Subject Matter and Alternate Coordinates

Many sports such as football or soccer are played on a nearly flat field that forms a rigid planar patch over which the analysis may be conducted. After each of the frames undergoes the appropriate coordinate transformation to bring it into the same coordinate system as the reference frame, the sequence can be played back showing only the players (and the image boundaries) moving. Markings on the field (e.g., numbers and lines) remain at a fixed location, which makes subsequent analysis and summary of the video content easier. These data make a good test case for the algorithms because video is noisy and players violate the assumption of a static scene.

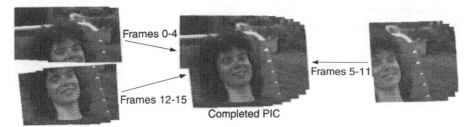

Figure 6.17 Subcomposites are each made from subsets of the images that share high quantities of mutual support and low estimates of mutual error, and then combined to form the final composite.

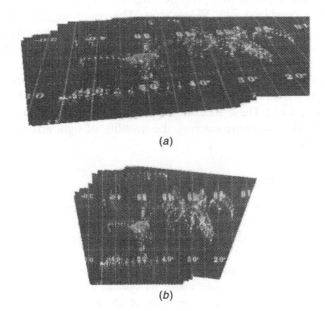

Figure 6.18 Image composite made from 16 video frames taken from a television broadcast sporting event. Note the "Edgertonian" appearance, as each player traces out a stroboscopic path. The proposed method works robustly, despite the movement of players on the field. (a) Images are expressed in the coordinates of the first frame. (b) Images are expressed in a new useful coordinate system corresponding to none of the original frames. The slight distortions due to the fact that football fields are never perfectly flat but raised slightly in the center.

Despite the moving players in the video, the proposed method successfully registers all of the images in the orbit, mapping them into a single high-resolution image composite of the entire playing field. Figure 6.18a shows 16 frames of video from a football game combined into a single image composite, expressed in the coordinates of the first image in the sequence. The choice of coordinate system was arbitrary, and any of the images could have been chosen as the reference frame. In fact a coordinate system other than one chosen from the input images could even be used. In particular, a coordinate system where *parallel lines never meet*, and periodic structures are "dechirped" (Fig. 6.18*b*) lends itself well to machine vision and player-tracking algorithms [132]. Even if the entire playing field is not visible in a particular image, collectively the video from an entire game will reveal every square yard of the playing surface at one time or another, enabling a composite to be made of the entire playing surface.

6.6   AGC AND THE RANGE OF LIGHT

6.6.1   Overview

In this section the Wyckoff [63] photoquantigraphic imaging principle presented in Chapter 5 is combined with VideoOrbits. The result suggests that a camera rotated about its center of projection, may be used as a measuring instrument. The look-and-paint metaphor of this chapter will now provide not just a picture of increased spatial extent but a way to "paint" a set of photoquantigraphic *measurements* onto an empty "canvas," as the camera is swept around. (In the case where the camera is the eye, the painting is accomplished by gaze-based measurement spaces.) These measurements describe, up to a single unknown scalar constant (for the entire canvas), the quantity of light arriving from every direction in space.

6.6.2   Turning AGC from a Bug into a Feature

In Chapter 5 much was said about and done with differently exposed images. Now we will consider images that differ not only in exposure but also in projection. They are related by a projective coordinate transformation, in addition to the change in quantity of light of Chapter 5.

Consider a static scene and fixed center of projection at which a camera is free to zoom, pan, tilt, and rotate about its optical axis. With an ideal camera, the resulting images are in the same orbit of the projective group-action, and each pixel of each image provides a measurement of a ray of light passing through a common point in space. Unfortunately, as noted at the beginning of this chapter, most modern cameras have a built in automatic gain control (AGC), automatic shutter, or auto-iris that cannot be turned off. Many modern digitizers to which cameras are connected have their own AGC, which also cannot be disabled. With AGC, the characteristic response function of the camera varies, making it impossible to accurately describe one image as a projective coordinate transformed version of another.

Below, a solution to this problem is proposed, as well as a means of turning AGC into an asset. It turns out that AGC is the very element that produces differently exposed images. When we point the camera at bright objects, the gain decreases, so darker objects in the periphery may be grossly underexposed. When the camera is centered on dark objects, the periphery is grossly overexposed. Since the same objects often appear in the periphery of both overexposed and underexposed images, we obtain, without expending any conscious thought or effort, pictures of overlapping subject matter in which the same subject matter is available at a wide variety of exposures. Therefore, even in cases where AGC could be disabled, we will most likely choose not to turn it off.

6.6.3   AGC as Generator of Wyckoff Set

Say we take two pictures using the same settings (in manual exposure mode), the same scene, and a fixed common location (where the camera is free to zoom, pan, tilt, and rotate about its optical axis between taking the two pictures). Both pictures capture the same pencil of light (we neglect the boundaries of the sensor array and assume that both pictures have sufficient field of view to capture all of the objects of interest). Yet each picture projects this information differently onto the film or image sensor. Neglecting that which falls beyond the borders of the pictures, the images are in the same orbit of the projective group of coordinate transformations. The use of projective (homographic) coordinate transformations to automatically (without use of explicit features) combine multiple pictures of the same scene into a single picture of greater resolution or spatial extent was first described in 1993 [63]. These coordinate transformations were shown to capture the essence of a camera at a fixed center of projection (COP) in a static scene.

Note that the projective group of coordinate transformations is not Abelian, and that there is thus some uncertainty in the estimation of the parameters associated with this group of coordinate transformations [73]. We may first estimate parameters of Abelian subgroups (e.g., the pan/tilt parameters, approximating them as a 2-D translation so that Fourier methods [127] may be used). Estimation of zoom (scale) together with pan and tilt, would incorporate noncommutative parameters (zoom and translation don't commute), but could still be done using the *multiresolution Fourier transform* [133,134], at least as a first step, followed by a repetitive parameter estimation procedure over all parameters. An iterative approach to the estimation of the parameters of a projective (homographic) coordinate transformation between images was suggested in [63], and later in [129] and [98].

Lie algebra is the algebra of symmetry. It pertains to the behavior of a group in the neighborhood of its identity. With typical video sequences, coordinate transformations relating adjacent frames of the sequence are very close to the identity. Thus we may use the Lie algebra of the group when considering adjacent frames of the sequence, and then use the group itself when combining these frames together. For example, to find the coordinate transformation, p_{09}, between $F_0(x, y)$, frame 0 and $F_9(x, y)$, frame 9, we might use the Lie algebra to estimate p_{01} (the coordinate transformation between frames 0 and 1) and then estimate p_{12} between frames 1 and 2, and so on. Each transformation is found in the neighborhood of the identity. Then to obtain p_{09}, we use the *true law of composition* of the group: $p_{09} = p_{01} \circ p_{12} \circ \ldots \circ p_{89}$.

6.6.4 Ideal Spotmeter

Recall the ideal spotmeter, presented in Chapter 6. It is a perfectly directional lightmeter that measures the quantity of light, q, arriving from the direction in which it is pointed (parameterized by its azimuth, θ, and its elevation, ϕ). In Chapter 5 we saw how an ordinary camera could be linearized by simply analyzing a collection of differently exposed images. Here we will see how a camera with time-varying gain (e.g., one with AGC) can be made to function as closely as possible, to a collection of the idealized spotmeters of Chapter 6, similar to that depicted in Figure 5.2, although typically with only three color channels (red, green, and blue).

The basic philosophy of Chapter 5 is that the camera may be regarded as an array of (nonmetric) spotmeters, measuring rays of light passing through the center of projection (COP). To each pair of pixel indexes of the sensor array in a camera, we may associate an azimuth and elevation. Eliminating lens distortion [106] makes the images obey the laws of projective geometry so that they are (to within image noise and cropping) in the same orbit of the projective group action. (Lens distortion may also be simply absorbed into the mapping between pixel locations and directions of arrival.)

In Chapter 5 we found that using a pixel from a camera as a lightmeter raises many interesting problems. The output of a typical camera, f, is not linear with respect to the incoming quantity of light, q. For a digital camera, the output, f, is the pixel value, while for film, the output might be the density of the film at the particular location under consideration. It was assumed that the output was some unknown but monotonic function of the input. (Monotonicity being a weaker constraint than linearity.)

Parametric and nonparametric methods of estimating this nonlinearity, in pictures that differ only in exposure, were presented in Chapter 3, and these methods facilitated the use of an ordinary camera as an array of metric spotmeters, measuring, to within a single unknown constant, the quantity of light arriving from each direction in space.

In this chapter, one of the methods developed in Chapter 5 is selected to illustrate the parametric method for estimating f based on automatically determining the parameters of the classic response curve [75] given in equation (4.51) from pictures that differ only in exposure. This method is emphasized here as it is introduced into VideoOrbits. However, any method of Chapter 5 may be similarly combined with VideoOrbits.

6.6.5 AGC

If what is desired is a picture of increased spatial extent or spatial resolution, the nonlinearity is not a problem so long as it is not image dependent. However, most low-cost cameras have built-in automatic gain control (AGC), electronic level control, auto-iris, and other forms of automatic exposure that cannot be turned off or disabled. (For simplicity all such methods of automatic exposure

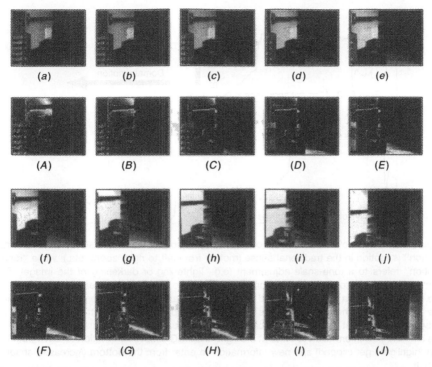

Figure 6.19 The fire-exit sequence, taken using a camera with AGC. (a)–(j) frames 0 to 9: As the camera pans across to take in more of the open doorway, the image brightens and shows more of the interior, while at the same time, clipping highlight detail. Frame 0 (a) shows the writing on the white paper taped to the door very clearly, but the interior is completely black. In frame 5 (f) the paper is completely obliterated. It is so washed out that we cannot even discern that there is a paper present. Although the interior is getting brighter, it is still not discernible in frame 5 (f), but more and more detail of the interior becomes visible as we proceed through the sequence, showing that the fire exit is blocked by the clutter inside. (A)–(J) "certainty" images are corresponding to (a) to (j).

control are referred to as AGC, whether or not they are actually implemented using gain adjustment.) This means that the unknown response function, $f(q)$, is image dependent. It will therefore change over time, as the camera framing changes to include brighter or darker objects.

AGC was a good invention for its intended application, serving the interests of most camera users who merely wish to have a properly exposed picture without having to make adjustments to the camera. However, it has thwarted attempts to estimate the projective coordinate transformation between frame pairs. Examples of an image sequence, acquired using a camera with AGC appear in Figure 6.19.

A joint estimation of the projective coordinate transformation and the tone-scale change may be regarded as "motion estimation" problems if we extend the concept of motion estimation to include both domain motion (motion in the traditional sense) and range motion (Fig. 6.20).

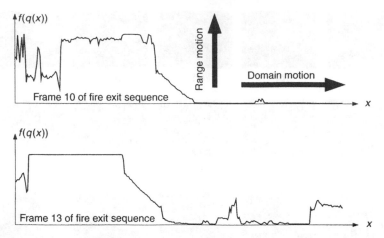

Figure 6.20 One row across each of two images from the fire-exit sequence. "Domain motion" is motion in the traditional sense (motion from left to right, zoom, etc.), while "range motion" refers to a tone-scale adjustment (e.g., lightening or darkening of the image). The camera is panning to the right, so domain motion is to the left. However, when panning to the right, the camera points more and more into the darkness of an open doorway, causing the AGC to adjust the exposure. Thus there is some upward motion of the curve as well as leftward motion. Just as panning the camera across causes information to leave the frame at the left, and new information to enter at the right, the AGC causes information to leave from the top (highlights get clipped) and new information to enter from the bottom (increased shadow detail).

6.7   JOINT ESTIMATION OF BOTH DOMAIN AND RANGE COORDINATE TRANSFORMATIONS

As in [129], we consider one-dimensional "images" for purposes of illustration, with the understanding that the actual operations are performed on 2-D images. The 1-D projective-Wyckoff group is defined in terms of the group of projective coordinate transformations, taken together with the one-parameter group of image darkening/lightening operations:

$$p_{a,b,c,k} \circ f(q(x)) = g\left(f\left(q\left(\frac{ax+b}{cx+1}\right)\right)\right) = f\left(kq\left(\frac{ax+b}{cx+1}\right)\right),$$

where g characterizes the lightening/darkening operation.

The law of composition is defined as: $(p_{abc}, p_k) \circ (p_{def}, p_l) = (p_{abc} \circ p_{def}, p_k \circ p_l)$ where the first law of composition on the right-hand side is the usual one for the projective group, and the second one is that of the one-parameter lightening/darkening subgroup.

Two successive frames of a video sequence are related through a group-action that is near the identity of the group. Thus one could think of the Lie algebra of the group as providing the structure locally. As in previous work [129] an approximate model that matches the "exact" model in the neighborhood of the identity is used. For the projective group, the approximate model has the form $q_2(x) = q_1((ax + b)/(cx + 1))$.

For the Wyckoff group (which is a one-parameter group isomorphic to addition over the reals, or multiplication over the positive reals), the approximate model may be taken from (4.51) by noting that

$$g(f(q)) = f(kq) = \alpha + \beta(kq)^\gamma = \alpha - k^\gamma \alpha + k^\gamma \alpha + k^\gamma \beta q^\gamma$$
$$= k^\gamma f(q) + \alpha - \alpha k^\gamma. \tag{6.36}$$

Thus we see that $g(f)$ is a linear equation (is affine) in f. This affine relationship suggests that linear regression on the comparagram between two images would provide an estimate of α and γ, while leaving β unknown. This result is consistent with the fact that the response curve may only be determined up to a constant scale factor.

From (6.36) we have that the (generalized) brightness change constraint equation is

$$g(f(q(x, t))) = f(kq(x, t))$$
$$= f(q(x + \Delta x, t + \Delta t))$$
$$= k^\gamma f(q(x, t)) + \alpha - \alpha k^\gamma$$
$$= k^\gamma F(x, t) + \alpha(1 - k^\gamma), \tag{6.37}$$

where $F(x, t) = f(q(x, t))$. Combining this equation with the Taylor series representation:

$$F(x + \Delta x, t + \Delta t) = F(x, t) + \Delta x F_x(x, t) + \Delta t F_t(x, t), \tag{6.38}$$

where $F_x(x, t) = (df/dq)(dq(x)/dx)$, at time t, and $F_t(x, t) = G(x, t) - F(x, t)$ is the frame difference of adjacent frames where $G(x, t) = g(f(q(x, t)))$. So we have

$$k^\gamma F + \alpha(1 - k^\gamma) = F + \Delta x F_x + \Delta t F_t. \tag{6.39}$$

Thus the brightness change constraint equation becomes

$$F + u F_x + F_t - k^\gamma F - \alpha(1 - k^\gamma) = \varepsilon \tag{6.40}$$

where we have normalized $\Delta t = 1$.

Substitution of the approximate model, as was used in (6.24) (e.g., that of Equation 6.23) into (6.40) gives:

$$F + (q_2 x^2 + q_1 x + q_0) F_x + F_t - k^\gamma F + \alpha k^\gamma - \alpha = \varepsilon. \tag{6.41}$$

Minimizing $\sum \varepsilon^2$ yields a linear solution in parameters of the approximate model:

$$\begin{bmatrix} \sum x^4 F_x^2 & \sum x^3 F_x^2 & \sum x^2 F_x^2 & \sum x^2 F F_x & \sum x^2 F_x \\ \sum x^3 F_x^2 & \sum x^2 F_x^2 & \sum x F_x^2 & \sum x F F_x & \sum x F_x \\ \sum x^2 F_x^2 & \sum x F_x^2 & \sum F_x^2 & \sum F F_x & \sum F_x \\ \sum x^2 F F_x & \sum x F F_x & \sum F F_x & \sum F^2 & \sum F \\ \sum x^2 F_x & \sum x F_x & \sum F_x & \sum F & \sum 1 \end{bmatrix}$$

$$\begin{bmatrix} q_0 \\ q_1 \\ q_0 \\ 1 - k^\gamma \\ \alpha k^\gamma - \alpha \end{bmatrix} = - \begin{bmatrix} \sum x^2 F_x F_t \\ \sum x F_x F_t \\ \sum F_x F_t \\ \sum F F_t \\ \sum F_t \end{bmatrix}.$$

The parameters of the approximate model are related to those of the exact model, as was illustrated earlier in this chapter (using the feedback process of Fig. 6.10).

This new mathematical result enables images to be brought not just into register in the traditional domain motion sense, but also into the same tonal scale through antihomomorphic gain adjustment. The combination of a spatial coordinate transformation combined with a tone-scale adjustment is referred to as a "spatiotonal transformation." In particular, it is the spatiotonal transformation of antihomomorphic homography that is of interest (i.e., homographic coordinate transformation combined with antihomomorphic gain adjustment). This form

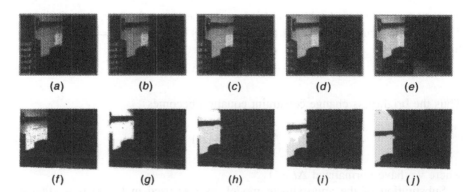

(a)   (b)   (c)   (d)   (e)

(f)   (g)   (h)   (i)   (j)

Figure 6.21 Antihomomorphic homographies. All images are expressed in spatiotonal coordinates of the first image in the sequence. This means that each image is comparadjusted (tonally registered) as well as coordinate transformed (spatially registered) with the first image in the image sequence.

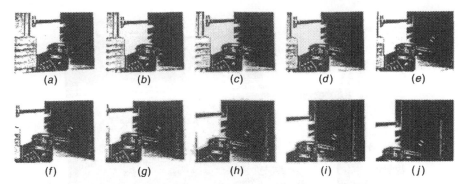

Figure 6.22 Antihomomorphic homographies. All images are expressed in spatiotonal coordinates of the last image in the sequence.

of spatiotonal transformation is illustrated in Figure 6.21 where all the images are transformed into the coordinates of the first image of the sequence, and in Figure 6.22 where all the images are transformed into the coordinates of the last frame in the image sequence. Here, because a tele-lens is used, the perspective is not as dramatic as it was in some of the image sequences observed earlier in this chapter, but it is still quite pronounced. Thus we have succeeded in simultaneously estimating the underlying gain change as well as the projective coordinate transformation relating successive pairs of images in the image sequence.

6.8 THE BIG PICTURE

To construct a single floating-point image of increased spatial extent and increased dynamic range, each pixel of the output image is constructed from a weighted sum of the images whose coordinate-transformed bounding boxes fall within that pixel. The weights in the weighted sum are the so-called certainty functions [59], which are found by evaluating the derivative of the corresponding effective response function at the pixel value in question. While the response function, $f(q)$, is fixed for a given camera, the effective response function, $f(k_i(q))$ depends on the exposure, k_i, associated with frame, i, in the image sequence. By evaluating $f_q(k_i(q_i(x, y)))$, we arrive at the certainty images (Fig. 6.19). Lighter areas of the certainty images indicate moderate values of exposure (midtones in the corresponding images), while darker values of the certainty images designate exposure extrema—exposure in the *toe* or *shoulder* regions of the response curve where it is difficult to discern subtle differences in exposure.

The photoquantigraphic estimate may be explored interactively on a computer system (Fig. 6.23). However the simultaneous wide dynamic range and ability to discern subtle differences in grayscale are lost once the image is reduced to a tangible form (i.e., a hardcopy printout).

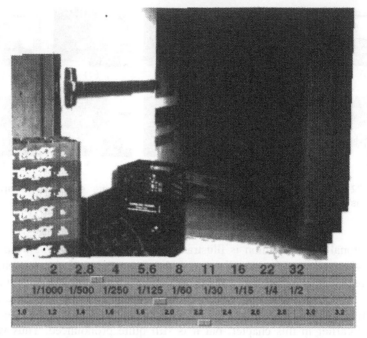

Figure 6.23 Floating-point photoquantigraphic image constructed from the fire-exit sequence. The dynamic range of the image is far greater than that of a computer screen or printed page. The photoquantigraphic information may be interactively viewed on the computer screen, and not only as an environment map (with pan, tilt, and zoom) but also with control of exposure and contrast. With a virtual camera we can move around in the photoquantigraph, both spatially and tonally.

6.8.1 Paper and the Range of Light

Print paper typically has a dynamic range that is much lower than that of photographic emulsion (film).[22] Standard photographic processes may be used to mitigate this effect to a limited extent. For example, through careful choice of chemical developers used in processing the film, a lateral inhibition effect can be produced (very similar to the lateral inhibition that happens in the human visual system) that violates the monotonicity constraint we have emphasized so strongly. Print paper instead returns an image where the grayscale value at a given point depends not only on the quantity of light arriving at that point but also on the grayscale values of neighboring regions. Alternatively, for negative film, contrast masks may be made which help in the photographic printing process.

More recently computational methods of reducing the dynamic range of images have been explored [58]. Just as these methods were applied to the images of Chapter 5, they may be applied to the photoquantigraphic image composites of

---

[22] The dynamic range of some papers is around 100 : 1, while that of many films is around 500 : 1.

Figure 6.24 Fixed-point image made by tone-scale adjustments that are only locally monotonic, followed by quantization to 256 graylevels. We can see clearly both the small piece of white paper on the door (and can even read what it says — "COFFEE HOUSE CLOSED"), as well as the details of the dark interior. We could not have captured such a nicely exposed image using an on-camera fill-flash to reduce scene contrast, because the fill-flash would mostly light up the areas near the camera (which happen to be the areas that are already too bright), while hardly affecting objects at the end of the dark corridor which are already too dark. One would then need to set up additional photographic lighting equipment to obtain a picture of this quality. This image demonstrates the advantage of a small lightweight personal imaging system built unobtrusively into a pair of eyeglasses. In this setup an image of very high quality was captured by simply looking around, without entering the corridor. This system is particularly useful when trying to report a violation of fire-safety laws, while at the same time not appearing to be trying to capture an image. The present image was shot some distance away from the premises (using a miniaturized tele lens that the author built into his eyeglass-based system). The effects of perspective, though present, are not as immediately obvious as in some of the other extreme wide-angle image composites presented earlier in this chapter.

this chapter. As with the photographic lateral inhibition, these methods also relax the monotonicity constraint.

Thus, in order to print a photoquantigraph, it may be preferable to relax the monotonicity constraint, and perform some local tone-scale adjustments (Fig. 6.24).

6.8.2   An Extreme Example with Spatiotonal Processing of Photoquantities

To fully appreciate the benefits of photoquantigraphic image processing, combined with VideoOrbits, let us consider a seemingly impossible scene to photograph in a natural way without bringing in lighting equipment. Figure 6.25 depicts a scene in which there is a dynamic range in excess of a million to one. Two pictures were captured with several orders of magnitude difference

(a)   (b)

(c)

Figure 6.25 Extreme illustration of nonmonotonic processing. (a) An underexposed picture shows details such as the horizon and the sail of a boat, as seen through an open doorway, even though the sail is backlit with extremely bright light. (b) The picture is taken from inside an abandoned fortress with no interior light. Light coming in from the open door is largely lost in the vastness of the dark interior. A much longer exposure is needed to show any detail of the inside of the fortress. (c) Sharpened (filtered) photoquantigraphic estimate $\hat{f}\{k_d S\hat{q}[(\hat{A}_2 x + \hat{b}_2)/(\hat{c}_2 x + \hat{d}_2)]\}$ expressed in the projective coordinates of the right-hand image ($i = 2$). A dynamic range in excess of a million to one was captured in $\hat{q}$, and the estimate was then photoquantigraphically sharpened, resulting in a lateral inhibition effect so that the output is no longer monotonically related to the input. Notice, for example, that the sail is as dark as some shadow areas inside the fortress. Because of this filtering, a tremendous dynamic range has been captured and reduced to that of printed media while still revealing details of the scene. © Steve Mann, 1991.

between the two exposures. Thus the photoquantigraphic estimate $\hat{q}$ has far greater dynamic range than can be directly viewed on a television or on the printed page. Display of $\hat{f}(\hat{k}_1 q)$ would fail to show the shadow details, while display of $\hat{f}(\hat{k}_2 q)$ would fail to show the highlight details.

In this case, even if we had used the virtual camera architecture depicted in Figure 4.5, there would be no single value of display exposure k_d for which a display image $f_d = \hat{f}(k_d \hat{q})$ would capture both the inside of the abandoned fortress and the details looking outside through the open doorway.

Therefore a strong highpass (sharpening) filter, S was applied to $\hat{q}$, to sharpen the photoquantity $\hat{q}$, as well as provide lateral inhibition similar to the way in which the human eye functions. Then the filtered result,

$$\hat{f}\left(k_d S \hat{q} \left(\frac{\hat{A}_2 \mathbf{x} + \hat{\mathbf{b}}_2}{\hat{\mathbf{c}}_2 \mathbf{x} + \hat{d}_2}\right)\right),$$

was displayed on the printed page (Fig. 6.25c), in the projective coordinates of the second (rightmost) image, $i = 2$. Note the introduction of spatial coordinates **A**, **b**, **c**, and d. These compensate for projection (which occurs if the camera moves slightly between pictures), as described in [2,77]. In particular, the parameters of a projective coordinate transformation are typically estimated together with the nonlinear camera response function and the exposure ratio between pictures [2,77].

As a result of the filtering operation, notice that there is no longer a monotonic relationship between input photoquantity q and output level on the printed page. For example, the sail is as dark as some shadow areas inside the fortress. Because of this filtering the dynamic range of the image can be reduced to that of printed media, while still revealing details of the scene. This example answers the question, Why capture more dynamic range than you can display.

Even if the objective is a picture of limited dynamic range, perhaps where the artist wishes to deliberately wash out highlights and mute down shadows for expressive purposes, the proposed philosophy is still quite valid. The procedure captures a measurement space, recording the quantity of light arriving at each angle in space, and then from that measurement space, synthesizes the tonally degraded image. This way as much information about the scene as possible becomes embedded in a photoquantigraphic estimate, and then "expressed" into that estimate (by throwing away information in a controlled fashion) to produce the final picture.

6.9 REALITY WINDOW MANAGER

6.9.1 VideoOrbits Head-Tracker

In virtual reality environments one ordinarily needs to install a special head-tracker, with head-tracking devices installed in the environment around the user. However, this installation assumes a cooperative environment.

In certain situations the environment is not cooperative. Extreme examples of noncooperative environments might include criminal settings, gambling casinos, and commercial operations, run by crooks. In a department store owned by a criminal organization, or in any other establishment that might be a money-laundering front, it is doubtful that a customer wearing a camera would be welcome, let alone infrastructure being provided to make the photographing better.

Accordingly, for day–to–day use in ordinary environments like department stores, banks, and out on the street, the visual prosthetic must not depend entirely on the environment to function well. The VideoOrbits system provides a featureless environment (object) tracker so that, as the user looks around, the apparatus has a sense of where one is looking in the scene. This means that the user does not need a special separate head tracking device that might otherwise require a cooperative environment.

6.9.2 A Simple Example of RWM

Reality window managers (RWMs) often provide the ability to have a large virtual screen, and to move around within that virtual screen. When the VideoOrbits head-tracker is used, the mediation zone of a reality mediator can become a viewport into this virtual screen (Fig. 6.26).

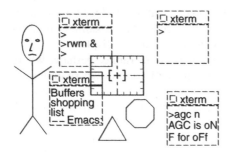

Embodiment of wearcam invention, as seen while looking through viewfinder

(a)

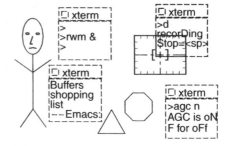

Foveated embodiment of wearable camera system --- --- as seen while looking through vviewfinder

(b)

Figure 6.26 Reality window manager (RWM). The viewport is defined by an EyeTap or laser EyeTap device and serves as a view into the real world. This viewport is denoted by a reticle and graticule with crosshairs. The mediation zone over the visual perception of reality can be altered. There is a virtual screen. Portions of windows inside the viewport are denoted by solid lines, and portions of windows outside the viewport are denoted by dotted lines. Actual objects in the scene are drawn as solid lines, and are of course always visible. (a) Initially the mediation zone is in the center of the virtual screen. (b) When it is desired to select a window, one looks over to the desired window. This selects the window. The user then presses "d" to select "recorD" (r selects rewind, etc.).

6.9.3   The Wearable Face Recognizer as an Example of a Reality User Interface

Once an RWM is running, it can also be used for many other purposes. It can provide a constantly running automatic background process such as face recognition in which virtual name tags exist in the wearer's own visual world. These virtual name tags appear as illusory planar patches arising through the process of marking a reference frame [73] with text or simple graphics. By calculating and matching homographies of the plane using VideoOrbits, as described earlier in this chapter an illusory rigid planar patch appears to hover upon objects in the real world, and this allows a form of computer-mediated collaboration [1].

This collaborative capability holds promise for the application of HIs as aids for the visually challenged or the elderly with visual memory disabilities [14]. In HI systems a computer program, or remote expert (be it human or machine), could assist users in negotiating their paths, or provide photographic/videographic memories, such as the ability to associate a name with a face (see Fig. 6.27).

In the figure note that the tracking remains at or near subpixel accuracy even when the subject matter begins to move out of the mediation zone, and in fact even after the subject matter has left the mediation zone. This is due to the fact that the tracking is featureless and global.

With the RWM turned on one could leave a grocery list on the refrigerator to be read by a selected individual, since not everyone wearing the special glasses would see the message. Only the person wearing the glasses and on the list of intended recipients, has this capability.

Note that the message could be sent right away, and "live" dormant on the recipient's WearComp until an image of the desired object "wakes up" the

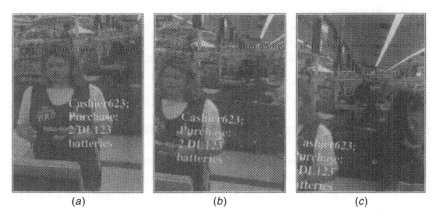

(a)   (b)   (c)

Figure 6.27 Mediated reality as a photographic/videographic memory prosthesis. RWM provides a window into reality, in which the virtual window tracks the real scene to within subpixel accuracy. (a) Wearable face-recognizer with virtual "name tag" (and grocery list) appears to stay attached to the cashier, (b) even when the cashier is no longer within the field of view of the video camera and transmitter (c).

Figure 6.28 Virtual message left on the wall under the entrance to the grocery store. When the recipient of the message approaches the store wearing a reality mediator, the message left there will suddenly appear. As the wearer moves his/her head, the message will appear to be attached to the wall. This is because the homography of the plane is tracked, and a projective coordinate transformation is performed on the message before it is inserted into the wearer's reality stream. (*Top*) Lens distortion in WearCam results in poor registration. (*Bottom*) After correcting for lens distortion using the Campbell method [106] the sub-pixel registration is possible. (Data captured by author and processed later on base station; thanks to J. Levine for assisting author in porting VideoOrbits to SGI architecture used at base station.)

message, as illustrated in Figure 6.28. This message includes a virtual Post–It note (to use Feiner's Post–It metaphor), in addition to the name. The note provides additional information, associated with (bound to) the face of the cashier. The additional information pertains to the purchase. These notes could be notes that the wearers give to themselves, or notes that wearers send to other people.

A recent example appears in Figure 6.28. Observe how the flowfield of the rigid planar patch in the scene is tracked, and the virtual object (message) is inserted onto the flat surface. This message will be seen only by the recipient through a WearCam.

This illusory rigid planar patch could, of course, be photoquantigraphic. The patch then could be responsive to the automatic gain control of the camera, and the quantity of virtual light would be proportional to the quantity of real light that it replaces, to within a single scalar constant for the entire system.

6.10   APPLICATION OF ORBITS: THE PHOTONIC FIREWALL

Imagine an unauthorized user able to remotely log into your computing facility, and then running a large computer program on your computer without your knowledge or consent. Many people might refer to this as "theft" of CPU cycles (i.e., obtaining computing services without payment).

In many ways advertising does the same thing to our brains. The idea behind advertisements is to break into consumer brains by getting past their mental filters that have evolved to block out extraneous information. Like the banner ads on the WWW that try to simulate a second cursor, real-world ads try to trick the brain into paying attention. This sort of "in-band" signaling continually evolves in an attempt to try to bypass the mental filters we have developed to filter it out.

Like an intelligence arms race, both our coping mechanisms and the ads themselves escalate the amount of mental processing required to either filter them out or process them. In this way thefts of the brain's CPU cycles are increasing rapidly.

Ads are also being designed to be responsive. Consider the talking ads above urinals that trigger on approach; it is as if we have a multimedia spectacle that watches and responds to our movements. This is a closed-loop process involving the theft of personal information (called humanistic property, analogous to intellectual property) followed by spam that is triggered by this stolen information.

To close the control system loop around a victim (e.g. to make the human victim both *controllable* as well as *observable*), perpetrators of humanistic property violations will typically commit the following violations:

- *Steal* personal information from the victim. This theft involves the violation of acquisitional privacy.
- *Traffick* in this stolen information. This trafficking involves the violation of disseminational privacy.
- *Spam* the victim. This spamming involves the violation of the victim's solitude.

It has been argued that intellectual property is already excessively protected [135]. Proponents of intellectual property have used the word "piracy" to describe making "unauthorized" copies of informational "wares." Of course, this immediately evokes villains who attack ocean-going vessels and kill all on board, tying the bodies to life rafts and setting them adrift to signal to rival pirates not to tread on their turf. Thus some consider the making of "unauthorized" copies of information wares equal in culpability to piracy. Mitch Kapor, cofounder of the Electronic Frontier Foundation (EFF), has criticized this equivalence between copying floppy disks and "software piracy" as the software industry's propaganda (see also http://wearcam.org/copyfire.html).

Thus the use of terms "steal" and "traffick" is no more extreme when applied to humanistic property than to intellectual property.

6.11 ALL THE WORLD'S A SKINNER BOX

The fundamental issue is the manipulation of the individual through observability and controllability. A block diagram, in which the human is part of a feedback loop, is shown in Figure 6.29. This "observability controllability" theory is closely related to behaviorist psychology which concerned itself primarily with measurable (observable) data, and for the most part excluded consideration of inner mental state of the person under control.

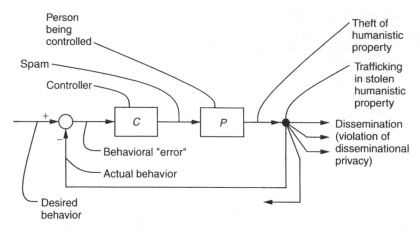

Figure 6.29   Block diagram depicting person, P, controlled by feedback loop comprising the three steps of external controllability: theft of humanistic property, followed by trafficking in said stolen property, followed by spamming. P is said to be *observable* when such theft is possible, and *controllable* when such spam is possible. Note also that desired behavior is subtracted from the actual behavior to obtain a behavioral "error" signal that is used by the controlling entity C to generate customized spam targeted at behavioral modification.

John B. Watson, a psychologist in the United States, was the "father" of behaviorist psychology as a purely objective (experimental) branch of science. B.F. Skinner pioneered the idea of behavior modification through reward and punishment, by modifying observable behavior instead of thoughts and feelings.

Skinner's "operant conditioning" relied on the ability to observe the subject and apply reward and punishment based on observed behavior. Thus Skinner's approach was a closed–loop control of sorts. It's no small wonder that the hottest trend in dog training — hotter than pawnshop televisions and stolen cars — is "operant conditioning."

French philosopher Michel Foucault provided a good critical analysis in his classic work *Surveiller et Punir* [136]. Somehow modern psychology has forgotten the lessens learned from basing a society on surveillance and torture, however mild or subtle. (Foucault documents how punishment has become weaker but more pervasive as time has evolved, and this theory is extended by the author to include the notion of micropunishments and microcrimes, in the limit as the process becomes infinitesimal [2].)

Fortunately behavioral psychology has recently come under much-needed criticism, as has evolutionary psychology. See, for example, Angier's analysis of psychologists (particularly evolutionary psychologists) [137]. Her use of the abbreviation "psycho" to refer to psychologists ("psychos" for plural) is indicative of a growing trend to call into question the goals of psychology, particularly branches of psychology that reduce human dignity to the level of animals or machines.

6.12 BLOCKING SPAM WITH A PHOTONIC FILTER

The problem summarized in Figure 6.29 provides us with the seeds of its own solution. Notably, if we can find a way to break open this feedback loop, we will find a way to subvert the hegemony of the controller.

This section deals primarily with solitude, defined as the freedom from violation by an inbound channel controlled by remote entities. Solitude, in this context, is distinct from privacy. For the purposes of this discussion, privacy is defined as the freedom from violation by an outbound channel controlled by remote entities.

While much has been written and proposed in the way of legislation and other societal efforts at protecting privacy and solitude, We concentrate here on a personal approach at the level of the point of contact between individuals and their environment. A similar personal approach to privacy issues has already appeared in the literature [138]. The main argument in [138] and [2] is that personal empowerment is possible through wearable cybernetics and humanistic intelligence.

This section applies a similar philosophical framework to the issue of solitude protection. In particular, the use of mediated reality, together with the VideoOrbits-based RWM, is suggested for the protection of personal solitude.

6.12.1 Preventing Theft of Personal Solitude by Putting Shades on the Window to the Soul

If it is true that the eyes are the window to the soul, this window is often left often unlocked. Anyone with enough money to construct a billboard can steal one's personal solitude with their real-world spam. Some writers have referred to advertising signs as pollution. Hardin [139] observes how advertising signs contribute further to the tragedy of the commons:

> In a reverse way, the tragedy of the commons reappears in problems of pollution. Here it is not a question of taking something out of the commons, but of putting something in — sewage, or chemical, radioactive, and heat wastes into water; noxious and dangerous fumes into the air; and *distracting and unpleasant advertising signs* into the line of sight. The calculations of utility are much the same as before. The rational man finds that his share of the cost of the wastes he discharges into the commons is less than the cost of purifying his wastes before releasing them. Since this is true for everyone, we are locked into a system of "fouling our own nest," so long as we behave only as independent, rational, free enterprisers. ... the air and waters surrounding us cannot readily be fenced, and so the tragedy of the commons as a cesspool must be prevented by different means, ... Indeed, our particular concept of private property, which deters us from exhausting the positive resources of the earth, favors pollution. The owner of a factory on the bank of a stream — whose property extends to the middle of the stream — often has difficulty seeing why it is not his natural right to muddy the waters flowing past his door. ... (emphasis added)

The owner of a building or other real estate can benefit directly from erecting distracting and unpleasant (at least unpleasant to some people) advertising signs into the line of sight of all who pass through the space in *and* around his or her property. Such theft of solitude allows an individual to benefit at the expense of others (i.e., at the expense of the commons).

Legislation is one solution to this problem. However, here, a diffusionist [138] approach is proposed in the form of a simple engineering solution in which the individual can filter out unwanted real-world spam. Since WearComp, when functioning as a reality mediator, has the potential to create a modified perception of visual reality, it can function as a visual filter.

WearComp, functioning as a reality mediator can, in addition to augmenting reality, also diminish or otherwise alter the visual perception of reality. Why would one want a diminished perception of reality? Why would anyone buy a pair of sunglasses that made one see worse?

An example of why we might want to experience a *diminished* reality is when we drive and must concentrate on the road. Sunglasses that not only diminish the glare of the sun's rays but also filter out distracting billboards could help us see the road better, and therefore drive more safely.

An example of the visual filter (operating on the author's view in Times Square) is shown in Figure 6.30. Thanks to the visual filter, the spam (unwanted advertising material) gets filtered out of the wearer's view. The advertisements, signs, or billboards are still visible, but they appear as windows, containing alternate material, such as email, or further messages from friends and relatives. This personalized world is a world of the wearer's own making, not the world that is thrust down our throats by advertisers.

Let us see how MR can prevent theft of visual attention and mental processing resources for the spam shown in Figure 6.30. In the figure light enters the front of the apparatus as is depicted in the image sequence, which is used to form a photoquantigraphic image composite. This photoquantigraphic representation follows the gaze of the wearer of the apparatus, and thus traces what the wearer would normally see if it were not for the apparatus.

Using a mathematical representation, the WearComp apparatus deletes or replaces the unwanted material with more acceptable (nonspam) material (Fig. 6.31). The nonspam substitute comprises various windows from the wearer's information space. As the mathematical representation is revised by the wearer's gaze pattern, a new sequence of frames for the spam-free image sequence is rendered, as shown in Figure 6.31. This is what the wearer sees. Note that only the frames of the sequence containing spam are modified. The visual filter in the wearcomp apparatus, makes it possible to filter out offensive advertising and turn billboards into useful cyberspace.

Unlimited Screen Real Estate

A common problem with computer screens is the limited screen real estate; that is, a limited number of pixels can be represented by the screen. This limitation

(a) (b)

(c) (d)

(e) (f)

(g) (h)

Figure 6.30 Successive video frames of Times Square view (frames 142–149).

can be overcome by using the VideoOrbits head-tracker of Figure 6.11. This apparatus attain an essentially unlimited screen size, where different windows are opened on different subject matter in the real world. If one wishes more screen real estate, one simply walks further down the street to discover new billboards.

The version of VideoOrbits described in this chapter makes a zero parallax assumption (that the billboards are flat). It could of course be generalized to arbitrary three-dimensional objects. Nevertheless, the flat object paradigm (i.e., rigid planar patch) is intuitive within the context of our being accustomed to flat display media such as television screens, paper, and signage, even when viewed

Figure 6.31 Filtered video frames of Times Square view (frames 142–149 filtered). Note the absence of spam within regions of images where spam was originally present. To prevent the theft of solitude, spam may be deleted, or replaced, with useful material such as personal email messages, the text of a favorite novel, or a favorite quote. Here the spam was replaced with window diagrams and a table of equations from the wearer's WWW site (http://wearcam.org/orbits).

from off axis. We are used to seeing, for example, a flat movie screen from one side of a theater and perceiving it as correct. Therefore we can quite comfortably use the VideoOrbits head-tracker to experience the windowing system that we call a reality window manager (RWM).

In some situations a single window in the RWM environment may be larger than the field of view of the apparatus. When this occurs we simply look into the space and find a larger window (see Figs. 6.32 and 6.33).

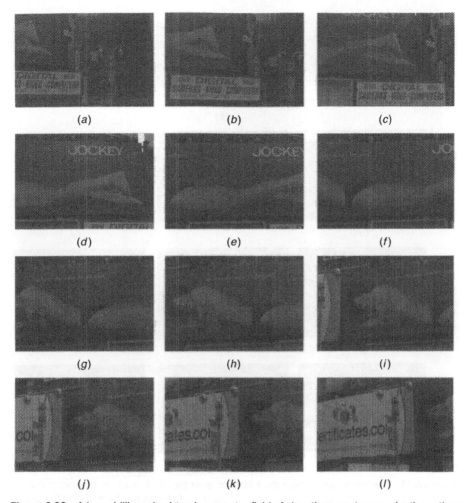

Figure 6.32 A large billboard subtends a greater field of view than can be seen by the author who is too close to such a large billboard to see its entire surface.

6.13 EXERCISES, PROBLEM SETS, AND HOMEWORK

6.13.1 The VideoOrbits Head-Tracker

In a mediated reality environment, such as with the WearCam viewfinder-based wearable face recognizer, an illusion of a rigid planar patch is sustained by a head-tracking system. In virtual reality, head-trackers are fixed in the environment because the headset can only be used in a specific environment. However, personal imaging systems are used in ordinary day-to-day life, such as in department stores, banks, or on the street. We cannot expect these organizations to install head-trackers for our convenience, especially since they generally prohibit

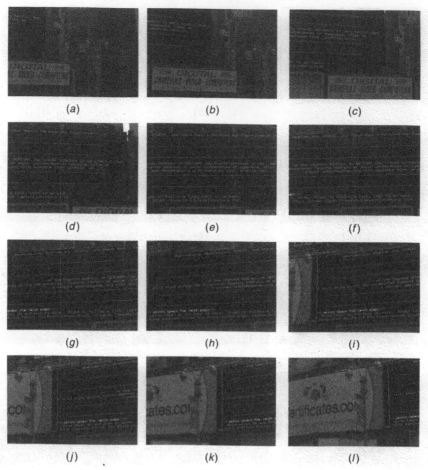

Figure 6.33   A window can replace the billboard even though it is larger than what can be seen by a person who is too close to a large billboard. The wearer of the apparatus simply looks around to see the entire screen. The experience is like being very close to a very high definition video display screen.

photography on their premises. Therefore if one wishes to do collaborative shopping with a shared viewfinder cursor (e.g., when a remote spouse must help select fruits and vegetables at the grocery store or help pick out a new sofa), the head-tracker will depend entirely on the WearCam. The proposed VideoOrbits head-tracker, is based on comparing successive images and looking at the projective coordinate transformation that relates them.

Consider the two "pictures" of the same scene or objects in Figure 6.34. To make this question simple, the "pictures" are both one-dimensional. It is more important that you understand the basic principle here than slog through a lot of math, so that is why it is presented in 1-D. The problem is not hard, just try to think about what is happening here.

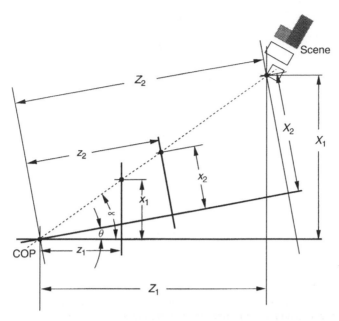

Figure 6.34 Projective coordinate transformation for two pictures of the same scene or objects.

A particular point has been selected in the scene. Measured along the optical axis of the first camera, the distance to the point in question is Z_1; It is measured as Z_2 along the optical axis of the second camera. These are the same camera in two different positions, but they are drawn as two optical axes in order to simplify matters. Camera 1 (the first picture) has zoom setting z_1, while camera 2 (the second picture) has zoom setting z_2. (By "zoom setting," what is meant is the principal distance.) Derive a mathematical expression for the relationship between coordinates x_1 and x_2 as a function of the angle between the cameras, θ, and the zoom settings, z_1 and z_2. [Hint: The answer should not contain α, since that is just the angle between the first optical axis and an arbitrary point in the scene.]

If your answer contains trigonometric functions that depend on x_1 or x_2, simplify your expression to remove any trigonometric functions that depend on x_1 or x_2. (Your head-tracker will later need to run on a small battery-powered computer system, so computational efficiency will be important.)

Sketch a rough graph of x_2 as a function of x_1 to show its general shape.

6.13.2 Geometric Interpretation of the Three-Parameter Model

The geometry of the situation depicted in Figure 6.8*b* and Figure 6.2*d* and shown in Figure 6.9 corresponded to a 45 degree pan of the camera. Consider now a 30 degree camera pan, as illustrated in Figure 6.35. This situation corresponds to $\mathbf{p'} = \{1, 2, 30°\}$. To what values of the three-parameter projective operator, $\mathbf{p}$,

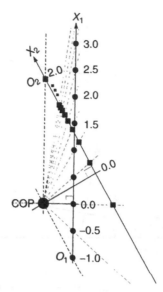

Figure 6.35 Graphical depiction of a situation in which two pictures are related by a zoom from 1 to 2, and a 30 degree angle between the two camera positions.

does this situation correspond? What is the value of chirpiness c' corresponding to this situation? Plot the operator function of this situation.

6.13.3 Shooting Orbits

Obtain a small collection of images in the same orbit of the projective group of coordinate transformations. For now, collect these images at the same exposure if possible, but with slightly different camera orientations. You may wish to use your own camera, or you may wish to sign out a quickcam and use the quickcam program in `http://wearcam.org/freewear/quickcam` vf.c (erlichr, mann) together with the libraries, and other features there.

See also some of the orbits sequences in `http://wearcam.org/lieorbits` to get an idea of how these can be shot.

6.13.4 Photoquantigraphic Image Composite (PIC)

Create a PIC as described in `http://wearcam.org/orbits` with the program that's made available there. This is free thought, and can be run on the WearComps or on a desktop PC, or the like.

6.13.5 Bonus Question

Implement a wearable wireless webcam. This runs by sending images wirelessly (e.g. use vf.c) and running orbits on a base station (ask for account on n1nlf-1 or `eyetap.org` if necessary) to cement the images together into a PIC for each set of images transmitted.

APPENDIX A

SAFETY FIRST!

The importance of personal safety in this new computing paradigm must be emphasized. Since electrical connections are often in close proximity to the body, and are often made directly to the body (e.g., as when fitting the undergarment with electrodes that connect to the bare flesh of the user, in the chest area, for ECG waveform monitoring), the inputs to which these connections are made must be fully isolated. In the present prototypes, this isolation is typically accomplished by using a length of fiber optic cable between the measurement hardware and the host computer. This is essential because the host computer may be connected to other devices such as head-mounted displays containing voltages from 500 Volts to as high as 9 kV (in the case of head-mounted displays containing cathode ray tubes).

The presence of high voltages in the eyeglasses themselves, as well as in other parts of the system (as when it is interfaced to an electronic flash system which typically uses voltages ranging from 480 V to 30 kV), requires extra attention to insulation. In fact it is harder to free oneself from the apparatus when it is worn than when it is merely carried. For example, a hand-held electronic flash can be dropped to the ground should it become unstable, while a wearable system embodies the danger of entrapment in a failing system.

Since batteries may deliver high currents, there is the risk of fire, and the prospect of being trapped in burning clothing. So precautions are taken in limiting current flow. In addition to improved high-voltage insulation, there is also the need to install current limiting fuses, and the like, throughout the garment.

As a further precaution all garments are made from flame-proof material. In this regard, especially with the development of early prototypes over the last 20 years, it was felt that a healthy sense of paranoia was preferable to carelessness that might give rise to a dangerous situation.

APPENDIX B

MULTIAMBIC KEYER FOR USE WHILE ENGAGED IN OTHER ACTIVITIES

Humanistic intelligence arises in a natural cybernetic way by maintaining a constancy of user-interface by way of a computer system. This chapter describes a handheld multiambic keyer that can be easily custom-built for a user, and activated while doing other things such as jogging, running, and climbing stairs. The keyer can also be used to secretly type messages while standing and conversing with other people in a natural manner.

B.1 INTRODUCTION

What is described is a simple conformable multiambic keyer for use with computer systems that work in close synergy with the human user. The synergy between computers and users is achieved through a *user-interface* to signal-processing hardware that is both in *close physical proximity* to the user and *constant*.

The WearComp apparatuses of the 1970s and early 1980s were examples of an interactionally constant wearable multimedia computer system for collaboration in computer-mediated reality spaces. Physical proximity and constancy were simultaneously realized by the WearComp. This was a first attempt at building an intelligent "photographer's assistant" around the body. WearComp comprised a computer system attached to the body, a display means constantly visible to one or both eyes, and a means of signal input including a series of pushbutton switches and a pointing device (Fig. B.1) that the wearer could hold in one hand to function as a keyboard and mouse do, but still be able to operate the device while walking around. In this way the apparatus re-situated the functionality of a desktop multimedia computer with mouse, keyboard, and video screen, as a physical extension of the user's body. While the size and weight reductions of WearComp over the last 20 years have been quite dramatic, the basic qualitative elements and functionality have remained essentially the same, apart from the obvious increase in computational power.

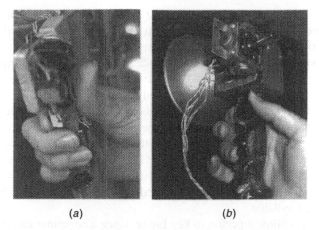

(a)   (b)

Figure B.1 Some of author's early keyer inventions from the 1970s (keyers and pointing devices) for WearComp. (a) Input device comprising pushbutton switches mounted to a wooden lamp pushbroom handgrip; (b) input device comprising five microswitches mounted to the handle of an electronic flash. A joystick (controlling two potentiometers), designed as a pointing device for use in conjunction with the WearComp project, is also present.

An important aspect of the WearComp has been the details of the keyer, which serves to enter commands into the apparatus. The keyer has traditionally been attached to some other apparatus that needs to be held, such as a flashlamp and a lightcomb, so that the effect is a hands-free data entry device (hands free in the sense that one only needs to hold onto the flashlamp, or light source, and no additional hand is needed to hold the keyer).

B.2 BACKGROUND AND TERMINOLOGY ON KEYERS

A distinction will be made from among similar devices called keyboards, keypads, and keyers. Often all three are called "keyboards," conflating very different devices and concepts. Therefore these devices and the underlying concepts and uses will be distinguished in this appendix as follows:

A keyboard will be considered to be a device with keys attached to a board, meant to be used while seated. The board upon which the keys are attached rests on a desk, or the lap of a user, in the case of a laptop computer.

A keypad will be considered to be a similar device, sometimes having fewer keys, and often mounted on a wall, on an object, or otherwise mounted to some device.

A keyer will be considered to be a device with one or more keys that are operationally separate from a device, in the sense of use. When there are multiple keys, a defining attribute of a keyer is that keys typically face in different directions.

Another difference is that keyers require multiple keypresses. This means that one either presses the same key more than once, or presses more than one key at the same time, in order to generate a single letter or symbol.

Like keyboards and keypads, keyers are devices for communicating in symbols such as letters of the alphabet, numbers, or selections. The simplest keyer is a pushbutton switch or telegraph key pressed a short time (for a "dot"), or a long time (for a "dash"), to key letters using a code, such as Morse code.

The next most complicated keyer is the so-called *iambic* keyer having two keys, one to generate a "dot" and the other to generate a "dash." The term "iambic" derives from Latin *iambus*, and Greek *iambos*, and denotes the use of a line of verse, such as the iambic pentameter, comprised of one short syllable followed by one long syllable or comprised of one unstressed syllable followed by one stressed syllable.

Iambic keyers allow a person to key faster, since a computer can do the timing to time the length of a dot or a dash. Most iambic keyers contain some kind of microprocessor, although similar early units were based on a mechanical resonant mass on a stiff spring steel wire.

In this appendix the term "bi-ambic" will be used to denote the iambic keyer, so that it can be generalized as follows:

- uni-ambic: one pushbutton switch or key, could also be taken to mean "un-iambic" (as in not iambic)
- bi-ambic: two pushbutton switches or keys
- tri-ambic: three pushbutton switches or keys
- . . .
- pentambic: five pushbutton switches or keys
- . . .
- septambic: seven pushbutton switches or keys
- . . .
- multiambic: many pushbutton switches or keys

B.3   OPTIMAL KEYER DESIGN: THE CONFORMAL KEYER

Unlike the keyboard or keypad, the keyer is preferably customized to the individual user. It functions as a true extension of the mind and body, as if it were an integral part of the user. Early keyers were made by the author, and shaped specifically to fit the author's own hand. Switches were often hand picked, for each finger, so that different switches were used for different fingers (the smallest finger used a switch with a very weak spring, etc.).

Figure B.2 shows how the author formed a keyer to perfectly fit his left hand. A plastic sheet of relatively low melting temperature was heated in boiling water,

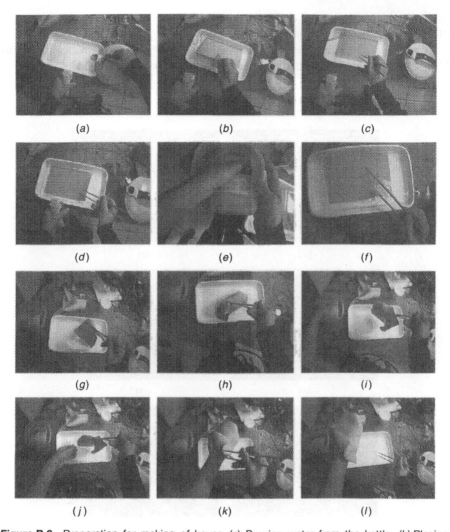

Figure B.2 Preparation for making of keyer. (*a*) Pouring water from the kettle. (*b*) Placing low-temperature plastic in the hot water; (*c*) wooden chopsticks are used to handle the hot plastic; (*d*) the soft plastic is tested for consistency; (*e*) the hand is cooled in icewater; (*f–k*) the soft plastic is lifted out of the hot water in one quick movement while the hand is taken out of the ice bath; (*l*) finishing up with soft plastic on the hand. If the pain threshold is reached, the process can be repeated with more cooling of the hand.

and applied to the hand to conform to the shape of the hand. These pictures were captured by the author wearing a modern embodiment of the wearable photographic apparatus (WearComp). This figure also shows the usefulness of the wearable photographic apparatus in documenting scientific experiments from the perspective of the individual scientist (i.e., first-person perspective). Thus the apparatus itself can serve a useful function in the context of automated collection of experimental data and their documentation.

Next the soft-heated plastic is shaped to perfectly fit the hand as shown in Figure B.3. Excess material is trimmed away as shown in Figure B.4.

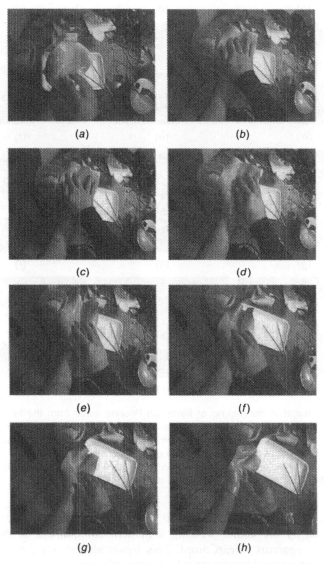

(a)   (b)

(c)   (d)

(e)   (f)

(g)   (h)

Figure B.3 Shaping the soft-heated plastic to perfectly fit the hand. (a) Here a left-handed keyer is in the making; (b–c) soft-heated plastic is pressed down to form nicely between the fingers so that the keyer will conform perfectly to the hand's shape; (d–h) when the right hand's taken away, the material should feel comfortable and naturally stay in position on the left hand.

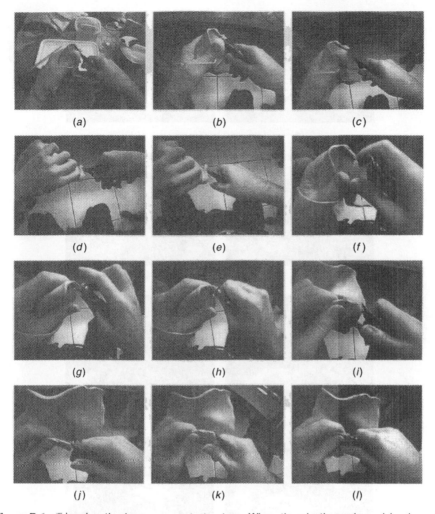

Figure B.4 Trimming the keyer support structure. When the plastic cools and hardens, it should fit perfectly to the hand in the interior region of the plastic. At the edges will be rough and will need to be trimmed. (*a–h*) the initial rough trimming is done while the support structure is worn, so that it can be trimmed to the hand's shape; (*i–l*) then the plastic is removed and the rough edges are easily rounded off.

Now the keyer is ready to be finished off by selecting appropriate switches, mounting them, and building an interface circuit so that the keyer can plug into a standard PS/2 keyboard connector. This process is illustrated in Figure B.5.

B.4 THE SEVEN STAGES OF A KEYPRESS

Early keyers designed and built by the author in the 1970s were used in conjunction with wearable photographic apparatus.

Figure B.5 Finishing off a keyer. (*a*) Selecting appropriate pushbutton switches; (*b*) testing for positioning of the switches; (*c*) getting the thumb switches in position is most important; (*d*) material being cut away and switches glued into place all while wearing the keyer; (*e*) keyer being interfaced to WearComp by way of a Programmable Interface Controller, using a circuit board designed by Wozniak (assembled by author) and a PIC program designed by Wozniak, Mann, Moncrieff, and Fung; (*f*) circuit board (in author's right hand) that interfaces key switches to standard PS/2 connector (in author's left hand); (*g*) the RJ45 connector used with eight wires, one for each of the seven switches and the eighth for common; (*h*) the keyer being plugged in by way of the RJ45 connector. The author has standardized the connections so that any member of the community having difficulty with their keyer can temporarily swap with someone else to determine whether the problem is in the keyer or in the conversion circuit.

For example, the original pentambic keyer had five keys, one for each of the four fingers, and a fifth one for the thumb, so that characters were formed by pressing the keys in different combinations. The computer could read when each key was pressed, and when each key was released, as well as how fast the key was depressed. Since the switches were double throw, the velocity sensing capability arose from using both the naturally closed (NC) and naturally open (NO) contacts, and measuring the time between when the common contact (C) leaves the NC contact and meets the NO contact.

There are seven stages associated with pressing a combination of keys on a multiambic keyer (see Fig. B.6). The Close–Sustain–Release progression exists only in the intentionality of the user, so any knowledge of the progression from within these three stages must be inferred, for example, by the time delays.

Arbitrary time constants could be used to make the keyer very expressive. For example, characters could be formed by pressing keys for different lengths of time. Indeed, a uniambic keyer, such as one used to tap out Morse code, relies heavily on time constants. Two keys gave the iambic paddle effect, similar to that described in a January 12, 1972, publication, by William F. Brown, U.S. Pat. 3,757,045, which was further developed in U.S. Pat. 5,773,769. Thus there was no need for a heavy base (it could thus be further adapted to be used while worn).

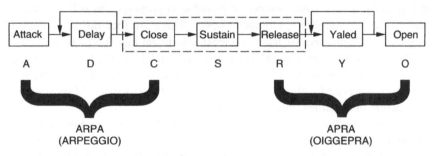

Figure B.6 The seven stages of the keypress. (**A**) Attack is the exact instant when the first switch is measurably pressed (when its common moves away from its first throw if it is a double throw switch, or when the first switch is closed if it is a single throw switch). (**D**) Delay is the time between Attack and when the last switch of a given chord has finished being pressed. Thus Delay corresponds to an arpeggiation interval (ARPA, from Old High German harpha, meaning harp, upon which strings were plucked in sequence but continued to sound together). This Delay may be deliberate and expressive, or accidental. (**C**) Close is the exact instant at which the last key of a desired chord is fully pressed. This Closure of the chord exists only in the mind (in the first brain) of the user, because the second brain (i.e., the computational apparatus, worn by, attached to, or implanted in the user) has no way of knowing whether there is a plan to, or plans to, continue the chord with more switch closures, unless all of the switches have been pressed. (**S**) Sustain is the continued holding of the chord. Much as a piano has a sustain pedal, a chord on the keyer can be sustained. (**Y**) Yaled is the opposite of delay (yaled is delay spelled backward). Yaled is the time over which the user releases the components of a chord. Just as a piano is responsive to when keys are released, as well as when they are pressed, the keyer can also be so responsive. The Yaled process is referred to as an APRA (OIGGEPRA), namely ARPA (or arpeggio) spelled backward. (**O**) Open is the time at which the last key is fully (measurably) released. At this point the chord is completely open, and no switches are measurably pressed.

Another example of time-dependent input devices include those with a Sustain feature, such as keyboards with the well-known "Typematic" (auto repeat) function of most modern keyboards. A key held down for a long time behaves differently than one pressed for a short time. The key held down for a short time produces a single character, whereas the key held down for a long time produces a plurality of the same character.

Some problems arise with time-dependent keying, however. For example, a novice user typing very slowly may accidentally activate a timing feature. Although many input devices (ordinary keyboards and mice, as well as ordinary iambic paddles) have user-adjustable timing constants, the need to adjust or adapt to these constants is an undesirable feature of these devices.

There are other problems and issues of velocity sensing, which is itself a timing matter. Some problems associated with velocity sensing include the necessity of selecting a switch with less deadband zone ("snap") than desired, for the desirable amount of tactile feedback. There were some other undesirable attributes of the velocity sensing systems, so for simplicity in this appendix the nonvelocity sensing version will be described.

Without using any timing constants whatsoever and without using any velocity sensing (nor Sustain, nor measurement of the timing in the Delay and Yaled stages as in Fig. B.6), a very large number of possible keypresses can still be attained. Consider first, for simplicity, a biambic keyer. There are four possible states: 00 when no keys are pressed, 01 when the least significant key (LSK) is pressed, 10 when the most significant key (MSK) is pressed, and 11 when both are pressed. It is desired to be able to have a rest position when no characters are sent, so 00 is preferably reserved for this rest state; otherwise, the keyer would be streaming out characters at all times, even when not in use.

In a dynamic situation, keys will be pressed and released. Both keys will be pressed at exactly the same time, only on a set of measure zero. In other words, if we plot the time the LSK is pressed on the abscissa, and the time that the MSK is pressed on the ordinate, of a graph (see Fig. B.7), each keypress will be a point, and we will obtain a scatterplot of keypresses in the plane. Simultaneity exists along the line $t_0 = t_1$, and the line has zero measure within the plane. Therefore any symbol that requires simultaneous pressing of both keys (or simultaneous release of both) will be inherently unreliable, unless we build in some timing tolerance. Timing tolerances require timing information, such as a timing constant or adaptation. For now, for simplicity, let us assume that such timing tolerances are absent. We need only to concern ourselves with whether or not the key presses overlap, and if they do, which key was pressed first, and which was released first.

This limitation greatly simplifies programming (e.g., for programming on a simple 6502 microprocessor) and greatly simplifies learning, as the progression from novice to expert does not involve continually changing timing parameters and any other subjectively determined timing constants. Without any timing constants or timing adaptation, we can, with only two switches, obtain six possible

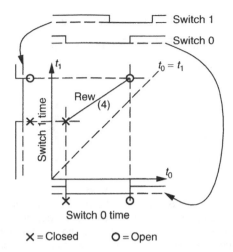

Figure B.7 Cybernetic keyer timing. Two keys would be pressed or released at exactly the same time, only on a set, denoted by the line $t_0 = t_1$. This has measure zero in the (t_0, t_1) plane, where t_0 is the time of pressing or releasing of SWITCH 0, and t_1 is the time of pressing or releasing of SWITCH 1. To overcome this uncertainty, the particular meaning of the chord is assigned based ordinally, rather than on using a timing threshold. Here, for example, SWITCH 0 is pressed first and released after pressing SWITCH 1 but before releasing SWITCH 1. This situation is for one of the possible symbols that can be produced from this combination of two switches. This particular symbol will be numbered (4) and will be assigned the meaning of REW (rewind).

unique symbols, excluding the Open chord (nothing pressed) as in the diagram of Figure B.8.

The operation of the cybernetic keyer is better understood by way of a simple example, illustrated in Figure B.9. The time space graph of Figure B.7 is really just a four-dimensional time space collapsed onto two dimensions of the page. Accordingly, we can view any combination of key presses that involves pressing both switches within a finite time as a pair of ordered points on the graph. There are six possibilities. Examples of each are depicted in Figure B.10.

B.5 THE PENTAKEYER

With three switches instead of two, there are many more combinations possible. Even if the three switches are not velocity sensing (i.e., if they are only single throw switches), there are still 51 combinations. They can be enumerated as follows:

- Choose any one of the three switches (one symbol each).
- Choose any pair of switches (omit any one of the three switches from the chord). For each of these three choices, there are four possible symbols (corresponding to the symbols 3 through 6 of Fig. B.8).

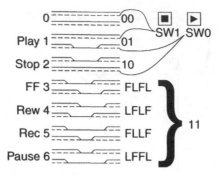

Figure B.8 The cybernetic keyer. Timing information is depicted as dual traces: SWITCH 0 is depicted by the bottom trace and SWITCH 1 by the top trace. The zeroth symbol 00 depicts the open chord (no switches pressed). The first symbol 01 depicts the situation where only SWITCH 0 is pressed. The second symbol 10 depicts the situation where only SWITCH 1 is pressed. The third through sixth symbols 11 arise from situations where both switches are pressed and then released, with overlap. The third symbol FLFL depicts the situation where SWITCH 1 is pressed First, switch 0 is pressed Last, SWITCH 1 is released First, and switch 0 is released Last. Similarly LFLF denotes Last First Last First (fourth symbol). FLLF denotes the situation where SWITCH 1 is held down while SWITCH 0 is pressed and released (fifth symbol). LFFL denotes the situation in which SWITCH 0 is held down while SWITCH 1 is pressed and released (sixth symbol). The zeroth through sixth symbols are denoted by reference numerals 0 through 6, respectively. Each of the active ones (other than the Open chord, 0) are given a meaning in operating a recording machine, with the functions PLAY, STOP, FastForward (FF), REWind, RECord, and PAUSE.

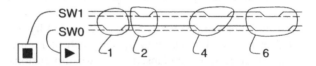

Figure B.9 Cybernetic keyer timing example. In this example, the top trace denotes SWITCH 1, and the bottom trace SWITCH 0. Initially SWITCH 0 is pressed and then SWITCH 1 is pressed. However, because there is no overlap between these switch pressings, they are interpreted as separate symbols (e.g. this is not a chord). The separate symbols are 1 (PLAY) and 2 (STOP). This results in the playing of a short segment of video, which is then stopped. A little while later, SWITCH 0 is pressed and then SWITCH 1 is pressed. However, because there is now overlap, this action is considered to be a chord. Specifically it is an LFLF (Last First Last First) chord, which is interpreted as symbol number 4 (REWIND). A REWind operation on a stopped system is interpreted as high-speed rewind. A short time later, SWITCH 0 is held down while SWITCH 1 is pressed briefly. This action is interpreted as symbol number 6 (PAUSE). Since PAUSE would normally be used only during PLAY or RECORD, the meaning during REWIND is overloaded with a new meaning, namely slow down from high-speed rewind to normal speed rewind. Thus we have full control of a recording system with only two switches, and without using any time constants as might arise from other interfaces such as the iambic Morse code keyers used by ham radio operators.

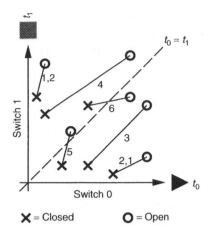

Figure B.10 Cybernetic keyer timings. The symbol "X" denotes pressing of the two keys, and exists in the first pair of time dimensions, t_0 and t_1. The releasing of the two keys exists in the first second pair of dimensions, which, for simplicity (since it is difficult to draw the four-dimensional space on the printed page), are also denoted t_0 and t_1, but with the symbol "O" for Open. Examples of symbols 3 through 6 are realized. Two other examples, for when the switch closures do not overlap, are also depicted. These are depicted as 1,2 (symbol 1 followed by symbol 2) and 2,1 (symbol 2 followed by symbol 1).

- Using all three switches, at the ARPA (arpeggio, Fig. B.6) stage:
  1. There are three choices for First switch.
  2. Once the first switch is chosen, there remains the question as to which of the remaining two will be pressed Next.
  3. Then there is only one switch left, to press Last.

  Thus at the ARPA stage, there are $3 * 2 * 1 = 6$ different ways of pressing all three switches. At the APRA (oiggepra, Fig. B.6) stage, there are an equal number of ways of releasing these three switches that have all been pressed. Thus there are six ways of pressing, and six ways of releasing, which gives $6 * 6 = 36$ symbols that involve all three switches.

The total number of symbols on the three switch keyer is $3 + 12 + 36 = 51$. That is a sufficient number to generate the 26 letters of the alphabet, the numbers 0 through 9, the space character, and four additional symbols.

Uppercase and control characters are generated by using the four additional symbols for SHIFT and CONTROL, for example, of the letter or symbol that follows. Thus the multiplication sign is SHIFT followed by the number 8, and the @ sign is SHIFT followed by the number 2, and so on.

It is best to have all the characters be single chords so that the user gets one character for every chord. Having a separate SHIFT chord would require the user to state (i.e., remember) whether the SHIFT key was active, and that would also slow down data entry.

Accordingly, if a fourth switch is added, we obtain a larger possible combination of choices:

- Choose any one of the four switches (one symbol each).
- Choose any pair of switches. For each of these $4!/2(4-2)! = 6$ choices, there are four possible symbols (corresponding to the symbols 3 through 6 of Fig. B.8).
- Choose any three switches (i.e., omit any one of the four switches from the chord). For each of these four choices, form the chord in any of the $3*2*1 = 6$ possible ways, and unform the chord in any of six possible ways, giving $6^2 = 36$ ways to create and uncreate the chord of the three chosen switches, as described in the three-switch example above.
- Use all four switches at the ARPA (arpeggio) stage:
  1. There are four choices for First switch.
  2. Once the first switch is chosen, there remains the decision which of the remaining three switches should be pressed Second.
  3. Once the second switch is chosen, there remains decision which of the remaining two switches should be pressed Third.
  4. Then there is only one switch left, to press Last.

Thus at the ARPA stage, there are $4*3*2*1 = 4! = 24$ different ways of pressing all four switches. At the APRA (oiggepra) stage, there are an equal number of ways of releasing these four switches that have all been pressed. Thus there are 24 ways of pressing, and 24 ways of releasing, which gives $24*24 = 576$ symbols that involve all four switches.

The total number of symbols on the four switch keyer is

$$\frac{4!}{1!(4-1)!}(1!)^2 + \frac{4!}{2!(4-2)!}(2!)^2 + \frac{4!}{3!(4-3)!}(3!)^2 + \frac{4!}{4!(4-4)!}(4!)^2$$

$$= 4*1^2 + 6*2^2 + 4*6^2 + 1*24^2 = 748. \tag{B.1}$$

This number is sufficient to generate the 256 ASCII symbols, along with 492 additional symbols that may be each assigned to entire words, or to commonly used phrases, such as a sig (signing off) message, a callsign, or commonly needed sequences of symbols. Thus a callsign like "N1NLF" is a single chord. A commonly used sequence of commands like ALT 192, ALT 255, ALT 192, is also a single chord. Common words like "the" or "and" are also single chords.

The four switches can be associated with the thumb and three largest fingers, leaving out the smallest finger. Claude Shannon's information theory, however, suggests that if we have a good strong clear channel, and a weaker channel, we can get more error-free communication by using both the strong and weak channels than we can by using only the strong channel. We could and should use the weak (smallest) finger for at least a small portion of the bandwidth, even though the other four will carry the major load. Referring back to Figure B.1, especially Figure B.1b, we see that there are four strong double-throw switches for the thumb and three largest fingers, and a fifth smaller switch having a very long lever for the smallest finger. The long lever makes it easy to press this switch with the weak finger but at the expense of speed and response time. In fact each of the five switches has been selected upon learning the strength and other attributes of what will press it. This design gives rise to the pentakeyer.

The result in (B.1) can be generalized. The number of possible chords for a keyer with N switches, having only single-throw (ST) switches, and not using any looping back at either the Delay or Yaled (Fig. B.6) stages of chord development, is

$$\sum_{n=1}^{n=N} \frac{N!}{n!(N-n)!}(n!)^2. \tag{B.2}$$

Equation (B.2) simplifies to

$$\sum_{n=1}^{n=N} \frac{N!n!}{(N-n)!} \tag{B.3}$$

Thus the pentakeyer gives us $5 + 40 + 360 + 2880 + 14,400 = 17,685$ possible chords, without the use of any loopback, velocity sensing, or timing constants.

B.6 REDUNDANCY

The pentakeyer provides enough chords to use one to represent each of the most commonly used words in the English language. There are, for example, enough chords to represent more than half the words recognized by the UNIX "spell" command with a typical /usr/share/lib/dict/words having 25,143 words.

However, if all we want to represent is ASCII characters, the pentakeyer gives us $17,685/256 > 69$. That is more than 69 different ways to represent each letter. This suggests, for example, that we can have 69 different ways of typing the letter "a," and more than 69 different ways of typing the letter "b," and so on. In this way we can choose whichever scheme is convenient in a given chord progression.

In most musical instruments there are multiple ways of generating each chord. For example, in playing the guitar, there are at least two commonly used G chords, both of which sound quite similar. The choice of which G to use depends on which is easiest to reach, based on what chord came before it, and what chord will come after it, and so on. Thus the freedom in having two different realizations of essentially the same chord makes playing the instrument easier.

Similarly, because there are so many different ways of typing the letter "a," the user is free to select the particular realization of the letter "a" that's easiest to type when considering whatever came before it and whatever will come after it. Having multiple realizations of the same chord is called "chordic redundancy." Rather than distributing the chordic redundancy evenly across all letters, more redundancy is applied where it is needed more, so there are more different ways of typing the letter "a" than there are of typing the letter "q" or "u." Part of this reasoning is based on the fact that there are a wide range of letters that can come before or after the letter "a," whereas, for example, there is a smaller range of, and tighter distribution on, the letters that can follow "q," with the letter "u" being at the peak of that relatively narrow distribution.

Redundancy need not be imposed on the novice. The first-time user can learn one way of forming each symbol, and then gradually learn a second way of forming some of the more commonly used symbols. Eventually an experienced user will learn several ways of forming some of the more commonly used symbols.

Additionally some chords are applied (in some cases even redundantly) to certain entire words, phrases, expressions, and the like. An example with timing diagrams for a chordic redundancy based keyer is illustrated in Figure B.11.

This approach, of having multiple chords to choose from in order to produce a given symbol, is the opposite of an approach taken with telephone touchpad-style keypads in which each number could mean different letters. In U.S. Pat. 6,011,554, issued January 4, 2000, assigned to Tegic Communications, Inc. (Seattle, WA), Martin T. King; (Vashon, WA); Dale L. Grover; (Lansing, MI); Clifford A. Kushler (Vashon, WA); and Cheryl A. Grunbock; (Vashon, WA) describe a disambiguating system in which an inference is made as to what the person might be trying to type. A drawback of this Tegic system is that the user must remain aware of what the machine thinks he or she is typing. There is an extra cognitive load imposed on the user, including the need to be constantly vigilant that errors are not being made. Using the Tegic system is a bit like using command line completion in Emacs. While it allegedly purports to speed up the process, it can, in practice, slow down the process by imposing an additional burden on the user.

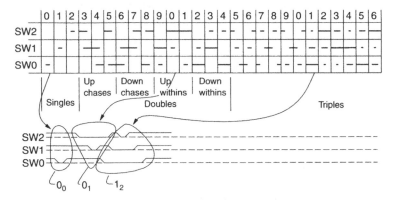

Figure B.11 Keyer with a functional chordic redundancy generator or keyer having functional chordic redundancy. This keyer is used to type in or enter the numbers from 0 to 9 using three single throw switches. Each symbol (each number from 0 to 9) may be typed in various ways. If we wish to type "001," we can do this as follows: first press and release switch SW0, to obtain symbol 0_0 (the zeroth embodiment of symbol 0). Then to speed up the process (rather than press the same switch again), we press switch SW1 while holding SW2, to obtain symbol 0_1 which is another realization of the symbol 0. We next choose a realization of the symbol 1, namely 1_2, that does not begin with switch SW2. Thus before the chord for symbol 0_1 is completely released (at the Yaled stage), we begin entering the chord for symbol 1_2, starting with the available switch SW0.

In some sense the Tegic system is a form of antiredundancy, giving the user less flexibility. For example, forming new words (not in the dictionary) is quite difficult with the Tegic system, and when it does make mistakes, they are harder to detect because the mistakes get mapped onto the space of valid words. Indeed, chordic redundancy (choice) is much more powerful than antiredundancy (antichoice) in how characters can be formed.

B.7   ORDINALLY CONDITIONAL MODIFIERS

A modifier key is a key that alters the function of another key. On a standard keyboard, the SHIFT key modifies other letters by causing them to appear capitalized. The SHIFT key modifies other keys between two states, namely a lowercase state and an uppercase state.

Another modifier key of the standard keyboard is the control key. A letter key pressed while the control key is held down is modified so that it becomes a control character. Thus the letter "a" gets changed to "Â" if it is pressed while the control key is held down.

With the cybernetic keyer, an approach is to have a modifier that is ordinally conditional, so that its effect is responsive to where it is pressed in the chord. See Figure B.12 for an example of how a four-key ordinally conditional modifier is implemented.

B.8   ROLLOVER

One reason that chording keyers can be slow is that they often don't provide rollover. A regular QWERTY ... keyboard allows for rollover. For example, the

| | | | | | | | ^ | ^ | ^ | ^ | ^ | | ~ | ~ | ~ | ~ | ~ | | | | | | | |
	e	t	a	o	n	...	E	T	A	O	N	...	e	t	a	o	n	...	e	t	a	o	n	...
SWt		−						−						−										
SWi	−		⊢─┐		−	⊢─┐			−		⊢─┐													
SWm	−		⊢─┐	−			⊢─┐	−			⊢─┐	−												
SWr						⊢ ⊢ ⊢ ⊢ ⊢							─┤─┤					┤ ┤ ┤ ┤ ┤						

Figure B.12 Example of keyer with ordinally conditional modifier. Letters are arranged in order of letter frequency, starting with the letter "e" which is the most commonly used letter of the alphabet. Each of the 26 letters, the 10 numbers, and some symbols are encoded with the 51 possible chords that can be formed from 3 switches, a middle finger switch, SWm, an index finger switch, SWi, and a thumb switch, SWt. (The more common letters, such as e, t, and a, are also encoded redundantly so that there is more than one way to enter, for example, the letter "e.") A ring finger switch, SWr, is the ordinally conditional modifier. If SWr is not pressed, an ordinary lowercase character is assumed. If a chord leads with SWr, the character is assumed to be an uppercase character. If the chord is entered while holding SWr, the character is assumed to be a control character. If a chord trails with SWr, it is assumed to represent a meta character. The ordinally conditional modifier is also applied to numbers to generate some of the symbols. For example, an exclamation mark is entered by leading with SWr into the chord for the number 1.

classic 1984 IBM model M keyboard, still to this day a favorite of many users, will be responsive to any key while the letter "q" is held down. When the letters "q" and "w" are held down, it is responsive to most keys (i.e., all those except keys in the q and w columns). When the letters "q," "w," and "e" are held down, it is responsive to other keys except from those three columns. When "q," "w," "e," and "r" are held down, it is still responsive to keys in the right-hand half of the keyboard (i.e., keys that would ordinarily be pressed with the right hand). Only when five keys are held down, does it stop responsing to new keypresses. Thus the model M has quite a bit of rollover. This means that one can type new letters before finishing the typing of previous letters. This ability to have overlap between typing different letters allows a person to type faster because a new letter can be pressed before letting go of the previous letter. Commercially available chording keyers such as the Handykey Twiddler and the BAT don't allow for rollover. Thus typing on the Twiddler or BAT is a slower process.

A goal of the cybernetic keyer is to be able to type much more quickly. Therefore the important features are the trade-off between loopbacks at the Delay and Yaled stages (Fig. B.6) and rollover. If we decide, by design, that there will be no loopback at the Delay or the Yaled stages, we can assume that a chord has been committed to at the Release stage. Thus, once we reach the Release stage, we can begin to accept another chord, so long as the other chord does not require the use of any switches that are still depressed at the Release stage. However, because of the 69-fold chordic redundancy, it is arranged that for most of the commonly following letters, there exists at the Release stage at least one new chord that can be built on keys not currently held down.

B.8.1 Example of Rollover on a Cybernetic Keyer

With reference to the two-switch keyer, suppose that we press SWITCH 1, and then press SWITCH 0 and release SWITCH 1. We are now at the Release stage, and can enter a new command with SWITCH 1, since we know that there will be no Yaled loopback (i.e., we know that the chord will not involve pressing SWITCH 1 again). Thus pressing SWITCH 1 again can be safely used as a new symbol, prior to releasing SWITCH 0. In this way symbols can rollover (overlap).

B.9 FURTHER INCREASING THE CHORDIC REDUNDANCY FACTOR: A MORE EXPRESSIVE KEYER

The number of possible chords can be increased from 17,685 to $7 + 84 + 1260 + 20,160 + 302,400 + 3,628,800 + 25,401,600 = 29,354,311$ by simply adding three switches at the thumb position. This provides more than 29 million symbols, which is enough since each word in the English language can be represented in approximately a thousand different ways. This degree of chordic redundancy could provide for some very fast typing if this many chords could be remembered. However, rather than increasing the number of switches, it is preferable to increase, instead, the expressivity of each one.

The pentakeyer is a crude instrument that lacks an ability to provide for tremendous "expression" and sensitivity to the user. It fails to provide a rich form of humanistic intelligence in the sense that the feedback is cumbersome, and not continuous. A guitar, violin, or real piano (i.e., an old fashioned mechanical piano, not a computerized synthetic piano data input keyboard) provides a much richer user experience because it provides instant feedback, and the user can experience the unique response of the instrument.

Even using both rails of each switch (i.e., double throw and even velocity sensing) fails to provide a truly expressive input device. Accordingly a better keyer was built from continuous transducers in the form of phonographic cartridges salvaged from old record players. These devices provide continuous flow of pressure information along two axes (each phono cartridge is responsive to pressure along two independent axes at right angles to one another, originally for playing stereo sound recordings from the grooves of a record). The dual sensor is depicted in Figure B.13, and it may comprise either a continuous sensor or two on–off switches operable on separate axes.

In this embodiment the keyer described here is similar to the ternary data entry keyboard described by Langley, October 4, 1988, in U.S. Pat. 4,775,255. Namely there are also two axes to each key. A given key can move toward or away from the operator, and the key has a central "off" position and a spring detent to make if return to the central position in the absence of pressure from the finger. An important difference is that the keyboard of U.S. Pat. 4,775,255 has no ability to sense how fast, how hard, or how much each switch is pressed, other than just the ternary value of 0, +1, or −1. Further, in the keyer of U.S. Pat. 4,775,255, the axes are not independent (i.e., one cannot press +1 and −1 at the same time).

The sensor pair of Figure B.13, on the other hand, provides two independent continuous dimensions. Thus a keyer made from five such sensor pairs provides a much more expressive input. Even if the transducers are quantized, to binary outputs, there are four possibilities: 0, −1, +1, and ±1. With five continuous transducers, one for each finger or thumb position, the user interface involves squeezing out characters, rather than clicking out characters. The input space is a very richly structured 10-dimensional time space, producing 10 traces of

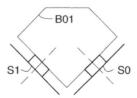

Figure B.13 Dual sensor keyer. Sensors S0 and S1 may be switches or transducers or other forms of sensory apparatus. Sensors S0 and S1 are operable individually, or together, by way of rocker block B01. Pressing straight down on block B01 will induce a response from both sensors. A response can also be induced in only one of sensors S0 or S1 by pressing along its axis.

time-varying signals. This 10-dimensional time space is reduced to discrete symbols according to a mapping based on comparison of the waveforms with reference waveforms stored in a computer system. Since comparison with the reference waveforms is approximate, it is done by clustering, based on various kinds of similarity metrics.

B.10   INCLUDING ONE TIME CONSTANT

If we relax the ordinality constraint, and permit just one time constant, pertaining to simultaneity, we can obtain eleven symbols from just two switches. Such a scheme can be used for entering numbers, including the decimal point.

```
        00 (Open chord not used)
0       01
1       10
2       FLFL
3       FLLF
4       FLW
5       LFFL
6       LFLF
7       LFW
8       WFL
9       WLF
.       WW
```

Using this simple coding scheme, the number zero is entered by pressing the LSK. The number one is entered by pressing the MSK. The number four, for example, is entered by pressing the MSK first, then pressing the LSK, and then releasing both at the same time, Within a certain time tolerance for which time is considered the same. (The letter "W" denotes Within tolerance, as illustrated in Fig. B.14.) The decimal point is entered by pressing both switches at approximately the same

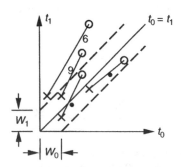

Figure B.14 Example showing keyer chords within timing tolerances W_0 and W_1. Time differences within the tolerance band are considered to be zero, so events falling within the tolerance band defined by W_0 and W_1 are considered to be effectively simultaneous.

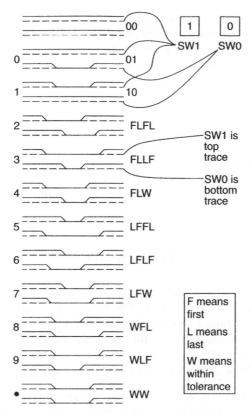

Figure B.15 Chordic keyer with timing tolerances. In addition to the unused Open chord, there are 11 other chords that can be used for the numbers 0 through 9, and the decimal point.

time, and releasing both at approximately the same time. The "approximately the same time" is defined according to a band around the line $t_0 = t_1$ in Figure B.7. Such a timing band is depicted in Figure B.15.

This number system can be implemented either by two pushbutton switches or by a single vector keyswitch of two components, as illustrated in Figure B.13. In the latter case the entire set of number symbols can be entered with just one switch, by just one finger. Note that each number involves just a single keypress, unlike what would be the case if one entered numbers using a small wearable Morse code keyer. Thus the cybernetic chordic keyer provides a much more efficient entry of symbols.

B.11   MAKING A CONFORMAL MULTIAMBIC KEYER

Wearable keyers are known in the art of ham radio. For example, in U.S. Pat. 4,194,085, March 18, 1980, Scelzi describes a "Finger keyer for code transmission." The telegraphic keyer fits over a finger, preferably the index finger, of an operator, for tapping against the operator's thumb or any convenient object. It is used for transmission of code with portable equipment. The keyer is wearably operable when walking, or during other activities.

All keyers, including previously known keyers and the proposed keyers, such as the pentakeyer and the continuous 10-dimensional keying system, are much easier to use if they are custom-made for the user. The important aspect is getting the hand grip to fit well.

A subject of ongoing work, therefore, is designing ways of molding the keyers to fit the hand of the wearer. Presently this is done by dipping the hand in icewater, as was shown in Figure B.2, and draping it with heated plastic material that is formed to the shape of the hand. Once the handpiece is formed, sensors are selected and installed so the keyer will match the specific geometric shape of the user's hand.

B.12   COMPARISON TO RELATED WORK

The keyer described in this chapter is closely related to other work done on so-called chording keyboards. Since this field is so rapidly changing, a list of references is maintained dynamically, online, as a constantly evolving and updated bibliography and resource for the wide variety of keyers and keyer-related research [140,141].

Two essential differences should be noted, however:

- The multiambic keyer enables a variety of absolute timing, ordinal timing (order), and other fine structure, as well as phenomena such as redundancy. Chording keyboards of the prior art fail to provide these features. However, these so-called chording keyboards (which often don't have a "board," and so should perhaps be called keyers rather than keyboards) may be regarded as special cases of the more general keyer described in this article.

- The multiambic keyer described in this chapter is customized to the individual user, much like prescription eyeglasses, a mouthguard, or shoes and clothing. Therefore it takes an important departure from traditional computing in which the interface is mass produced. Although there are some obvious problems in manufacture, such customization is not without precedent. For example, we commonly fit shoes and clothing for an individual person, and do not normally swap shoes and clothing at random, and expect them to serve any person at random. Likewise it is believed by the author that many individual persons might someday have their own keyers, and use these as their own personal input devices.

The customization of the keyer marks a sharp departure from the environmental intelligence paradigms in which the environment simply adapts or is alleged to adapt to our needs [142]. Instead of having cameras and microphones everywhere, watching us, and feeding into a network of pervasive computing, we simply have the computer attached to our own body. Thus, through our own cybernetic personalized keyer interface, we have computing at our call whenever we need it. Interfaces to the outside world are then mediated by our own computer under our own control.

Additionally there has been much recent interest in voice-activated wearable computing. However, it has been the author's experience, first with a voice-activated wearable computer system in the 1970s (finalized and then abandoned in the early 1980s) and later with other similar voice activated systems, that these systems do not work very well. Although the technical problems were not so pronounced (e.g., in some wearable photographic applications only a few commands are needed, and sometimes just one command to generate each new exposure), it is more because of the social problems that this interface was abandoned. Especially in situations from ordinary life (walking down the street, standing in line at the bank, etc.), voice activation is highly undesirable. The keyer, on the other hand, provides an unobtrusive means of keying in commands quietly and without disturbing others.

Moreover, during a lecture, where one might wish to take down personal notes triggered by thoughts of the instructor (but in one's own words), one can use the keyer to take notes without talking over the instructor. Such personalized notes are far more valuable than merely recording what the instructor says. The keyer can be easily hidden in a pocket, or discreetly used under a table, without the usual distractions to others that are caused when using a laptop computer. Even a pocket organizer or a pen and paper are distracting to others.

The author often finds that people stop talking or become disturbed as soon as a pen and paper are pulled from a pocket to take notes of an informal conversation. However, no such problem exists with the keyer because people often have no idea whether or not the keyer is being used, especially if held down at the side of the body, out of sight of others.

Thus the keyer provides a much more private and unobtrusive input device than speech recognition, keyboards, or handwriting.

B.13 CONCLUSION

Learning to use the pentakeyer is not easy, just as learning how to play a musical instrument is not easy. The pentakeyer evolved out of a different philosophy, more than 20 years ago. This alternative philosophy knew nothing of so-called user-friendly, user-interface design, and therefore evolved along a completely different path.

Just as playing the violin is much harder to master than playing the TV remote control, it can also be much more rewarding and expressive. Thus, if we were only to consider ease of use, we might be tempted to teach children how to operate a television because it is easier to learn than how to play a violin, or how to read and write. But if we did this, we would have an illiterate society in which all we could do would be things that are easy to learn. It is the author's belief that a far richer experience can be attained with a lifelong computer interface that is worn on the body, and used constantly for 10 to 20 years. On this kind of time scale, an apparatus that functions as a true extension of the mind and body may result. Just as it takes a long time to learn how to see, or to read and write, or to operate one's own body (e.g., it takes some years for the brain to figure out how to operate the body so that it can walk, run, swim, etc. effectively), it is expected that the most satisfying and powerful user interfaces will be learned over many years.

B.14 ACKNOWLEDGMENTS

Simon Haykin, Woodrow Barfield, Richard Mann, Ruth Mann, Bill Mann, and Steve Roberts (N4RVE) helped in the way of useful feedback and constructive criticism as this work evolved.

Dr. Chuck Carter volunteered freely of his time to help in the design of the interface to WearComp2 (a 6502-based wearable computer system of the early 1980s), and Kent Nickerson similarly helped with some of the miniature personal radar units and photographic devices involved with this project throughout the mid-1980s.

Programming of one of the more recent embodiments of the Keyer was done in collaboration with Adam Wozniak, and elements of the recent embodiment borrow code from Wozniak's PICKEY. Students, including Eric Moncrieff, James Fung, and Taneem Ahmed, are continuing with this work.

The author would also like to thank Corey Manders, Maneesh Yadav, and Adnan Ali, who recently joined in this effort.

The author additionally extends his thanks to Xybernaut Corp., Digital Equipment Corp., and Compaq, for lending or donating additional equipment that made these experiments possible.

APPENDIX C

WEARCAM GNUX HOWTO

This appendix is somewhat specific to the ECE1766 class taught at University of Toronto, based on a class set of Xybernat wearable computer systems. The details here pertain to the Xybernaut systems, as originally shipped, (research units in early production, typically having low, e.g., 2 digit serial numbers). The details of this appendix may not pertain to other wearable computers in general.

However, the appendix is provided for the benefit of a typical class teaching example.

> WARNING: Do not "make bootable" the WearComp GNUX partition (e.g. do not install LILO) or you may clobber the hard drive and set yourself back a couple of weeks. Unlike desktop computers, the wearcomps are ruggedized systems in which the hard drive is very well sealed inside, and difficult to remove and recover from a clobbered master boot record.

The LILO installation is often very insidiously named something like "make bootable" under the deselect menu. Ordinarily this would not be a problem. However the ruggedized nature of the WearComps and makes it difficult to remove the hard drives to recover from problems with LILO on these WearComps, since the WearComps typically do not have a floppy drive with proper booting support.

C.1 INSTALLING GNUX ON WEARCOMPS

The goal of this exercise is to familiarize the student with some of the typical situations that arise in getting a WearComp to boot a free-source operating system.

GNUX (GNU + LinUX) has been chosen as the basis for the WearComp operating system (WOS) and picture transfer protocol (PTP). It will therefore be used for this exercise. WOS will continue to be developed on top of GNUX.

The student should install the GNUX operating system on a computer that has no floppy disk drive or ethernet card. The GNUX runs in a ramdisk so that, there is no dependence on hard drive. This exercise can be either done on one of the standard issue WearComps (class set) or on any desktop computer that has no GNUX file systems on the hard drive, and either has no floppy drive or has the floppy drive disabled in order to simulate the condition of having no floppy drive present. If you are using a WearComp, simply proceed. If you do not have a WearComp, simply find a suitable computer with i386 type architecture; make sure that there are no GNUX filesystems on any of the hard drives. Preferably there should only be one DOS partition on the hard drive, of size 500 megabytes, in order to simulate the condition present on the WearComps. Various open source freeDOS systems are preferred to proprietary DOS. The student can install freeDOS, then, from the BIOS, disable the floppy drive, and shut down the ethernet to simulate a typical WearComp situation.

C.1.1   GNUX on WearCam

In this exercise we will use the Debian distribution of GNUX. This distribution tends to be the most free, that is the closest in spirit to completely open source headers, engineering and research (COSHER) of the distributions, in terms of purity of the scientific values.

Obtain the boot portion "debboot" onto another computer (one that is connected to the Internet). This material will be available at `http://wearcam.org/free-wear/debboot/` and may be downloaded for placement on the WearComp. The instructions below will further clarify the placement.

Install this material on the DOS partition, and then use loadlin to boot to ramdisk, as described in what follows.

C.2   GETTING STARTED

Assuming that you are using the WearComp, familiarize yourself with the Wear-Comp system. Currently it has on it DOS, as well as a virus called "win." By virus, what is meant is a program in which there has been deliberate attempt to obfuscate its principle of operation (i.e., by Closed Source) as in the formal definition of "virus" proposed in the USENIX98 closing keynote address. `http://wearcam.org/usenix98/index.html` (note that the virus spreads by way of human users who write programs or develop applications that depend on it, so it propagates by the need to install it to run these other applications.)

The following section discusses how to eradicate the automatic running of this virus.

C.3   STOP THE VIRUS FROM RUNNING

Copy autoexec.bat to autoexec.ori to save the original file (preserve original file in autoexec.ori).

Remove lines of the autoexec.bat file that invoke "win," that is in a standard issue WearComp, lines 15 to the end (line 15 to 20 inclusive) of autoexec.bat using the dos "edit" command, assuming that line 15 is the line with the "win" command on it. Removing these 6 lines includes removal of the line with the *win* command (the line that starts the virus).

Now the WearComp should boot into DOS only. DOS is not a particularly good operating system but forms a satisfactory boot monitor from which to load another operating system such as GNUX. On a WearComp it is preferable to use loadlin, rather than LILO. Also using loadlin means that you will not continually need to rewrite the MBR every time you want to change the default boot kernel.

If there is already LILO present, it can be removed with the "FDISK /MBR" command which restores the Master Boot Record (MBR). You may want to add the line "doskey" to the end of the autoexec.bat file. This is useful because it will allow you to use the up/down arrows to get commands from a command history.

C.4   MAKING ROOM FOR AN OPERATING SYSTEM

We need to make room on the hard drive for GNUX, so delete some of the unnecessary files. On a standard issue WearComp, proceed as follows:

- Delete `386spart.par`. This is a hidden file (a win swap file). To delete the file, you first need to unhide it: `attrib -h -r -s 386spart.par`; this removes the hidden attribute and the readonly attribute the system file attribute (because you can't unhide a system file). Now you can delete 386spart.par: `del 386spart.par`.
- Get rid of all checkdisk files: `del *.chk`.
- Do the following to delete the not needed directories recursively, using the DOS `deltree` command:

  deltree aol25
  deltree apache
  deltree cdrom
  deltree fmpro
  deltree ifloldpi
  deltree ifls (takes a few minutes to delete)
  deltree mmworks
  deltree mtb30
  deltree picture
  deltree pman15
  deltree policed
  deltree powerpnt
  deltree project1
  deltree puzzle

deltree sidecar

deltree temp

deltree tigers (takes about 30 seconds delete)

deltree verbex (takes about a minute to delete)

deltree voiceage

Keep the "dos" utilities, and the "win" directory (running the "win" virus can tell you certain useful things about the system, what kind of mouse it has, etc.).

C.5 OTHER NEEDED FILES

There are several files that are needed and can be obtained from the `wearcam.org/freewear` site. You will need access to a network connected PC to which you can access the serial or parallel port. This is a good exercise in transferring files to and from the WearComp.

The best way to get the files onto the WearComp is to get them onto your desktop computer in the DOS partition. From GNUX on your desktop computer (or by any other means) obtain the following from wearcam.org which you will put in the dos partition of your desktop computer:

- All the files in `wearcam.org/freewear/debian`
- All the files in `wearcam.org/freewear/fips`
- All the files in `wearcam.org/freewear/loadlin`

Create directories on the WearComp DOS computer with directory names:

- debian
- fips
- loadlin

When you obtain these files, make sure that they have the same filesize and contents as the ones on `wearcam.org`, since some Web browsers, in the presence of certain viruses such as Virus95, will corrupt files during transfer. In particular, it is common under Virus95 for binary files to have something appended to the end of the files. Thus double-check to make sure that your browser has not appended a virus to the end of any of the files that you download.

The DOS programs interlnk and intersvr may be used to transfer files. If you are not already in DOS, restart your computer in DOS, and use the DOS utilities `interlnk` and `intersvr` to transfer these to the WearComp into the appropriate directories.

After you've transferred the additional files over, your directory structure should look something like this:

autoexec.bak	cardsoft	dblspace.bin	linux	setup.bat
autoexec.bat	cardview	debbase	loadlin	wina20.386
autoexec.exp	command.com	debboot	mouse	windows
backfmt.com	config.exp	disk1	msdos.sys	
backpack.sys	config.flp	dos	pk	
cap	config.sys	fips	ppcfd.sys	
cardcam	config.vdg	io.sys	ps_off.exe	

Edit the `autoexec.bat` and `config.sys` appropriately for the new material added, and the old material deleted. For example, add directories such as *loadlin* to your path, and delete paths to nonexistent directories, to shorten your path if it gets too long. (Remember that if you goof `autoexec.bat` and `config.sys`, you might have to hold down F8 while booting just before the prompt says "`booting msdos`."

C.6 DEFRAG

Run the `defrag` program to degragment the drive. This is very important thing to do.

Make sure you do a full `defrag`. If the disk is already less than 1% fragmented, it will run a defrag of files only. If this occurs, make sure you still force it to do a complete `defrag`.

Be careful not to "clobber" DOS, or you will have "killed" the WearComp, since you will then have no way to boot it (it has no floppy drive, CD ROM, etc). There is currently no convenient way to remove the hard drive, or to connect a floppy disk or CD ROM. This is typical of WearComp systems. Consider yourself lucky that it boots *something*. Do your best to keep it that way (i.e., keep it so that it boots something).

C.7 FIPS

Before running fips, make sure that the `defrag` program has run. Be careful that nothing happens during fips (e.g., tripping over the cable or pulling out power, which can kill the WearComp). This is the time to be careful that nothing gets clobbered.

Use *fips.exe* to reduce the partition size of the DOS partition to 100 megabytes. When fips asks you if you want to make a backup, you will have to specify *n* (no) because there is no way to make a backup at this time. Use the up/down arrows in fips to specify the partition size. Select 100.4 MB and cylinder number 204. This leaves 399.2 MB for GNUX.

Once fips exits, you will need to reboot the computer before the size change takes effect. Do not mess around creating or deleting files, as this can kill the computer. Reboot as soon as fips exits. You will now see a smaller amount of free space, and the computer will behave, in DOS, as if it has a 100 megabyte hard drive instead of a 500 megabyte hard drive. The remaining 400 megabytes (invisible to DOS except for fdisk) will be used for GNUX.

Although DOS fdisk can see the new 400 megabyte partition, don't use DOS fdisk to do anything to the new partition; just leave the remaining 399.2 MB as it is for now (unformatted). This will later be repartitioned using GNUX fdisk, and formatted using GNUX mke2fs.

C.8 STARTING UP IN GNUX WITH RAMDISK

Reboot, go into debian directory, and type `install` to run the install.bat file.

C.8.1 When You Run *install.bat*

See `http://wearcam.org/freewear/debian/README`. *Install.bat* runs loadlin, which creates a ramdisk and loads a kernel that has initrd in it. This loads *root.bin* which has the install programs in it, as well as other things like fdisk.

Once GNUX starts, it will continue to run the install program. Alternatively, you can, in loadlin, use command line parameters load_ramdisk = 1initrd = root.bin. Once you are booted in ramdisk, you can run GNUX fdisk, create another partition of type ext2, and install GNUX.

You can run mke2fs or mkfs to make the filesystem, and proceed to put Debian GNUX on it, and get it up and running. You will need to remove first the second partition made by FIPS, which was also made as a DOS-type partition (keep only the first DOS partition, not 2 DOS partitions). Remove the third partition, if any, which is the 0.5 megabyte left over.

Once you have only the one DOS partition, you can use GNUX fdisk to make a single ext2 type partition. Then edit your `linux.bat` file in the loadlin directory to change it from ramdisk to the new partition you just created.

After you are up and running, you can use PLIP or SLIP to connect to your main computer. On your main computer you should also install GNUX. You may even want to build IPFWADM into the kernel so that you can talk to the Internet directly using the WearComp (i.e., so your desktop computer acts as an IP Masq gateway).

If you've never done GNUX before, you might want to team up with someone who has.

C.8.2 Assignment Question

Summarize briefly any problems you encountered while installing GNUX on a computer that has no floppy drive or ethernet card. What did you learn from this exercise?

HOW TO BUILD A COVERT COMPUTER IMAGING SYSTEM INTO ORDINARY LOOKING SUNGLASSES

For the WearComp reality mediator to be of use in everyday life, it must not have an unusual appearance, especially given its use in corrupt settings such as dishonest sales establishments, gambling casinos, corrupt customs borders stations, and political institutions where human rights violations are commonplace or where objections are likely to be raised to recording apparatus.

Accordingly it has been proposed that the apparatus must pass the so-called casino test [37]. Once the apparatus has successfully passed the scrutiny of the most paranoid individuals, like the croupiers and pit bosses of criminally funded organizations, it will then have reached what one might call a state of looking normal.

A brief historical time line of the "computershades" (covert reality mediator) follows:

- 1995, author designed and built covert rig (computershades95) grayscale only (published in *IEEE Computer*, February 1997).
- 1996, author designed and built covert rig (computershades96) full color.
- 1998, author designed and built covert rig (computershades98) based on Kopin cyberdisplay (low-cost kopin system based on M1, but reproducible for mass production).
- 2000, various other students and hobbyists begin to build covert sunglass-based rigs, mostly based on the computershades98 design.

Some examples appear in Figure D.1.

Computershades95 and 96 were very difficult to make at the time, but computershades98 were designed to be easily reproduced by others. This appendix serves as a rough "howto" for getting started with the computershades98 design that was featured on the cover of *Toronto Computes*, September 1999.

(*a*)   (*b*)

Figure D.1   Covert embodiments of WearComp suitable for use in ordinary day-to-day situations. Both incorporate fully functional UNIX-based computers concealed in the small of the back, with the rest of the peripherals, such as analog to digital converters, also concealed under ordinary clothing. Both incorporate camera-based imaging systems concealed within the eyeglasses. While these prototype units are detectable by physical contact with the body, detection of the apparatus by others was not found to be a problem. This is, of course, because normal social conventions are such that touching of the body is normally only the domain of those known well to the wearer. As with any prosthetic device, first impressions are important to normal integration into society, and discovery by those who already know the wearer well (i.e., to the extent that close physical contact may occur) typically happens after an acceptance is already established. Other prototypes have been integrated into the clothing in a manner that feels natural to the wearer and to others who might come into physical contact with the wearer. (*a*) Lightweight black-and-white version completed in 1995. (*b*) Full-color version completed in 1996 included special-purpose digital signal-processing hardware based on an array of TMS 320 series processors connected to a UNIX-based host processor, which is concealed in the small of the back. A cross-compiler for the TMS 320 series chips was run remotely on a SUN workstation, accessed wirelessly through radio and antennas concealed in the apparatus.

D.1   THE MOVE FROM SIXTH-GENERATION WEARCOMP TO SEVENTH-GENERATION

In a sixth-generation system the processor is typically a small single-board computer that can be placed in a small metal box. This setup is a favorite among hobbyists because of its flexibility and ease of interface. For example, a 64 pin ribbon cable can be attached to the industry standard architecture (ISA) bus of the computer, and connected to a small solderless breadboard in the system. Such sixth-generation systems are used in teaching three courses at University of Toronto (ECE385, ECE431, and ECE1766).

Traditionally one of the problems with wearable computing has been that the wearer tends to look odd. Like any new invention the early prototypes have often had an unusual appearance by modern standards. The computer has now been made quite small. For example, in a seventh-generation system the components are distributed and concealed in a structure similar to an athletic tank top for being worn under casual clothing. This structure also allows the device to pick up physiological measurements, such as respiration, heart rate, and in fact the full ECG waveform. Alternatively, when it is not necessary to collect physiological data, we sometimes use small-size commercial off-the-shelf computers, such as the Expresso pocket computer, which can fit in a shirt pocket and can be concealed under casual clothing without much difficulty.

Batteries can be distributed and are easy to conceal. In and of themselves, the processor and batteries are easily to concealed, and even the keyer can be concealed in a pocket, or under a table during a meeting.

The display device is perhaps the most cumbersome characterizing feature of the WearComp. Even if a 20-year-old backpack-based wearable computer, or a 15-year-old jacket-based computer, is worn, it is the display that is most objectionable and usually first noticed. Of all the various parts of the WearComp, the information display is that which makes it most evident that a person is networked, and it is usually also the most unnerving or disturbing to others.

A display system, even if quite small, will be distracting and annoying to others, simply because it is right at the eye level. Of course, this is the area where people pay the most attention when engaged in normal conversation. Thus one might want to consider building a covert display system.

The seventh-generation WearComps (started in 1995) were characterized by a display concealed inside what appear to be ordinary sunglasses. Some of the sunglasses had more than just displays. Some were EyeTap devices that functioned as cameras. However, for simplicity, we will look at the example of a simple display device.

The simplest display medium is the Kopin CyberDisplay. The original Kopin display system, selling for approximately U.S. $5,000 was donated to the author by Kopin, and formed the basis for many of these experiments. Presently, however, the cost has come down considerably, and units are now selling for less than $100.

Originally the author had some connectors manufactured to connect to the Kopin CyberDisplay. However, later, in order to keep the overall size down, the size was reduced by soldering wires directly to the Kopin CyberDisplay, in one of two ways:

1. To the fat end where the contacts widen.
2. To the slender part, after cutting off the part where the contacts widen, and eating away at the insulation with a solvent.

Assuming that most students (especially with the growing emphasis on soft computing) are novices at soldering, we will focus on the first method which is a lot easier, especially for the beginning student.

D.2   LABEL THE WIRES!

The very first step is to *number the wires*. The importance of numbering the wires cannot be overemphasized. After soldering the wires on, you will find it somewhat difficult to determine which wire is which by following each wire. Since the whole item is very fragile, it is strongly recommended that the wires be numbered before soldering any of them to anything.

Take 20 or so wires (depending on if you want to connect up all the lines, or just the ones that are actually used — check the Kopin specifications for signal levels, etc., and what you are going to use), and bring them into a bundle and label them as shown in Figure D.2.

The author prefers to use all black wires because they are easier to conceal in the eyeglass frames. Usually number 30 wire (AWG 30) is used. Sometimes black number 30 stranded, and sometimes black number 30 solid are used. If you're a novice at soldering, use number 30 solid and splice it to number 30 stranded inside the eyeglass frames. Solid is a lot easier to solder to the Kopin cyberdisplay.

D.3   SOLDERING WIRES DIRECTLY TO THE KOPIN CYBERDISPLAY

With the reduction by more than a factor of 50 times in cost (from U.S. $5,000 down to less than U.S. $100), we can afford to take more risks and solder directly to the device to avoid the bulk of a connector that should be concealed.

Figure D.2 Use of black wires for all the wires instead of color coding the wires. Using all black wire makes them easier to conceal into the frames with optical epoxy, rather than using variously colored wires. One begins by labeling (numbering) the wires. Here is what a bundle of wires looks like when it is labeled. The 6 (''six'') is underlined so that, when it is upside down, it does not alias into the number 9.

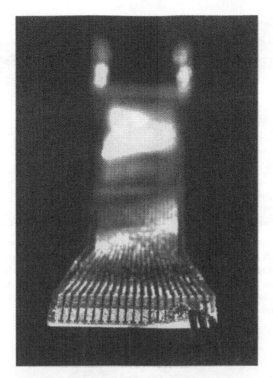

Figure D.3 Begin soldering at one end, and work across carefully, since it is much easier to solder when one side is free than to solder into the middle of a row of wires.

To solder the wires to the Kopin CyberDisplay, a fine tip iron is best. The author usually uses, a Weller 921ZX iron, which is the sleekest and most slender commercially produced soldering iron; it also takes the finest tip, number U9010.

Begin soldering at one end, and work across carefully. It is a lot easier to solder when one side is free than to go back and fix a bad connection in the middle of a row of wires as indicated in Figure D.3.

D.4   COMPLETING THE COMPUTERSHADES

You're now ready to install the unit into eyeglasses. The display requires a backlight, and a circuit to drive it. If you're versed in the art of field programmable gate arrays (FPGAs), you should have no trouble designing a driver circuit for the display. Alternatively, you could purchase a product that uses the Kopin CyberDisplay. An example of a product that uses the Kopin CyberDisplay is the M1 product made in Canada. If you purchase an M1, you will be able to test your eyeglasses while you continue development of a smaller-sized drive circuit.

There are now two versions of the M1: one with remote driver board, and the other in which the driver board is put inside the main box. The one with

Figure D.4 Completed covert eyeglass rig: Here only the right eye position is shown wired. The second eye (left eye) position has not yet been installed. A second eyeglass safety strap and a second display is next installed. Both can now be tested with the M1 drive circuit. The next step is to build a smaller circuit that drives two Kopin CyberDisplays. Not shown in this system is the installation of the cameras, which are each reflected off the back of the optical element used for the display.

Figure D.5 Completed unit as it appeared on the cover of *Toronto Computes*, September 1999. The computershades enable a fashionable, or at least normal-looking existence in the world of wearable computing.

remote driver board will tend to give a better picture (less image noise) because of the reduced distance of signal path. In this case (see Fig. D.4), a short (e.g., 18 inch) set of wires from the eyeglasses to the driver board can be concealed in an eyeglass safety strap.

Not shown in Figure D.4 is the installation of the cameras. The cameras would each be reflected off the back of the optical element shown for the display. If you are just using the computer for normal computational applications, you don't need to worry about the camera or the second eye. Enjoy your covert seventh-generation WearComp.

A complete version of the partially constructed eyeglasses pictured above, appeared on the cover of the September 1999 issue of *Canada Computes* (Fig. D.5), where we can see that wearable computing can appear fashionable, or at the very least normal looking.

A NOTE ON SAFETY: Neither the author nor the publisher can assume any liability for any bad effects experienced. Displays can be distracting and cause death or injury because of the distraction. Also care is needed to avoid optical elements getting into the eye, if struck, falling down, or the like, while wearing the apparatus. Finally, excessive brightness over long-term usage can be bad, (clear glasses turn up brightness and lead to eye damage). If you use a high-voltage source for the backlight, beware of possible bad effects from it being close to the eye, and with exposed wires. The electric shock, which feels like a bad mosquito bite, even at low current, can also cause distraction. So, even if the voltage is not harmful in itself, it may cause other injury. Remember SAFETY FIRST!

BIBLIOGRAPHY

[1] Steve Mann. Wearable computing: A first step toward personal imaging. *IEEE Computer*, 30(2):25–32, Feb. 1997. http://wearcam.org/ieeecomputer.htm.

[2] Steve Mann. Humanistic intelligence/humanistic computing: "Wearcomp" as a new framework for intelligent signal processing. *Proc. IEEE*, 86(11):2123–2151 + cover, Nov. 1998. http://wearcam.org/procieee.htm.

[3] William A. S. Buxton and Ronald M. Baecker. *Readings in Human-Computer Interaction: A Multidisciplinary approach*. Morgan Kaufmann, 1987, chs. 1, 2.

[4] Simon Haykin. *Neural Networks: A Comprehensive Foundation*. Mcmillan, New York, 1994.

[5] Simon Haykin. Radar vision. Second International Specialist Seminar on Parallel Digital Processors, Portugal, Apr. 15–19, 1992.

[6] D. E. Rumelhart and J. L. McMlelland, eds. *Parallel Distributed Processing*. MIT Press, Cambridge, 1986.

[7] Tomaso Poggio and Federico Girosi. Networks for approximation and learning. *Proc. IEEE*, 78(9):1481–1497, Sep. 1990.

[8] Bart Kosko. *Fuzzy Thinking: The New Science of Fuzzy Logic*. Hyperion, New York, 1993.

[9] Bart Kosko and Satoru Isaka. Fuzzy logic. *Scientific American*, 269:76–81, July 1993.

[10] Marvin Minsky. Steps toward artificial intelligence. In Phillip Laplante, ed., *Great Papers on Computer Science*, Minneapolis/St. Paul, 1996 (paper in IRE 1960).

[11] D. C. Engelbart. Augmenting human intellect. a conceptual framework. Research Report AFOSR-3223, Stanford Research Institute, Menlo Park, 1962. http://www.histech.rwth-aachen.de/www/quellen/engelbart/ahi62index.html.

[12] Douglas C. Engelbart. A conceptual framework for the augmentation of man's intellect. In P. D. Howerton and D. C. Weeks, eds., *Vistas in Information Handling*. Spartan Books, Washington, DC, 1963.

[13] Method and apparatus for relating and combining multiple images of the same scene or object(s). Steve Mann and Rosalind W. Picard, U.S. Pat. 5706416, Jan. 6, 1998.

[14] Steve Mann. Wearable, tetherless computer–mediated reality: WearCam as a wearable face–recognizer, and other applications for the disabled. TR 361, MIT Media Lab Perceptual Computing Section. Also appears in *AAAI Fall Symposium*

on Developing Assistive Technology for People with Disabilities, Nov. 9–11, 1996, MIT. http://wearcam.org/vmp.htm. Cambridge, Feb. 2 1996.

[15] Stephen M. Kosslyn. *Image and Brain: The Resolution of the Imagery Debate*. MIT Press, Cambridge, 1994.

[16] S. Mann. "WearStation": With today's technology, it is now possible to build a fully equipped ham radio station, complete with internet connection, into your clothing. *CQ-VHF*, pp. 1–46, Jan., 1997.

[17] S. Mann. "Mediated reality." TR 260, MIT Media Lab vismod, Cambridge, 1994. http://wearcam.org/mr.htm.

[18] James D. Meindl. Low power microelectronics: Retrospect and prospect. *Proc. IEEE* 83(4):619–635, Apr. 1995.

[19] Steve Mann. An historical account of the "WearComp" and "WearCam" projects developed for "personal imaging". In *Int. Symp. on Wearable Computing*, IEEE, Cambridge, MA, Oct. 13–14, 1997.

[20] Steve Mann. *Personal Imaging*. Ph.D. thesis. Massachusetts Institute of Technology. 1997.

[21] Steve Mann. Further developments on "headcam": Joint estimation of camera rotation + gain group of transformations for wearable bi-foveated cameras. In *Proc. Int. Conf. on Acoustics, Speech and Signal Processing*, vol. 4, Munich, Germany, Apr. 1997. IEEE.

[22] Eric J. Lind and Robert Eisler. A sensate liner for personnel monitoring application. In *First Int. Symp. on Wearable Computing*. IEEE, Cambridge, MA, Oct. 13–14, 1997.

[23] R. W. Picard and J. Healey. Affective wearables. In *Proc. First Int. Symp. on Wearable Computers*, IEEE pp. 90–97, Cambridge, MA, Oct. 13–14, 1997.

[24] Steve Mann. Smart clothing: The wearable computer and wearcam. *Personal Technologies*, 1(1):21–27, Mar. 1997.

[25] Simon Haykin, Carl Krasnor, Tim J. Nohara, Brian W. Currie, and Dave Hamburger. A coherent dual-polarized radar for studying the ocean environment. *IEEE Trans. on Geosciences and Remote Sensing*, 29(1):189–191, Jan. 1991.

[26] Brian W. Currie, Simon Haykin, and Carl Krasnor. Time-varying spectra for dual-polarized radar returns from targest in an ocean environment. In *IEEE Conf. Proc. RADAR90*, pp. 365–369, Arlington, VA, May 1990. IEEE Aerospace and Electronics Systems Society.

[27] D. Slepian and H. O. Pollak. Prolate spheroidal wave functions, Fourier analysis and uncertainty, I. *Bell Syst. Tech. J.*, 40:43–64, Jan. 1961.

[28] Steve Mann and Simon Haykin. The chirplet transform: A generalization of Gabor's logon transform. *Vision Interface '91*, pp. 205–212, June 3–7, 1991.

[29] G. Strang. Wavelets and dilation equations: A brief introduction. *SIAM Rev.*, 31(4):614–627, 1989.

[30] I. Daubechies. The wavelet transform, time-frequency localization and signal analysis. *IEEE Trans. Inf. Theory*, 36(5):961–1005, 1990.

[31] D. Mihovilovic and R. N. Bracewell. Whistler analysis in the time-frequency plane using chirplets. *J. Geophys. Res.*, 97(A11):17199–17204, Nov. 1992.

[32] Richard Baraniuk and Doug Jones. Shear madness: New orthonormal bases and frames using chirp functions. *Trans. Signal Processing*, 41, Dec. 1993. Special issue on wavelets in signal processing.

[33] M. A. Saunders, S. S. Chen, and D. L. Donoho. Atomic decomposition by basis pursuit. http://www-stat.stanford.edu/~-donoho/Reports/1995/30401. pdf, pp. 1–29.

[34] H. M. Ozaktas, B. Barshan D. Mendlovic, and L. Onural, Convolution, filtering, and multiplexing in fractional fourier domains and their relation to chirp and wavelet transforms, *J. Opt. Soc. America*, A11(2):547–559, (1994).

[35] Steve Mann and Simon Haykin. The chirplet transform: Physical considerations. *IEEE Trans. Signal Processing*, 43(11):2745–2761, Nov. 1995.

[36] Don Norman. *Turn Signals Are the Facial Expressions of Automobiles*. Addison Wesley, Reading, MA, 1992.

[37] Steve Mann. "Smart clothing": Wearable multimedia and "personal imaging" to restore the balance between people and their intelligent environments. In *Proc. ACM Multimedia 96*. pp. 163–174, Boston, Nov. 18–22, 1996. http://wearcam.org/acm-mm96.htm.

[38] Steve Mann. Humanistic intelligence. Invited plenary lecture, Sept. 10, In *Proc. Ars Electronica*, pp. 217–231, Sept. 8–13, 1997. http://wearcam.org/ars/ http//www.aec.at/fleshfactor. Republished in Timothy Druckrey, ed., *Ars Electronica: Facing the Future, A Survey of Two Decades*. MIT Press, Cambridge, pp. 420–427.

[39] R. A. Earnshaw, M. A. Gigante, and H Jones. *Virtual Reality Systems*. Academic Press, San Diego, CA, 1993.

[40] Sutherland. A head mounted three dimensional display. In *Proc. Fall Joint Computer Conf.*, Thompson Books, Washington, DC, 1968, pp. 757–764.

[41] S. Feiner, B. MacIntyre, and D. Seligmann. Knowledge-based augmented reality. *Commun. ACM*, 36(7):52–62, July 1993.

[42] S. Feiner, B. MacIntyre, and D. Seligmann. Karma (knowledge-based augmented reality for maintenance assistance). 1993. http://www.cs.columbia.edu/grap-hics/projects/ karma/karma.html.

[43] Henry Fuchs, Mike Bajura, and Ryutarou Ohbuchi. Teaming ultrasound data with virtual reality in obstetrics. http://www.ncsa.uiuc.edu/Pubs/ MetaCenter/SciHi93/ 1c.Highlights-BiologyC.html.

[44] David Drascic. Papers and presentations, 1993. http://vered.rose.utoronto. ca/people/david_dir/ Bibliography.html.

[45] S. Mann. Wearable Wireless Webcam, 1994. http://wearcam.org.

[46] Ronald Azuma. Registration errors in augmented reality: NSF/ARPA Science and Technology Center for Computer Graphics and Scientific Visualization, 1994. http://www.cs.unc.edu/~/azuma/azuma_AR.html.

[47] George M. Stratton. Some preliminary experiments on vision without inversion of the retinal image. *Psycholog. Rev.*, 3: 611–617, 1896.

[48] Hubert Dolezal. *Living in a World Transformed*. Academic Press, Orlando, FL, 1982.

[49] Ivo Kohler. *The Formation and Transformation of the Perceptual World*, Vol. 3(4) of *Psychological Issues*. International University Press, New York, 1964.

[50] Simon Haykin. *Communication Systems*, 2d ed. Wiley, New York, 1983.

[51] G. Arfken. *Mathematical Methods for Physicists*, 3rd ed. Academic Press, Orlando, FL, 1985.

[52] K. Nagao. Ubiquitous talker: Spoken language interaction with real world objects, 1995. `http://www.csl.sony.co.jp/person/nagao.html`.

[53] Michael W. McGreevy. The presence of field geologists in mars-like terrain. *Presence*, 1(4):375–403, Fall 1992.

[54] Stuart Anstis. Visual adaptation to a negative, brightness-reversed world: Some preliminary observations. In Gail Carpenter and Stephen Grossberg, eds., *Neural Networks for Vision and Image Processing*. MIT Press, Cambridge, 1992, pp. 1–15.

[55] Wilmer Eye Institute. Lions Vision Research and Rehabilitation Center, Johns Hopkins, 1995. `http://www.wilmer.jhu.edu/low_vis/low_vis.htm`.

[56] Bob Shaw. *Light of Other Days*. Analog, August 1966.

[57] Harold E. Edgerton. *Electronic Flash/Strobe*. MIT Press, Cambridge, 1979.

[58] T. G. Stockham Jr. Image processing in the context of a visual model. *Proc. IEEE*, 60(7):828–842, July 1972.

[59] S. Mann and R. W. Picard. Being "undigital" with digital cameras: Extending dynamic range by combining differently exposed pictures. Technical Report 323, MIT Media Lab Perceptual Computing Section, Cambridge, 1994. Also appears, IS&T's 48th Ann. Conf., pp. 422–428, May 7–11, 1995, Washington, DC. `http://wearcam.org/ist95.htm`.

[60] P. Pattie Maes, Treror Darrell, Bruce Blumberg, and Alex Pentland. The alive system: Full-body interaction with animated autonomous agents. TR 257, MIT Media Lab Perceptual Computing Section, Cambridge, 1994.

[61] Steve Mann. Eyeglass mounted wireless video: Computer-supported collaboration for photojournalism and everyday use. *IEEE ComSoc*, 36(6):144–151, June 1998. Special issue on wireless video.

[62] W. Barfield and C. Hendrix. The effect of update rate on the sense of presence within virtual environments. *Virtual Reality: Research, Development, and Application*, 1(1):3–15, 1995.

[63] S. Mann. Compositing multiple pictures of the same scene. In *Proc. 46th An. IS&T Conf.*, pp. 50–52, Cambridge, MA, May 9–14, 1993. Society of Imaging Science and Technology.

[64] Steve Mann. Personal imaging and lookpainting as tools for personal documentary and investigative photojournalism. *ACM Mobile Networking*, 4(1):23–36, 1999.

[65] R. J. Lewandowski, L. A. Haworth, and H. J. Girolamo. Helmet and head-mounted displays iii. *Proc. SPIE, AeroSense 98*, 3362, Apr. 12–14, 1998.

[66] T. Caudell and D. Mizell. Augmented reality: An application of heads-up display technology to manual manufacturing processes. *Proc. Hawaii Int. Conf. on Systems Science*, 2:659–669, 1992.

[67] Microvision, `http://www.mvis.com/`.

[68] Graham Wood. The infinity or reflex sight, 1998. `http://www.graham-wood.freeserve.co.uk/1xsight/finder.htm`.

[69] Stephen R. Ellis, Urs J. Bucher, and Brian M. Menges. The relationship of binocular convergence and errors in judged distance to virtual objects. *Proc. Int. Federation of Automatic Control*, June 27–29, 1995.

[70] S. Mann. Comparametric equations with practical applications in quantigraphic image processing. *IEEE Trans. Image Proc.*, 9(8):1389–1406, Aug. 2000.

[71] B. Horn and B. Schunk. Determining optical flow. *Artificial Intelligence*, 17:185–203, 1981.

[72] M. Irani and S. Peleg. Improving resolution by image registration. *Computer Vision Graphics Image Processing*, 53:231–239, May 1991.

[73] S. Mann and R. W. Picard. Video orbits of the projective group; a simple approach to featureless estimation of parameters. TR 338, Massachusetts Institute of Technology, Cambridge. See `http://hi.eecg.toronto.edu/tip.html`, 1995. Also appears in *IEEE Trans. Image Proc.*, 6(9):1281–1295, Sep. 1997.

[74] R. Szeliski. Video mosaics for virtual environments. *Computer Graphics and Applications*, 16(2):22–30, Mar. 1996.

[75] Charles W. Wyckoff. An experimental extended response film. *SPIE Newsletter*, pp. 16–20, June–July 1962.

[76] Charles W. Wyckoff. An experimental extended response film. Technical Report B-321, Edgerton, Germeshausen & Grier, Inc., Boston, MA, Mar. 1961.

[77] Steve Mann. "Pencigraphy" with AGC: Joint parameter estimation in both domain and range of functions in same orbit of the projective-Wyckoff group. Technical Report 384, MIT Media Lab, Cambridge, December 1994. `http://hi.eecg.toronto.edu/icip96/index.html`. Also appears in *Proc. IEEE Int. Conf. on Image Processing* (ICIP–96), pp. 193–196, Lausanne, Switzerland, Sep. 16–19, 1996.

[78] Charles Poynton. *A Technical Introduction to Digital Video*. Wiley, New York, 1996.

[79] `http://wearcam.org/gamma.htm`.

[80] J. Aczél. *Lectures on Functional Equations and Their Applications*, vol. 19. Academic Press, New York, 1966. Mathematics in science and engineering, a series of monographs and textbooks edited by Richard Bellman, University of Southern California.

[81] Berthold Klaus and Paul Horn. *Robot Vision*. MIT Electrical Engineering and Computer Science Series. McGraw-Hill, New York, 1986, chs. 1, 2, 6, 9, 10 and 12.

[82] K. P. Berthold Horn and E. J. Weldon Jr. Direct methods for recovering motion. *Int. J. Comput. Vision*, 2 No.1, pp. 51–76, 1988.

[83] O. D. Faugeras and F. Lustman. Motion and structure from motion in a piecewise planar environment. *Int. J. Pattern Recognition and Artificial Intelligence*, 2(3):485–508, 1988.

[84] S. Laveau and O. Faugeras. 3-D scene representation as a collection of images. In *Proc. IEEE Conf. on Computer Vision and Pattern Recognition*, Seattle, WA, June 1994.

[85] S. C. Woon. Period-harmonic-tupling jumps to chaos and fractal-scaling in a class of series. *Chaos, Solitons, and Fractals*, 5(1):125–30, Jan. 1995.

[86] M. A. Berger. Random affine iterated function systems: Curve generation and wavelets. *SIAM Rev.*, 31(4):614–627, 1989.

[87] William J. Mitchell. *The Reconfigured Eye*. MIT Press, Cambridge, 1992.

[88] E. H. Adelson and J. R. Bergen. The plenoptic function and the elements of early vision. In M. Landy and J. A. Movshon, eds., *Computational Models of Visual Processing*, MIT Press Cambridge MA, pp. 3–20, 1991.

[89] Compiled and edited from the original manuscripts by Jean Paul Richter. *The Notebooks of Leonardo Da Vinci*, 1452–1519 vol. 1. Dover, New York, 1970.

[90] Graham Saxby. *Practical Holography*, 2nd ed., Prentice-Hall, Englewood Cliffs, New Jessey, 1994.

[91] B. R. Alexander, P. M. Burnett, J. -M. R. Fournier, and S. E. Stamper. Accurate color reproduction by Lippman photography. In *SPIE Proc. 3011–34 Practical holography and holographic materials*, Bellingham WA 98227. Feb. 11, 1997. Photonics West 97 SPIE, Cosponsored by IS&T. Chair T. John Trout, DuPont.

[92] Steve Mann. Lightspace. Unpublished report (paper available from author). Submitted to SIGGRAPH 92. Also see example images in http://wearcam.org/lightspace, July 1992.

[93] Cynthia Ryals. Lightspace: A new language of imaging. *PHOTO Electronic Imaging*, 38(2):14–16, 1995. http://www.peimag.com/ltspace.htm.

[94] S. S. Beauchemin, J. L. Barron, and D. J. Fleet. Systems and experiment performance of optical flow techniques. *Int. J. Comput. Vision*, 12(1):43–77, 1994.

[95] A. M. Tekalp, M. K. Ozkan, and M. I. Sezan. High-resolution image reconstruction from lower-resolution image sequences and space-varying image restoration. In *Proc. Int. Conf. on Acoustics, Speech and Signal Proc.*, pp. III–169, San Francisco, CA, Mar. 23–26, 1992. IEEE.

[96] Qinfen Zheng and Rama Chellappa. A Computational Vision Approach to Image Registration. *IEEE Trans. Image Processing*, 2(3):311–325, 1993.

[97] L. Teodosio and W. Bender. Salient video stills: Content and context preserved. *Proc. ACM Multimedia Conf.*, pp. 39–46, Aug. 1993.

[98] R. Szeliski and J. Coughlan. Hierarchical spline-based image registration. *Computer Vision Pattern Recognition*, pp. 194–201, June 1994.

[99] George Wolberg. *Digital Image Warping*. IEEE Computer Society Press, Los Alamitos, CA, 1990. IEEE Computer Society Press Monograph.

[100] G. Adiv. Determining 3D motion and structure from optical flow generated by several moving objects. *IEEE Trans. Pattern Anal. Machine Intell.*, PAMI-7(4):384–401, July 1985.

[101] Nassir Navab and Steve Mann. Recovery of relative affine structure using the motion flow field of a rigid planar patch. *Mustererkennung 1994, Tagungsband.*, 5 186–196, 1994.

[102] R. Y. Tsai and T. S. Huang. Estimating three-dimensional motion parameters of a rigid planar patch I. *IEEE Trans. Accoust., Speech, and Sig. Proc.*, ASSP(29):1147–1152, Dec. 1981.

[103] Amnon Shashua and Nassir Navab. Relative affine: Theory and application to 3D reconstruction from perspective views. *Proc. IEEE Conf. on Computer Vision and Pattern Recognition*, Jun. 1994.

[104] H. S. Sawhney. Simplifying motion and structure analysis using planar parallax and image warping. *International Conference on Pattern Recognition*, 1:403–908, Oct. 1994. 12th IAPR.

[105] R. Kumar, P. Anandan, and K. Hanna. Shape recovery from multiple views: A parallax based approach. *ARPA Image Understanding Workshop*, Nov. 10, 1994.

[106] Lee Campbell and Aaron Bobick. Correcting for radial lens distortion: A simple implementation. TR 322, MIT Media Lab Perceptual Computing Section, Cambridge, Apr. 1995.

[107] M. Artin. *Algebra*. Prentice-Hall, Englewood Clifs, NJ, 1991.

[108] S. Mann. Wavelets and chirplets: Time-frequency perspectives, with applications. In Petriu Archibald, ed., *Advances in Machine Vision, Strategies, and Applications*. World Scientific, Singapore, 1992.

[109] L. V. Ahlfors. *Complex Analysis*, 3rd ed., McGraw-Hill, New York, 1979.

[110] R. Y. Tsai and T. S. Huang. *Multiframe Image Restoration and Registration*. Vol 1, in Advances in Computer Vision and Image Processing 1984. pp. 317–339.

[111] T. S. Huang and A. N. Netravali. Motion and structure from feature correspondences: A review. *Proc. IEEE*, 82(2):252–268, Feb. 1984.

[112] Nassir Navab and Amnon Shashua. Algebraic description of relative affine structure: Connections to Euclidean, affine and projective structure. MIT Media Lab Memo 270, Cambridge, MA., 1994.

[113] Harry L. Van Trees. *Detection, Estimation, and Modulation Theory*. Wiley, New York, 1968, part I.

[114] A. Berthon. Operator Groups and Ambiguity Functions in Signal Processing. In J. M. Combes, ed. *Wavelets: Time-Frequency Methods and Phase Space*. Springer Verlag, Berlin, 1989.

[115] A. Grossmann and T. Paul. *Wave functions on subgroups of the group of affine canonical transformations*. Resonances — Models and Phenomena, Springer-Verlag, Berlin, 1984, pp. 128–138.

[116] R. K. Young. *Wavelet Theory and its Applications*. Kluwer Academic, Boston, 1993.

[117] Lora G. Weiss. Wavelets and wideband correlation processing. *IEEE Sign. Process. Mag.*, pp. 13–32, Jan. 1994.

[118] Steve Mann and Simon Haykin. Adaptive "chirplet" transform: An adaptive generalization of the wavelet transform. *Optical Eng.*, 31(6):1243–1256, June 1992.

[119] John Y. A. Wang and Edward H. Adelson. Spatio-temporal segmentation of video data. In *SPIE Image and Video Processing II*, pp. 120–128, San Jose, CA, Feb. 7–9, 1994.

[120] J. Bergen, P. J. Burt, R. Hingorini, and S. Peleg. Computing two motions from three frames. In *Proc. Third Int. Conf. Comput. Vision*, pp. 27–32, Osaka, Japan, Dec. 1990.

[121] B. D. Lucas and T. Kanade. An iterative image-registration technique with an application to stereo vision. Proc. 7th Int. Joint conf. on Art. Intell. In *Image Understanding Workshop*, pp. 121–130, 1981.

[122] J. Y. A. Wang and Edward H. Adelson. Representing moving images with layers. *Image Process. Spec. Iss: Image Seq. Compression*, 12(1):625–638, Sep. 1994.

[123] Roland Wilson and Goesta H. Granlund. The uncertainty principle in image processing. *IEEE Trans. on Patt. Anal. Mach. Intell.*, 6:758–767, Nov. 1984.

[124] J. Segman, J. Rubinstein, and Y. Y. Zeevi. The canonical coordinates method for pattern deformation: Theoretical and computational considerations. *IEEE Trans. on Patt. Anal. Mach. Intell.*, 14(12):1171–1183, Dec. 1992.

[125] J. Segman. Fourier cross-correlation and invariance transformations for an optimal recognition of functions deformed by affine groups. *J. Optical Soc. Am., A*, 9(6): 895–902, June 1992.

[126] J. Segman and W. Schempp. Two methods of incorporating scale in the Heisenberg group. *Journal of Mathematical Imaging and Vision* special issue on wavelets, 1993.

[127] Bernd Girod and David Kuo. Direct estimation of displacement histograms. *OSA Meeting on Image Understanding and Machine Vision*, June 1989.

[128] Yunlong Sheng, Claude Lejeune, and Henri H. Arsenault. Frequency-domain Fourier-Mellin descriptors for invariant pattern recognition. *Optical Eng.*, 27(5):354–357, May 1988.

[129] S. Mann and R. W. Picard. Virtual bellows: Constructing high-quality images from video. In *Proc. IEEE First Int. Conf. on Image Processing*, pp. 363–367, Austin, TX, Nov. 13–16, 1994.

[130] Peter J. Burt and P. Anandan. Image stabilization by registration to a reference mosaic. ARPA Image Understanding Workshop, Nov. 10, 1994.

[131] M. Hansen, P. Anandan, K. Dana, G. van der Wal, and P. J. Burt. Real-time scene stabilization and mosaic construction. ARPA Image Understanding Workshop, Nov. 10, 1994.

[132] S. Intille. Computers watching football, 1995. http://www-white.media.mit.edu/vismod/demos/football/football.html.

[133] R. Wilson, A. D. Calway, E. R. S. Pearson, and A. R. Davies. An introduction to the multiresolution Fourier transform. Technical Report, Department of Computer Science, University of Warwick, Coventry, UK, 1992. ftp://ftp.dcs.warwick.ac.uk/reports/rr-204/.

[134] A. D. Calway, H. Knutsson, and R. Wilson. Multiresolution estimation of 2-D disparity using a frequency domain approach. In *British Machine Vision Conference*. Springer-Verlag, Berlin, 1992, pp. 227–236.

[135] Seth Shulman. *Owning the Future*. Houghton Mifflin, Boston, 1999.

[136] Michel Foucault. *Discipline and Punish*. Pantheon, New York, 1977. Trans. from *Surveiller et punir*.

[137] Natalie Angier. *Woman, An Intimate Geography*. Houghton Mifflin, Boston, 1999.

[138] Steve Mann. Reflectionism and diffusionism. *Leonardo*, 31(2):93–102, 1998. http://wearcam.org/leonardo/index.htm.

[139] Garrett Hardin. The tragedy of the commons. *Science*, 162:1243–1248, 1968.

[140] Current list of references for keyers, chording keyboards, etc. http://wearcam.org/keyer_references.htm.

[141] Online list of links and resources for keyers, chording keyboards, etc. http://about.eyetap.org/tech/keyers.shtml.

[142] J. R. Cooperstock, S. S. Fels, W. Buxton, and K. C. Smith. Reactive environments: Throwing away your keyboard and mouse, 1997. http://www.csl.sony.co.jp/person/ jer/pub/cacm/cacm.html.

INDEX

Printed and bound by CPI Group (UK) Ltd, Croydon, CR0 4YY

27/10/2024

14580331-0001